Visual FoxPro to Visual Basic .NET

Les Pinter

800 East 96th Street, Indianapolis, Indiana 46240

Visual FoxPro to Visual Basic .NET

International Standard Book Number: 0-672-32649-3

Library of Congress Catalog Card Number: 2003099326

Printed in the United States of America

First Printing: May 2004

07   06   05   04   4   3   2

Trademarks

Warning and Disclaimer

Bulk Sales

Sams Publishing offers excellent discounts on this book when ordered in quantity for bulk purchases or special sales. For more information, please contact

U.S. Corporate and Government Sales

1-800-382-3419

corpsales@pearsontechgroup.com

For sales outside of the U.S., please contact

International Sales

1-317-428-3341

international@pearsontechgroup.com

Associate Publisher
Michael Stephens

Acquisitions Editor
Loretta Yates

Development Editor
Sean Dixon

Managing Editor
Charlotte Clapp

Project Editor
George E. Nedeff

Copy Editor
Margaret Berson

Indexer
Ken Johnson

Proofreader
Elizabeth Scott

Technical Editor
Martìn Salìias

Publishing Coordinator
Cindy Teeters

Multimedia Developer
Dan Scherf

Book Designer
Gary Adair

Contents at a Glance

Table of Contents

About the Author

Les Pinter is the author of six books and more than 280 articles on database development. He received a master's degree from Rice University in Houston, Texas, and finished the coursework for both an MBA and a Ph.D. from the University of Houston. He joined with Mike Griffin and Bill Radding in 1980 to market the Magic Wand, the fourth word processor ever written for the CP/M operating system, and sold the source code to a 23-year-old Bill Gates, who used it to build Microsoft Word a year later.

He moved into the database field with dBASE II and dBASE III, then migrated to FoxBASE during a project at LucasFilm's Skywalker Ranch in 1987. He published the Pinter FoxPro Letter for 10 years in the United States and for four years (together with Dmitry Artemov and Igor Medvedev) in Russia.

Les is Contributing Editor of Universal Thread Magazine, published in Montréal, Quebec, Canada. He is a member of the INETA Speakers' Bureau, and frequently speaks on database development in Latin America. Les was selected as a Microsoft Visual FoxPro MVP in Fall of 2003. Les does seminars and conferences on FoxPro and Visual Basic .NET in English, Spanish, French, Portuguese, and Russian. He lives with his wife Ying-Ying in San Mateo, California. Les is also a private pilot.

Dedication

This book is dedicated to the memory of my son, John Sebastian Pinter, who began the project of writing this book with me two years ago. It would have been a far better book, and this a far better world, if he were still alive. His share of the proceeds from the sale of this book will go to the Bay Area Outreach and Recreation Program (www.BORP.org) where he served as president, and where he developed so many of the qualities that made him a hero to hundreds of Bay Area children with physical challenges.

Acknowledgments

I want to thank Loretta Yates for shepherding this book through the process. Thanks to Sean Dixon for his careful read of every single word in the manuscript and valuable suggestions that made this a much better book than it otherwise would have been. Thanks to Margaret Berson for dotting the I's and crossing the T's, and for correcting the spelling of this sentence when she sees it. Thanks to George Nedeff for keeping the many files straight. Thanks to Martín Salías, my boss at Universal Thread magazine, who agreed to do the technical edit of this book. Your considerable talents and knowledge of FoxPro have added value to this book in ways that no one else could have done.

Special thanks to Michael Stephens, associate publisher at Sams, who I ran into by chance at the Tech-Ed in Dallas last summer. Michael was editor of the *Cobb Group Clipper* newsletter years ago when I was publishing the *Pinter FoxPro Letter*. He remembered that he liked my writing and asked if I had a manuscript. Business was so bad that I really couldn't afford to attend that show, but INETA offered me a free ticket. I stopped by Michael's booth, and that made all the difference.

Les

We Want to Hear from You!

As the reader of this book, *you* are our most important critic and commentator. We value your opinion and want to know what we're doing right, what we could do better, what areas you'd like to see us publish in, and any other words of wisdom you're willing to pass our way.

As an associate publisher for Sams Publishing, I welcome your comments. You can email or write me directly to let me know what you did or didn't like about this book—as well as what we can do to make our books better.

Please note that I cannot help you with technical problems related to the topic of this book. We do have a User Services group, however, where I will forward specific technical questions related to the book.

When you write, please be sure to include this book's title and author as well as your name, email address, and phone number. I will carefully review your comments and share them with the author and editors who worked on the book.

Email: feedback@samspublishing.com

Mail: Michael Stephens
             Associate Publisher
             Sams Publishing
             800 East 96th Street
             Indianapolis, IN 46240 USA

For more information about this book or another Sams Publishing title, visit our Web site at www.samspublishing.com. Type the ISBN (excluding hyphens) or the title of a book in the Search field to find the page you're looking for.

Introduction

About This Book

There are lots of different kinds of software. There are communications tools, graphics packages, Web page development tools, and Internet add-ins of seemingly endless variety. C# and C++ are good for all these kinds of applications. But my favorites are database applications. And of all of the languages sold by Microsoft, Visual FoxPro and Visual Basic .NET are the two most suitable for database application development.

Databases are simply collections of tables, each containing a single kind of record. By using software to relate records from various tables, you can build complex systems to deal with data for accounting, contact management, medical information, tax collection, law enforcement, space vehicle development, and anything else. Alan Greenspan attributes the increasing prosperity of the United States to computer software, and I don't think he's talking about software for drawing pictures. Databases are *awesome*.

Database development, as a profession, is about as good as it gets. I can't wait to get to my office every morning. Every new project offers a chance to extend my skills. Every day produces a new plateau of achievement. I can't recommend it enough to young people who are looking for a great job and the pay ain't bad.

Microsoft is the world's largest vendor of software development tools. Its flagship product, Visual Studio, supports four of Microsoft's languages: C++, C#, J#, and Visual Basic. Microsoft also sells Visual FoxPro, a language originally conceived solely for database application development. Visual FoxPro has its own IDE, is not a part of Visual Studio, and does not integrate natively with Visual Studio languages.

Visual Basic .NET is a complete rewrite of the Visual Basic language, with a well-thought-out architecture that is methodologically elegant and robust. It represents a huge step forward in Microsoft's strategy to provide a full range of tools for application development. Visual Basic .NET's architecture moves commands and functions out of the language and into *objects*, a trend that is bound to continue. I see the best of Delphi, FoxPro, Visual Basic 6, and even C++ in Visual Basic .NET.

This is not to say that Visual FoxPro applications are unsophisticated compared to those written in Visual Basic .NET. In fact, they're very similar. But Visual FoxPro is easier to learn. You can write your first working application in a few hours.

Microsoft spends huge amounts of money advertising Visual Studio. FoxPro, on the other hand, is practically invisible. I won't speculate on Microsoft's reasons for not advertising FoxPro. It is a spectacular product. It is easier to learn; it takes less time to develop comparable applications; and Visual FoxPro applications run faster than anything written in Visual Basic .NET. But if you don't have clients, it's not a job; it's a hobby.

Visual Basic .NET is the database application development tool of the future. Its architecture is elegant and extensible. It gives you dozens of controls and components, drawing features from Visio, integrated UML support, integrated SQL Server administration and query support, Crystal Reports designer, an HTML editor, and everything else you can imagine. With power comes complexity, but the feature list is impressive. And it has Microsoft's support, without which no product can survive.

Who Should Read This Book

Demand for database applications seems to have no limits. There's not a corporation on this planet that couldn't make double or triple its initial investment in a database application that allowed their employees to work more efficiently. In some cases, applications of this type pay for themselves in a month! The average company considers itself lucky if a particular machine pays for itself in two years, but a 200% annual rate of return is easy to achieve in the database world. So when you walk into the office of a potential client or employer, you're selling something that pays for itself faster than just about any other investment the company could make. That's a pretty good resume.

Database development is fun, the pay is great, and you get to be a hero. We even get more credit than we deserve. For some reason, if a guy comes over and fixes your toilet, he's just a plumber; but when your cousin Danny, a 14-year-old with a bad complexion, gets an Internet connection working again, they call him a computer genius. Doesn't make much sense to me, but take advantage of it. What we do is *cool*.

Database application development is an excellent career choice. Many young people get an undergraduate degree in one of the soft sciences, like Sociology, Anthropology, or Economics, only to find out that the only jobs they qualify for are trainee jobs. But not everyone wants to get a job in Engineering or Pharmacy. And computer science departments seem determined to teach skills that are not in high demand—compiler design and ray tracing graphics are important, but how many operating systems and graphics packages do we need?

I also recommend database development as a second career to professionals who have already achieved mastery of one set of skills, and are looking for something to integrate into their professional life and synthesize a new direction. I've known doctors, dentists, veterinarians, chemists, biologists, actors, teachers—a variety of people who had a decade or two of successes under their belt, but who were still hungry for a new adventure—and made the shift to database development. Databases go with everything.

If you think you missed the boat and lost your chance to prepare for a good career, you're dead wrong. I first saw FoxPro's predecessor, FoxBASE, in 1986, when I was 38 years old. That's when my database career *started* (unless you count a dozen years with COBOL, which I try to forget). So if you're 24 and think you're too old to start a career, don't make me laugh. (You might be too young, though. Sow those wild oats; then come see me when you're ready to get serious about your future.)

Go through this book and learn how the code works. Make the application work, understand what it's doing, and how it does it. When you're done, you'll have a real career—the kind others dream of.

You can travel all around this little planet, meet other programmers, share your successes, pass on your discoveries, and generally have a wonderful time with this career. The languages change every few years, so you won't be bored. And you'll never, ever master database programming, because it's endless. There's always something more to learn, some new challenge to solve, and solutions to be found for your colleagues who think something can't be done. You can push the limits as far as you want. Database development can become the foundation for a successful life.

How This Book Is Organized

This book begins with a review of the major differences between Visual FoxPro and Visual Basic .NET. It shows examples of object-oriented programming in both languages by demonstrating a class-based FoxPro example first, then providing the equivalent in Visual Basic .NET. Finally, it covers specific topics, allowing you to compare the two languages in much more detail. Go to www.samspublishing.com to download the code examples in this book.

What's Not Included

A number of topics are not included in this book. I was unable to include a detailed treatment of thin client development and the construction of installers, due to page count limitations. I excluded the treatment of the Visual FoxPro Toolkit for .NET written by Kamal Patel (www.KamalPatel.net) for the same reason that I excluded the VisualBasic Namespace; because, the whole point of using .NET is to discover its capabilities and use them, rather than depending on legacy features. I've left out remoting and reflection because they are advanced topics that are not required to build many basic database applications.

I didn't talk about third-party products such as RapTier and Visible Developer, both of which will save countless hours, because they build middle-tier code that you will and should know how to write yourself. You can always go out and buy this kind of tool once you understand what they do for you. Finally, I didn't mention Visual CE, a great tool for building Pocket PC applications, because FoxPro doesn't provide a mechanism for programming Windows CE.

With Visual Basic .NET, you can do things that you can't do with FoxPro. However, if you start at the beginning and work through the chapters, writing and testing the code as you go, by the time you finish the book you'll be able to build the same kind of database applications in Visual Basic that you've built in FoxPro. This should get you started on the rest of your career.

An Offer You Can't Refuse

To all readers wherever you live, I'll make you an offer you can't refuse: My email address is les@lespinter.com. If you have any problems with this book, or can't get something to work, or just need a little encouragement, send me an email. When I'm gone, my life will be measured by the number of people whose lives I've affected. So I'd consider it an honor to hear from you. And if you need assistance migrating to .NET, give me a call. My entire consulting practice is focused on migrating Visual FoxPro applications to .NET, and I'd be happy to share the experience with you.

Les Pinter

CHAPTER 1

Differences Between Visual FoxPro and Visual Basic .NET

A Whole New World

When I first began to look at Visual Basic .NET a couple of years ago, it reminded me of the movie *Alien*. Nothing looked familiar!

Where's the command window? And when you find it, what is it for? In Visual FoxPro, you can practically dispense with the menu and just type commands in order to do your work. For example, instead of selecting File, Open, Project from the menu, you can type MODIFY PROJECT (or MODI PROJ as most FoxPro commands can be abbreviated to four characters) and the project name, or just let the list of matching files pop up and press the spacebar to pick the first one. In Visual Basic, although there is a command window, the list of commands that you can type is pretty short.

And while I'm at it, where have all the functions gone? Recent versions of FoxPro (and of Visual Basic, for that matter) have around two thousand commands and functions. Visual Basic .NET has only a couple of hundred. Where did they go?

In FoxPro, commands and functions are in many cases simply wrappers for calls to DLLs that are themselves components of Windows. The developers of FoxPro enclosed all such method calls in **wrappers** to produce the commands and functions that you see when you enter HELP. For example, the UPPER function converts a string to uppercase. In Visual Basic .NET, the Upper method belongs to string objects. So UPPER(mVar) in FoxPro is mVar.Upper in Visual Basic.NET.

Other methods belong to classes, such as Strings and Math. Thanks to IntelliSense, you can type "Strings." Or "Math.", and when you press the period, in each case several dozen familiar method names will appear. But you have to know in which class to look. In FoxPro, you're relieved of the responsibility of knowing which Dynamic Link Library (DLL) the method came from.

Most methods are only exposed when you instantiate an object based on a particular class. For example, TableUpdate() in FoxPro is like a dataset's AcceptChanges() method. But to get to the point where you can use it, you would have to create a dataset, which requires creating a new connection, opening it, creating a new dataadapter, using its Fill method to create a dataset, displaying the dataset in a table to allow the user to make changes, then executing the dataset's AcceptChanges() method to save the changes, like this:

```
Imports System.Data.SQLClient

Public ds as Dataset

Dim cn as New SQLConnection("server=localhost;database=North Wind;UID=sa;PWD=;"
Cn.open()
Dim da as New SQLDataAdapter("SELECT * FROM Customers",cn)
ds = New DataAdapter
Da.fill(ds)
DataGrid1.DataSource = ds.Tables(0)
...
' Save commandbutton Click event handler:
Ds.AcceptChanges()
...
' Code to save changes back to data store
```

That would be two lines of code in FoxPro:

```
BROWSE
TableUpdate(.T.)
```

One of the characteristics of the .NET languages that looks strangest to Visual FoxPro (VFP) developers is that most of what were commands and functions in FoxPro are methods of some two hundred class libraries (called namespaces in .NET) containing over two thousand classes. If you want to use a method, you instantiate an object based on the class that contains it. Then when you type the object's name and a period, IntelliSense kicks in, and the entire list of properties, events, and methods is laid out before you like a banquet table. In order to get to this point, however, you have to know which of the approximately two thousand classes contains the method you want. In some sense, you have to know what you're looking for in order to find it.

Some classes are directly accessible, without requiring that you first instantiate an object based on them. For example, type "Strings.", and as soon as you type the period, a list of dozens of familiar functions appears, again thanks to IntelliSense. Similarly, typing "Math." Displays most of the math functions you know and love in FoxPro. So as long as you know to start by typing the name of the Namespace that contains the functions you need, they're only a word away.

FoxPro FUNCTION and PROCEDURE declarations are as simple as can be. In Visual Basic .NET, Sub and Function declarations seemed to include keywords of endless variety: Overrideable, Shadow, Protected, MustOverride—what did these mean? And did I really have to know about all of them and use all of them in my code? And variable declarations in Visual Basic .NET have a different but equally perplexing variety of options. Do I need to use some of these options? All of them?

And what's up with events? The handling of events in Visual Basic escaped me for years. My eyes glazed over every time I saw the word WithEvents. How was it possible that Visual Basic relied so completely on a feature that you don't even have in FoxPro? You can do everything that events are used for in Visual Basic .NET transparently in FoxPro, without any special effort. I spent hours trying to think of a reason to create an event that FoxPro didn't already have so that I'd have a reason to "raise" it.

I also discovered that data binding, one of FoxPro's greatest strengths, is Visual Basic .NET's greatest weakness. Data binding is so intrinsic in Visual FoxPro that you don't even think about it (at least not until you change to a different data store than the DBF). In .NET, data access is disconnected; there are *always* additional steps required—sometimes lots of them—to send edited data back where it came from.

After months of experimentation, I finally concluded that most of the things I do in FoxPro are done in very similar ways in Visual Basic .NET. Little by little I've found equivalences that make me feel more at home. And sometimes, I even find something in Visual Basic that I like more than the analog in FoxPro. Other than minor name changes, there are only a few things that are truly different.

In most cases, you can ignore many of the powerful but irrelevant features in Visual Basic .NET and use only a subset that's just right for database development. In saying this, I know that I run the risk of incurring the territorial wrath of some guy who's just written an article about how critically important it is to use overloading in *all* of your applications—because if I'm right, he's just wasted your time *and* a tree. (There's a lot of money to be made by saying that things are harder than they really are, because if you're a consultant, and if you know about it and they don't and if they *really, really* need it, they had *better* hire you.) But I'm not afraid of controversy, as you may know. Someone has to point out that the emperor's naked.

Before you start building applications, let's review the principal differences between Visual FoxPro and Visual Basic .NET. I've summarized these differences in this chapter under 12 major subject headings. After reviewing these differences, you should be able to read Visual Basic .NET code and have a general idea of what the code is trying to do.

The Integrated Development Environment (IDE)

Visual Basic .NET is similar to the latest version of FoxPro. Features like the Visual FoxPro 8 Toolbox and the Task Pane appear to have been ported directly from .NET. As you'll see, many of the differences stem from the fact that Visual Basic .NET can build many kinds of applications—Windows Forms, ASP.NET Web pages, Web Services, Smart Devices (Pocket PC and Tablet PC applications), console applications, services that run when your computer starts up, and others. Visual FoxPro only builds two (executables and DLLs).

FoxPro can create `.app` and `.exe` files as well as `.dlls`. However, the `.app` and `.exe` files contain tokenized FoxPro, not machine code. The `.app` files can only be called by other FoxPro programs. The `.exe` files are `.app` files with a loader that Windows can use to run the encapsulated `.app`. DLLs in FoxPro are pretty much used only in XML Web Services. So the generation of a DLL for each project in .NET looks strange to FoxPro developers. FoxPro apps don't have to be compiled into an executable unless they're going to be used with the FoxPro runtime.

Many of the differences between the two languages stem from the fact that so many more output options are available in Visual Basic .NET. In the following sections, we'll look at the main differences in the components of the respective IDEs one by one.

Typing Commands in the Command Window

FoxPro has a command window, which appears automatically when you start up. If the command window isn't visible, you can activate it using Ctrl+F2. The command window is crucial to FoxPro. In it, you can type commands to do virtually everything that you can by clicking on a menu bar. In fact, I use commands so extensively that I've occasionally watched another FoxPro developer do something using the menu and wondered "Why did I never see that before?" Some menu selections actually insert the text of the corresponding command into the command window and execute it there, in effect using the command window as the shell.

The closest equivalent in Visual Basic .NET is Immediate mode in the command window. Although the command window is central to Visual FoxPro, you can use Visual Basic for months without ever opening it. In fact, I haven't opened it up in months. I had to do so just to remember enough to write this paragraph. So, although it's not as central to your work as it is in FoxPro, it can be used in testing and debugging.

Immediate mode in Visual Basic .NET is only available during program execution. You can either set a breakpoint or add `Debugger.Break` (like `SET STEP ON`) to your code. (To set a breakpoint, you can click on the left margin in the Code editor, insert the line

`Debugger.Break`, or press Ctrl+B and specify a breakpoint condition: function name and line number, a variable to monitor for changes, or some other condition.) You can then use the command window (or the Locals window, or one of the four Watch windows) to examine variables. You can use IntelliSense to expose their PEMs (Properties, Events, and Methods). You can execute their methods, run subroutines and functions from the currently executing program, and assign values to object properties.

FoxPro's command window saves prior commands. You can use the UpArrow or PgUp keys to find and execute previously entered commands, or use the keys to cut and paste code into your programs. Visual Basic .NET toggles between Mark and Immediate mode. In Visual Basic .NET's Immediate mode, the up/down arrow keys cycle through recent commands; in Mark mode (which is like the FoxPro variant), you can cut and paste. You can use the shortcuts Ctrl+Alt+I and Ctrl+Shift+M to switch between Mark mode and Immediate mode.

However, Visual Basic .NET doesn't have commands like `MODIFY PROJECT`, `CREATE TABLE`, or any of the dozens of commands that you use in FoxPro. Scroll back through your Visual FoxPro command window; every single command you see there will have to be done in Visual Basic .NET either through an IDE menu selection, a builder in one of Visual Basic .NET's windows, an external program (like the Query Analyzer or the SQL Server Enterprise Manager) or through your own program code. As a result, the Visual Basic .NET IDE exposes the equivalents of Visual FoxPro commands, where they exist, as menu selections. That's yet another reason to become very familiar with the .NET IDE before you go too far. (Appendix A, "A Comparison of FoxPro and Visual Basic .NET Commands and Functions," provides a concordance of Visual FoxPro commands and their Visual Basic counterparts.)

The Toolbox

In FoxPro you add controls to your forms using the Form Controls toolbar, which can display either the FoxPro base control classes, your current selection of registered OCXs and DLLs, or any combination of your own class libraries and the excellent classes that ship with FoxPro. Starting with FoxPro 7 you can also drag and drop classes from the Component Gallery. Beginning with FoxPro 8, you have the Toolbox, with tabs for the Component Gallery and a customizable toolbox where you can store your own classes.

The Toolbox is the only way to drag and drop controls onto forms in Visual Basic .NET. In that sense, it replaces FoxPro's Form Controls toolbar. But it does much more. The FoxPro and Visual Basic .NET toolboxes are very similar. Visual FoxPro's Toolbox has bars for text scraps (it's initially seeded with a bug report template and a commented program header, but you can add entries by highlighting and dragging them to the Toolbox). The Visual Basic .NET equivalent is the Clipboard, to which code fragments are automatically added whenever you highlight code or text and press Ctrl+C. Figure 1.1 shows the Visual Basic .NET Toolbox.

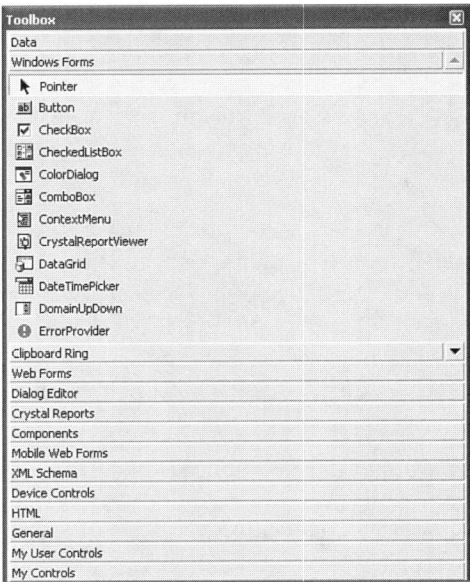

FIGURE 1.1   The Visual Basic .NET Toolbox.

The .NET toolbox contains collections of objects for every conceivable environment: Data, Device Controls, XML Schema, Dialog Editor, Mobile Web Forms, Web Forms, Components, Windows Forms, HTML, the Clipboard Ring, Crystal Reports, and any other toolboxes that you might want to add and customize.

When the Visual FoxPro Screen Designer is open, the Toolbox entries for the FoxPro Base Classes, the Foundation Classes, and My Base Classes permit you to drag and drop screen design elements from the toolbox instead of dragging them from the Form Controls toolbar. Any ActiveX controls that you've registered in the Tools, Options, Controls dialog page will appear here as well, so you don't have to switch between your class library toolbar and the ActiveX Controls toolbar. And you can also use the Form Controls toolbar and the Toolbox at the same time.

In Visual Basic .NET, the Toolbox is your one-stop-shopping source for screen controls and components. As you move from one design context to another, the toolbar elements change to reflect what's appropriate. For example, if you're building an ASP .NET form, you can select from either HTML controls or Web Forms controls. Visual Basic .NET provides a collection of components, such as `FileSystemWatcher`, `MessageQueue`, and others that you just don't have in FoxPro.

In Visual Basic .NET, you can build your own user controls, just as you can build your own classes in FoxPro and then add them to the User Controls toolbar. In Chapter 2, "Building Simple Applications in Visual FoxPro and Visual Basic .NET," you'll learn how to add a

Windows Control Library to your project, after which any user controls you add to it will automatically be displayed in the User Controls toolbar. As in FoxPro, you use these controls instead of the standard Visual Basic controls on your forms. And because all of your user controls show up here, regardless of which Windows Control Library they came from, you don't have to switch between VCXs as you do in FoxPro.

TIP

Unlike FoxPro, where each open class library is a selection on the Class Picker toolbar context menu, there's only one User Controls toolbar in Visual Basic .NET.

Tab Ordering

Tab ordering of controls is a little different in VB .NET as well. In FoxPro, you can use the Tools, Options, Forms dialog to select either interactive or list ordering of your form controls. If you use interactive ordering, you click on controls in the order in which you want the user to be able to tab through them, then click somewhere on the form surface to tell FoxPro you're done. I usually prefer tab ordering by list.

In Visual Basic .Net, interactive tab ordering is the only way that's available. To start the process, select Tab Ordering from the View menu pad. When you're done, select Tab Ordering from the menu pad again; clicking somewhere on the form won't do a thing.

Projects and Solutions

FoxPro's basic container for building an application is the **project**. FoxPro stores the pieces of a project in a **project file**, which is a table and associated memo file with the same structure as a DBF and the extensions PJX and PJT. When the Project Manager screen is open, a Project menu pad with the relevant options (including Set Main, Exclude from Project, and Build Executable/DLL) appears in the FoxPro menu. Although FoxPro has had the ability to build DLLs for several versions, in general FoxPro developers haven't warmed up to them. Files that are located in the current directory are not necessarily listed in the project; files can be listed but excluded, which documents the files' importance to the project. These files remain freestanding elements not included in the executable.

Visual Basic .NET adds one more layer on top of the projects layer: the solution. I think the marketing guys had a hand in this, because where I come from, it's not a solution until it solves something. But I suppose they had to call it something. And I like what it does.

Visual Basic .NET applications sometimes consist of a data server that sends and receives data in XML format, a Windows Forms, and/or an ASP.NET application that uses that data. Because each of these is a project, it's useful to group them in such a manner as to be able to associate the data source with the data consumer. Solutions do just that. If you have only one project, it's still enclosed in a solution. But if there are several related projects, the solution keeps them together for administrative purposes.

Figure 1.2 shows a Visual Basic. NET solution containing a Web service and a Windows form application that uses the Web service. The two FoxPro projects in Figure 1.3 do the same thing, but you just have to remember that they're related to one another. In both cases the Web service and the application that uses it are in different directories.

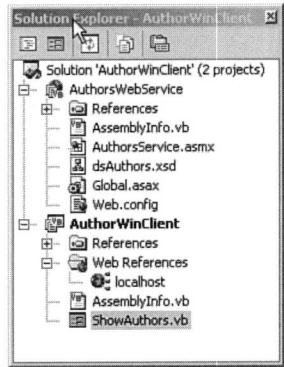

FIGURE 1.2   A Visual Basic. NET solution containing a Web service and a Windows form application that uses the Web service.

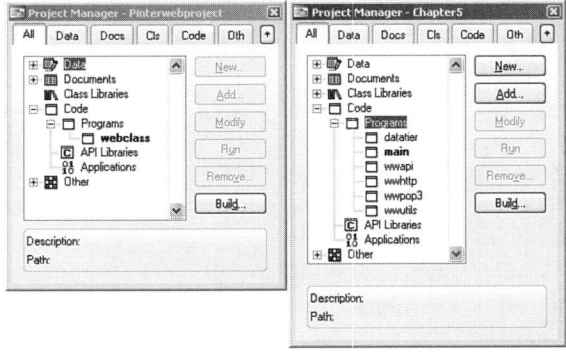

FIGURE 1.3   Two FoxPro projects.

However, the solution doesn't produce an executable. Executables or DLLs are the result of compiling **projects**. Solutions are simply a bookkeeping mechanism. In a solution, there will always be one project designated as the Startup project. That's the one that will run if you press F5. It can't be a class library because they're not executable. But it can be a Web page, a Web service, or any kind of executable.

Compiler Output Formats

In FoxPro, although you can compile to APP, DLL, or EXE format, you generally build EXE files. APP files can only be called from another FoxPro application and DLLs require some additional work that generally isn't worth the bother. In Visual Basic .NET (and in earlier versions of Visual Basic), it's common practice to build components as Dynamic Link Libraries (DLLs). Typically, at least one of the projects in the solution compiles to EXE format. DLLs built from other projects in the solution—class libraries, user controls, and the like—are used as components of the executable.

When you build a FoxPro project, you can build an APP, an EXE, a single-threaded DLL, or a multithreaded DLL. APPs can be called by the FoxPro runtime, but I almost always use EXEs. I've only used DLLs for Web services and seldom even then. You can either click on the Build button, press Alt+D, or type BUILD EXE *Name* FROM *Name* (BUILD DLL *Name* FROM *Name*, or BUILD MTDLL *Name* FROM *Name* for multithreaded DLLs).

In Visual Basic .NET, DLLs are used as you might use class libraries in FoxPro. For example, you can build an inheritable form (a Form Template class in FoxPro) as a DLL and inherit from it in another form, after you include the DLL as a reference in your project. When you build a Class Library project in Visual Basic .NET (by right-clicking on the project name in the Solution Explorer, selecting Properties, and setting the Output option to Class Library), the project compiles to a DLL.

> **NOTE**
>
> The name Dynamic Link Library (DLL) derives from the fact that they are linked when called (dynamically) rather than when the executable is created. So, you can run them from within other programs. They are said to run **in-process** as opposed to **out-of-process** in the non-FoxPro world, where components are compiled as DLLs; for us, the distinction is meaningless.

When you build a project, the type of project you select determines which references to .NET class library components will be automatically included. You can then add any other references (DLLs or namespaces) that you need. For example, if you want to inherit from an inheritable form that you had built previously, you would add a reference to the inheritable form DLL in your project before trying to add the inherited form. In that way, the project knows where to look for and display any available inheritable forms.

The nearest FoxPro equivalent would be adding class libraries to a project. (The other case where you add references, when you add ActiveX controls to forms, involves using the Tools, Options, Controls page to add ActiveX controls to the Selected list. This causes them to be displayed in the Form Controls toolbar ActiveX menu. However, ActiveX components don't explicitly appear in the Project Manager's file list.)

In Visual Basic .NET you first designate the Startup project because a solution may contain several projects. You can see this if you build my favorite .NET walkthrough, *Creating a Distributed Application*. (This walkthrough can be found in the Visual Studio .NET, Samples and Walkthroughs Help selection. In it, you build a solution containing a Web service, then add a Windows client application, and finally add a Web client application.) You can designate any of the three as the startup project. If you choose the Web service, a test page is automatically built and presented to you to test those of your Web services that are testable with keyboard input (that is, those that don't have a diffgram [a dataset containing changes made to another dataset] or other type of dataset as the input parameter). Change the Startup Project selection in the Solution Explorer and you can test either of the other projects. It beats fumbling around trying to remember the name of your latest FoxPro Web Service directory.

The Code Window

The code window for a Windows Forms project is shown in Figure 1.4. Unlike FoxPro, which puts each code snippet in a separate window, they're concatenated in Visual Basic. The Text Editor toolbar contains elements for indenting text, setting and jumping to bookmarks, and displaying object and parameter information.

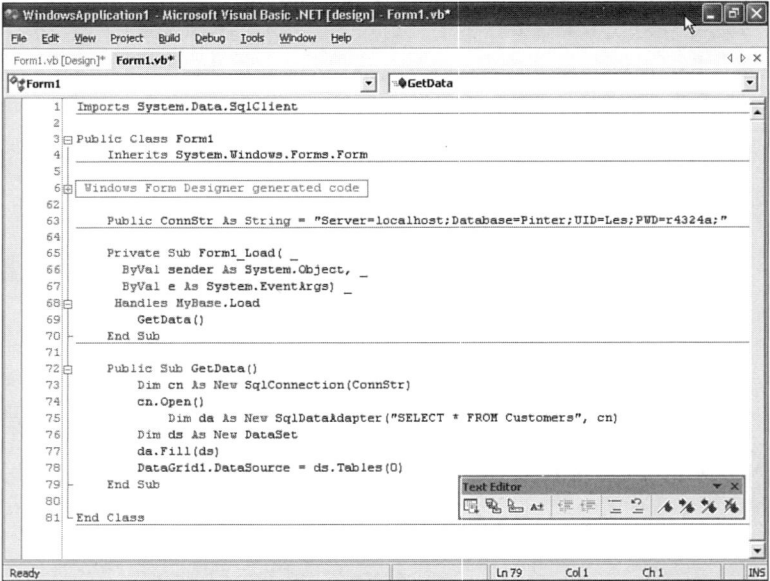

FIGURE 1.4   The code window for a Windows Forms project.

The Document View Window

FoxPro's Document View window automatically displays all of the events and methods in the current form or class where you've already written some code and lets you click to jump to the selected code snippet.

There is no Document View window in the Visual Basic IDE. However, the Class view does just about the same thing, and exposes all of the classes in your project, not just the currently open file. And if you enter comments preceded by a single quote and the word TODO at the beginning of each routine, the Task List (activated from the menu using Alt+V, K, A) will display an entry for each TODO item. Double-clicking on an item takes you straight to the comment line in the code. So with a tiny amount of effort you get the same capability, and in fact, a little more.

To jump to a code snippet that you haven't yet coded in a Visual Basic .NET form, you select the object (for example, the form or a button or list box) from the drop-down list at the upper left of the code window screen, and then select the corresponding event or method from the drop-down list at the upper right of the screen. Just as in FoxPro, the names of snippets containing code appear in boldface. In FoxPro you can open the Properties window and pick the Methods tab, and then double-click on an event or method name to open its code snippet; you can't do that in Visual Basic .NET because events and methods don't appear in the Properties window page. It makes more sense in Visual Basic .NET, but the convenience of FoxPro is nice, too.

Bookmarks and Task Lists

Bookmarks and a Task List are both available in both Visual FoxPro and Visual Basic, and perform very similar functions. To create a bookmark in FoxPro, Shift+Double-click or use Alt+Shift+F2. In Visual Basic .NET, use Ctrl+K, which is a toggle. You can also click on the Toggle Bookmark button (the little blue flag) in the Text Editor toolbar. In fact, there are four command buttons in the Text Editor toolbar for managing all aspects of bookmarks; in FoxPro, you have to use the context menu.

The Server Explorer

In FoxPro, using DBFs is extremely easy. The USE command opens a table. CURSORSET-PROP("Buffering",5) turns on optimistic table buffering, so that APPEND BLANK or record changes are not finalized until and unless you issue a TableUpdate() call. TableRevert() undoes anything done since optimistic buffering was enabled. If you're using a DBF, TableUpdate() commits changes back to the file on disk, and you're truly done.

There is no Visual Basic .NET equivalent to FoxPro's DBF in terms of ease of use. You must create a connection to find the data source, a data adapter (or at least a command object) to retrieve the data, and a dataset (an XML schema and container) to hold the data while you work with it. Then you must explicitly send an INSERT or UPDATE command back to the data source. There's even a CommandBuilder object that will use your SELECT command to infer the other three commands for you.

Visual Basic .NET doesn't have a USE command. To connect to a table, you need to define a connection using a connection string such as this one:

```
Server=(local);Database=Northwind;UID=sa;PWD=;
```

Visual Basic's Server Explorer exposes some of the capabilities of FoxPro's `BROWSE` command. After you've defined a connection, you can open a table in the connected database, return all rows, and optionally type changes or additions, which will be sent back to the data source. It allows access not only to ODBC/OLEDB data sources (your FoxPro tables, for example), but also to SQL Server databases.

Thus you can open a database and then view, edit, or add data without opening up the SQL Server Enterprise Manager or the Query Analyzer. You can also create tables, indexes, and relations. Still, the connection to your tables seems a little removed compared to FoxPro. And there's a slight delay when you access any data table. However, you can do all of the things that you can do with FoxPro tables, albeit in more roundabout ways.

In FoxPro, you use `CREATE` *TableName* to open up the schema design tool, or `MODIFY STRUCTURE` to change an existing one. `USE` *TableName* opens the table and points to the first row, whereas `BROWSE` returns the number of rows that you see in the resulting grid. There is no perceptible delay in either a `USE` or a `BROWSE` in FoxPro because little or no data is moved from the data source to the workstation.

In FoxPro, we use local tables because they're cheap and because they're fast. In fact, as of this writing, Microsoft doesn't sell a faster data store for single-user workstation applications than FoxPro DBFs with CDX files. (Actually, they don't sell it; they give it away.)

In Visual Basic .NET, using local data sources (like DBFs or Access MDB files) implies exactly the same degree of difficulty as does the use of SQL Server. As a programmer, you save your client no programming costs if you use local tables, as would have been the case with FoxPro.

I would love to have FoxPro's ease of access to local tables in Visual Basic .NET. Still, using the Server Explorer to build connections and data adapters is much easier than it used to be in Visual Basic, so to Visual Basic 6 programmers it's a step up.

What Can You DO in the IDE?

In FoxPro you type `DO` *AppName* to run an APP, an EXE, or a PRG. You can type `DO MAIN.PRG` and run your entire application within the IDE, rather than compiling and running an executable with `MAIN` as the entry point. You can also `DO FORM` *FormName* to run a form standalone.

You can't do that in Visual Basic; you can only execute an executable. But it's easy. Press F5 and the designated Startup project runs. To test a form, you'll need to add a couple of lines of code in your main form menu to instantiate the form class as an object and call its `Show()` method, like this:

```
Dim Frm as new CustForm
Frm.Show()
```

That's two lines of code instead of one, but it's almost as easy as `DO FORM` *CustForm*.

The Class Browser and Visual Basic .NET's Class View

Both FoxPro and Visual Basic .NET have a class browser. If you need to become familiar with a class in a FoxPro VCX, you can use the Class Browser to examine its structure (although you can't edit the method code in the Class Browser). Also, you'll need to use the Open dialog to locate and open a class. Visual Basic .NET's Class view automatically shows all of the classes in the current solution in a tree view, and permit code editing. To jump to the code for a method, double click on its name.

The Object Browser

For your own classes, you use the Class Browser; for all other objects, there's the Object Browser. FoxPro's Object Browser lets you open a type library from any of the registered classes on your computer and browse through the class hierarchy, whereas Visual Basic's Object Browser uses the currently open solution to navigate (although you can browse objects that aren't in the project as well.). It lists the objects of whichever project you click on in the Solution Explorer. Visual Basic .NET's Object Browser not only knows what's in your project, but remembers selected components from session to session. FoxPro's Object Browser is not connected to the current project.

The Properties Window

FoxPro's Properties windowopens with Alt+W, P (Windows, Properties), whereas in Visual Studio, F4 brings up the Visual Studio Properties window. You can view properties on .NET's built-in controls, or properties on your own classes.

In both Visual FoxPro and Visual Basic .NET, properties can be listed either alphabetically or grouped by categories. These categories are fixed in FoxPro, whereas in Visual Basic .NET you can add your own by preceding property procedures with the `<Category("XYZ")>` attribute (provided that you've included `Imports System.ComponentModel` at the top of your class). Precede your custom categories with an asterisk (for example, `*XYZ`) and they'll appear right at the top of the Properties window.

The most important difference between the two languages in this regard is that in FoxPro, properties are like public variables of classes and have immediate visibility in the Class Designer as well as in classes that inherit from the class. In Visual Basic you need to write a **property procedure** (as follows) consisting of about eight lines of code for each and every property that you want to see in the Properties window.

To create a property procedure in a class, you type

```
Public Property (name)
```

As soon as you press Enter, the IDE adds six lines of code.

You're expected to do three things:

1. Declare a private variable in the Declarations section of the class; the name should be an underscore followed by the name you used for the property procedure. A good time to do this would be just before creating the property procedure.

2. Add a `Return _PropName` statement in the Getter.

3. Add a `_PropName = Value` statement in the Setter.

Furthermore, unlike FoxPro, in Visual Basic .NET you only see your properties in classes that inherit from your class—not in the class itself. So if you define property procedures in a class, you won't see them in the Properties window. As soon as you inherit from that class, the inherited object's Properties window will expose the property.

Getters and Setters Versus `ASSIGN` and `ACCESS` Methods

Property procedures do more than simply expose the property in the Properties window; they also provide a trappable event at the moment of assigning or retrieving a property value. That's what the `Get` and `Set` methods (often called Getters and Setters) in a Visual Basic .NET property procedure do. (These will be discussed in more detail in the discussion of the Properties window because they're very important, very different, and you'll use them every day.)

FoxPro properties by default do nothing when you assign them a value, unless you indicate that you want to include Assign and/or Access methods when you add a property in the Class Designer. If you do, FoxPro adds procedures (methods) to the class with the name of the property followed by either `_Assign` or `_Access`. You can type code into these methods, and when you either assign a value to the property or request its value, the corresponding property procedure code will execute.

If you're writing classes in a `.prg` file and you want `Assign` and `Access` methods for your properties, simply use the name of the property with `_Assign` or `_Access` added to the end of the property name as the procedure name, and it will indeed fire when the property is assigned a value or when the value is read, respectively.

I've only had occasion to use `Assign` and `Access` methods twice in my professional career, so I don't think they're very important. Requiring eight lines of code for every single property in a class on the off chance that you *might* want to use `Assign` and `Access` methods seems to me to be a case of the tail wagging the dog. However, you absolutely have to use property procedures if you want to use properties as you do in FoxPro.

Shortcut Keys

The IDE is where you spend your day, so it's important to know where everything is. By this point in your career, you probably don't even need to look for things. When you want to open up the Properties window, your hands type Ctrl+W, P without any conscious effort on your part.

You need to develop the equivalent reflexes for Visual Basic .NET. The task is somewhat complicated by the fact that FoxPro is a command window-based IDE, so that all of the features that are accessible from the menu, or from toolbars, are generally accessible as well by typing a command string.

In both languages, the menus are context-sensitive. For example, the Project menu pad is only visible after you've opened a project. For example, the Form Designer shown in Figure 1.5 must be open in order to right-click on the designer surface and expose the context menu that lets you activate the Properties window.

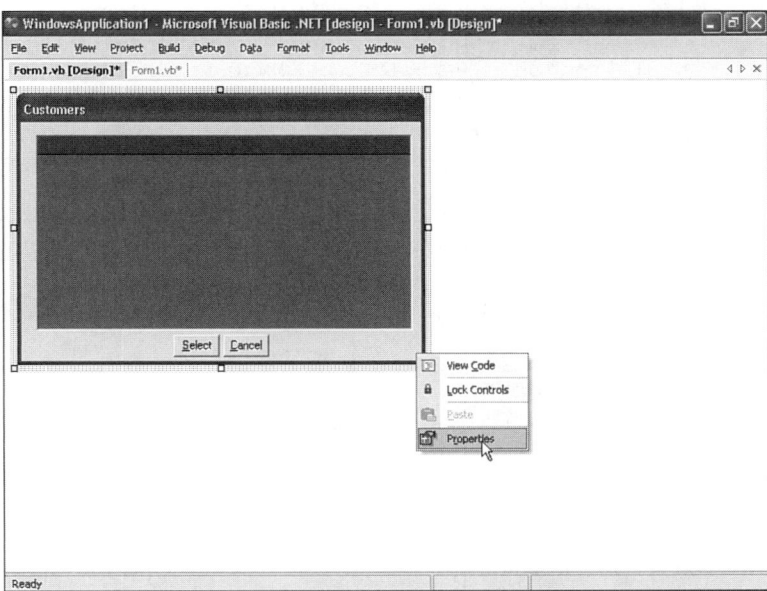

FIGURE 1.5 The Form Designer.

Table 1.1 summarizes the menu shortcut or the command that activates the main functionalities of the respective Integrated Development Environments. (The entries in the table assume that the target context is available—for example, the hotkey for a Form Designer feature is only available if the Form Designer is open.)

TABLE 1.1   Keyboard Shortcuts in Visual Basic .NET and Visual FoxPro

Feature	Visual Basic .NET	Visual FoxPro
Properties sheet	F4	Alt+W,P
Solution Explorer	Ctrl+Alt+L	Alt+W,Project Mgr, or Alt+F, New Project to create
Server Explorer	Ctrl+Alt+S	Like the Database Container or Data Environment
Class view	Ctrl+Shift+C	Alt+T, C
Object Browser	Ctrl+Alt+J	Alt+T, J
Compile and Run	F5	Ctrl+D, then select

The Tools, Options Dialog

FoxPro can be managed from the Tools, Options dialog. The Tools, Options page contains a page frame with 14 pages, containing settings that have huge implications for the way the IDE, and your applications, work. Some of these pages have equivalents in Visual Basic .NET, but a few of them don't. For example, the Data and the Remote Data pages, which handle access to DBFs and to SQL using remote views respectively, are irrelevant in Visual Basic .NET; the Data page controls access to DBFs in FoxPro, and in Visual Basic .NET DBFs are just another OLEDB or ODBC data source. Also, the purpose of Remote views in FoxPro is to provide access to SQL Server table data in a way that's very similar to the way we use DBFs.

The Options page I wish Visual Basic .NET had is the Field Mapping page, which controls which of your classes are used to automatically populate a form. There is no equivalent feature in Visual Basic .NET. The Data Form Wizard does some things that are interesting, but I use inheritance for forms, and the wizard doesn't. It's the greatest shortcoming of the form design environment.

Visual Basic .NET also has a Tools, Options menu selection. The resulting dialog uses a tree view for navigation instead of a page frame. In addition, some of the settings found in FoxPro's Tools, Options dialog are to be found in the Solution and Project Properties sheets, respectively. Right-click on either the solution or a project and select Properties from the resulting context menu.

Table 1.2 shows the location of equivalents to the FoxPro Tools, Options Page elements in the .NET IDE.

TABLE 1.2   Equivalents to the FoxPro Tools, Options Page Elements in the .NET IDE

FoxPro	Visual Basic .NET
View	Tools, Options, Environment, General.
General	No equivalent (FoxPro-specific).
Data	Connection- and `DataAdapter`-specific.
Remote Data	Connection- and `DataAdapter`-specific.
File Locations	N/A; Visual Studio controls file locations.

TABLE 1.2   Continued

FoxPro	Visual Basic .NET
Forms	Tools, Options, Windows Form Designer; for templates, use Add Inherited Form from Solution Explorer context menu.
Projects	Source Control, General tab for SourceSafe settings
Controls	Add References in the Solution Explorer exposes the Add Reference dialog; the COM page lists registered COM objects, and has a BROWSE button for unregistered COM objects.
Regional	Environment, International Settings controls most; use the locale property of the dataset to set CultureInfo; FormatCurrency function; System.Globalization Namespace components can be used to override the System and User language and currency specifications.
Debug	Environment, Fonts and Colors sets colors in various windows. VS .NET debug settings involve features that Visual FoxPro doesn't have.
Editor	Text Editor, Basic and Text Editor, General tabs; The Visual FoxPro equivalent of some Visual Basic Text editor settings are found in the Edit, Properties dialog available while editing a text file. The Visual FoxPro Tools, Options IDE tab is used to set many of the VS Text Editor tab settings.
Field Mapping	FoxPro specific; I wish there were a Visual Basic equivalent.
IDE	Text Editor, Basic; Environment, Fonts and Colors;
Reports	In a Crystal Report, right click on the design surface and select Designer, Default Settings

The Task Pane Manager

The FoxPro Task Pane is a command center that brings together resources for learning FoxPro, samples of code, and links to related Web sites. This is similar to the Online Resources panel of the .NET Start Page. Some elements of the Task Pane are to be found in the Tools, Options dialog, under Environment, General (for example, what to show when the IDE starts up). But the FoxPro Task Pane manager doesn't have an exact duplicate in the Visual Basic .NET IDE.

The Output Window and Your Application Menu

FoxPro's output goes by default to _Screen, the background screen for FoxPro and by default any FoxPro application that you build. You can use a combination of a form's DeskTop, MDIForm, and ShowWindow properties to change that, but many developers use FoxPro's _Screen as their background and as the container for their menu (which replaces FoxPro's _MSYSMENU), as well as for all of the forms in their application. The simple application we'll write in Chapter 2 does just that.

No similar default background exists in Visual Basic .NET. Your first form is the container for all other forms. You manually drop a `MainMenu` control on the form and use Visual Basic .NET's delicious menu designer, which I would have loved to have in FoxPro.

When an IDE action such as a compile produces output, it opens the Output window by default at the bottom of the screen. If you have compile errors, they'll appear here. You can double-click on an error to be taken directly to the offending code.

Customizing the IDE

In FoxPro, I usually put the form that I'm working on at the upper-left corner of the screen; the Project Manager, Properties window, and the command window over on the right. I reduce the screen resolution to the smallest size that doesn't give me a headache, then expand the Properties sheet to fill almost all of the vertical size of the screen; the Project Manager and the command window split what's left at the lower-right corner of the screen. The Toolbox goes somewhere on top of the properties window whenever I need it.

In Visual Basic .NET I have a more convenient option: I open the Properties window using F4, then open the Solution Explorer with Ctrl+Alt+L and drop it on top of the Properties window. It becomes a member of the same container. I do the same thing with the Toolbox. As I drop these elements, tabs with their names appear at the bottom of the container. All three can thus share in the same space, each coming to the foreground when its tab is clicked.

FoxPro IDE components can be right-clicked and characterized as dockable, which controls whether or not they stay put and behave as expected. I generally make them dockable. Visual Basic .NET components can be configured with more specificity, although I have a 21-inch monitor and it's still not big enough. If the truth be told, though, it's not big enough for FoxPro application development either.

Getting used to the IDE is important if you want to enjoy application development. And it's a never-ending task. I even learned a bunch of new IDE tweaks from Cathy Pountney at the DevTeach Conference in Montreal, and I've been doing this for 15 years. Productivity is the name of the game, and the fine folks in Redmond have given us some great tools. So take the time to learn where things are in the IDE and what they can do for you. It's a small investment that will return a big dividend.

The Visual Basic .NET Solution Explorer

The distinction between FoxPro's Project Manager and Visual Basic .NET's Solution Explorer was touched on earlier, but there are additional important differences.

FoxPro groups every project into five classes of elements, as indicated by the tabs at the head of the Project Manager:

- Data lists excluded tables as well as files that define queries and views.

- Documents contains screens (forms), reports, and labels.

- Classes lists all Visual Class Libraries contained in your project.

- Code includes PRG files for standalone programs, procedures, or class libraries in code.

- Other holds menus, graphics, and miscellaneous text files.

Items can be listed in the project file but are marked as excluded, so that they are not part of the executable and can be modified. For example, by default DBFs are marked as excluded in the Project Manager. If a DBF (say a table of States) is included in the executable, it can be read but can't be modified. This is sometimes useful, but rarely. Items that are in the current directory but haven't been included in the project don't appear in the Project Manager files list.

> **TIP**
>
> I once saw a clever use of a DBF embedded in the executable. In a multiuser FoxPro application running on a Local Area Network (LAN), the programmer added a "licenses" table containing 10 records. Then, whenever a user logged on, he used LOCATE FOR NOT RLOCK(). If he found a record, he issued an RLOCK(). As users logged out, the records were unlocked. After 10 users, no more records could be found.

Finally, if you create an empty project and add your MAIN program, the BUILD PROJECT command will start by reading all components referenced in MAIN and then follow the rabbit trail until the project has been rebuilt.

There is no corresponding automatic discovery process in Visual Basic .NET. You have to add files to a project manually, one at a time. Click on the Show All Files button to see files that are located in the project directory. The icon beside each file's name indicates whether it's included in the project or not.

In Visual Basic .NET, when you create a project, a solution of the same name is also created, with a hierarchy consisting of a bin and a debug directory. In the Solution Explorer there's a Show All Files button; when you click it, all of the files in the application directory are displayed. You can right-click on them and include them in the build. Once the files are included, the Properties window gives you several options for the build **action**—none, content, compile, or embedded resource.

All of the code files in a project must be written in the same language. However, you can build a solution with one Visual Basic (.vb) project and one C# (.cs) project, and they'll make beautiful music together. This is, of course, because both have been translated to Intermediate Language by the time the solution is built, and neither one cares which boat the other's ancestors arrived on.

Intermediate Language

Intermediate language is the result of the compilation project in Visual Studio .NET, regardless of which language you use to write the code. It looks a bit like assembler. When you first run an executable on a workstation, the internal IL is compiled to machine codeas pieces of your application are invoked. This happens each time the application is run, and a noticeable delay occurs during compilation.

The FoxPro IDE does something similar. If you DO a PRG inside FoxPro and if an .fxp file exists with an earlier time stamp, FoxPro automatically compiles the PRG to produce an FXP. If the FXP is more recent, it's run, and the PRG is ignored. Of course, we don't send PRGs to our customers, and the FoxPro runtime can't compile them; but the analogy is useful.

In general, project elements are either code or data. If they contain code, their extension indicates which language you chose for your project (currently .vb, .cs, or .js for Visual Basic, C#, and J#). There are also a host of extensions that have been created for various components of a Visual Studio solution or project component. Generally, these are tables in XML format. In FoxPro we use DBFs with other extensions; the notion is precisely the same.

Some files have companion files under certain circumstances. For example, forms have a .resx (resource) file, which contains information about the form. Open it up, and you'll be able to see the contents either as XML or in table form.

Similarly, .xsd (schema) files have an associated .vb or .cs file if they represent a typed dataset. Typed datasets allow FoxPro developers to do something near and dear to our hearts—use the Table.Field syntax in Visual Basic .NET that we have always had in FoxPro. To do so in Visual Basic .NET, there must be a class with one property procedure for each field name in the table in question. These classes are automatically generated by the Generate Dataset phase of the DataAdapter Wizard dialog.

If you generate a typed dataset (an XML schema file with an .xsd extension), the .xsd file will have a .vb file behind it with one property procedure for each column in the table. You have to click the Show All Files button to see it. Typed datasets are the only way you'll be able to type employee.lastname in Visual Basic .NET. You don't even want to know what you have to type to refer to a field without them. I imagine that FoxPro does something similar internally, although not knowing about it has never bothered me.

TIP

You can generate typed datasets directly from the command line if you have an XML schema. You can get the XML Schema from SQL Server using the FOR XML AUTO&Root=Root option, or from any other source. Open a Visual Studio command window, use the command XSD (file-name.xml) to create an XSD file, and then use XSD (filename.xsd) -c /1:VB to generate a Visual Basic typed dataset class. Or you can simply right-click on a data adapter at the bottom of a form and select Generate Dataset.

Other files in the project use XML files to store tables of information concerning how to manage and build the project. An XML file in its simplest form describes rows and columns, so it's exactly like a DBF without the ability to have an index and thus be searched quickly. You can think of them as dumbed-down DBFs. Generally, if you double-click on a file with a .vbproj, .sln, .xsd, or other extension, you'll get XML; and at the lower-left corner of the screen you'll see a Data tab. Click on it to see a tabular representation of the XML.

DLLs

A solution can consist of multiple projects. Typically, one of them is an executable, and the rest are class libraries, which are compiled into Dynamic Link Libraries (DLLs).

There is a fundamental belief in the non-FoxPro world that components should be bullet-proofed, then shared as DLLs and patched together. What would be a class library in FoxPro is generally built as a separate DLL in Visual Basic, and shared with other developers. FoxPro developers generally view their class libraries as an integral part of the forms that use them, and continue to modify forms and the class libraries that use them simultaneously. Because sharing DLLs is a normal practice in the non-FoxPro developer communities, they're often looked at as a final product, and subjected to quality assurance procedures of some sort.

That's not the world of the rapid prototyper, the world we as database developers live in. My clients' requirements shift daily, sometimes hourly. I simply can't send out a memo requesting changes in a DLL, and then wait a few weeks for them to code, test, and ship back the result for me to test.

In FoxPro, although you can do this, I've never felt the need to build components and stitch them together to build the executable. It just never occurred to me—and still doesn't, come to think of it. I don't see changing our thinking to accept black-box DLLs as a normal component of application development in FoxPro. But in Visual Basic .NET, classes compile to DLLs—there is no equivalent to FoxPro's VCX file.

Other Characteristics of a Visual FoxPro Project

FoxPro uses a current directory concept. At any time you can type CD in the command window to see "where you are"—that is, what the current directory is. You can also type ? SET("DEFAULT") or ? CURDIR() to display the current directory in the output window (_Screen). You can use CD (path) or SET DEFAULT TO (path) to change it. Before creating a project, you use CD and MD commands to create and navigate to the folder the project will occupy.

The mere fact that files are located in this directory doesn't make them part of the project, and in fact a project isn't strictly necessary. FoxPro is unique in that you can run programs without compiling them. If you type DO MAIN in the command window, the program will run *exactly* as if you had compiled it and run the executable. And even if you do build an executable, if FoxPro can't find a program, screen, menu, or class file in the executable, it searches first in the current directory, and then along any paths specified with a SET PATH TO command (for example, SET PATH TO Classes;Menus;Programs).

Using Tables to Store FoxPro Project Components

If you type CREATE Table1, a dialog opens to allow you to build a table schema and store it in a file with a .dbf extension (and optionally an additional file with the same name and the extension .fpt if your table schema contains variable-length fields called "memo fields"). Any DBF that has variable-length fields has an associated memo file with the extension "FPT". There are other extensions that are used for other types of files. I'll introduce each of them.

Projects are stored in one of these file pairs with the extensions .pjx and .pjt respectively. The "PJX" is the "DBF" file, and the "PJT" is the "FPT" file. It shouldn't surprise you that FoxPro uses a table to store the project details. Screens, classes, and reports use the same scheme of pairs of files with extensions that suggest their usage.

Visual Studio uses HTML files for similar purposes. For example, each page in an ASP.NET application is stored in an HTML file with the extension "aspx", which is essentially a table containing the descriptive elements of the page. The code is stored separately in a "code-behind" file. But if you change the page, you don't have to recompile, because it's just data—exactly as if it were coming from a DBF.

By default, any files you create for a project will go in the current directory. When you create a project using the MODIFY PROJECT Name command, the .pjx and .pjt files are created. Subsequently, as you add other files like MAIN.PRG, they are put by default into the current directory.

> **NOTE**
>
> Long ago, Windows performed poorly when more than 127 files were located in any single folder. As a result, it was customary to distribute the elements of Visual FoxPro projects into Screens, Reports, Data, and Other folders. That's no longer necessary.

If you build a menu, an MNX/MNT file pair is created. If it's included in a project, in the project record for the MNX file an MPR file with the same filename and the extension .mpr is designated as the **outfile**. The compiled code for the resulting compiled MPX file is stored in the Object memo field.

If you create a form (screen), a pair of files with .scx and .sct extensions are added. Again, if there's no project, FoxPro will compile and run the SCX file using the DO FORM FormName command. The SCX/SCT files don't have to be part of a project.

If you create a class library, a VCX/VCT pair is created. It has exactly the same column layout as an SCX/SCT file pair. (Think about that for a while. This is the reason that you can select Save As Class in the Form Designer and then instantiate a form object from the saved form class using `frm = CREATEOBJECT("`*`formclassname`*`")` followed by `frm.Show()`—almost exactly the same syntax used in Visual Basic .NET.)

TIP

If you want to ship someone your screens or class libraries without giving them source code, you can compile both VCX and SCX files, and erase the code in the Methods memo field. The compiled code in the ObjCode field is all the user's FoxPro compiler needs to build the executable.

If you use a FoxPro project file, when you build the application, any included PRG files are compiled, and the generated FXP code is added into the corresponding `MAIN.PRG` record in the object memo field. If you called an MPR (menu) program, it is compiled into an MPX file and the MPX is included in the executable. Any SCX (screen) and VCX (class) files are compiled and added to the executable.

After the source files have been compiled, you don't need to ship any of them to your users; the executable contains everything. However, if there's no project, FoxPro will look for and execute the MPX file if it exists; if not, it will look for and compile the MPR file, and then run the resulting MPX file. It won't automatically build an MPR file from an MNX file, though; you have to do that in the Menu Builder, or let the Project Manager do it for you at build time.

Similarly, any referenced screen files are called as needed. Class library files, on the other hand, whether in VCX or as `DEFINE CLASS` statements located in PRG files, must be referred to in the code with `SET CLASSLIB TO` *`VCXFileName`* `ADDITIVE` and `SET PROCEDURE TO` *`PrgFileName`* `ADDITIVE` in order for FoxPro to know how to use their contents.

Reports are stored in FRX/FRT pairs. It's common practice to exclude report files from the project and then simply build a list of available FRX files for the user to select. In this way, customized reporting is easy to support.

File Types Used in Visual Basic Projects

Unlike Visual FoxPro, Visual Basic puts your project in the directory you name when you create the project. By default the project directories you create are created under a default projects folder, which you can and should change when you start using Visual Studio.

For each project, .NET creates a project folder using the project name you supply, within your default projects folder. It also automatically creates a solution (with the extension `.sln`) with the same name as the project. A solution is a grouping of related items such as a form and the routine that returns data to it, or a Web page and a Web service. There can be any number of projects in a solution, but only one of them is the startup project that runs if you press F5.

FoxPro doesn't have this additional layer. I wish it did. I have to write down which Web service goes with which applications on little sticky notes. A little bookkeeping help would be nice.

Whereas FoxPro uses tables to store projects, screens, menus, and classes, Visual Basic uses either .vb files or XML text files to store solution details.

Project Information

If you're fond of customizing your projects in FoxPro using Ctrl+J, you'll be interested to know that you can right-click on the solution and select Properties to set a number of characteristics of the solution. Similarly, you can right-click on a project and select Properties from the resulting context menu to set project properties. However, if you want to set the program's name, the company's name, versioning information and so forth, double-click on the AssemblyInfo.vb file in the project and fill in the Assembly attributes you'll find there.

Command Syntax

When you first look at Visual Basic code, there are so many unrecognizable constructs that it's often difficult to tell what you're looking at. But they usually have equivalents in FoxPro.

For that reason, you should take a few minutes to go over Table 1.3 and familiarize yourself with some of the principal similarities and differences in command syntax.

This is not meant to be an exhaustive list; we'll save that for Appendix A at the end of the book, where you can find a concordance of Visual FoxPro and Visual Basic equivalents.

TABLE 1.3   Command Syntax Differences

Item	Visual Basic	Visual FoxPro
Continuation character	_ (underscore)	; (semicolon)
Comments	' (single quote)	* (asterisk) at the beginning of a line, && (two ampersands) anywhere else
Data type indicators	Deprecated in Visual Basic	{} (curly braces) around dates
Boolean literals	True|False	.T.|.F. or T|F
String delimiters	" "	" ", ' ', [ ]
Null	Nothing (the word)	.Null. or Null
Character literals	"abc"c	"abc"
Attributes of functions	<attr("value")>	No equivalent
Option Explicit On	Variables can't be used unless previously declared	No equivalent
Option Strict On	Narrowing conversions not allowed; default is Off	No equivalent

TABLE 1.3   Continued

Item	Visual Basic	Visual FoxPro
`Option Compare Text`	Case insensitivity	Must be explicit in FoxPro, for example, `IF UPPER(a)=UPPER(b)...`
Refer to class libraries	`Imports` (top of file)	`SET CLASSLIB TO` *Name* `ADDITIVE` or `SET PROCEDURE TO` *Name* `ADDITIVE`
Refer to base class	`Inherits`	*ClassLibrary* name shown in the Properties sheet, or declared with "as *classname* of *sourcefilename*" in code.
Namespace	Prefixes for classes	No equivalent
Array dimensioning	`Dim X(2)` is 3 long; `X(0)` is first one; all elements same type	`Dim X(2)` is 2 long; `X(1)` is first one; elements can be of different types
Array initialization	Can assign values, for example, `Dim x(2) as new integer = {1,4}`	`DIMENSION X(2)` or `DECLARE X(2)`, then assign individual cells' values one line at a time
Parameters	Specified in `Function` or `Sub` statement in parentheses, with type declaration	Before Visual FoxPro7, specified in `PARAMETERS` or `LPARAMETERS` statement; beginning with Visual FoxPro7, same style as in Visual Basic .NET
Properties	Create property procedures with `GET` and `SET` methods, using a private variable as the get/set target; property name appears in Properties sheet of derived classes.	Enter the property name in the Class Designer, or assign a value to a variable name at the top of a class definition in code; the property appears immediately in the Properties sheet of the Class Designer
Default prefix block	`WITH/ENDWITH`	`WITH/ENDWITH`
Events	Used to call as yet unnamed functions in other modules	Don't have 'em, don't need 'em
Delegates	`Var = AddressOf FunctionName`; used to pass functions as parameters	Don't have 'em, don't need 'em
Determine variable type	`TypeOf Var IS Typename` or `GetType()`	`TYPE()` or `VARTYPE()`
Argument lists	Either positional or `(Name:=Value)`	Positional only
Variable or object creation	`Dim VarName as Class;` `VarName = New Class;` `VarName = Value`, or `Dim VarName as New Class = Value`	`SET CLASSLIB TO XYZ; VarName = CREATEOBJECT("Class")`, or `VarName = NEWOBJECT("Class", "Lib.VCX")`

TABLE 1.3   Continued

Item	Visual Basic	Visual FoxPro
Object creation from a COM object	`CreateObject` `("Word.Application")`	`CreateObject("Word.Application")` or `GetObject("Word.Application")`
Cast operators	`CTYPE()`	Individual cast functions like `DTOC()` or `STR()`
Reference to container	`ME`	`THIS, THISFORM`
If statement syntax	`IF` *Expr* `Then; End If`	`IF` *Expr*; `ENDIF`
Case statements	`Select Case VarName;` `Case "abc"; Case else;` `End Select`	`DO CASE; CASE Name="abc"; OTHERWISE;` `ENDCASE`

Flow of Control

Branching, looping, and conditional execution are the fundamental building blocks of programming. Almost every one of the mechanisms listed in Table 1.4 is slightly syntactically different in the two languages, although clearly, you can accomplish the same things in either language.

Following the table, I've made a few notes on how each construct works. `IIF` and `SWITCH` are included here as well because they replace what used to be four or five lines of `IF/ENDIF` or `CASE/ENDCASE` code.

TABLE 1.4   Flow of Control

Action	Visual Basic	Visual FoxPro
Call a procedure	*Name*`()` or `CALL` *Name*	*Prog*`()` or `DO` *Prog*
Exit a block	`Exit Sub, Exit While, Exit <block>`	`Exit`
End the program	`End`	`Quit`
Looping	`DO/Loop, For/Next, For Each/Next,` `While/End While`	`DO/ENDDO, FOR` `[EACH]/ENDFOR¦NEXT,` `SCAN/ENDSCAN`
Conditional branching	`Choose, IF/Then/Else, Select Case, Switch`	`IF/ELSE/ENDIF, DO` `CASE`
Procedure definitions	`Function, Sub, Property procedure`	`Function, Procedure`
Immediate If	`IIF()`	`IIF()`

Calling a Function, Procedure, or Method

To call a procedure called `ProcName` in FoxPro, you either type `DO ProcName` or simply `ProcName()`. The parentheses are required. The second variant is the way you call a subroutine or function in Visual Basic .NET.

If you instantiate an object named `MyObj` that has a method called `ProcName`, you call it using `MyObj.ProcName`. If it has parameters, you can add parentheses after the name and put the parameters within them. Otherwise, the parentheses are not required.

In Visual Basic .NET the syntax is exactly the same, except that `DO ProcName()` is not supported.

String handling

The well-known Canadian developer Steven Black has pointed out in several articles that string handling in FoxPro is thousands of times faster than it is in Visual Basic 6. In Visual Basic .NET, the String module contains dozens of methods that are more efficient. Type the word "String" and a period in a code window, and Intellisense will show you what's available.

In addition to the string functions found in FoxPro, String.Format can be used like TextMerge:

```
FoxPro:
 Name = "Fred"
 Age = 32
 SET TEXTMERGE ON NOSHOW
 TEXT TO X
 <<Name>> is <<TRANSFORM(age)>> years old.
 ENDTEXT
 ? X


VB:
 Dim Name As String = "Fred"
 Dim Age As Integer = 32
 Label1.Text = String.Format("{0} is {1} years old", Name, Age)
```

Ending Your Program

In FoxPro, `RETURN` takes you out of the current procedure, `THISFORM.Release` closes the current form, and `QUIT` ends the program. `RETURN` from the MAIN program also ends the application, unless you're running MAIN from inside the FoxPro IDE. So a compiled application can use `RETURN` to end the program.

In Visual Basic .NET, `CLOSE()` closes a form; `End` ends the program. You can't end a program with `Return` in Visual Basic.

Do...ENDDO and Other Loops in Visual FoxPro

In FoxPro, `DO...ENDDO` is used to do something repetitively until a condition is satisfied. In the following FoxPro example, we test a printer object, and if its `ErrorOccurred` property is set to .T., or if its `PrintedOk` property is set to `True`, we exit the loop; otherwise, we keep trying.

```
DO WHILE .T.
   oPrinter.Test
   IF oPrinter.ErrorOccurred or oPrinter.PrintedOk
      EXIT
   ENDIF
ENDDO
```

`DO WHILE` is not as frequently used as its cousin `FOR ... ENDFOR` or `FOR...NEXT`. The syntax is either

```
FOR I = 1 TO N
   - do something -
ENDFOR ¦ NEXT
```

or

```
FOR EACH obj IN Collection
   - do something -
ENDFOR ¦ NEXT
```

Finally, in FoxPro, where we have tables and cursors, there is a special command pair to traverse the table or cursor from top to bottom:

```
SCAN
   - do something -
ENDSCAN
```

The Visual Basic equivalent is to use a FOR EACH *row* IN *table* loop:

```
Dim dr as datarow
For each dr in dataset.tables(0)
...
End For
```

Loops in Visual Basic .NET

In Visual Basic .NET, the equivalent of `FOR...NEXT` is very similar:

```
FOR I = 1 TO N
   - do something -
NEXT I
```

However, `DO...LOOP` has four variants. The first two check the expression at the beginning of the loop, whereas the last two check the expression at the end of the first loop:

- `Do While:`

```
Do While condition
    statements
Loop
```

- `Do Until:`

```
Do Until condition
    statements
Loop
```

- `Do...Loop While:`

```
Do
    statements
Loop While condition
```

- `Do...Loop Until:`

```
Do
    statements
Loop Until condition
```

If that isn't enough, there's a `While...Wend` construct that's similar to `DO...LOOP`, except that it doesn't support `Exit`:

```
While condition
    statements
Wend
```

Conditional Execution in Visual FoxPro

In Visual FoxPro you can use either of these two mechanisms to execute only a certain block of code:

```
IF Expr
   - Execute if true -
ELSE
   - Execute if not true -
ENDIF
```

or

```
DO CASE
   CASE Expr1
   - Execute if Expr1 is true -
   CASE Expr2
   - Execute if Expr2 is true -
ENDCASE
```

It's a peculiarity of FoxPro's DO CASE construct that the expressions evaluated in the CASE statements don't have to refer to the same variable. It's very flexible.

Conditional Execution in Visual Basic .NET

As usual, Visual Basic .NET has more constructs. I don't know if that's good or bad: Sometimes although we're offered several ways of doing things, one of them is really the preferred method.

Choose returns the numbered entry from a list of choices, for example:

```
Return Choose(idx, "Lions", "Tigers", "Bears")
```

Choose is a primitive construct from years ago, and will seldom if ever be the best choice. It has been deprecated.

```
If Expr Then...Else...End If
```

If the evaluated expression is true, the first statement is executed; if Else is present and a second statement follows it, the second statement is executed, for example:

```
If Salary > 1000000.00 Then
   Bonus =  1000000.00
 Else
   Bonus = 25.00
End If
```

Note that a single line implementation is permitted. If it improves readability, use it. When I'm writing code for publication I use the single-line implementation. You can also include several statements separated by colons, but it gets hard to read pretty fast.

```
If Salary > 1000000 Then Bonus = 1000000
If Salary > 1000000 Then Bonus = 1000000 Else Bonus = 25
If Salary > 10000 Then Salary = Salary * 2 : Bonus = 10000
Else Salary = Salary / 2: Bonus = 25
```

```
Select Case
```

This command evaluates a single variable's values, for example:

```
Select case StateName
      Case "CA"
            Governor = "Arnold"
      Case Else
            Governor = "Someone else"
End Select
```

Switch(*VisualBasic Namespace*)

This statement evaluates a series of pairs of expressions and their corresponding return values and returns the first value whose expression evaluates to True, for example:

```
Return Microsoft.VisualBasic.Switch( _
 CityName = "London", "English", _
 CityName = "Rome", "Italian", _
 CityName = "Paris", "French")
```

Note that the Switch function name is not unique in the .NET namespaces and so must be qualified. This version is from the Visual Basic compatibility namespace provided for people who are inordinately fond of Visual Basic6. I'd be sparing about using this function; it looks a little dated.

In summary, both languages offer very similar capabilities in the flow of control area. I like FoxPro's DO CASE statement, which allows all sorts of expressions, not just different values for the named variable or expression. But the differences are small.

Variables, Enums, Arrays, Collections, and Fields

Variable declaration in FoxPro is very straightforward because there are only a few options. But in Visual Basic .NET it's more complicated. Public, Private, Protected, Local, Hidden, Overrides, Overrideable, Shadow, and Friend are declarations that are used in Visual Basic .NET to define scope and accessibility not only of variables, but also of methods, functions, and procedures. Even in FoxPro, most developers have not fully considered their usage. We only have three options (Public, Protected, and Hidden) and we just make everything Public. In Visual Basic .NET, they are considerably more intimidating. But as usual, there's a simple answer.

Data Types

Data type declarations in FoxPro take two forms: fields in tables and memory variable creation. Scope declarations can be used to declare data types in FoxPro, for example:

```
LOCAL Salary as Double
```

In addition, function and procedure declarations can describe parameter types and return value types. However, it's an illusion; FoxPro data is stored internally as variants, and typing is not enforced. For example, the following Visual FoxPro function will cheerfully concatenate a pair of strings passed to it as parameters:

```
FUNCTION Test (One as Integer, two as String) as String
RETURN TRANSFORM( one, "@L ###") + Two
```

And the following code runs fine in FoxPro:

```
LOCAL MyVar AS Integer
MyVar = "Oops!"
```

In FoxPro, although there are 14 possible choices for a field type in a table, for in-memory data representation there are only six types: Character, Currency, Numeric, Date, DateTime, and Logical. Finer data resolution only happens when you store the data to a table. Visual Basic's insistence on converting to many more data types doesn't matter in FoxPro. The TYPE and VARTYPE functions report back objects as type "O".

Table 1.5 compares the data types available in Visual Basic to the FoxPro data types and to FoxPro DBF Field types.

TABLE 1.5   Data Types in Visual Basic .NET and Visual FoxPro

Data Type	Visual Basic	Visual FoxPro memvar	Visual FoxPro Field
Logical	Boolean	Logical/Boolean	Logical(L)
Byte	Byte	Char	Char(C)
Money	-none-	Currency	Currency(Y)
Date	-none-	Date	Date(D)
DateTime	Date	DateTime	DateTime(T)
Decimal	Decimal	Numeric	Numeric(N)
Double	Double	Numeric	Double (B)
Integer	Integer	Integer	Integer(I)
Long	Long	Floating	Numeric(F)
Object	Object	Object,Variant	General(OLE objects)
Short	Short	Integer	Integer(I)
Single	Single	Numeric	Numeric(N)
String	Text	Memo	Memo(M)
Binary String	Binary Text	Memo Binary	Memo Binary(M)

Variable Scope Declaration in Visual FoxPro

In Visual FoxPro, some confusion results from the fact that PUBLIC, PRIVATE, and LOCAL refer to *variable* scope, whereas PROTECTED and HIDDEN refer to property and *method* visibility, and PROTECTED will always be part of a FUNCTION or PROCEDURE declaration in a class definition; no confusion there. But PUBLIC can refer to either a variable or to a property or method of a class.

PUBLIC, PRIVATE, and LOCAL are declarations that precede variables and determine their scope. If a variable is declared in a program, by default it's visible in that routine and in any routine below it. For example, if MAIN contains a line like Name=[Les] and uses DO FORM CUSTOMERS to show a form, within the form you can type THISFORM.Caption = [Les] in the form's LOAD event and the form's caption will appear as "Les". If you move the line Name=[Les] to the CUSTOMERS form and change the Load code to read

```
Name=[Les]
THISFORM.Caption = Name
```

the form's caption will change, but as soon as the form closes, the variable Name disappears. Technically, it is said to **go out of scope**.

LOCAL means that a variable exists only within the procedure in which it's named, whereas PRIVATE means that it exists in the procedure in which it's created as well as in any procedure called by that procedure.

For example, variables can be scoped before a value is assigned using a PUBLIC, PRIVATE, or LOCAL declaration:

```
PUBLIC Address        && will be available after exiting this procedure
Address = FileToStr ( ClientAddressTextFile )

LOCAL I
FOR I = 1 TO 2        && does not conflict with any global instance of I
    ? "Hi"
ENDFOR
```

Within a program, we declare variables to store values. The declaration of and use of variables in Visual Basic looks confusing to FoxPro developers because it requires an extra step that's optional in FoxPro. And the reason for it is that in Visual Basic, all variables are actually objects.

In FoxPro, you declare a variable by assigning it a value:

```
X = 3
```

Similarly, you declare a class property by assigning it a value:

```
DEFINE CLASS Person AS Custom
FirstName = []
LastName = []
ENDDEFINE
```

FoxPro generally declares all variables as variants, which means you can assign any value to them. In fact, you can change their data type in the middle of the program—usually inadvertently and with confusing results. It's not a good idea, but it's possible. However, you can declare types using the PUBLIC, PRIVATE, and LOCAL declarations:

```
LOCAL LastName AS String
PUBLIC I AS Integer
```

You can also declare objects based on classes in your class libraries, or from the FoxPro base classes:

```
LOCAL oDoc as Word.Document
oDoc = CREATEOBJECT ( "Word.Document")
```

However, all variables declared with the LOCAL, PUBLIC, or PRIVATE declarations have an initial value of .F., and can be changed to any other data type any time you want. So why bother?

Type declarations in FoxPro are used to permit specification of parameters for creating Dynamic Link Libraries (DLLs), which require a type library (TLB) entry that specifies parameter data types in a universally accepted format. Because FoxPro didn't have anything but variants, type declarations were added to the language to permit building Web services, which must specify their parameters and output types. But internally, they're pretty much ignored except for supporting IntelliSense.

Similarly, classes can have PRIVATE and PUBLIC properties and methods. IntelliSense reveals the public ones, whereas private ones are not visible.

Essentially, PUBLIC variables are accessible any time after being declared, as if they had been initialized in the MAIN program. PRIVATE variables are declared in the procedure in which they are created and in procedures called by the creating procedure. LOCAL variables are available only within the creating procedure, so they're perfect for loop counters. In general, the idea is to avoid inadvertently overwriting a variable. That's the story on variable declarations in FoxPro. Pretty simple, isn't it?

Variable Declarations in Visual Basic .NET

Visual Basic .NET is rendered more confusing because there are scope declarations for functions and procedures as well as for variables. We'll look at these in great detail shortly.

In Visual Basic, variables are objects. In fact, you can't use variables unless you first declare them with a statement that specifies which object they're derived from. Best practices dictate that you use Option Strict On and Option Implicit Off, so that the compiler will stop you from trying to assign an integer to a string variable. This can catch a certain type of programmer error that can be hard to diagnose.

This is the reason that many functions in FoxPro are methods of objects in Visual Basic. For example, in Visual FoxPro you use the `UPPER(StringVar)` function to convert a string to uppercase. In Visual Basic .NET, strings are objects, with dozens of built-in methods. The string object's methods include a `ToUpper` method. So the Visual Basic .NET equivalent of `UPPER(StringVar)` is `StringVar.ToUpper`. In a way it's better: Type a string variable's name, press the period key, and IntelliSense shows you all of the object's methods. In FoxPro, you'd be searching Help about now.

Variables are created from the named type using the `DIM` statement, which has the following syntax:

```
[ <attrlist> ] [{ Public ¦ Protected ¦ Friend ¦ Protected Friend ¦
                Private ¦ Static }] [ Shared ] [ Shadows ] [ ReadOnly ]
             Dim [ WithEvents ] name[ (boundlist) ]
                   [ As [ New ] type ] [ = initexpr ]
```

If any of the first nine declaratives are used, `Dim` can be omitted. An explanation of each of these options follows:

- `Public`—Variables declared with this keyword have no restrictions on their accessibility. (`Public` is used only at module, namespace, or file level; you can't declare public variables inside a procedure.)

- `Protected`—Variables declared with this keyword are accessible only from within their own class or from a derived class. Protected access is not a superset of friend access. `Protected` is used only at class level, to declare members of the class.

- `Friend`—Variables declared with this keyword are accessible from within their declaration context and from anywhere else in the same program. `Friend` can be used at module, namespace, or file level, but can't be declared inside a procedure.

- `Protected Friend`—Variables declared with these keywords can be used by code anywhere in the same program, by code in their own class, and by code in any derived classes. `Protected Friend` can be used only at class level; you can declare protected friend variables inside a class but not inside a procedure, and not at module, namespace, or file level, and only to declare members of the class.

- `Private`—Variables declared with this keyword are accessible only from within their declaration context, including from members of any nested types such as procedures. You can declare private variables inside a module, class, or structure, but not at namespace or file level and not inside a procedure.

- `Static`—Variables declared with this keyword remain in existence and retain their latest values after termination of the procedure in which they are declared. You can declare static variables inside a procedure or a block within a procedure, but not at class or module level.

- `Shared`—The variable is not associated with a specific instance of a class or structure. You can access a shared variable by qualifying it either with the class or structure name, or with the variable name of a specific instance of the class or structure. You can declare shared variables in a source file or inside a module, class, or structure, but not inside a procedure.

- `Shadows`—The variable shadows an identically named programming element, or set of overloaded elements, in a base class. You can shadow any kind of declared element with any other kind. A shadowed element is unavailable from within the derived class that shadows it, unless the shadowing element is inaccessible, for example, `Private`. You can declare shadowing variables in a source file or inside a module, class, or structure, but not inside a procedure.

- `ReadOnly`—Variables declared with this keyword can only be read and not written. Used to create constants of a particular type, such as an object variable with preset data members. `ReadOnly` can't be used inside a procedure.

- `WithEvents`—The variable is an object based on a class for which **events** have been created, so it needs to have the additional harness added to monitor for said events and respond accordingly using any added **handlers**, to be discussed later.

- `Type`—Any of the data types that Visual Basic supports. The list is slightly longer than that of FoxPro, but you'll always know what type to use. String is character, int is integer, double is numeric. Believe me; knowing the corresponding names of data types is the least of your problems.

Any of these attributes can be used with the `DIM` statement to allocate memory for variables. `DIM` comes from `DIMENSION`, which was the only way to allocate memory for variables in the early version of BASIC and was never replaced by `ALLOC` as it should have been. The `DIM` keyword is optional if any of these others are used, so it's often left out. If only `DIM` is used, it defaults to `Private`. That's part of the source of the confusion. Just think of `Public`, `Protected`, and so on as alternate ways of saying `Dim`. If you want to use variables in classes as we use them in FoxPro, you can generally use `Public` or `Friend`. Inside a procedure, just use `Dim`.

Enumerations, Arrays, and Collections

There are three variations on variables that demonstrate important differences between Visual FoxPro and Visual Basic .NET. We'll look at them here.

Enumerations

Visual Basic is rife with names of possible choices for everything. For example, if you type

```
MsgBox ("Hi",
```

Thanks to IntelliSense, you'll see a drop-down list of 19 `MsgBoxStyle` keywords from which you can choose the next parameter. These enumerations are surrogates for numbers, as those who use FoxPro know. In Visual Basic, it's customary to list them as words instead of numeric values. I must admit, it's easier to read

```
If MsgBox(
   "Print", _
     MsgBoxStyle.Question _
 and MsgBoxStyle.YesNo _
 and MsgBoxStyle.DefaultButton1) _
   = MsgBoxStyle.Yes
```

than it is to read

```
If MessageBox ( "Print", 4 + 32 + 256 ) = 6
```

as we do in FoxPro.

In FoxPro, we use include files full of `#CONST` declarations in place of enums. For example, if you open the `foxpro.h` header file in the home directory (the `home()` function returns the name of the directory where Visual FoxPro is installed), you can read the numeric equivalents for these enumerations. In FoxPro, we have a few dozen such enumerations, and they're all found in this one header file. In general, as you enter function or command parameters in Visual FoxPro, IntelliSense displays the selections that are available to you based on the context.

In Visual Basic, there are *hundreds and hundreds* of them. They are one of the reasons why IntelliSense is a part of Visual Basic. IntelliSense is nice to have in FoxPro; Visual Basic would be *dead* without IntelliSense.

Enumerations are ubiquitous in Visual Basic. Every time you're poised to set a property, you can expect to pick from an enumeration. The closest equivalent we have in FoxPro is in the Properties window, where available choices appear in a drop-down list box. Sometimes you simply have to know the name, for example, `ControlChars.CrLf` for `CHR(13)+CHR(10)`. The real challenge of IntelliSense is knowing what to type before you press the period key—after that, it's easy.

If you want to provide names for your lists of numeric values that are assignable in code, you can use an enum to provide IntelliSense support. After you define your enumeration, the editor will pick it up and use it the way it uses the enumerations that are built into the language. Enums can be integers (one, two, or four bytes) .

Here's what an `Enum` looks like:

```
Enum SecurityLevel
   IllegalEntry = -1
   MinimumSecurity = 0
   MaximumSecurity = 1
End Enum
```

Arrays

Arrays are one of the most powerful features available in programming. The good news is that arrays in both languages support FOR EACH <obj> IN ArrayName. However, there are important differences. And some of them are just silly.

To specify an array in Visual Basic, use parentheses after the name:

```
Dim x() as String  ' the array will be dimensioned by the mechanism that creates it
```

or

```
Dim x(5) as Integer ' the array will have six elements, to be filled in later
```

Visual Basic array elements start with 0. The first element is ArrayName(0), and the last element is one number smaller than the number of elements in the array. That is, when you dimension an array using ArrayName(3), you've created an array with four elements. Heaven knows why this ridiculous notion wasn't killed in Visual Basic .NET. Actually, they tried, but Visual Basic6 developers fought them off. If you're a FoxPro developer, you will never, ever get used to this.

Arrays in FoxPro can contain elements of different data types; that's why SCATTER TO ARRAY (name) works. You use DIMENSION or DECLARE to create an array and then assign values to its elements. A subsequent DIMENSION or DECLARE statement can increase or decrease the size of the array. Arrays, like variables, can be PUBLIC, PRIVATE, or LOCAL. Arrays in Visual FoxPro are either one- or two-dimensional. The size of an array named X is given by ALEN(X) or ALEN(X,0); the number of rows in a two-dimensional array is given by ALEN(X,1); and the number of columns by ALEN(X,2).

FoxPro arrays can be either one- or two-dimensional. Arrays in Visual Basic .NET can have any number of dimensions. I don't know how often you need to program in cubes, but you can do it in Visual Basic without going through the gyrations that were required in FoxPro.

In Visual Basic, all array elements must be of the same type. REDIM resizes an array, and REDIM PRESERVE does so without erasing the contents. We don't have PRESERVE in FoxPro because array contents are never removed if an array is redimensioned; if you want to do so, you RELEASE and DIMENSION the array anew.

As in FoxPro, you can either dimension an array initially, or simply declare the fact that it's an array and let some subsequent process determine its dimensionality. In FoxPro, the sequence

```
DIMENSION X(1)
X(1) = "Hi there"
DIMENSION X(4)
```

expands the array from one element to four. The contents of the first element of the array are not changed. The VB equivalent might be this:

DIM X() As String = {"Hi there}
ReDim X(3) Preserve

Table 1.6 summarizes the handling of arrays in Visual FoxPro and Visual Basic.

TABLE 1.6   Array Handling

Action	Visual FoxPro	Visual Basic
Verify an array	No equivalent	`IsArray()`
Declare and initialize	DIMENSION, DECLARE	`Dim, Private, Public, ReDim`
Find limits	`LBOUND()`, `UBOUND()`	`ALEN(name,1)` for rows, `ALEN(Name,2)` for columns
Resize	`DIM x(n)`	`Redim x(n) Preserve`

You can add anything to a collection in FoxPro. For example,

```
X = CREATEOBJECT("Collection")
x.Add(_Screen,"one")
```

adds the FoxPro background screen to a collection named x. You can subsequently display the FoxPro window caption using this:

```
WAIT WINDOW x("one").Caption
```

You can also set properties or call methods on the object as a collection member, for example:

```
X("one").WindowState = 1
```

So as you might suspect, in Visual Basic .NET, if you need an array of dissimilar data types (say, the values of the fields in a record—the *columns* in a *row*, as they say in Visual BasicSpeak), you can use a collection.

Table 1.7 summarizes the handling of collections in Visual FoxPro and Visual Basic.

TABLE 1.7   Collection Handling

Action	Visual FoxPro	Visual Basic .NET
Create a collection	`X=CREATEOBJECT("Collection")`	`Dim x as collection`
Add an item	`x.Add("key","value")`	`x.Add("key","value")`
Remove an item	`x.Remove("key")` or `x.Remove(n)`	`x.Remove("key")` or `x.Remove(n)`
Refer to an item	`x("key")` or `X.item(n)`	`x("key")` or `X.item(n)`

Fields

We can't leave the subject of variables without discussing table fields. In FoxPro, if you USE (TableName), or if you SELECT (TableName) subsequently, you expose the fields of the table as if they were memory variables. In fact, if you issue the SCATTER MEMVAR command, FoxPro creates duplicate memvars for all of your fields. How can you distinguish them?

Just remember that the field is the default. If both exist, the current table's field is assumed to be what you want, unless you preface the memvar with "m.". It's actually a common hard-to-find bug. The best fix for this is to preface the field name with its table name and a period, for example, Customers.Address, and to preface memvars with "m.". Alternatively, you can preface all memvars with an additional m. It seems like overkill, but FoxPro developers are used to it.

Visual Basic .NET doesn't have fields. Well, it does, but **field** in Visual Basic .NET means what we'd call a local variable in a class in FoxPro. But as you'll see, typed datasets act pretty much like FoxPro tables do in this regard. A typed dataset is a Visual Basic program, usually (make that always) generated by a program, that adds one property procedure for each field in a table. That is, when you create a dataset (an .xsd file, which is actually an XML file), if you ask the wizard to create a typed dataset, it will generate the code for you.

There are third-party tools available that will do this job for you, and I suspect that Whidbey (the next version of Visual Basic .NET) will do so as well. RapTier from SharpPower.com builds a robust data tier. Visible Developer and DeKlarit do even more. All of these are better than typing these things in yourself, or using the one that's automatically generated by the IDE.

Typed datasets allow you to do data binding using a syntax that looks just like FoxPro's; for example, you fill in *tablename.fieldname* in the DataBindings - Text property (the equivalent of the FoxPro controlsource property). However, data binding goes only as far as the dataset, which is a local cursor. It doesn't write the data back to the source table, wherever that is. For that you need a command object, as you'll see shortly.

Functions and Subroutines (Procedures)

In both FoxPro and Visual Basic .NET, code is divided into modules called functions and procedures (subroutines in Visual Basic .NET). These can be modules, or they can be methods in classes. You use Name() to call a function or procedure, and obj.Name() to call a method of a class.

When you define a class, whether in a PRG or in a VCX, you can add methods, which either return a value or don't. (In Visual FoxPro there is no distinction between function methods and procedure methods.)

When you add a method to either a Visual Class Library (VCX) or a class in a PRG, you designate it as Public, Protected, or Hidden. This determines the method's visibility when instantiated. If you define the class and its methods in a PRG, that is, a procedure library, you precede method names with PROTECTED or HIDDEN (the unstated default is PUBLIC):

- PUBLIC methods can be called when you instantiate an object based on the class.

- PROTECTED methods can be seen by other developers in the Class Browser and in the Properties sheet, but can't be invoked except by members of the class itself. You can even select them via IntelliSense, but any attempted call produces an error.

- HIDDEN methods can't be seen or invoked except by members of the class itself.

When you create an object from a class definition stored in a VCX or PRG using CREATEOBJECT() or NEWOBJECT(), all of the base class properties and methods are exposed. There may be dozens of them. However, if you use a PRG that starts with the statement

```
DEFINE CLASS <name> AS CUSTOM OLEPUBLIC
```

and ends with ENDDEFINE and compile it as a single-threaded DLL (STDLL) or a multi-threaded DLL (MTDLL), then when you instantiate an object from the resulting DLL, IntelliSense will only show you the PUBLIC properties and methods. It only takes two additional lines of code, and provides a cleaner way for others to use your class's methods.

Function Declarations

But even the many variations on declaring variables discussed in the preceding section don't cause as much confusion as subroutine and function declarations. For one thing, functions and subroutines in FoxPro have always been a bit amorphous; either one can return or not return a value.

Visual Basic .NET is very particular about this. Functions *must* return a value, and it *must* be of the type specified in the RETURN statement. To make matters worse, someone in Redmond (and I think I know who it was) once decided that assigning the function's value to its name was a good way to hide the RETURN statement, or save a line of code, or who knows what. So you see code like this:

```
FUNCTION DollarsToCharacters (inputval as double) AS String
DollarsToCharacters = CSTR(inputval,10,2)
END FUNCTION
```

Functions and Procedures in FoxPro

You can define functions and classes either in a PROCEDURE library or a program. Procedure libraries are simply collections of FUNCTION and PROCEDURE blocks stored inline in a text file ending with the extension .prg. They are opened for use as procedure libraries using the statement

```
SET PROCEDURE TO <filename> ADDITIVE
```

Typically this is done early in the MAIN program, after which the contained functions and procedures can be referred to as if they were FoxPro functions, that is, with no object name preceding them.

Functions are declared with the FUNCTION *<name>* ... ENDFUNC and PROCEDURE *<name>*... ENDPROC blocks. Methods in visual class libraries (VCX files) are not characterized as either functions or procedures, because fundamentally, FoxPro doesn't care whether you return a value or not.

FoxPro traditionally uses the PARAMETERS statement to collect passed values. More recent versions of FoxPro permit the use of the Visual Basic syntax. So you can now write either

```
FUNCTION DollarsToCharacters
PARAMETERS InputVal
RETURN STR(InputVal,10,2)
ENDFUNC
```

or

```
FUNCTION DollarsToCharacters ( InputVal as Numeric ) AS String
RETURN STR(InputVal,10,2)
ENDFUNC
```

In FoxPro, that's about all you have to know.

Functions and Subroutines in Visual Basic .NET

Brace yourself for the Visual Basic .NET equivalent. First, I'll show you the formal definitions. (Note that the only difference between functions and subroutines is the As *type* clause in the function declaration, which indicates what data type will be returned.)

The following is the SUB declaration in Visual Basic .NET:

```
[ <attrlist> ] [{ Overloads ¦ Overrides ¦ Overridable ¦
NotOverridable ¦ MustOverride ¦ Shadows ¦ Shared }]
[{ Public ¦ Protected ¦ Friend ¦ Protected Friend ¦ Private }]
Sub name [(arglist)] [ Implements interface.definedname ]
   [ statements ]
   [ Exit Sub ]
   [ statements ]
End Sub
```

The following is the FUNCTION declaration in Visual Basic .NET:

```
[ <attrlist> ] [{ Overloads ¦ Overrides ¦ Overridable ¦
NotOverridable ¦ MustOverride ¦ Shadows ¦ Shared }]
[{ Public ¦ Protected ¦ Friend ¦ Protected Friend ¦ Private }]
Function name[(arglist)] [ As type ] [ Implements interface.definedname ]
   [ statements ]
   [ Exit Function ]
   [ statements ]
End Function
```

The first group of options in a function or subroutine declaration determine how the routine relates to any identically named function in the base class. An explanation of each of these options follows. However, you probably don't need any of this. I'll explain at the end of this section:

- Overloads—This and several other functions with the same but different parameter lists (called signatures in .NET) will be defined in the class or module, and all of them will do the same thing using different parameters. This is good if you're building a compiler, but is not important for database applications.

- Overrides—This function procedure overrides an identically named procedure in a base class. The number and data types of the arguments, and the data type of the return value, must exactly match those of the base class procedure.

- Overridable—This function procedure can be overridden by an identically named procedure in a derived class. This is the default setting for a procedure that itself overrides a base class procedure.

- NotOverridable—This function procedure cannot be overridden in a derived class. This is the default setting for a procedure that does not itself override a base class procedure.

- MustOverride—This function procedure is not implemented in this class, and must be implemented in a derived class for that class to be creatable. Use this as a reminder to another member of the programming team to build his own function.

- Shadows—Like Overrides, except that parameters don't have to match. This means "Ignore the method of the same name in the base class and use this one instead."

- Shared—This can be called either directly from the class (without instantiating an object from the class) or by instantiating an object based on the class.

The second qualifier determine **visibility**, that is, where the function or procedure can be seen.

- Public—No restrictions on the accessibility of public procedures.

- Protected—Accessible only from within their own class or from a derived class. Can be specified only on members of classes.

- Friend—Accessible from anywhere in the same program.

- Protected Friend—Union of protected and friend access. Can be specified only on members of classes.

- Private—Accessible only from within their declaration context.

Constructors: Init vs. New

In FoxPro, you can include a PARAMETERS or LPARAMETERS statement as the first line of code in a class's Init procedure, then pass parameters to it in the CreateObject() or NewObject() function call that instantiates an object based on the class. Init is called the class constructor.

In .NET, the New() function is the constructor, and it can also be used to pass parameters while creating an instance of a class. However, it's common in the .NET Namespaces to have several overloads of the New method, so that you can instantiate an object and pass it several types of parameters. The only difference between different overloads is their parameter lists; for example, when creating a DataAdapter object, you can either pass it a SQL select statement and a connection string, like this:

```
Dim da as New SQLDataAdapter("SELECT * FROM Customers",
"server=(local);database=NorthWind, PWD=sa;")
```

or a SQL select statement and an object reference to an open connection, like this:

```
Dim cn as New SQLConnection("server=(local);database=NorthWind, PWD=sa;")
Cn.Open()
Dim da as New SQLDataAdapter("SELECT * FROM Customers", cn)
```

So even if you don't ever overload any of your own methods, you'll use overloaded .NET methods every day. When you do so, you'll need to add the statement

```
MyBase.New()
```

as the first line of your overloaded method, to call the object's original constructor.

Implementing Interfaces

Finally, you can declare a function signature (a collection of properties and methods) known as an **interface**, and then include an Implements clause in your function or subroutine declaration that checks to see that you did it right. It's a sort of project control feature.

> Implements—Indicates that this function procedure implements a function procedure defined by an interface.

If you're asked to add a specific functionality to your class that's been implemented elsewhere, you can build a list of the properties and methods you want to expose and include them in an Interface declaration. You can then include the statement Implements (*interface name*) in another class, and the compiler will report an error if the class doesn't reference all of the properties and methods in the interface.

For example, define a class called Class1 as shown in Listing 1.1.

LISTING 1.1   Declaring an Interface

```
Public Class Class1

    Public Interface Foo
        Property Banana() As String
        Sub One(ByVal a As String)
        Function Two(ByVal b As String) As String
    End Interface

End Class
```

Now, open another class named Class2, and on line 2, type Implements Class1.Foo. (The "Foo" will appear thanks to IntelliSense when you press the period key.) Prototyped declarations for the property, the subroutine, and the function will automatically be inserted into your code (see Listing 1.2).

LISTING 1.2   Implementing an Interface in a Class

```
Public Class Class2
    Implements Class1.Foo
    Public Property Banana() As String Implements Class1.Foo.Banana
        Get

        End Get
        Set(ByVal Value As String)

        End Set
    End Property

    Public Sub One(ByVal a As String) Implements Class1.Foo.One

    End Sub

    Public Function Two(ByVal b As String) As String Implements Class1.Foo.Two

    End Function

End Class
```

It's pretty hard to screw this up if you use these declarations. And as an added bonus, if the Interface definition in Class1 is changed, its implementation in Class2 produces a compiler error. On the other hand, you have to be pretty sure what you want Class1 to do before you define the Foo interface.

Defining interfaces and then using the `Implements` keyword to check your math is not a bad idea. You can do it in FoxPro as well (when working with Component Object Model [COM] objects), although I've never had occasion to do so. It's helpful, but it's not necessary. So unless someone tells you to use them, ignore `Interface` declarations and `Implements` clauses. In a team environment, they become more useful.

Summary of Visual Basic Declarations

The following summary of function scope declarations describes the available options. After I describe them, I'll suggest a simple approach.

- `Public` and `Friend` can refer to any of the following elements: `Class`, `Const`, `Declare`, `Delegate`, `Dim`, `Enum`, `Event`, `Function`, `Interface`, `Module`, `Property`, `Structure`, or `Sub`; `Protected` and `Private` can be used with all of these except `Module`, which can only be `Public` or `Friend` (the default).

- `Static` means that the variable continues to exist after the routine in which it was created is over. In that sense it's like FoxPro's `PUBLIC` declaration. Note that you can't specify `Static` with either `Shared` or `Shadows`.

- `Shared` means that you can refer to the property without instantiating an object based on the class. It allows you to use the class itself as an object based on the class. We don't have that in FoxPro.

- `Shadows` means that a variable completely replaces the identically named element in a base class. This is the default in FoxPro: If you write code in the method code window of a derived form class, it completely replaces the code that was written in the base form class. FoxPro doesn't check whether the signatures match or not. Ever.

So What Should I Use?

It's very, very simple. In FoxPro, put the initial assignment of variables in MAIN to default them to `PUBLIC` scope, and then declare variables as `PRIVATE` in all called routines that themselves might call other routines that might need the private values—for example, a screen that set up titles for a report. Use `LOCAL` for all variables that are definitely used only in a single routine (for example, loop counters). You can completely ignore method scope and make them all `PUBLIC`, the default. And remember that in general, variables that are used only by methods of a class should be public properties of that class, not `PUBLIC` variables in MAIN.

In Visual Basic, you can do the same thing. The greater variety of declarations in Visual Basic .NET implies that it's desirable to take advantage of every one of the options. However, as database developers, *we don't need most of them.*

Make all methods of your classes `Shared Public`, and *ignore* all of the nuances. Don't use `Overrides` and `Overloads`. And if you find yourself using `Shadows` a lot, consider redesigning your base class or writing two different classes.

A footnote on overloaded methods in .NET

The fact that you don't need to create multiple overloads of subs and functions doesn't mean, however, that you won't see them every day of your programming life. A great many of the .NET classes have overloaded methods. Let's say you want to create a connection to SQL Server. If you do this

Dim cn As SQLClient.SQLConnection(

when you press the left parenthesis, nothing happens. However, if you type this:

Dim cn As **New** SQLClient.SQLConnection(

you will be presented with a little tooltip box that informs you that you're about to use overload 2 (of 2 available overloads), which accepts a connection string. Multiple overloads of New() methods for .NET classes are ubiquitous, and rather helpful. I still don't think you need to overload your own methods, but you'll use overloaded methods every day.

Classes, Namespaces, Properties, and Forms

Many FoxPro developers began with version 1, which didn't have object orientation. We built forms that did what we wanted. If we needed a similar form, we cloned and modified the code. There was a template capability that allowed us to migrate features to the template and then stamp out similar forms like a cookie-cutter. But subsequent design changes could be painful.

When Visual FoxPro came out, for the first time we had the ability to write generic form class code and inherit forms from it. My own approach was to build a basic form and then slowly move code out of it into an underlying class, changing form references to a specific table name to the contents of a property, so if I changed

```
SELECT EMPLOYEES
```

to

```
SELECT ( THISFORM.MainTable )
```

I could base a form on this "form template," assign a value to the MainTable property, and the form would run as expected. Gradually, most if not all of the code in the original form migrated to the class. I ended up with a form that did what I needed if I set a dozen or so properties; if I needed a similar form, I just used

```
Create form xxx as MyForm FROM PinterLIB
```

And set the same dozen properties, and the form was up and running in minutes. I was in heaven! My customers got more software for less money, and I could win every single bid I made.

Visual Basic .NET is similarly object-oriented.

However, classes don't work exactly the same way. For one thing, FoxPro form classes are usually stored in a table with the extension .vcx (and an associated memo file with the same name and a .vct extension). Visual Basic .NET forms are source code files that don't look any different from program files. They have the extension .vb.

However, the general idea is the same: Classes have properties and methods. You instantiate an object based on the class, assign values to its public properties, and call its public methods. It uses its private properties as variables, and calls private methods to do its work. In this regard, FoxPro and Visual Basic .NET are identical.

However, the devil is in the details. And there are lots of details that differ. For one thing, FoxPro classes are stored either as VCX files or PRG files. If they're stored as VCX files, you use the Class Designer to add properties and methods, which can be either Public, Private, or Protected. If they're defined in a PRG, the file starts with this line of code

```
DEFINE CLASS Foobar AS CUSTOM (OLEPUBLIC)
```

and ends with

```
ENDDEFINE
```

The OLEPUBLIC keyword is required if you want to compile to a DLL, which is required for Web Services applications, and is generally not used by FoxPro developers unless they use COM+.

Properties are created simply by assigning them values, one per line, after the DEFINE CLASS statement and before the first FUNCTION or PROCEDURE statement. A single PRG can have one or more class definitions in it. They're instantiated using either

```
SET CLASSLIB TO VCXNAME ADDITIVE or
SET PROCLIB TO CLSLIB.PRG ADDITIVE
```

followed by

```
oName  = CREATEOBJECT ( "ClassName" )
oName2 = CREATEOBJECT ( "OtherClass" )
```

or you can skip the SET CLASSLIB and SET PROCLIB statements and use a shorter approach:

```
oName  = NEWOBJECT ( "ClassName", "VCXNAME.VCX" )
oName2 = NEWOBJECT ( "OtherClass", "CLSLIB.PRG" )
```

If you have parameters in a class's Init method, you can add the parameters at the end of the CREATEOBJECT() or NEWOBJECT() function call and pass them directly to the Init constructor. Inside the class, THIS refers to a property or method of the class itself. That's about the size of creating and using classes in FoxPro.

In Visual Basic .NET, classes are defined in code. There is no Visual Class Library. However, if the class is a form you can use the Form Designer to build it visually; and if it's a user control, you get a little container in which your control component or components appear.

The use of namespaces is confusing to FoxPro developers. Namespaces are just there to add an additional level of naming. For example, the class library shown in Listing 1.3 defines two classes in Visual Basic .NET. Note that the project name for this class library is NameSpaceDemo. This is important because the name of the project is the default name of the generated DLL, which becomes the first part of the class name.

LISTING 1.3   Namespace Declarations

```
Imports System.IO

Namespace PinterConsulting

    Public Class Functions
        Private _FileName As String
        Private sep As Char

        Public Property FileName()
            Get
                Return _FileName
            End Get
            Set(ByVal Value)
                _FileName = Value
            End Set
        End Property

    End Class

    Public Class Objects

        Public Class Person
            Private _FirstName As String
            Private _LastName As String
            Private sep As Char

            Public Property FirstName() As String
                Get
                    Return _FirstName
                End Get
                Set(ByVal Value As String)
                    _FirstName = Value
```

LISTING 1.3   Continued

```
                Select Case _FirstName
                    Case "Bob"
                    Case "Fred"
                    Case "Eddie"
                    Case Else
                End Select
            End Set
        End Property

        Public Property LastName() As String
            Get
                Return _LastName
            End Get
            Set(ByVal Value As String)
                _LastName = Value
            End Set
        End Property

        Public ReadOnly Property FullName()
            Get
                Return FirstName + " " + LastName
            End Get
        End Property

    End Class

  End Class

End Namespace
```

I've added a form in the same project that uses the classes. Notice that because the project name was NameSpaceDemo and the NameSpace was PinterConsulting, the name for the Imports statement (which is like SET CLASSLIB ... ADDITIVE) is the concatenation of the two. Listing 1.4 shows the form code:

LISTING 1.4   Using a Namespace in an Imports Statement

```
Imports NameSpaceDemo.PinterConsulting

Public Class Form1
```

LISTING 1.4 Continued

```
Inherits System.Windows.Forms.Form

Dim NameMgr As New PinterConsulting.Objects.Person

Private Sub Form1_Load( _
 ByVal sender As System.Object, ByVal e As System.EventArgs) _
 Handles MyBase.Load
End Sub

Private Sub txtFirst_TextChanged( _
 ByVal sender As System.Object, ByVal e As System.EventArgs) _
 Handles txtFirst.TextChanged
    NameMgr.FirstName = txtFirst.Text
    Label1.Text = NameMgr.FullName
End Sub

Private Sub txtLast_TextChanged( _
 ByVal sender As System.Object, ByVal e As System.EventArgs) _
 Handles txtLast.TextChanged
    NameMgr.LastName = txtLast.Text
    Label1.Text = NameMgr.FullName
End Sub

Private Sub txtFileName_TextChanged( _
 ByVal sender As System.Object, ByVal e As System.EventArgs) _
 Handles txtFileName.TextChanged
    Dim o As New PinterConsulting.Functions
End Sub

End Class
```

Note that I could have left out the Objects class because it only contains one nested class. But I could have added more classes within Objects, and they would also have been exposed via IntelliSense.

This is why I say that IntelliSense is merely nice to have in FoxPro, but in Visual Basic .NET you'd be dead without it. But I can imagine complex projects that need namespaces to document functionality of class members and classes, and it's just a naming convention. I just can't escape concluding that FoxPro works just fine without namespaces and wouldn't be enhanced if we had them. I understand the theory, but isn't anyone else out there cognizant of the divergence between theory and reality, and gutsy enough to eschew the theory?

Instantiating objects in Visual Basic .NET

One thing that will come up constantly in .NET is the creation and use of objects based on .NET classes. For example, the following code opens a table and displays its contents in a datagrid (the .NET equivalent of FoxPro's BROWSE):

```
Dim cn As New SqlConnection("Server=(local);Database=Northwind;UID=sa;PWD=;")
cn.Open()
Dim da As New SqlDataAdapter("SELECT * FROM CUSTOMERS", cn)
Dim ds As New DataSet
da.Fill(ds)
DataGrid1.DataSource = ds.Tables(0)
```

The statement Dim cn As SQLConnection is like FoxPro

LOCAL cn As String

It doesn't create the variable. It just announces your intention to do so at some future date. Sounds goofy, but it's true. (It actually feeds IntelliSense - in both cases.) It's supposed to be followed by the statement that actually creates the variable. It can either be done with a New statement, or by referring to a member of an existing object. If you leave out the word New in the Dim cn statement above, you won't be able to pass the connection string in as a parameter. In the fourth line of the same code, you can leave out the word New without incurring a syntax error, but the following line will bomb because Fill only works with an existing Dataset, and the statement Dim ds As Dataset doesn't create one – it only declares one.

Property Procedures in Visual Basic .NET

For years, Visual Basic developers got used to the idea of trapping the assignment of a value to a property and doing something when that assignment occurred. For example, I used to use a communication package that used the following syntax to read data from a telephone line:

```
OModem.Setting = 14
OModem.Action = 4     ' Read
```

The way this worked was that the moment of assigning a value to a property was trapped in what is called the `Property Set` method. At that instant, other code can be called. So they used that when they couldn't declare a "Do-it" method. It was a workaround for Visual Basic's inability to give us any way to simply write `oModem.Read`. After a while, the workaround seemed normal. Goofy but true.

The tradition continues. If you type

```
PUBLIC PROPERTY FullName AS String
```

and press Enter, Visual Basic will add complete the routine by adding the following six lines of code:

```
Public Property FullName() As String
    Get

    End Get
    Set(ByVal Value As String)

    End Set
End Property
```

You have to add three more lines of code, one before the routine and two within it, to end up with this:

```
Private _FullName As String
Public Property FullName() As String
    Get
        Return _FullName
    End Get
    Set(ByVal Value As String)
        _FullName = Value
    End Set
```

If you have two properties, you'll have two of these. If you have 20 properties, you'll have 20. Notice that a separate private variable (by convention the name is the property procedure's name preceded by an underscore) is required in order to store the value manipulated by the property procedure, and it must be declared outside of the property procedure.

This is the equivalent of the `Assign` and `Access` methods that FoxPro allows you to create when you add a property to a class. As you may know, you can add code to the `Assign` method code to do other tasks when the property is assigned a value. That's the idea behind property procedures.

However, in Visual FoxPro property procedures (that is, `Assign` and `Access` methods) are completely optional; I've only had occasion to use them twice in years of client development.

In Visual Basic .NET, you can't see either class properties or public class variables in the Properties sheet for the class. However, you can't see public class variables in the Properties sheet. And you can only see them in subclasses that inherit from your classes. That's right; to get what you call a property in FoxPro, you *must* create a public property procedure in Visual Basic .NET. Strange but true. So even if you don't need the `Assign` and `Access` methods (called Getters and Setters in Visual Basic), you need property procedures. The fact that Visual Basic writes most of the code diminishes the pain, but I think it's goofy, and hope that it will be replaced by FoxPro's much simpler and clearly adequate counter-part some day.

Forms

Forms are classes in Visual Basic .NET. If you refer to one in a menu, it will take either two or three lines of code to display the form:

```
Dim frm as new CustomerForm    ' can be written as 2 lines of code
Frm.Show
```

In FoxPro you just write

```
Do form Customer
```

However, have you ever looked at the structure of an SCX file? It has *exactly* the same structure as a VCX file. And in fact, if you save a form as a class, the code to run the form changes to this:

```
Frm = CREATEOBJECT ( "FormClassName", "VCXFILE.VCX" )
Frm.Show()
```

So they're more similar than you might have thought.

Forms have a section of code called the "Windows Form Designer generated code." When you're in the form designer, things that you do, like adding controls on the form, moving things around, and assigning values to properties, are actually stored in source code. The designer merely uses this code to create a visual display of the code's contents. If you manually change this code, it will be overwritten whenever a change is made in the designer and the file is saved.

However, sometimes it's useful to write code that is saved as part of the form's initialization sequence – for example, using property values to open tables and populate some standard controls. If you have such code, you can place it in the Public Sub New() method, after the word InitializeComponent(). It's the only place in the Form Designer generated code that you can include code that won't be overwritten by the designer.

Events

For a FoxPro developer, events constitute one of the strangest things in Visual Basic .NET. I looked for the equivalent in FoxPro for the longest time, and I just couldn't find it. It turns out that there are two kinds of events in Visual Basic .NET, and they bear little resemblance to one another. FoxPro only has one kind of event. Visual Basic actually uses events to call methods in other objects; hence the confusion. I hope this part of the chapter will clear it up for you.

Events in Visual FoxPro

FoxPro's classes have properties, events, and methods. Properties are variables, and methods are functions and procedures. But you can't add events. When you subclass a base class, you can add properties and methods at will. You can also add your own code to the existing methods. For example, when you refresh a form, you can add code to SEEK() records in all related tables so that bound fields displayed on the form will be coordinated.

Events are different. Events happen. When they do, any code that you add to the event's code window is executed, in addition to the default behavior of the event. But events happen when they happen—when you click, or double-click, or mouse over, or whatever. You don't add events in FoxPro.

Each of FoxPro's base classes comes with a generous but fixed list of events. You can't add to FoxPro's events; you're stuck with the list of events that each class was born with. In FoxPro, the name of an event implies what it handles. TextBox1.Click tells you which object the Click event responds to. There is no Handles clause at the end. It's not needed. You don't even see the mechanism that handles it. It's transparent.

To add code for an event, you pick the event from the Method Name/Members combo box of the code window navigation bar (at the upper-right side of the screen).

FoxPro's IDE supplies any necessary parameters. The code, in the form of an LPARAMETERS statement, is inserted when the code window opens. If you erase the LPARAMETERS line and leave the code window empty, the LPARAMETERS line will be put back in the next time you open the code window. For example, open a new MouseDown event code window and you get this:

```
LPARAMETERS nButton, nShift, nXCoord, nYCoord
```

> **NOTE**
>
> We'll look at the event argument parameter generated for this same event in Visual Basic by the .NET IDE in the next section. It does essentially the same thing.

There is no Event statement in FoxPro. (There are three new functions [BindEvent, RaiseEvent and ReleaseEvents] related to events in Visual FoxPro8, but it's difficult to come up with a reason to use them.) Looking at the list of events for a typical FoxPro control, I can't imagine why I'd want to add more events. That's why the Event statement in Visual Basic has always confused me. And why "raise" an event? Aren't events things that just happen, like "Click"?

> **NOTE**
>
> The closest things we have to events in FoxPro are the Assign and Access methods for form properties. They allow you to trap the instant when a value is assigned to or retrieved from a

> class property. But that's unrelated to the use of `RaiseEvents` in Visual Basic. It's interesting that in FoxPro we use the Visual Basic naming convention. If you add a `MyPropName_Assign` method to your class, the code in it will fire when the property is assigned a value.

This is at the heart of the reason that FoxPro developers can't easily understand Visual Basic events. The events that are declared for the purpose of calling them with `RaiseEvent` have nothing to do with the events that come with controls. That's not what `RaiseEvent` is used for in Visual Basic.

Events in Visual Basic .NET

One of the really huge differences between FoxPro and Visual Basic .NET is Visual Basic's use of events. FoxPro objects have events, and you can write code in the event snippets that will run when the event fires. It's transparent. In Visual Basic, event handling is not transparent. You get to watch.

If you create a Windows Form project and add a text box to the form, you'll find the following generated code in the form's codebehind:

```
Friend WithEvents TextBox1 As System.Windows.Forms.TextBox
...
    'TextBox1
    '
    Me.TextBox1.Location = New System.Drawing.Point(110, 54)
    Me.TextBox1.Name = "TextBox1"
    Me.TextBox1.TabIndex = 0
    Me.TextBox1.Text = "TextBox1"
    Me.Controls.Add(Me.TextBox1)
```

If the `WithEvents` clause were not included, the program would ignore any of the control's events. Presumably, doing so causes the program to run faster; otherwise, why would the `WithEvents` clause exist? This allows us to add a `Handles` clause to a subroutine, regardless of its name, that "reacts" when the named event occurs. So what is the Visual Basic default—*without events*? Oddly enough, *it is*.

The IDE writes the code for you if you open the code window and select an object from the Objects drop-down list at the upper-left corner of the window, and then select an event from the drop-down list at the upper-right corner of the same window.

For example, the following code changes the text box back to black text on a white background when the cursor leaves the control:

```
Private Sub TextBox1_LostFocus( _
        ByVal sender As Object, _
        ByVal e As System.EventArgs) _
```

```
    Handles TextBox1.LostFocus
      TextBox1.ForeColor = Color.Black
      TextBox1.BackColor = Color.White
  End Sub
```

Although a subroutine name that references the event name is generated when you add
the code, the name is in fact functionally unrelated to what the routine does. You can
change the name, and the program will work exactly the same. The `Handles` clause at the
end is what causes the subroutine to execute when the event fires. Or, as they like to say
in Redmond, when the event is *raised*.

RANT

<rant>That's actually part of the problem as well. The guys who developed Visual Basic took
considerable liberties with the language. You *throw* and *catch* an error. (Why? Because they had
seen the Mariners the night before, and because they could. There were no language police. The
first little guy high on Coca-Cola at three a.m. gets to pick a name.) Similarly, you *raise* an event.
Don't even get me started on persisting, depersisting, and consuming XML. By capriciously
assigning terms that don't particularly reflect what's being done, they made the language that
much harder to understand. But I digress... </rant>

The two parameters in parentheses that follow the subroutine name are always `ByVal`
`sender As Object` (a reference to the calling object) and an **event argument** whose type
is based on what kind of parameters the called event needs. For example, if you add a
MouseDown event routine, you get the following code:

```
  Private Sub Form1_MouseDown( _
    ByVal sender As Object, _
    ByVal e As System.Windows.Forms.MouseEventArgs) _
  Handles MyBase.MouseDown
  Debugger.Break   ' like SET STEP ON
  End Sub
```

I've included a breakpoint so that you can type "e" into the Watch window and see what
it is. It's a structure containing the values needed to respond to a mousedown event: X
and Y coordinates, among others. So it's pretty much the same thing that FoxPro is doing
with its generated `LPARAMETERS` statements. One more mystery solved.

If this were the only use for events in Visual Basic .NET, you could simply ignore them
and let the IDE generate event-related code whenever it felt like it. The developers of
FoxPro apparently felt that the confusion resulting from optionally exposing events in this
way was not worth the bother. Generally, they were correct.

RaiseEvent

Events in Visual Basic are also used as a workaround for a characteristic of the Visual Basic compiler that prevents it from calling functions and procedures that aren't resolved at compile time. In particular, although you can instantiate an object based on a class and call the object's methods at will from within a form, you can't do the opposite in Visual Basic. For example, in FoxPro, you can't call `THISFORM.Refresh` from inside a class, like this:

```
DEFINE CLASS Utilities AS CUSTOM

PROCEDURE CoordinateTables
THISFORM.Refresh          && in whatever form is active
ENDPROC

ENDDEFINE
```

You can, however, use `_Screen.ActiveForm.CoordinateTables`. You can even use `PEMSTA-TUS ( Object, MethodName, 5 )` to determine whether the method exists before calling it. So we have workarounds in FoxPro. But in Visual Basic they don't. (Well, there is reflection, but it's new. `RaiseEvents` has been around since Visual Basic4 at least, so that's how they do it.)

In Visual Basic you can't call a method in a form from inside an object without resorting to some trick. `RaiseEvent` is that trick. That's why it's so confusing. Here we are trying to think up events that might go beyond clicking or double-clicking. The use of `RaiseEvent` is a trick with mirrors to overcome a limitation in the compile process for Visual Basic. You don't need to try to invent events in FoxPro. There's no reason to. You can do what you need to do without them. In Visual Basic, you can't.

This is why FoxPro developers have a hard time understanding events in Visual Basic. All of FoxPro's events are always trappable; there is no need to use `WithEvents` to declare that the events for a control are subject to handling; they just *are*. And the second reason for using events in Visual Basic is unnecessary in Visual FoxPro!

In Visual Basic, `Public Sub XXX Handles ObjectName.EventName` can be used to respond to the line `RaiseEvent EventName` in a class. So a form can contain a subroutine that is called when the event named in the `Handles` clause of the subroutine fires (or is raised, as they like to say).

How to Declare an Event in a Class

To declare an event in a class, include the statement

```
Public Event <Name> ( Parameters )
```

Instantiate your object:

```
Dim oObj as New <ClassName>
```

Then, within the code, invoke it using the RaiseEvent command:

```
RaiseEvent <Name> ( Parameters )
```

This "raises" the event and passes any parameters to it. Finally, trap the event using the Handles clause of a subroutine in the form:

```
Public sub xxx ( Parameters as string ) Handles oObj.EventName
```

Using this mechanism, I've created a "hook" that lets me call any method in the form when something happens in the class. Note that I could simply call a method in the class using oObj.MethodName (Parameters), as I do in the Update button code in Listing 1.5. But if I want to call form methods from the class, this is actually a pretty clean way to do it.

Here's an example, based on the "Visual Basic .NET How-To N-Tier Data Form App" sample included in the "101 Visual Basic .NET Samples" library available for free from the MSDN site. I can't say enough about this code library, which gives you good examples of how to do a huge variety of things in Visual Basic .NET. I've added a few properties so that it's more flexible and easier to configure.

Using Events in a Data Access Class

The benefits of separating the implementation of data access from the form are immediate. The data access class is external to the form, so you can change the data source without making any changes to the form. This allows (for example) using MSDE during development, then changing to SQL Server at a later date with minimal disruption. Listing 1.5 shows the example class.

LISTING 1.5   A Data Access Class

```
Option Strict On
Imports System.Data.SqlClient

Namespace DataAccessLayer

Public Class DataAccess

    Protected Const CONNECTION_ERROR_MSG As String = "Couldn't connect to SQL"
    Protected Const SQL_CONNECTION_STRING As String = _
                "server=(local);database=Northwind;uid=sa;pwd=;"
```

LISTING 1.5   Continued

```
Public da As SqlDataAdapter
Public ds As DataSet

Public _MainTable As String
Public _KeyField As String

Protected DidPreviouslyConnect As Boolean = False
Protected strConn As String = SQL_CONNECTION_STRING

Public Event ConnectionStatusChange(ByVal status As String)
Public Event ConnectionFailure(ByVal reason As String)
Public Event ConnectionCompleted(ByVal success As Boolean)

Public Property MainTable() As String
    Get
        Return _MainTable
    End Get
    Set(ByVal Value As String)
        _MainTable = Value
    End Set
End Property

Public Property KeyField() As String
    Get
        Return _KeyField
    End Get
    Set(ByVal Value As String)
        _KeyField = Value
    End Set
End Property

Public Function CreateDataSet() As DataSet

    Dim ds As DataSet
    If Not DidPreviouslyConnect Then
        RaiseEvent ConnectionStatusChange("Connecting to SQL Server")
    End If
    Dim IsConnecting As Boolean = True
    While IsConnecting
        Try
            Dim scnnNW As New SqlConnection(strConn)
            Dim strSQL As String = "SELECT * FROM " + MainTable
```

LISTING 1.5   Continued

```
                Dim scmd As New SqlCommand(strSQL, scnnNW)
                da = New SqlDataAdapter(scmd)
                Dim cb As New SqlCommandBuilder(da)
                ds = New DataSet
                da.Fill(ds, MainTable)
                IsConnecting = False
                DidPreviouslyConnect = True
            Catch exp As Exception
                If strConn = SQL_CONNECTION_STRING Then
                    RaiseEvent ConnectionFailure(CONNECTION_ERROR_MSG)
                End If
            End Try
        End While
        RaiseEvent ConnectionCompleted(True)
        da.Fill(ds, MainTable)
        Return ds

    End Function

    Public Sub UpdateDataSet(ByVal inDS As DataSet)
        If inDS Is Nothing Then
            Exit Sub
        End If
        Try
            If (da Is Nothing) Then
                CreateDataSet()
            End If
            inDS.EnforceConstraints = False
            da.Update(inDS, MainTable)
        Catch exc As Exception
            RaiseEvent ConnectionFailure("Unable to update the data source.")
        End Try
    End Sub

End Class
End Namespace
```

There are four RaiseEvent calls in this code. Each call is made when the result of an attempt to connect to the database is known. Because you don't know which form is going to call these methods, or even what the form is going to do when this occurs, all you provide is the mechanism for notifying the form that it needs to do something.

This is called **messaging**. Internally, Windows threads send each other messages. Each thread listens for a message, and responds when the message is received.

RANT

<rant>There was once a book written about FoxPro that went on and on about "messaging." I thought it was silly. When I start my car, it causes thousands of gasoline explosions per second. But I don't say "I'm going to explode some gasoline." I say "I'm going to drive to the store." The less I know about what's under the hood, the better. In fact, the one criticism I have of .NET at this point is that it gives me way too much information. I can't imagine why I need to see the code that instantiates text boxes and positions them on the form.</rant>

So in summary, the stage is set for the class code to "call" related methods in a form to be named later. In the form code shown in Listing 1.6, you'll see how this is done.

The Form

The form code answers the question "What do I do when these events occur?" The Data Access Layer class is instantiated as object m_DAL. The events are referred to with the prefix m_DAL because they belong to the object. See Listing 1.6.

LISTING 1.6   A Form That Uses a DAL Component with Events

```
Option Strict On
Imports System.Data.SqlClient
Imports DataAccessLayer

Public Class frmMain
    Inherits System.Windows.Forms.Form

...Windows Form Designer generated code goes here...

    Protected DidPreviouslyConnect As Boolean = False
    Private ds As DataSet
    Private dt As DataTable
    Private dv As DataView

    Public MainTable As String = "Customers"
    Public KeyField As String = "CustomerID"

    Protected WithEvents m_DAL As DataAccess

    Dim frmStatusMessage As New frmStatus
```

LISTING 1.6 Continued

```
    Private Sub btnNext_Click( _
      ByVal sender As System.Object, _
      ByVal e As System.EventArgs) _
     Handles btnNext.Click
        NextRecord()
    End Sub

    Private Sub btnPrevious_Click( _
      ByVal sender As System.Object, _
      ByVal e As System.EventArgs) _
     Handles btnPrevious.Click
        PreviousRecord()
    End Sub

    Private Sub btnRefresh_Click( _
      ByVal sender As System.Object, _
      ByVal e As System.EventArgs) _
     Handles btnRefresh.Click
        frmMain_Load(Me, New System.EventArgs)
    End Sub

' Call the UpdateDataSet method:
    Private Sub btnUpdate_Click( _
      ByVal sender As System.Object, _
      ByVal e As System.EventArgs) _
     Handles btnUpdate.Click
     m_DAL.UpdateDataSet(ds.GetChanges())
        frmMain_Load(Me, New System.EventArgs)
    End Sub

    Protected Sub dt_PositionChanged( _
      ByVal sender As Object, _
      ByVal e As System.EventArgs)
        BindGrid()
    End Sub

    Private Sub frmMain_KeyDown( _
      ByVal sender As Object, ByVal e _
      As System.Windows.Forms.KeyEventArgs) _
     Handles MyBase.KeyDown
        If e.KeyCode = Keys.Right Then NextRecord()
        If e.KeyCode = Keys.Left Then PreviousRecord()
    End Sub
```

LISTING 1.6   Continued

```
Private Sub frmMain_Load( _
  ByVal sender As Object, _
  ByVal e As System.EventArgs) _
 Handles MyBase.Load
    frmStatusMessage = New frmStatus
    GetDataSet()
    BindGrid()
End Sub

Private Sub grd_CurrentCellChanged( _
  ByVal sender As Object, _
  ByVal e As System.EventArgs) _
 Handles grd.CurrentCellChanged
    grd.Select(grd.CurrentCell.RowNumber)
    If TypeOf (grd.Item(grd.CurrentRowIndex, 2)) Is DBNull Then
        grd.Item(grd.CurrentRowIndex, 2) = _
            grd.Item(grd.CurrentRowIndex, 0)
    End If
End Sub

Private Sub grdClick( _
  ByVal sender As System.Object, _
  ByVal e As System.EventArgs) _
 Handles grd.Click
    BindGrid()
End Sub

* Handle the ConnectionCompleted event:
   Private Sub m_DAL_ConnectionCompleted( _
     ByVal success As Boolean) _
    Handles m_DAL.ConnectionCompleted
       frmStatusMessage.Close()
   End Sub

* Handle the ConnectionFailure event:
   Private Sub m_DAL_ConnectionFailure( _
     ByVal reason As String) _
    Handles m_DAL.ConnectionFailure
       MsgBox(reason, MsgBoxStyle.Critical, Me.Text)
       End
   End Sub
```

LISTING 1.6   Continued

```
* Handle the ConnectionStatusChanged event:
    Private Sub m_DAL_ConnectionStatusChange( _
      ByVal status As String) _
     Handles m_DAL.ConnectionStatusChange
        frmStatusMessage.Show(status)
    End Sub

    Sub BindGrid()
        With grd
            .CaptionText = MainTable
            .DataSource = dv
        End With
    End Sub

    Sub GetDataSet()
        frmStatusMessage.Show("Retrieving Data From Data Access Layer")
        ds = m_DAL.CreateDataSet()
        dt = ds.Tables(MainTable)
        dv = dt.DefaultView
    End Sub

    Public Sub NextRecord()
        grd.UnSelect(grd.CurrentRowIndex)
        grd.CurrentRowIndex += 1
        grd.Select(grd.CurrentRowIndex)
    End Sub

    Public Sub PreviousRecord()
        grd.UnSelect(grd.CurrentRowIndex)
        If grd.CurrentRowIndex > 0 Then
            grd.CurrentRowIndex -= 1
        End If
        grd.Select(grd.CurrentRowIndex)
    End Sub

End Class
```

frmStatus is just a simple form with a label control in the center of the screen and an override of the form's Show method code:

```
Public Overloads Sub Show(ByVal Message As String)
    lblStatus.Text = Message
    Me.Show()
    System.Threading.Thread.CurrentThread.Sleep(500)
    Application.DoEvents()
End Sub
```

This displays the form with a message and resumes execution after a half-second delay.

To summarize: If you want to use events in your classes to call methods in forms when you don't yet know which form and which methods, do this:

1. Create a solution containing a project named, say, "A", output type "Class Library", which contains a class named, say, "B".

2. In class B, define an event like this:

   ```
   PUBLIC Event ABC ( ByVal xxx As String )
   ```

3. In the class, call using this:

   ```
   RaiseEvent ABC ( parms )
   ```

4. Add a Windows Form project.

5. In the form, include this:

   ```
   Imports A                    'so that it will know to use the class
   ```

6. Add this:

   ```
   Protected Withevents C AS B    'instantiate an object based on the class
   ```

7. In the form, add a subroutine or function with a `Handles` clause:

   ```
   Private Sub XYZ ( parms ) Handles C.ABC
   ```

8. Use the sub/function's parameter list to pass the event's parameters.

Compiler Directives

In FoxPro, the `#CONST` directive can be used to specify a value that is substituted for occurrences of the named constant in the code at compile time. The `#IF` `#ELSE` `#ENDIF` construct can be used to deliver source code that will include only the code that will compile correctly given the compiler version. `#DEF`, `#UNDEF`, and `#IFDEF` can similarly be used to determine what code gets compiled. The `#Include` directive reads in a text file, and is like the `#ExternalSource` directive in Visual Basic.

In Visual Basic .NET, the #Const compiler directive also exists, and the #IF/#ELSE/#ENDIF construct works much like its counterpart in FoxPro, although not to support multiple language versions because there's only one at this time; besides, Visual Basic doesn't allow code that isn't syntactically correct to exist in the source code, as it compiles automatically when you close a code window.

The most interesting compiler directive in Visual Basic is the #Region *Name*/#End Region block, which allows you to group code elements and collapse them to a single label by clicking on the "+" beside the #Region directive. There's no equivalent in FoxPro, although the way that FoxPro groups code into snippets in the Form and Class Designers provides similar functionality, in the sense of letting you see only some of the code at one time.

Table 1.8 summarizes compiler directives in Visual FoxPro and Visual Basic.

TABLE 1.8   Compiler Directives

Action	Visual Basic	Visual FoxPro
Define a constant	#Const	#Const
Compile selected lines	#IF.. #ENDIF	#IF.. #ENDIF
Collapse part of code	#Region.. #End Region	No equivalent
Include a file	#ExternalSource	#Include

Data

Perhaps the greatest difference between Visual FoxPro and Visual Basic .NET is the handling of tables. It's a huge topic, and I'll just talk about general issues here. (It's covered in considerably more detail in Chapter 4, "A Visual Basic .NET Framework for SQL Server," and Chapter 7, "XML.") But I can give you a feel for the issues here.

FoxPro stores its data in either DBF files or in cursors. DBFs have a header of about 512 bytes that describes the nature of the table and its membership, if any, in a data base container (DBC). It then uses 32 bytes per field to describe all of the fields in the table. What follows are fixed-length records with a "delete byte" at the front, one per record. Cursors are in-memory representations of tables, having the same format except for the database container (DBC) information, which doesn't apply. When you USE a table or create a cursor using CREATE CURSOR or as the result of a SQL SELECT statement, FoxPro reads the header and uses its contents to interpret the fixed-length records that follow. BROWSE displays the table rows in a grid-like format.

Visual Basic .NET has no native data storage format. It always treats data as a foreign object. It usually reads it into a dataset, which is an XML representation of the data.

In its simplest form, XML consists of an XML header (a single line that says "I'm an xml string"), followed optionally by a Schema that describes the rows that follow, followed by a hierarchy of rows and fields that describe the table. A simple example follows:

```xml
<?xml version = "1.0" encoding="Windows-1252" standalone="yes"?>
<VFPData>
   <xsd:schema id="VFPData" xmlns:xsd="http://www.w3.org/2001/XMLSchema"  _
     xmlns:msdata="urn:schemas-microsoft-com:xml-msdata">
      <xsd:element name="VFPData" msdata:IsDataSet="true">
         <xsd:complexType>
            <xsd:choice maxOccurs="unbounded">
               <xsd:element name="customer" minOccurs="0" maxOccurs="unbounded">
                  <xsd:complexType>
                     <xsd:sequence>
                        <xsd:element name="name">
                           <xsd:simpleType>
                              <xsd:restriction base="xsd:string">
                                 <xsd:maxLength value="20"/>
                              </xsd:restriction>
                           </xsd:simpleType>
                        </xsd:element>
                        <xsd:element name="phone">
                           <xsd:simpleType>
                              <xsd:restriction base="xsd:string">
                                 <xsd:maxLength value="12"/>
                              </xsd:restriction>
                           </xsd:simpleType>
                        </xsd:element>
                     </xsd:sequence>
                  </xsd:complexType>
               </xsd:element>
            </xsd:choice>
            <xsd:anyAttribute namespace="http://www.w3.org/XML/1998/
➡ namespace" processContents="lax"/>
         </xsd:complexType>
      </xsd:element>
   </xsd:schema>
   <customer>
      <name>Les Pinter</name>
      <phone>650-344-3969</phone>
   </customer>
</VFProData>
```

It looks scary, but if you saw the FoxPro DBF header it would be equally scary. Oh, what the heck. Figure 1.6 shows what the data that was displayed in XML looks like as a FoxPro .DBF.

Address	0	1	2	3	4	5	6	7	8	9	A	B	C	D	E	F	Text
00000000	30	03	0A	04	01	00	00	00	68	01	21	00	00	00	00	00	0□□□□□□h□!□□□□□
00000010	00	00	00	00	00	00	00	00	00	00	00	00	03	00	00	00	□□□□□□□□□□□□□□□□
00000020	4E	41	4D	45	00	00	00	00	00	00	43	01	00	00	00	00	NAME□□□□□□C□□□□
00000030	14	00	00	00	00	00	00	00	00	00	00	00	00	00	00	00	□□□□□□□□□□□□□□□□
00000040	50	48	4F	4E	45	00	00	00	00	00	43	15	00	00	00	00	PHONE□□□□□□C□□□□
00000050	0C	00	00	00	00	00	00	00	00	00	00	00	00	00	00	00	□□□□□□□□□□□□□□□□
00000060	0D	00	00	00	00	00	00	00	00	00	00	00	00	00	00	00	□□□□□□□□□□□□□□□□
00000070	00	00	00	00	00	00	00	00	00	00	00	00	00	00	00	00	□□□□□□□□□□□□□□□□
00000080	00	00	00	00	00	00	00	00	00	00	00	00	00	00	00	00	□□□□□□□□□□□□□□□□
00000090	00	00	00	00	00	00	00	00	00	00	00	00	00	00	00	00	□□□□□□□□□□□□□□□□
000000A0	00	00	00	00	00	00	00	00	00	00	00	00	00	00	00	00	□□□□□□□□□□□□□□□□
000000B0	00	00	00	00	00	00	00	00	00	00	00	00	00	00	00	00	□□□□□□□□□□□□□□□□
000000C0	00	00	00	00	00	00	00	00	00	00	00	00	00	00	00	00	□□□□□□□□□□□□□□□□
000000D0	00	00	00	00	00	00	00	00	00	00	00	00	00	00	00	00	□□□□□□□□□□□□□□□□
000000E0	00	00	00	00	00	00	00	00	00	00	00	00	00	00	00	00	□□□□□□□□□□□□□□□□
000000F0	00	00	00	00	00	00	00	00	00	00	00	00	00	00	00	00	□□□□□□□□□□□□□□□□
00000100	00	00	00	00	00	00	00	00	00	00	00	00	00	00	00	00	□□□□□□□□□□□□□□□□
00000110	00	00	00	00	00	00	00	00	00	00	00	00	00	00	00	00	□□□□□□□□□□□□□□□□
00000120	00	00	00	00	00	00	00	00	00	00	00	00	00	00	00	00	□□□□□□□□□□□□□□□□
00000130	00	00	00	00	00	00	00	00	00	00	00	00	00	00	00	00	□□□□□□□□□□□□□□□□
00000140	00	00	00	00	00	00	00	00	00	00	00	00	00	00	00	00	□□□□□□□□□□□□□□□□
00000150	00	00	00	00	00	00	00	00	00	00	00	00	00	00	00	00	□□□□□□□□□□□□□□□□
00000160	00	00	00	00	00	00	00	00	20	4C	65	73	20	50	69	6E	□□□□□□□ Les Pin
00000170	74	65	72	20	20	20	20	20	20	20	20	20	36	35	30		ter 650
00000180	2D	33	34	34	2D	33	39	36	39								-344-3969

FIGURE 1.6   The same data as a FoxPro .DBF.

As you can see, neither one is really a "table." The program reads the file and uses it for whatever display mechanism you choose. As you can see, the tags that bracket each data element occupy quite a bit of space, compared to the positional format that fixed-length records permit; on the other hand, trimmed strings mean that extra blanks aren't transmitted. On balance, DBFs are somewhat smaller than their XML counterpart. So the idea that XML is less of a table than a DBF is just silly.

But the idea that XML is less efficient as a data storage mechanism is absolutely accurate. In fact, DBFs are extraordinarily efficient, especially when combined with the structural .cdx index files supported by FoxPro. I've demonstrated a SELECT that returned 30 matching records from more than a million in less than a tenth of a second. You can't get performance like that from SQL Server, which is a much more expensive data store. In some sense, XML is a dumbed-down DBF. Still, it does the job.

In FoxPro, on-screen controls use the ControlSource to bind to the data. Binding is bidirectional; change the contents of a text box, and the changes are automatically written back to the DBF. (There are a few caveats to observe, especially in multiuser environments, but this is basically how it works.) Grids have a RecordSource property that binds data to the grid in the same way that ControlSource does for controls.

Visual Basic .NET doesn't have tables or cursors. It has datasets. You fill a dataset by creating a SQLCommand or an OLEDBCommand object, specifying its SelectCommand CommandText, executing the SELECT, and then calling the Fill method of the Command object or DataAdapter object to fill the dataset. If that looks more complicated to you than USE (Table), you're right.

But wait, there's more. A dataset can contain several tables; in that sense it's more like a form's Data Environment. In fact, it's a *lot* like a form's Data Environment. A dataset can also contain indexes and relations, just as the DE does.

Things stop being equally simple about here. You can bind a recordset to a `DataGrid`, but you have to tell it which of the tables in the recordset to bind to first. If you don't, you'll get a little plus sign that you click on to display all available tables and choose one. Or you can specify the table. `Table(0)` is the first table, so if there's only one table, it's always the same code. You can also select the `DefaultView` of the dataset, which is `table(0)`, and assign that to the `DataGrid`'s `DataSource`:

```
SqlDataAdapter1.Fill(DsEmployee1)
Dim dv As DataView
dv = DsEmployee1.Tables(0).DefaultView
DataGrid1.DataSource = dv
```

This assumes that you previously dropped a `SQLDataAdapter` on the form and specified the connection to use to the ensuing wizard, and then right-clicked on the `DataAdapter` and selected Generate DataSet from the context menu, providing the name `dsEmployee` as the dataset name. Visual Basic .NET adds a 1, because it always adds a 1, even to the first instance of the class.

However, binding is one-way. In order to update the data source from whence the data came, you'll have to add code to get the changes made to the dataset and put them into a diffgram. Then you'll have to pass the diffgram to the `SQLDataAdapter`'s `Update` method, which was generated automatically when the `DataAdapter` was created. It's just a few more lines of code, but the fact that in FoxPro it's not necessary is notable.

But that's not entirely true. If you use DBFs it's not necessary. But if you use SQL or a Web service as the data store, you have to build a mechanism for executing the `UPDATE` statement that applies the changes that you made in the local cursor to the data store. So it's harder in Visual FoxPro as well.

The fact is that sending back new records or updates to a local table in Visual Basic .NET is exactly as difficult as sending them to SQL Server. So the programming cost saving of working with local tables in Visual Basic .NET is gone. You might as well print out the bill for some SQL Server licenses and hand them to your client.

Data Binding

In FoxPro, when you change a field's value on a screen and the corresponding data field in the underlying table is changed, you're taking a lot for granted. What's happening is called **data binding**.

Visual Basic .NET doesn't have data binding to the data store. Not really. What Visual Basic .NET does have is binding to the dataset, the XML string that holds the data you got from your data source. Assume you've built a form with a text box on it and then returned a typed dataset. (See Chapter 4, "A Visual Basic .NET Framework," for more information on the Customers table containing Phone fields.) Select the text box on the form, press F4 to open the Properties window, and click on the plus sign beside the `Databindings` property to open the two fields under the heading. Select Text, and then select Customers.Phone from the list of available dataset classes that automatically appears.

This will cause the dataset's Phone value to be copied to the text box's Text property when you get values for the rows in the dataset, and conversely it will move any value that's typed into the text box into the dataset's Phone column. That's what Visual Basic .NET calls data binding.

The dataset's AcceptChanges and RejectChanges methods correspond to FoxPro's TableUpdate() and TableRevert() functions, respectively. But that still doesn't get your data back to the data store. Think of the dataset as a cursor into which you've copied a record. You've saved the changes to the cursor, but you haven't copied the changed record back to wherever it came from. How you do that will have to wait until Chapter 4.

Error Handling and Debugging

After years of primitive error handling, both Visual Basic and Visual FoxPro have finally acquired real error-handling capabilities with the TRY...CATCH block. And Visual Basic .NET actually has more debugging features than does FoxPro.

TRY...CATCH

The syntax for TRY...CATCH is slightly different for Visual Basic .NET than for Visual FoxPro.

Here's the syntax in Visual FoxPro:

```
TRY
      Code here
Catch To oEx WHEN ERROR() = 1234
      What to do for this error
Catch To oEx WHEN ERROR() = 4321
      What to do for this error
Catch To oEx
      What to do for all other errors
Finally
      Do this whether there was an error or not
ENDTRY
```

At a minimum, you can print out the error details:

```
Msg = oEx.Message + CHR(13)+oEx.Details + CHR(13)+oEx.LineContents
MessageBox ( Msg, 32, "Error" )
```

And this is the syntax in Visual Basic .NET:

```
Try
     Code here
Catch oEx as ExceptionType1  (of about 60 exception types)
     Code to handle ExceptionType1
Catch oEx as ExceptionType2  (of about 60 exception types)
     Code to handle ExceptionType2
Catch oEx as Exception
     Code to handle all other Exceptions
Finally
     Do this under all circumstances
END Try
```

Similarly, you can print out `oEx.Message + CHR(13)+oEx.Source` to see the error message and offending code.

Visual Basic does have additional language elements (`Error`, `Raise`, `GetException`, `Err`, `On Error`, and `Resume`), but `Try...Catch` is a lot better.

Error trapping is meant to allow graceful handling of unavoidable errors in the program, due to device unavailability (CD-ROM, printers, floppy drives), incorrect input that can't be prevented, and other errors that are the result of normal program operation. Error trapping is not meant to be used to catch errors in program logic. Still, it's better than letting users see messages from the FoxPro or the .NET IDE.

In the code that appears in this book, we have left out error trapping in most code samples. That doesn't mean that we recommend leaving it out of your code. In fact, Try...Catch blocks are an excellent idea, and should be used in every case where a user or system error is possible. (It can even be helpful in finding your own coding errors during debugging, although that's not the purpose of Try...Catch.) But we've decided to focus on the main purpose of each code fragment, and adding error trapping to a single line of code tends to make the code harder to read. So with regard to error trapping, do as I say, not as I do.

Debugging

Debugging support is awesome in both languages. In FoxPro, you can either toggle a breakpoint by clicking in the selection margin of the code at the point where you want the code to break, or you can insert a `SET STEP ON` command. In Visual Basic .NET, you can either toggle a breakpoint by clicking in the selection margin of the code at the point where you want the code to break, or you can insert a `Debugger.Break` command.

FoxPro Debugging Aids

At this point FoxPro provides you with five windows:

- Trace (to step through the code)
- Locals (all variables and objects)

- Watch (type in the names of the variables to inspect)

- Call Stack (*A* called *B* called *C*, and so on)

- Debug Output (`Debug.print` output goes here)

In addition, you can add assertions to your code. Assertions are statements that only execute if they evaluate to `False`, and only if you `SET ASSERTS ON`. You'll get a little dialog window that asks if you want to debug. This permits bracketing of debugging code in a way that it can be turned on and off with a single command in the command window.

Visual Basic .NET Debugging Aids

In Visual Basic .NET, `Debugger.Break` (or a breakpoint entered in the Selection Margin of the code window) gives you a vast array of debugging windows:

- Modules

- Threads

- Call Stack

- Me

- Command window

- Locals

- Autos

- Watch (four of them!)

- Running Documents

- Breakpoints

Each of these windows gives you some of the information about your program's state at the breakpoint. You can either go to the command window in Immediate mode and print the contents of individual Variables and object properties, type the name of the object in a watch window, or look in the Locals window to see if it's there already.

It's clear that both languages offer excellent error trapping and debugging capabilities.

Summary

By now, I hope you've come to the same conclusion I have, which is that Visual Basic .NET is not nearly as different as it looks. The few things that appear truly strange are not really very important; the use of events, when it's necessary, can be reduced to a six-step cookie-cutter procedure; property procedures practically write themselves, and do the same thing as FoxPro properties do; and the additional effort get to your data can be relegated to a data access layer class that does the same thing FoxPro does, so that you don't ever have to think about it.

In Chapter 2 we'll build a FoxPro application using form classes and a data access class, permitting us to switch between DBFs and SQL Server as the data store. This application will serve as a model for developing your first Visual Basic .NET application in Chapter 3, using very similar coding. Then in Chapter 4 we'll compare data access to tables, SQL Server, and XML Web Services, in preparation for upgrading our applications to work with any of the three types of data stores.

CHAPTER 2

Building Simple Applications in Visual FoxPro and Visual Basic .NET

Most of us can remember the first database application we built in FoxBASE or FoxPro. The thrill of seeing everything work for the first time is hard to forget. That ability to do simple things quickly and easily made FoxPro the huge success that it became. You'll find the same to be true of Visual Basic .NET.

In this chapter, we'll build simple applications in both languages, using the techniques that are appropriate for a FoxPro application. Then we'll begin to differentiate the Visual Basic .NET model to take into account the idiosyncrasies of that platform and the slightly different expectations in that world.

Building a Simple Application in Visual FoxPro

The simplest Visual FoxPro application is a single user app with one or more screens. In this chapter we'll build a simple application consisting of a single screen to find, add, edit, and delete records in a Customers table. For this purpose, create a table called Customers by entering the following:

```
CREATE TABLE Customers ( ;
  CustomerID Integer,    ;
```

```
Name        Char(30),     ;
Address     Char(30),     ;
City        Char(30),     ;
State       Char( 2),     ;
Zip         Char(10),     ;
Phone       Char(10),     ;
Balance     Numeric(9,2),,;
LastOrder   Date(8)       )
```

There are a few FoxPro defaults that exist at the environment level that have to be changed. First, before you can insert a date into a table, you have to make sure that you've set the STRICTDATE setting to zero. I don't know why this setting defaults to the SQL Server syntax in a default installation, but it does. Also TALK defaults to ON, and displays all variable assignments in the _Screen background. Finally, MULTILOCKS must be set to ON in order to enable buffering. So issue these three commands either in the command window, or in the form's LOAD event before anything else happens:

```
SET STRICTDATE TO 0
SET TALK OFF
SET MULTILOCKS ON
```

After you've changed these settings, the following command will put one record into the new table:

```
INSERT INTO Customers VALUES ( ;
    1, "Joe's Hardware", "202 Main", "Dallas", "TX", ;
"94121", "212-331-2014", 243.21, {03/15/2004} )
```

Based on this table structure and this record, a typical customer screen might look like the one shown in Figure 2.1.

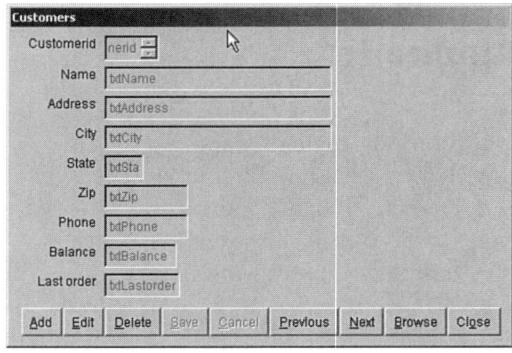

FIGURE 2.1   A simple application screen.

Creating a Simple Form Controls Class Library

To build our new application, we first need to create a class library with subclasses of the FoxPro base control classes. Type the following in the command window, using Ctrl+W to close the resulting designer window after each command:

```
CREATE CLASS mytext  OF pinter as textbox
CREATE CLASS mycheck OF pinter as checkbox
CREATE CLASS myedit  OF pinter as editbox
CREATE CLASS mycombo OF pinter as combobox
CREATE CLASS myspin  OF pinter as spinner
CREATE CLASS myradio OF pinter as optiongroup
CREATE CLASS mylabel OF pinter as label
CREATE CLASS mycmd   OF pinter as commandbutton
```

> **TIP**
>
> Use Alt+W, P to open the Properties sheet, and make sure that Dockable is not checked before you do this.

I do this because it's the simplest way to begin to take advantage of object-oriented programming. If you now open the class library and change the properties for selected commands as shown in Table 2.1, you'll see what I mean; these changes will now take effect on every single form you create that uses these classes. Change the font or color of the MyText class, and it changes in all instances on all of your forms.

TABLE 2.1   My Subclassed Controls with Important Property Settings

Control	Property	Setting
MyCommand	AutoSize	.T.
MyText	FontName	Courier New
MyText	Enabled	.F.
MyEdit	Enabled	.F.
MySpin	Enabled	.F.
MyCheck	Enabled	.F.
MyCombo	Enabled	.F.
MyLabel	BackStyle	0 (Transparent)

Field Mapping

Select Tools, Options, Field Mapping and match the controls shown in Table 2.1 with the data types used in your Customers table. If you cut and paste the class name Pinter.vcx into the Class Location field and use Alt+A to save each field mapping after you fill in the three fields in the Field Mapping dialog, the entire process of creating the classes and setting the mappings should take two minutes or less.

Creating the Form Using Your Subclassed Controls

After you've created your subclassed controls, type **CREATE SCREEN CUSTOMERS DEFAULT** to use the base FoxPro form class, open the Data Environment, and add the Customers table. Drag and drop the word Table from the top of the Customer table graphic onto the upper-left corner of the form, and you'll have the screen shown in Figure 2.1, minus the command buttons.

Form Methods

I know that I'll want to enable and disable controls and command buttons, so I might as well write methods to do this before I go any further.

In Visual FoxPro, you can traverse all controls in the form's `Controls` collection and set values based on the names of the form classes. I added a form property called `InputClasses` and populated it with the names of the input control classes in `pinter.vcx`:

```
InputClasses: MyText,MyEdit,MyCheck,MyCombo,MySpin
```

The code to enable or disable controls based on these classes, and to turn all of the form's command buttons on or off as needed, is this:

Form method **Input**

```
PARAMETERS OnOff
WITH THISFORM
FOR EACH Ctrl IN.Controls
    IF UPPER(Ctrl.Class) $.InputClasses
        Ctrl.Enabled = OnOff
    ENDIF
ENDFOR
.Buttons(OnOff)
ENDWITH
```

Form method **Buttons**

```
PARAMETERS OnOff
WITH THISFORM
    .SetAll ( "Enabled", NOT OnOff, "MyCommand" )
    .cmdSave.Enabled   = OnOff
    .cmdCancel.Enabled = OnOff
ENDWITH
```

Because the only controls that are enabled or disabled are the ones in the list, this approach permits us to put other controls (for example, list boxes) on the form without enabling or disabling them when inputs are enabled or disabled.

Adding the Command Buttons

Open the form, select View, Toolbars, and click on the Form Controls toolbar. Click on the three little books and select `pinter.vcx`. This changes the available controls to include only those contained in our class library. Drag and drop nine instances of the `MyCommand` control to the bottom of the form. Change their names, captions, and their `Enabled` property as shown in Table 2.2.

TABLE 2.2   Properties for the Command Buttons

Name	Caption	Enabled Property
cmdAdd	\<Add	[Default]
cmdEdit	\<Edit	[Default]
cmdDelete	\<Delete	[Default]
cmdSave	\<Save	.F.
cmdCancel	\<Cancel	.F.
cmdPrevious	\<Previous	[Default]
cmdNext	\<Next	[Default]
cmdBrowse	\<Browse	[Default]
cmdClose	Cl\<ose	[Default]

I've resized the form and changed both the form's `Name` and its `Caption` to Customers, its `AutoCenter` property to `.T.`, and its `ControlBox` property to `.F.`. It's beginning to look pretty good. Now it's time to code the buttons.

The Add Button Code

Given that this is a single-user application, you'd think that all I have to do is change the table's `Buffering` property to 3 (optimistic record), append a blank, and refresh the screen. However, `APPEND BLANK` moves the record pointer to the phantom record. If the user cancels, I want to redisplay the same record that was visible before the user clicked on Add. So I need to add a `BeforeAdd` property to the form by selecting Form, Add Property Menu. When that's done, the code for the Add button is this:

```
WITH THISFORM
SELECT ( [CUSTOMERS] )
.BeforeAdd = RECNO()
CursorSetProp ( [Buffering], 3 )
APPEND BLANK
.Refresh
.Inputs(.T.)
ENDWITH
```

This adds a blank record to the Customers table after turning `Buffering` on, which means that `TableUpdate()` can be used to cancel the operation and simply throw away the blank record. We save the `RECNO()` value in order to redisplay the record that was on the screen before adding the blank. Finally, we refresh the screen controls to display their blank values and enable all input fields.

Note that I didn't do anything about inserting a key value that is guaranteed to be unique. Generally, I call a function that takes a single parameter, a table name, and returns an integer. Here's the code:

```
FUNCTION NextKey
PARAMETERS pTableName
pTableName = UPPER(pTableName)
SaveAlias = ALIAS()
IF NOT USED ( [Keys] )
   USE KEYS IN 0
ENDIF
SELECT KEYS
LOCATE FOR UPPER(TableName) = pTableName
IF NOT FOUND
   APPEND BLANK
   REPLACE TableName WITH pTableName
ENDIF
REPLACE LastKey WITH LastKey + 1
SELECT ( SaveAlias )
RETURN LastKey
```

If you can be guaranteed that every table will have a unique integer key, you can include a call to this function in your code, using this:

```
NewKeyValue = NextKey ( THISFORM.TableName )
REPLACE ( THISFORM.KeyField ) WITH New I KeyValue
```

The Edit Button Code

The code for the Edit button is almost identical to the code for the Add button, except that the APPEND BLANK is not needed. Strictly speaking, saving the RECNO() value in BeforeAdd isn't necessary either, but it makes the Cancel button code easier to write because we don't need to know whether we're canceling an Add or an Edit:

```
WITH THISFORM
SELECT ( [CUSTOMERS] )
.BeforeAdd = RECNO()
CursorSetProp ( [Buffering], 3 )

.Refresh
.Inputs(.T.)
ENDWITH
```

The Save Button Code

To save any changes made by the user, we call the `TableUpdate()` function and then disable input fields:

```
WITH THISFORM
SELECT ( [CUSTOMERS] )
TableUpdate(.T.)
CursorSetProp ( [Buffering], 1 )
.Inputs(.F.)
ENDWITH
```

The Cancel Button Code

To cancel an Add or any changes made by the user, we call the `TableRevert()` function, turn buffering off, disable the input fields, return to the record number showing before the Add or Edit began, and then refresh the controls to reflect the data before the Add or Edit began:

```
WITH THISFORM
SELECT ( [CUSTOMERS] )
TableRevert(.T.)
CursorSetProp ( [Buffering], 1 )
.Inputs(.F.)
IF BETWEEN ( .BeforeAdd, 1, RECCOUNT() )
   GO       .BeforeAdd )
ENDIF
.Refresh
ENDWITH
```

The Delete Button Code

Deleting a record is straightforward. We only have to decide which record to display after deleting a record.

```
WITH THISFORM
SELECT ( [CUSTOMERS] )
DELETE
IF NOT EOF()
   SKIP
ELSE
   GO BOTTOM
ENDIF
.Refresh
ENDWITH
```

The Previous and Next Buttons

It's traditional to include Previous and Next buttons on FoxPro forms. Sometimes I think that we only offer these buttons because they're a single command (SKIP +/-n), and that users don't care and would prefer a good SEARCH command. But they'll serve to illustrate a point, as you'll see later in this chapter. Note that trying to go past BOF() or EOF() is an error in FoxPro:

cmdPrevious::Click

```
SELECT ( [CUSTOMERS] )
IF NOT BOF()
   SKIP -1
   IF BOF()
      GO TOP
   ENDIF
ENDIF
THISFORM.Refresh
```

cmdNext::Click

```
SELECT ( [CUSTOMERS] )
IF NOT EOF()
   SKIP
   IF EOF()
      GO BOTTOM
   ENDIF
ENDIF
THISFORM.Refresh
```

The Browse Button Code

Browsing is a simple navigation technology. We could simply include a ReadOnly grid on the screen because the record pointer is automatically bound to the grid. But that uses space on the form, and if space is scarce, the BROWSE command is a good alternative. I only have to provide for the possibility that the user presses Esc to cancel the BROWSE. FoxPro doesn't have automatic handling for this, but it's easy to provide. I also map the right mouse button and the Enter key to Ctrl+W to select the highlighted record and close the Browse window:

```
SELECT ( [CUSTOMERS] )
WhereWasI = RECNO()
ON KEY LABEL ENTER KEYBOARD CHR(23)
ON KEY LABEL RIGHTMOUSE KEYBOARD CHR(23)
BROWSE TITLE [Rightclick or press ENTER to select a record; ESC to cancel]
ON KEY LABEL ENTER
```

```
ON KEY LABEL RIGHTMOUSE
IF LASTKEY() = 27  && Esc
   GO ( WhereWasI )
ENDIF
THISFORM.Refresh
```

Finally, to close the form, the form's Release method is all we need:

```
THISFORM.Release
```

Enter this code and run the form. It ought to work.

Now, change the font for the MyText class in pinter.vcx, and notice that it changes every text box on the screen. That's a simple demonstration of the power of objects. But wait, there's more....

Creating a Form Template

Since we used the power of objects for our control classes, why not do the same thing with the form? Use MODIFY FORM Customers to open the form. Highlight all of the labels and controls except for the command buttons and *cut* them (don't copy, but cut them to keep them in the clipboard for later), and then choose Save As Class. Pick Pinter.vcx as the class library, use the name FlatFileForm for the class, and save it (see Figure 2.2). This also saves the form's properties and methods.

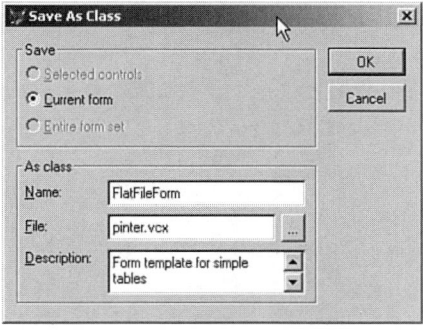

FIGURE 2.2   Saving the form and buttons as a class.

Now we're ready for some magic. In the command window, type

```
ERASE CUSTOMERS.SC?
```

to erase the SCX and SCT files containing the Customers form. Then, select Tools, Options, Forms from the IDE menu, click on Form Template, and select FlatFileForm from the Pinter.VCX Class Library. Click OK to close the dialog.

Now, type

```
MODIFY FORM Customers
```

You'll see a form with only the buttons across the bottom. (You'll also see the name Customers, but we'll deal with that shortly.) Presuming you haven't trashed the paste buffer, press Ctrl+V, and all of your labels and data controls will appear. They're all selected already, so use the up-arrow and left-arrow keys to move them all up and left eight pixels each, which is the amount of the automatic offset for cutting and pasting screen objects.

Changing Form Code into Class Code

The original code that we wrote for the form class is still there; however, it's specific to a single table. To make it generic, add a `TableName` and an `IndexTag` property to the `FlatFileForm` class. Then, change all instances of `[Customers]` in the class code to `(THIS-FORM.TableName)`. You can also change the `FlatFileForm` class `Caption` property to "Please supply a title".

> **TIP**
>
> If you've used `WITH THISFORM` in all of your methods, you only need `( .TableName )`.

In the `LOAD` event of the `FlatFileForm` class, put this:

```
WITH THISFORM
SELECT 0
USE ( .TableName )
IF NOT EMPTY    ( .IndexTag )
   SET ORDER TO ( .IndexTag )
ENDIF
ENDWITH
```

And in the class's `UNLOAD` event, put this:

```
USE IN ( THISFORM.TableName )
```

Finally, open the Customers form with `MODIFY FORM CUSTOMERS` and add Customers as the `TableName` property and the form `Caption`. If you've added an index for `CustomerID`, you can enter the name of the tag in the `IndexTag` property.

Cosmetics

Before you run the form, there are a few things you can do to tidy up your creation. For one thing, the tab order is probably not right. Choose Tools, Options, Forms to open the Forms dialog, and change the Tab Ordering to By List. Now, open the form and click on View, Tab Order. Click on the By Row button. Now, find the `cmdAdd` button and drag it to the top of the list. Drag the `cmdEdit` button to the second position in the list, and click OK.

Next, open the Properties sheet, select the form, and change the `BorderStyle` property to something other than 3. We don't really do resizing of this kind of form, so if users try to do so it will look funny. We'll just nip it in the bud.

Running the Form

Now, run the form. Again, it should work.

Open the form in the Form Designer and look at the code. *There isn't any!* That's the *right* way to build forms in Visual FoxPro.

This simple example used DBFs, the simplest way to deal with data in FoxPro. The `CursorAdapter` in Visual FoxPro 8 makes it about as easy to build a SQL Server or Web Service application as it is in Visual Basic .NET. I purposely didn't use the `CursorAdapter` in this example. We'll deal with the `CursorAdapter` in Chapter 6, "Data Access" and Chapter 7, "XML."

There are lots of enhancements that can be made to this template. It doesn't handle multi-user scenarios, where someone else might have changed the data. It doesn't handle classes of parent-child forms, although it could.

> **TIP**
>
> I once wrote a system to manage sales quotations, sales orders, invoices, shipping memos, purchase quotes, purchase orders, and receiving memos using a single template and was able to build the entire system in 10 working days, including a pretty serious inventory control subsystem. Nothing says you can't design your entire project around a couple of special-purpose form classes. In fact, that's the idea. Consider this `FlatFileForm` as the simplest possible case.

Next, we'll do the same thing we did in this example again in Visual Basic .NET. It's a little different, but the concepts are the same.

Building a Simple Application in Visual Basic .NET

The simplest Visual Basic .NET application is a single form managing a single table. It doesn't matter whether it's a "local" table stored in a FoxPro DBF or an Access MDB file or a table in an MSDE or a SQL Server database. The coding is exactly the same.

Creating a Customers Table

There is a command window in Visual Basic .NET, but it has very limited use. To create a new table, we'll first need to add a new database. Use Ctrl+S to open the Server Explorer, and expand the tree until SQL Server is visible. Expand its tree, right-click on Databases, and select New Database. Supply the name Chapter2, and use `sa` and blank for the userid and password respectively (see Figure 2.3).

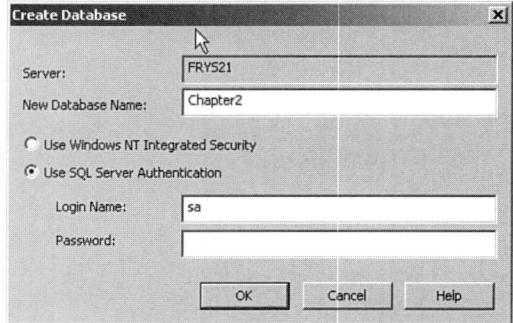

FIGURE 2.3   Adding the Chapter2 database.

Click on the Database to select it, and expand the tree to reveal the Tables branch. Right-click and select New Table. The Table Designer shown in Figure 2.4 will appear. Enter the fields and data descriptors used to create the FoxPro Customers.DBF earlier. You'll be asked for a name for the table when you close the designer; enter **Customers**, just as before.

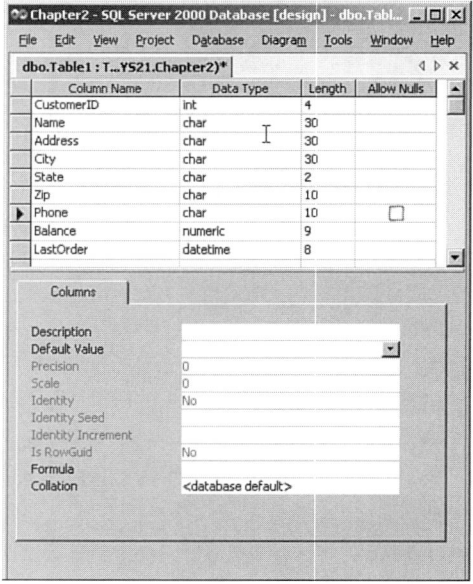

FIGURE 2.4   Specifying the Customers schema.

The structure is the same. The only peculiarity is that the database offered to store NULL values for any column entries not specified in an INSERT statement. We absolutely don't want that. I've wasted a significant portion of my professional life dealing with null fields, provided on the off chance that I might want to know whether those fields were specified or not. Blank is blank, and that's always been good enough in my line of work. So don't forget to uncheck the nulls.

At the bottom of the Table Designer, there is a toolbar with five choices:

Generate Change Script

Set Primary Key

Relationships

Manage Indexes and Keys

Manage Check Constraints

These are largely features that are supported either by the FoxPro Data Environment, or by the database container. Select the CustomerID field and click on Set Primary Key to create an index. Without this, Visual Basic .NET has no clue how to locate a specific record for updating or deleting because there is no RECNO() in SQL Server.

The other features won't enter into our simple example in this chapter, but you can be sure they come in handy at some point in a real-world application.

Again, reflecting the limited usefulness of Visual Basic .NET's command window, you can't type in an INSERT statement interactively. Data is entered graphically.

To enter a record into the table, right-click on the table name in the Solution Explorer and select Retrieve Data from Table. The resulting grid allows us to enter one row at a time. Type in the same values entered for CUSTOMERS.DBF, as shown in Figure 2.5.

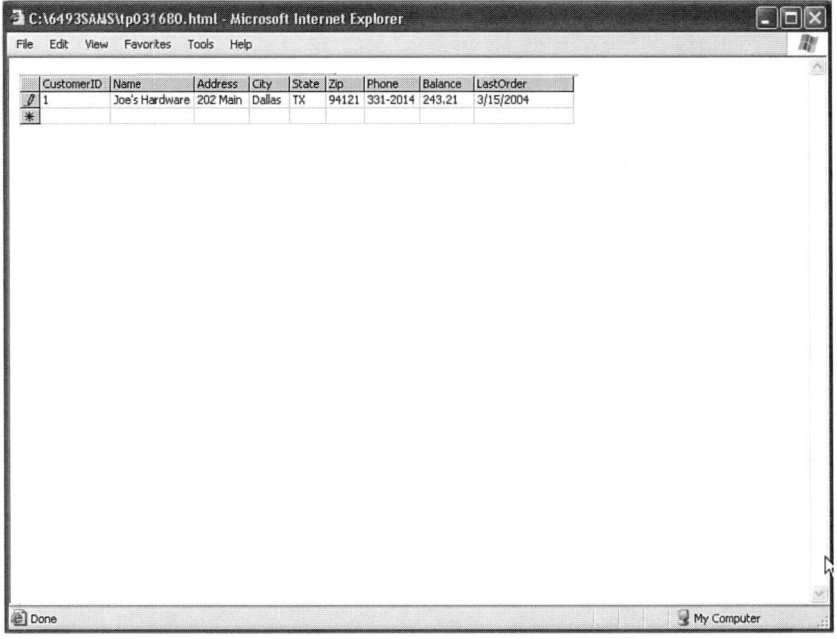

FIGURE 2.5   Entering a Customer record.

Designing the Form

Start by creating a Visual Basic Windows Application project called CustomersProject, as shown in Figure 2.6. It's created with one form named Form1.

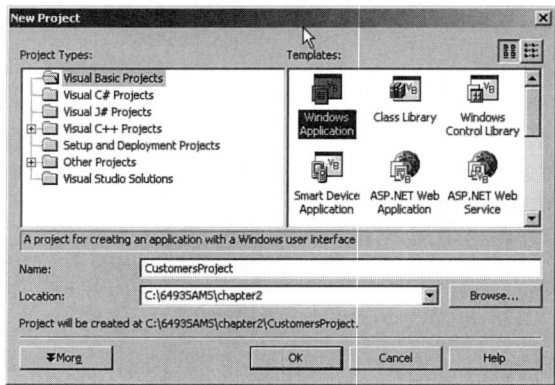

FIGURE 2.6   Creating the CustomersProject project.

Now for a little surprise: Open the Server Explorer with Ctrl+Alt+S, select the Customers table in the Chapter2 database, and drag it onto Form1. You get—a `DataAdapter`. What's a `DataAdapter`?

A `DataAdapter` is a middle-tier component that contains `SELECT`, `INSERT`, `UPDATE`, and `DELETE` statements that are automatically generated by Visual Basic .NET. In this case, dragging the table to the design surface meant `SELECT * FROM CUSTOMERS`. From there, Visual Basic .NET was able to infer the other three commands because it knows the key field (`CustomerID`).

In our Visual FoxPro example, the simple act of issuing the command `USE CUSTOMERS`, or `USE (THISFORM.TableName)` in the form class, in effect opened the data source and returned the entire table. There's a command in Visual Basic .NET that does the same thing. It's actually not a command; it's the `FILL` method of the `DataAdapter`. It takes two parameters; the first is the name of a dataset, and the second is a name to give the first table in the dataset.

Creating a Dataset

To create a dataset, select Generate Dataset from the Data pad of the IDE menu, using `dsCustomers` as the dataset name. You'll notice that a file named `dsCustomers.xsd` has been added to the project. There's more to it than that, but I'll tell you later. An instance named `dsCustomers1` has been added to the form, much as a `TextBox` class added to your form in Visual FoxPro will be named `TextBox1`.

Double-click on the form to open its Load event and type the following line:

```
SQLDataAdapter1.Fill(dsCustomers1,"Customers")
```

Building the Form

To build the form, drag nine labels, eight text boxes, and an UpDownNumeric control to the form. Assign the appropriate text to the labels' Text properties (in FoxPro we use Captions).

Data binding is what we expected to achieve when we dragged the table onto the form. But at least for now, it's a manual process in Visual Basic .NET. Open the Properties sheet, click on the first control, open the DataBindings property by clicking on the plus sign to the left of it, and add the CustomerID field of the Customer table of the dsCustomers1 dataset to the data bindings. You have to expand the tree each time for each control, so it's tedious. Later we'll see a routine that can use the control names to do this automatically.

Form Methods

We'll need the same two methods used in the FoxPro application. They're almost identical, except that in Visual Basic .NET you can't refer to a variable until it's been declared with Dim or some other modifier:

```
Public Sub Inputs(ByVal OnOff)
    Dim Ctrl As Control
    For Each Ctrl In Controls
        If Not Ctrl.Name.StartsWith("cmd") Then Ctrl.Enabled = OnOff
    Next
    Buttons(Not OnOff)
End Sub

Public Sub Buttons(ByVal OnOff As Boolean)
    Dim Ctrl As Control
    For Each Ctrl In Controls
        If Ctrl.Name.StartsWith("cmd") Then Ctrl.Enabled = OnOff
    Next
    cmdSave.Enabled = Not OnOff
    cmdCancel.Enabled = Not OnOff
End Sub
```

Because the command buttons begin with "cmd", I can direct the code to manipulate only command buttons or only controls other than command buttons.

Adding the Command Buttons

Drag and drop nine instances of the CommandButton control to the bottom of the form. Change their names, captions, and their enabled property as shown in Table 2.3.

TABLE 2.3   Properties for the CommandButton Controls

Name	Caption	Enabled Property
cmdAdd	&Add	[Default]
cmdEdit	&Edit	[Default]
cmdDelete	&Delete	[Default]
cmdSave	&Save	False
cmdCancel	&Cancel	False
cmdPrevious	&Previous	[Default]
cmdNext	&Next	[Default]
cmdBrowse	&Browse	[Default]
cmdClose	Cl&ose	[Default]

I've resized the form and changed both the form's Name and its Text property to Customers, its StartPosition to CenterScreen, and its ControlBox property to False. The properties and settings are either almost identical to those of FoxPro or easily recognizable.

The Add Button Code

The equivalent of APPEND BLANK is done by the AddNew() method of the BindingContext, which is automatically added to every Visual Basic form. The dataset and the table name are required parameters of the BindingContext because it manages all datasets and all tables contained within datasets:

```
Private Sub cmdAdd_Click( _
  ByVal sender As System.Object, ByVal e As System.EventArgs) _
  Handles cmdAdd.Click
    Adding = True
    BindingContext(DsCustomers1, "Customers").AddNew()
    Inputs(True)
End Sub
```

A Visual Basic .NET routine to add a unique key would be nice. However, if you define the CustomerID as an IDENTITY field in SQL Server, the next available key value is automatically returned. FoxPro 8 also has this capability. You can also write your own, as we did earlier, and this can be useful for systems that can go offline and then synchronize the tables upon reconnection.

The Edit Button Code

The Edit button code is extremely simple because datasets keep track of their changes automatically; the only kind of Buffering mode in Visual Basic .NET datasets is mode 5:

```
Private Sub cmdEdit_Click( _
  ByVal sender As System.Object, ByVal e As System.EventArgs) _
  Handles cmdEdit.Click
    Inputs(True)
End Sub
```

The Save Button Code

To save any changes made by the user, we call the Update() method of the corresponding DataAdapter, and then disable input fields:

```
Private Sub cmdSave_Click( _
  ByVal sender As System.Object, ByVal e As System.EventArgs) _
  Handles cmdSave.Click
    Inputs(False)
    Try
        With BindingContext(DsCustomers1, "Customers")
            .EndCurrentEdit()
        End With
        SqlDataAdapter1.Update(DsCustomers1, "Customers")
        DsCustomers1.AcceptChanges()
        BindingContext(DsCustomers1, "Customers").Position = 0
    Catch oEx As Exception
        MsgBox(oEx.Message, MsgBoxStyle.Critical, "Unable to save record")
    End Try
End Sub
```

The Cancel Button Code

To cancel an Add or any changes made by the user, we just disable the input fields:

```
Private Sub cmdCancel_Click( _
  ByVal sender As System.Object, ByVal e As System.EventArgs) _
  Handles cmdCancel.Click
    Inputs(False)
    Try
        With BindingContext(DsCustomers1, "Customers")
            .CancelCurrentEdit()
        End With
    Catch oEx As Exception
        MsgBox(oEx.Message, MsgBoxStyle.Critical, "Problem canceling edit")
    End Try
End Sub
```

The Delete Button Code

Deleting a record is straightforward:

```
Private Sub btnDelete_Click( _
  ByVal sender As System.Object, ByVal e As System.EventArgs) _
 Handles btnDelete.Click
    Try
        BindingContext(dsCustomers1, "Customers").RemoveAt(0)
        dsCustomers1.Tables("Customers").AcceptChanges()
        MsgBox("Record deleted", MsgBoxStyle.Information, "My app")
    Catch oEx As Exception
        MsgBox("Error:  " + oEx.Message)
    End Try
End Sub
```

The Previous and Next Buttons

The Previous and Next buttons are one-line commands in Visual Basic .NET, because there's no need to check for BOF() or EOF() before moving the BindingContext's position, the Visual Basic read-write equivalent of RECNO():

```
Private Sub cmdPrevious_Click( _
  ByVal sender As System.Object, ByVal e As System.EventArgs) _
    Handles cmdPrevious.Click
    BindingContext(DsCustomers1, "Customers").Position -= 1
End Sub

Private Sub cmdNext_Click( _
  ByVal sender As System.Object, ByVal e As System.EventArgs) _
    Handles cmdNext.Click
    BindingContext(DsCustomers1, "Customers").Position += 1
End Sub
```

The Browse Button Code

Because there's no BROWSE command in Visual Basic .NET, I decided to add the Visual Basic equivalent. I put a grid to the right of the screen, and then used the Browse button's Click event to widen the form to expose and enable the grid. I also changed the button's caption to Hide, to indicate that the grid can be hidden by clicking on it. The form with the grid showing appears in Figure 2.7.

```
Private Sub cmdBrowse_Click( _
  ByVal sender As System.Object, ByVal e As System.EventArgs) _
  Handles cmdBrowse.Click
    If cmdBrowse.Text = "Hide" Then
        Width = 445
```

```
        cmdBrowse.Text = "Browse"
    Else
        Width = 660
        cmdBrowse.Text = "Hide"
    End If
End Sub
```

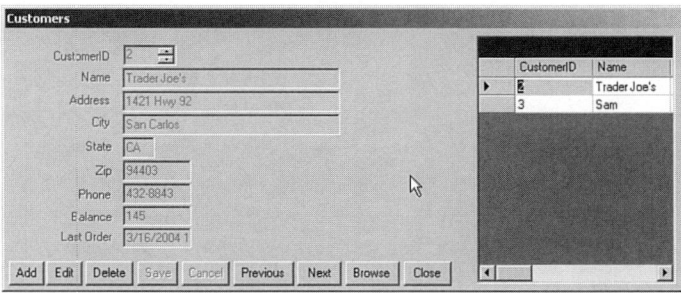

FIGURE 2.7 Simulating the FoxPro BROWSE command with a hidden grid.

The grid's `AfterCellChange` event moves the `BindingContext` position pointer:

```
Private Sub DataGrid1_CurrentCellChanged( _
  ByVal sender As Object, ByVal e As System.EventArgs) _
    Handles DataGrid1.CurrentCellChanged
    BindingContext(DsCustomers1, "Customers").Position = _
      DataGrid1.CurrentRowIndex
End Sub
```

Finally, to close the form, the form's `Close()` method is the Visual Basic .NET equivalent of `THISFORM.Release`:

```
Close()
```

I'll leave the exercise of creating an inherited form for Chapter 3, "Building a Visual Basic .NET Application for SQL Server."

Summary

I hope this chapter was enlightening. It's interesting to compare specific functionality side by side. The exact same functionality doesn't always exist, but in this simple case I would think that most FoxPro developers would feel that, other than syntax, there are more similarities than differences.

In the next chapter, we'll use a data access layer to add SQL support to a generic Visual FoxPro template, so that no code changes are needed to switch between DBF and SQL access. Then, in Chapter 4, "A Visual Basic .NET Framework for SQL Server," we'll build a generic inheritable form for Visual Basic .NET that treats all data sources equally.

CHAPTER 3

Building a Visual FoxPro Application for SQL Server

Even if you haven't started using three-tier data access in FoxPro, you certainly have heard of it. What's the big deal? Is this something that you need to learn? In this chapter, you'll discover that

• You absolutely need to learn three-tier data access.

• It's easy.

• The library described in this chapter can be used with your very next project.

In this chapter, we'll build a data access layer to communicate with either DBFs or SQL Server. And we'll build it in such a way that there is absolutely no code to change when you move from DBFs to SQL tables. We'll even include an upsizing wizard to migrate the data for you. We'll talk about the things that you don't want to do in SQL if you want to simplify programming (always a good thing). We'll use a data access layer, which gives you the ability to use DBFs, SQL Server, a WebConnection XML server, or XML Web services built in Visual FoxPro 8, the best upgrade yet. The code for this chapter is written to be compatible with Visual FoxPro 7, but in subsequent chapters we'll add features only available in versions 8 and higher. It might surprise Microsoft, but not everyone has the latest version of their languages.

Why Three-Tier?

Three-tier is a variant of n-tier: A calls B calls C, and so on. Each one does a part of the task. With server farms and ASP applications, there can be several data tiers, a page generation tier, and so forth. But for our purposes, three-tier is generally sufficient. In the usual three-tier diagrams (which we'll dispense with here), A is your form, B is a data access layer, and C is the place where the data is stored—usually DBFs in our world, but that's changing, and that's where the data access layer comes in.

In traditional FoxPro applications, our forms contain the code that gets and stores data. Our code snippets are full of SEEK and REPLACE commands. The problem arises when our client decides that they're tired of kicking everyone out of the application and rebuilding the indexes, or redoing a 400-file backup that just failed because a user didn't close the CONTROL file, or watching an APPEND BLANK take 30 seconds because the table has 900,000 records and the index is 9MB. DBFs are great, but they do have drawbacks. And the solution is spelled *S-Q-L*.

SQL has numerous benefits. When you back up a SQL database, you're backing up a single file. Backup can be run while users are in the system. And RESTORE is also a one-line command.

Security is another issue with FoxPro tables. Anyone with access to the DBF directory on the server can see your FoxPro tables. SQL Server, on the other hand, has complex security built in. So you can decide who does what. In today's increasingly risky environment, users can and will demand improved security. SQL Server is a good way to accomplish it.

So your client is sold. Install SQL Server. You can run SQL Server on your development machine just fine; in fact, it's a great idea. Be sure to install the Developer Edition, which has a Management Console. If all you have is MSDE, it will work fine, but you have to create the database, indexes, and logins programmatically, and it's just a little harder to learn some SQL tasks nonvisually.

SQL Server runs as a service. It "listens" for requests from workstations, does what is asked of it, and sends any result set back to the workstation. There is no index traffic because the indexes don't come back with the results. Most of the slowdown you might have experienced in FoxPro apps on a LAN are due to network traffic, so solving the slowdown problem can be sufficient motivation for migrating to SQL Server.

So you've installed SQL Server, and you need to migrate your application to use SQL Server tables. First, you have to migrate the data. There are several ways to do this, and all of them have problems. You can use the SQL Upsizing Wizard, but the resulting SQL tables can cause serious programming headaches. There's a DTS utility that is installed when you load SQL Server, and if you like writing your data recoding routines in Basic, go right ahead. I prefer FoxPro. So your best bet is to write your own data migration program. I've included one in the code for this chapter.

What's wrong with the Upsizing Wizard? For one thing, it defaults to permitting NULLs as values in uninitialized fields. If you've never run into NULLs, consider yourself lucky. Statisticians need to know whether a value of zero is a reported value or simply someone who didn't answer the question—for example, What is your age? You can't calculate average age by summing ages and dividing by zero if half of the respondents didn't want to answer. So you have to know which are *missing values*. SQL Server allows for missing values, and in fact defaults to them. But they nearly double the programming burden. ASP code goes bonkers with nulls. So unless you really, truly care about missing values, you absolutely don't want to use NULLs. That's why the preferred way to declare a column in T-SQL is

```
Age Integer NOT NULL DEFAULT 0,...
```

I *strongly* urge you to include NOT NULL in your column declarations and to supply a default value.

Secondly, SQL has **reserved words**, which have to be enclosed in square brackets if you use them as field names. I don't use them if I have my way. But we often have to support legacy applications, and that means using two systems in parallel for at least a while. So we'll want to enclose reserved word column names in square brackets while building the table definitions. The data conversion program provides for you to furnish a list of SQL keywords that you've used as field names. I've seeded the list with the usual suspects (for example, see line 21 of the LoadSQLTables.PRG file in Listing 3.2). Add other field names that you've used in your tables if SQL complains about them during the table creation process.

Finally, in order to make updating records easy, it's a good idea to provide a unique integer key as the primary key for each table, especially if you have another text field that you've been using as a key. The reason is that unique keys are essential if you want to make the coding of updates simple, so every table has to have one. In the FoxPro world we've developed the bad habit of using a compound key (for example, PONum+LineNum for the purchase order items file), which is simply a nightmare to code in some generic fashion.

SQL Server has an autoincrementing feature called IDENTITY. For example, you can declare an Integer field named MyKey and set IDENTITY(1,1) (begin with 1 and increment by 1), and every time you insert a record a new key value will appear. The problem is that if you need instant access to that value, you need to add a SELECT @@IDENTITY command after the INSERT command—for example, after adding an Invoice header and before inserting the related Invoice Detail Lines in order to provide the header key in the detail records for subsequent JOINs. And there are other reasons. If you have an IDENTITY field, you must not include its name in any INSERT commands. So your CommandBuilder code has to know to skip the key field if it's an IDENTITY field. You get the picture. Identity fields are more trouble than they're worth. So we'll do our own primary key generation instead of using SQL's IDENTITY feature.

To get a head start, open each of your application's tables and create a primary key field if it doesn't already have one (child tables are good candidates). Use the MODIFY STRUCTURE command, add the PKFIELD column name (you can use PKFIELD as the PRIMARY KEY column for every table if you want to), and then use this to add unique keys:

```
REPLACE ALL "pkfield" WITH RECNO()
```

or

```
REPLACE ALL "pkfield" WITH TRANSFORM(RECNO(),"@L #######")
```

for character fields.

When you're done, do a `SELECT MAX(KeyFieldName) FROM (TableName)` for each of your DBFs, and make sure that these are the values that appear in the table called Keys that you'll find in the zip file for this project. This table tells the application what the last primary key value used was in each of the tables in the application. This table exists both for DBF-based and for SQL-based systems. It's a loose end, and a commercial application that used this technique would need to include a goof-proof way to set these keys after migrating the data and before going live. You'll have to do it manually. Or you can write a little utility routine as an exercise. (Hint: You'll need a list of table names and their primary key fields in order to automate the process.)

Getting Our Test Data Ready

The `FlatFileForm` and `DataTier` classes will allow us to quickly create forms that work with both a DBF and a SQL table. But in order to test them, we'll need to have the same tables in both formats. Luckily, there's an easy way to accomplish this.

FoxPro ships with a sample data directory containing some good examples. Type the following in the command window:

```
USE C:\PROGRAM FILES\MICROSOFT VISUAL FOXPRO 8\SAMPLES\DATA\Customer
COPY TO CUSTOMER
USE C:\PROGRAM FILES\MICROSOFT VISUAL FOXPRO 8\SAMPLES\DATA\EMPLOYEE
COPY TO EMPLOYEE
```

When you have your two tables, you should add integer keys to the tables using `MODIFY STRUCTURE`. In this case, use `PKFIELD` `(Integer)` for both tables, and make it the first field in the table. Before leaving the schema designer, add `PKFIELD` as an index tag, or just type the following in the command window:

```
USE CUSTOMER EXCLUSIVE
INDEX ON PKFIELD TAG PKFIELD
USE CUSTOMER EXCLUSIVE
INDEX ON PKFIELD TAG PKFIELD
```

Finally, you can set the database name in the SQL `ConnectionString` and run the `LoadSqlTables` program to load your tables.

If you want to use your own tables from your own database, you can copy them to DBFs very easily, using the procedure shown in Listing 3.1; substitute your names for your database, userID, and password.

LISTING 3.1   Procedure to Copy a SQL Table to a DBF

```
PROCEDURE SQLToDBF
PARAMETERS TableName
ConnStr = [Driver={SQL Server};Server=(local);Database=(Name);UID=X;PWD=Y;]
Handle = SQLStringConnect( ConnStr )
SQLExec ( Handle, [SELECT * FROM ] + TableName )
COPY TO ( TableName )
MessageBox ( [Done], 64, [Table ] + TableName + [ copied from SQL to DBF], 1000 )
ENDPROC

Sample usage:
SQLToDBF ( [Customers] )
```

Creating the SQL Database and Loading Your Tables

We're ready to build the SQL database and load the data. The easy way is to open the Enterprise Manager and create the MDF and LDF files yourself, estimating the initial size of each. Or you can just use a CREATE DATABASE command and let SQL start you out with about half a megabyte each. You can specify where to put these files, but the default, which is probably Program Files\Microsoft SQL Server\MSSQL\Data, is usually best. You can also use three lines of code in the command window to create the database:

```
Handle = SQLStringConnect ( ;
     "driver={SQL Server};server=(local);database=Master;pwd=sa;uid=;")
Result = SQLExec ( Handle, "CREATE DATABASE MYDATABASE" )
SQLDisconnect(0)
```

I also strongly urge you to create a userID and password that takes you straight to your database. Again, you can do this in Enterprise Manager or in code, but doing so visually is easier. Use the Security tab to add a login, giving (for now) full rights to the userID. Let the DBAs worry about fine-tuning security. They want to keep people out; we want to let them in.

As you saw earlier, whenever you want to send a command to SQL Server, you'll need a handle, which is always a positive integer, for example, 1, 2, 3, and so on.

The following connection string gets you a handle:

```
Handle = SQLStringConnect ( ;
    "driver={SQL Server};server=(local);database=MyDatabase;pwd=sa;uid=;")
```

To close any and all open handles, use SQLDisconnect(0).

Now we're ready. The program shown in Listing 3.2 will ask you where your DBFs are and load them to the named database on SQL Server.

LISTING 3.2   LoadSQLTables.PRG

```
* Purpose....: Creates a duplicate of each DBF
*           : from your data directory in SQL Server
*             and copies the DBF's records to the SQL table.
*             The program puts brackets around named reserved words.
* If you get an error indicating illegal use of a reserved word, add it here:

SET TALK OFF
CLEAR
CLOSE ALL
SET STRICTDATE TO 0
SET SAFETY OFF
SET EXCLUSIVE ON
SET DATE AMERICAN
SET CONFIRM ON

ConnStr = [Driver={SQL Server};Server=(local);UID=sa;PWD=;Database=MyDatabase;]
Handle = SQLSTRINGCONNECT( ConnStr )
IF Handle < 1
   MESSAGEBOX( "Unable to connect to SQL" + CHR(13) + ConnStr, 16 )
   RETURN
ENDIF

ReservedWords = ;
 [,DESC,DATE,RESERVED,PRINT,ID,VIEW,BY,DEFAULT,CURRENT,KEY,ORDER,CHECK,FROM,TO,]

DataPath = GETDIR("Where are your DBFs?")
IF LASTKEY() = 27   && Escape was pressed
   RETURN
ENDIF
IF NOT EMPTY ( DataPath )
   SET PATH TO &DataPath
ENDIF
ADIR( laDBFS, ( DataPath + [*.DBF] ) )
ASORT(laDBFS,1)
* Load each of the tables to SQL
FOR I = 1 TO ALEN(laDBFS,1)
   USE ( laDBFS(I,1))
   _VFP.Caption = "Loading " + ALIAS()
   LoadOneTable()
ENDFOR

SQLDISCONNECT(0)
```

LISTING 3.2   Continued

```
_VFP.Caption = [Done]


PROCEDURE LoadOneTable
LOCAL I
cRecCount = TRANSFORM(RECCOUNT())
cmd  = [DROP TABLE ] + ALIAS()
SQLEXEC( Handle, Cmd )
* Skip tables we don't want to load
IF ALIAS() $ [COREMETA/DBCXREG/SDTMETA/SDTUSER/FOXUSER/]
* skip system tables, add yours here.
   ? [Skipping ] + ALIAS()
   RETURN
ENDIF


CreateTable()        && see below


SCAN
    WAIT WINDOW [Loading record ] + TRANSFORM(RECNO()) + [/] + cRecCount NOWAIT
    Cmd  = [INSERT INTO ] + ALIAS() + [ VALUES ( ]
    FOR I = 1 TO FCOUNT()
        fld  = FIELD(I)
        IF TYPE(Fld) = [G]
            LOOP
        ENDIF
        dta  = &Fld
        typ  = VARTYPE(dta)
        cdta = ALLTRIM(TRANSFORM(dta))
        cdta = CHRTRAN ( cdta, CHR(39),CHR(146) )   && remove any single quotes
        DO CASE
          CASE Typ $ [CM]
              Cmd = Cmd + ['] + cDta + ['] + [, ]
          CASE Typ $ [IN]
              Cmd = Cmd +       cDta       + [, ]
          CASE Typ = [D]
              IF cDta = [/  /]
                 cDta = []
              ENDIF
              Cmd = Cmd + ['] + cDta + ['] + [, ]
          CASE Typ = [T]
              IF cDta = [/  /]
                  cDta = []
              ENDIF
```

LISTING 3.2   Continued

```
                    Cmd = Cmd + ['] + cDta + ['] + [, ]
            CASE Typ = [L]
                    Cmd = Cmd + IIF('F'$cdta,[0],[1]) + [, ]
            CASE Typ $ [Y]
                    Cmd = Cmd
        ENDCASE
    ENDFOR
    Cmd = LEFT(Cmd,LEN(cmd)-2) + [ )]
    lr = SQLEXEC( Handle, Cmd )
    IF lr < 0
        ? [Error: ] + Cmd
        SUSPEND
    ENDIF
ENDSCAN
WAIT CLEAR

PROCEDURE CreateTable
LOCAL J
Cmd = [CREATE TABLE ] + ALIAS() + [ ( ]
AFIELDS(laFlds)
FOR J = 1 TO ALEN(laFlds,1)
    IF laFlds(J,2) = [G]
        LOOP
    ENDIF
    FldName = laFlds(J,1)
    IF [,] + FldName + [,] $ ReservedWords
        FldName = "[" + FldName + "]"
    ENDIF
    Cmd = Cmd + FldName + [ ]
    DO CASE
        CASE laFlds(J,2) = [C]
            Cmd = Cmd + [Char(] + TRANSFORM(laFlds(J,3)) ;
                + [)  NOT NULL DEFAULT '', ]
        CASE laFlds(J,2) = [I]
            Cmd = Cmd + [Integer  NOT NULL DEFAULT 0, ]
        CASE laFlds(J,2) = [M]
            Cmd = Cmd + [Text     NOT NULL DEFAULT '', ]
        CASE laFlds(J,2) = [N]
            N = TRANSFORM(laFlds(J,3))
            D = TRANSFORM(laFlds(J,4))
            Cmd = Cmd + [Numeric(] + N + [,] + D + [)  NOT NULL DEFAULT 0, ]
        CASE laFlds(J,2) $ [TD]
```

LISTING 3.2   Continued

```
            Cmd = Cmd + [SmallDateTime  NOT NULL DEFAULT '', ]
      CASE laFlds(J,2) = [L]
            Cmd = Cmd + [Bit  NOT NULL DEFAULT 0, ]
   ENDCASE
ENDFOR
Cmd = LEFT(Cmd,LEN(cmd)-2) + [ )]
lr = SQLEXEC( Handle, Cmd )
IF lr < 0
   _ClipText = Cmd
   ? [Couldn't create table ] + ALIAS()
   MESSAGEBOX( Cmd )
   SUSPEND
ENDIF
? [Created ] + ALIAS()
ENDPROC
```

For each DBF that's not in the "Skip These Tables" list at the top of the LoadOneTable routine, the program issues a DROP TABLE "Name" command, followed by a CREATE TABLE command, which it builds. It then scans all records in the DBF and creates and executes an INSERT statement for each record. Users are often amazed at how fast this loads their data. I'm not. It's FoxPro.

Writing the Sample Application

Now, you're ready to write your sample application. Begin by creating a project called Chapter3:

```
MODIFY PROJECT Chapter3
```

Leave it open because if you close a FoxPro project before you've added anything to it, it asks you if you want to delete the empty project file, and that's just one more thing to deal with.

My MAIN.PRG will create a few settings, put a title on the screen, instantiate my DataTier object, install the menu, and initiate the event loop (see Listing 3.3).

LISTING 3.3   MAIN.PRG

```
* Purpose.....:  MAIN program for application

CLEAR ALL
CLOSE ALL
CLEAR
CLOSE ALL
```

LISTING 3.3   Continued

```
SET TALK        OFF
SET CONFIRM     ON
SET MULTILOCKS  ON
SET CENTURY     ON
SET EXCLUSIVE   ON
SET SAFETY      OFF
SET DELETED     ON
SET STRICTDATE TO 0

WITH _Screen
.AddObject ( [Title1], [Title], 0, 0 )
.AddObject ( [Title2], [Title], 3, 3 )
.Title2.ForeColor = RGB ( 255, 0, 0  )
ENDWITH

ON ERROR DO ErrTrap WITH LINENO(), PROGRAM(), MESSAGE(), MESSAGE(1)

DO MENU.MPR

oDataTier = NEWOBJECT ( [DataTier], [DataTier.PRG] )
oDataTier.AccessMethod = [DBF]     && Required to execute Assign method code

IF NOT EMPTY ( oDataTier.AccessMethod )
   READ EVENTS
ENDIF

ON ERROR

SET PROCEDURE TO
SET CLASSLIB TO

SET SYSMENU TO DEFAULT

WITH _Screen
.RemoveObject ( [Title1] )
.RemoveObject ( [Title2] )
ENDWITH

DEFINE CLASS Title AS Label
Visible    = .T.
BackStyle  = 0
FontName   = [Times New Roman]
```

LISTING 3.3   Continued

```
FontSize  = 48
Height    = 100
Width     = 800
Left      = 25
Caption   = [My application]
ForeColor = RGB ( 192, 192, 192 )

PROCEDURE Init
LPARAMETERS nTop, nLeft
THIS.Top = _Screen.Height - 100
IF PCount() > 0
   THIS.Top = THIS.Top  - nTop
   THIS.Left= THIS.Left - nLeft
   THIS.ForeColor = RGB(255,0,0)
ENDPROC

ENDDEFINE

PROCEDURE ErrTrap
LPARAMETERS nLine, cProg, cMessage, cMessage1
OnError = ON("Error")
ON ERROR
IF NOT FILE ( [ERRORS.DBF] )
   CREATE TABLE ERRORS (   ;
    Date     Date,         ;
    Time     Char(5),      ;
    LineNum  Integer,      ;
    ProgName Char(30),     ;
    Msg      Char(240),    ;
    CodeLine Char(240)     )
ENDIF
IF NOT USED ( [Errors] )
   USE ERRORS IN 0
ENDIF
SELECT Errors
INSERT INTO Errors VALUES ( ;
  DATE(), LEFT(TIME(),5),  nLine, cProg, cMessage, cMessage1 )
USE IN Errors
cStr = [Error at line ] + TRANSFORM(nLine) + [ of ] + cprog + [:] + CHR(13)    ;
    + cMessage + CHR(13) + [Code that caused the error:] + CHR(13) + cMessage1
IF MESSAGEBOX( cStr, 292, [Continue] ) <> 6
   SET SYSMENU TO DEFAULT
```

LISTING 3.3   Continued

```
    IF TYPE ( [_Screen.Title1] ) <> [U]
        _Screen.RemoveObject ( [Title2] )
        _Screen.RemoveObject ( [Title1] )
    ENDIF
    CLOSE ALL
    RELEASE ALL
    CANCEL
  ELSE
    ON ERROR &OnError
ENDIF
```

Don't try to run it yet because that reference on line 25 to MENU.MPR refers to a menu that we haven't yet created. The menu is where requests to show forms are located, as well as the all-important CLEAR EVENTS command that will end the event loop and allow the program to march onward to its eventual self-destruction.

Next I'll add a menu. I want to be able to switch between DBF and SQL access at will, so that I can verify that my program works exactly the same way with both data stores. So my menu (in which I've already added calls to a couple of screens that we'll build in this chapter) looks like Listing 3.4.

LISTING 3.4   Menu.MPR

```
SET SYSMENU TO
SET SYSMENU AUTOMATIC

DEFINE PAD FilePad        OF _MSYSMENU PROMPT "File"
DEFINE PAD TablePad       OF _MSYSMENU PROMPT "Tables"
DEFINE PAD DataPad        OF _MSYSMENU PROMPT "Change data access"
ON PAD FilePad            OF _MSYSMENU ACTIVATE POPUP file
ON PAD TablePad           OF _MSYSMENU ACTIVATE POPUP tables

ON SELECTION PAD DataPad OF _MSYSMENU DO ChangeAccess IN MENU.MPR

DEFINE POPUP file MARGIN RELATIVE
DEFINE BAR 1 OF file PROMPT "E\<xit"
ON SELECTION BAR 1 OF file CLEAR EVENTS

DEFINE POPUP tables MARGIN RELATIVE SHADOW COLOR SCHEME 4
DEFINE BAR 1 OF tables PROMPT "Customers" SKIP FOR WEXIST([frmCustomer])
DEFINE BAR 2 OF tables PROMPT "Employees" SKIP FOR WEXIST([Employees]  )
```

LISTING 3.4   Continued

```
ON SELECTION BAR 1 OF tables do form frmCustomer
ON SELECTION BAR 2 OF tables do form Employee

PROCEDURE ChangeAccess
oDataTier.AccessMethod = ;
  UPPER(INPUTBOX("Data access method", "DBF/SQL/XML/WC", "DBF" ))
```

What's `oDataTier`? That's next. The `DataTier` controls everything about access to data. So the first thing we do is add a property called `AccessMethod`, use its `Assign` method to trap and validate the assignment, and then do whatever needs to be done based on the method chosen. More about that later. Type

```
BUILD EXE Chapter3 FROM Chapter3
```

or use the project's Build button. Then use `DO Chapter3`, or press either the Ctrl+D short-cut key or Alt+P, D to activate the menu and bring up the Do dialog screen and select `Chapter3.exe`.

Figure 3.1 shows the application's main screen. That third menu selection should look interesting. By the end of this chapter, you'll be able to click on it and try your forms using either data source. The source code is downloadable from the Sams Web site, `www.samspublishing.com`. Also, readers can download this or any other source code from my site, `www.LesPinter.com`.

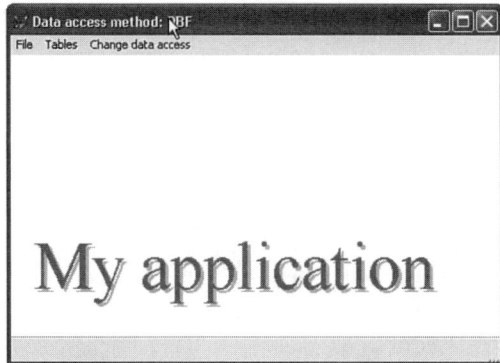

FIGURE 3.1   The main application screen.

We've already done something that would have stopped Visual Basic .NET in its tracks. The `DO` *FormName* references to the two forms that don't yet exist would be compiler errors in .NET. As far as FoxPro knows, the forms are right there in the application directory, or somewhere on the path; we simply have our reasons for excluding the forms from the build. Unlike Visual Basic .NET, FoxPro trusts us to come up with the forms by the time we ask for them.

The Form Template

The basic form template for this application is a flat file form. Most, if not all, applications have one or more of these, and some apps have dozens. So it's immediately useful, while still possessing sufficient simplicity to make the code easy to understand. When you catch on to the principles, more complex templates and data access methods should be easy to build.

What's a little tricky is understanding how form templates and the data tier interact. During the Depression, my father said that a humorous way of dismissing the difficult situation at hand was to say "If we had some ham we could have ham and eggs. If we had some eggs...." The form template and the data tier are each written with the other's function in mind. The reusable components go in the data tier, and the calls to use these components go in the template.

For example, Listing 3.5 shows the class code for my `FlatFileForm` template. I'll comment it as we go.

LISTING 3.5   The `FlatFileForm` Class

```
MainTable   = .F.      && Name of the main table for the form
KeyField    = .F.      && Name of the Primary Key for the Main Table
KeyValue    = .F.      && Value in the KeyField of the current record
Beforeadd   = .F.      && Record number before adding (used when Add is canceled)
SearchForm  = .F.      && Name of a "pick one" form called by the Find button
Adding      = .F.      && True at "Save" time if "Add" button was clicked
Inputfields = "MYTEXT,MYCHECK,MYEDIT,MYCOMBO,MYSPIN,MYDATE"
* Classes to enable/disable
Beforeadd   = 0        && Record pointer value before an add or edit begins
PROCEDURE Buttons      && Turns form buttons on or off as needed
LPARAMETERS OnOff
WITH THISFORM
.cmdAdd.Enabled     = OnOff
.cmdFind.Enabled    = OnOff
.cmdClose.Enabled   = OnOff
.cmdEdit.Enabled    = OnOff AND RECCOUNT() > 0
.cmdDelete.Enabled  = OnOff AND RECCOUNT() > 0
.cmdSave.Enabled    = NOT OnOff
.cmdCancel.Enabled  = NOT OnOff
.cmdClose.Cancel    = OnOff
.cmdCancel.Cancel   = NOT OnOff
ENDWITH
ENDPROC

PROCEDURE Inputs       && Enables/Disables form controls
```

LISTING 3.5   Continued

```
LPARAMETERS OnOff
WITH THISFORM
FOR EACH Ctrl IN .Controls
    IF UPPER ( Ctrl.Class ) $ UPPER ( .InputFields )
        Ctrl.Enabled = OnOff
    ENDIF
ENDFOR
.Buttons ( NOT OnOff )
ENDWITH
ENDPROC


PROCEDURE Load
*  Runs when an instance of this form class is instantiated
WITH THISFORM
IF EMPTY ( .MainTable )
   MESSAGEBOX( [No main table specified], 16, [Programmer error], 2000 )
   RETURN .F.
ENDIF
oDataTier.CreateCursor ( .MainTable, .Keyfield )
ENDWITH
ENDPROC


PROCEDURE Init       && Runs after buttons have been instantiated
THISFORM.Buttons ( .T. )
ENDPROC


PROCEDURE Unload       && Closes table or cursor opened by this form
WITH THISFORM
IF USED   ( .MainTable )
   USE IN ( .MainTable )
ENDIF
ENDWITH
ENDPROC


PROCEDURE cmdAdd.Click       && Adds a new record, autopopulating the key field
WITH THISFORM
cNextKey = oDataTier.GetNextKeyValue ( .MainTable )
SELECT ( .MainTable )
.BeforeAdd = RECNO()
CURSORSETPROP( [Buffering], 3 )
APPEND BLANK
IF TYPE ( .KeyField ) <> [C]
```

LISTING 3.5   Continued

```
    cNextKey = VAL ( cNextKey )
ENDIF
REPLACE ( .Keyfield ) WITH cNextKey
.Refresh
.Inputs ( .T. )
.Adding = .T.
ENDWITH
ENDPROC


PROCEDURE cmdEdit.Click      && Initiates an edit of the current record
WITH THISFORM
SELECT ( .MainTable )
.BeforeAdd = RECNO()
CURSORSETPROP( [Buffering], 3 )
.Inputs ( .T. )
.Adding = .F.
ENDWITH
ENDPROC


PROCEDURE cmdDelete.Click    && Deletes the current record
WITH THISFORM
IF MESSAGEBOX( [Delete this record?], 292, _VFP.Caption ) = 6
   oDataTier.DeleteRecord ( .MainTable, .KeyField )
   DELETE NEXT 1
   GO TOP
   .Refresh
ENDIF
ENDWITH
ENDPROC


PROCEDURE cmdSave.Click
*  Saves data in local cursor and then remotely (if not DBF)
WITH THISFORM
SELECT ( .MainTable )
TABLEUPDATE(.T.)
CURSORSETPROP( [Buffering], 1 )
.Inputs ( .F. )
oDataTier.SaveRecord( .MainTable, .KeyField, .Adding )
ENDWITH
ENDPROC


PROCEDURE cmdCancel.Click    && Cancels an Edit or Add
```

LISTING 3.5   Continued

```
WITH THISFORM
SELECT ( .MainTable )
TABLEREVERT(.T.)
CURSORSETPROP( [Buffering], 1 )
.Inputs ( .F. )
IF BETWEEN ( .BeforeAdd, 1, RECCOUNT() )
   GO      ( .BeforeAdd )
ENDIF
.Refresh
ENDWITH
ENDPROC


PROCEDURE cmdFind.Click
*  If they're using DBF and no search form is defined, use BROWSE
WITH THISFORM
IF EMPTY  ( .SearchForm ) AND oDataTier,AccessMethod = [DBF]
   SELECT ( .MainTable )
   .BeforeAdd = RECNO()
   ON KEY LABEL ENTER       KEYBOARD CHR(23)
   ON KEY LABEL RIGHTCLICK KEYBOARD CHR(23)
   BROWSE NOAPPEND NOEDIT NODELETE
   ON KEY LABEL ENTER
   ON KEY LABEL RIGHTCLICK
   IF LASTKEY() = 27
      IF BETWEEN ( .BeforeAdd, 1, RECCOUNT() )
         GO      ( .Beforeadd )
      ENDIF
   ENDIF
   ELSE
   DO FORM ( .SearchForm ) TO RetVal
   IF NOT EMPTY ( RetVal )
      oDataTier.GetOneRecord ( .MainTable, .KeyField, RetVal )
      .Refresh
      .Buttons ( .T. )
   ENDIF
ENDIF
ENDWITH
ENDPROC


PROCEDURE cmdClose.Click     && Da Svidaniya
THISFORM.Release
ENDPROC
```

How to Use the `FlatFileForm` Template

To use this template, you do the following eight steps:

1. Set Field Mappings to use `Pinter.VCX` and the appropriate controls (`MyText`, `MyChk`, and so on) for the data types you use in your tables.

2. Type the following in the command window:

   ```
   CREATE FORM "name" AS FlatFileForm FROM Pinter;
   ```

3. Open the form, add the DBF that's the `MainTable` to the Data Environment, drag and drop the fields to the form, and *remove* the table from the Data Environment.

4. Click on Tab Order and pick Rows, and then move the `cmdAdd` and `cmdEdit` objects to the top of the Tab Order list.

5. Set the form's `MainTable` and `KeyField` properties to the table name and key field name, respectively.

6. Remove any fields that you don't want users to enter or edit, like `CreateDate` or `RecordID`. (If you prefer, you can browse your SCX, find the controls you want to make noneditable, and change the value in the `Class` field of the SCX to `noedit`, which is a disabled `TextBox` control in `pinter.vcx`. Because it doesn't appear in the `InputFields` property list of editable fields, it never gets enabled.)

7. If you want the `KeyField` value to appear on the screen, add a label somewhere on the form, and add this code in the form's `Refresh` method:

   ```
   THISFORM.txtKeyField.Caption = ;
    TRANSFORM ( EVALUATE ( THISFORM.MainTable + [.] ;
    + THISFORM.KeyField ))
   ```

8. Add a `DO FORM "name"` bar to the menu. Recompile and run it, and it ought to work, except for the search form, which is next.

I've followed my instructions and built the little Customer form shown in Figure 3.2 in about 90 seconds.

That's a pretty simple form template, and you might wonder if it really does everything you need. It does if you include the data tier and the search form.

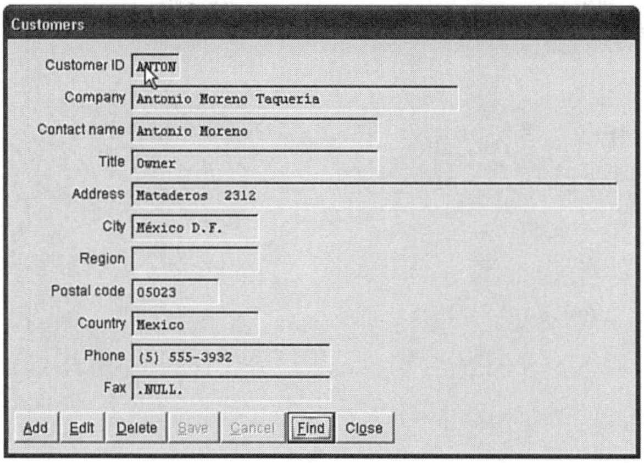

FIGURE 3.2   A sample customer form based on the `FlatFileForm` class.

A Search Form Template

I didn't include any navigation in the `FlatFileForm` template because Next/Previous/First/Last record is an artifact of the xBASE world. We could provide those four features with a single line of code each (not counting checking for `BOF()`/`EOF()` conditions). But users typically don't care about the previous or next record. They want to see a candidate list, point to the one they want, and click. Besides, it's nearly impossible if you use SQL Server, and that's what we're going to do next.

I've included a class called `EasySearch`. It allows you to add a search form with up to 4 searchable fields (and it's easy to extend that to 8 or 10 if you need them), to let users filter records and pick one, and to return the key value, from a DBF, SQL, or a Web service, with absolutely no coding in the form itself. You simply fill in three or four properties, name the input fields that you put on the search form with names SEARCH1, SEARCH2, SEARCH3, and SEARCH4, set the form's tab order to Row order, and you're done. The code for this class is shown in Listing 3.6.

LISTING 3.6   The EasySearch Class

```
DEFINE CLASS EasySearch AS modalform

tablename = ([])    && Table name to search
colwidths = ([])    && Comma-delimited list of the relative widths
colnames  = ([])    && Comma-delimited list of field names
orderby   = ([])    && "Order by" column name
colheadings = ([]) && Comma-delimited list if you don't want to use
*                      field names as headings
keyfield  = ([])    && Name of key field value to return
```

LISTING 3.6 Continued

```
PROCEDURE Init
WITH THISFORM
.Caption = [Search form - ] + .Name + [ (Main Table: ] ;
          + TRIM(.TableName)+[)  Data access: ] + .Access
NumWords = GETWORDCOUNT(.ColNames,[,])
IF NumWords > 4
   MESSAGEBOX( [This class only supports a maximum of 4 fields, sorry], ;
               16, _VFP.Caption )
   RETURN .F.
ENDIF
FOR I = 1 TO NumWords
    .Field(I)   = GETWORDNUM(.ColNames,   I,[,])
    .Heading(I) = GETWORDNUM(.ColHeadings,I,[,])
    .ColWidth(I)= GETWORDNUM(.ColWidths,  I,[,])
ENDFOR
WITH .Grid1
.ColumnCount        =  NumWords
.RecordSource       = THISFORM.ViewName
.RecordSourceType   = 1
GridWidth = 0
FOR I = 1 TO NumWords
    .Columns(I).Header1.Caption    =       THISFORM.Heading (I)
     GridWidth = GridWidth         +   VAL( THISFORM.ColWidth(I) )
     FldName   = THISFORM.ViewName + [.] + THISFORM.Field    (I)
    .Columns(I).ControlSource      = FldName
ENDFOR
Multiplier = ( THIS.Width / GridWidth ) * .90      && "Fudge" factor
FOR I = 1 TO NumWords
    .Columns(I).Width = VAL( THISFORM.ColWidth(I) ) * Multiplier
ENDFOR
.Refresh
ENDWITH
* Look for any controls named SEARCHn (n = 1, 2, ... )
FOR I = 1 TO .ControlCount
    Ctrl = .Controls(I)
    IF  UPPER(Ctrl.Name) = [MYLABEL]  && That is, if it starts with "MyLabel"
        Sub = RIGHT(Ctrl.Name,1)              && Determine the index
        IF TYPE([THISFORM.Search]+Sub)=[O]  && A search field #"Sub" exists
           Ctrl.Visible = .T.
           Ctrl.Enabled = .T.
           Ctrl.Caption = .Heading(VAL(Sub))
           .SearchFieldCount = MAX ( VAL(Sub), .SearchFieldCount )
```

LISTING 3.6   Continued

```
        ENDIF
    ENDIF
ENDFOR
.SetAll ( "Enabled", .T. )
ENDWITH
ENDPROC


PROCEDURE Load
WITH THISFORM
IF EMPTY ( .TableName )
    MESSAGEBOX( [Table name not entered], 16, _VFP.Caption )
    RETURN .F.
ENDIF
IF EMPTY ( .ColNames )
    Msg = [ColNames property not filled in.]
    MESSAGEBOX( Msg, 16, _VFP.Caption )
    RETURN .F.
ENDIF
IF EMPTY ( .ColWidths )
    .ColWidths = [1,1,1,1,1]
ENDIF
IF EMPTY ( .ColHeadings )
    .ColHeadings = .ColNames
ENDIF
.Access = oDataTier.AccessMethod
.ViewName = [View]  +  .TableName
oDataTier.CreateView ( .TableName )
ENDWITH
ENDPROC


PROCEDURE Unload
WITH THISFORM
IF USED   ( .ViewName )
    USE IN ( .ViewName )
ENDIF
RETURN .ReturnValue
ENDWITH
ENDPROC


PROCEDURE cmdShowMatches.Click
WITH THISFORM
Fuzzy = IIF ( THISFORM.Fuzzy.Value = .T., [%], [] )
```

LISTING 3.6   Continued

```
STORE [] TO Expr1,Expr2,Expr3,Expr4
FOR I = 1 TO .SearchFieldCount
    Fld = [THISFORM.Search] + TRANSFORM(I) + [.Value]
    IF NOT EMPTY ( &Fld )
        LDD = IIF ( VARTYPE( &Fld) = [D],        ;
                IIF ( .Access = [DBF],[{],['] ),  ;
                IIF(VARTYPE( &Fld) = [C], ['],[]) )
        RDD = IIF ( VARTYPE( &Fld) = [D],        ;
                IIF ( .Access = [DBF],[}],['] ),  ;
                IIF(VARTYPE( &Fld) = [C], ['],[]) )
        Cmp = IIF ( VARTYPE( &Fld) = [C], [ LIKE ],[ = ] )
        Pfx = IIF ( VARTYPE( &Fld) = [C], Fuzzy,   []    )
        Sfx = IIF ( VARTYPE( &Fld) = [C], [%],     []    )
        Exp = [Expr]  + TRANSFORM(I)
        &Exp = [ AND UPPER(] + .Field(I) + [)] + Cmp ;
             + LDD + Pfx + UPPER(ALLTRIM(TRANSFORM(EVALUATE(Fld)))) + Sfx + RDD
    ENDIF
ENDFOR
lcExpr = Expr1 + Expr2 + Expr3 + Expr4
IF NOT EMPTY ( lcExpr )
   lcExpr = [ WHERE ] + SUBSTR ( lcExpr, 6 )
ENDIF
lcOrder = IIF(EMPTY(.OrderBy),[],[ ORDER BY ] ;
        + ALLTRIM(STRTRAN(.OrderBy,[ORDER BY],[])))
Cmd     = [SELECT * FROM ] + .TableName + lcExpr + lcOrder
oDataTier.SelectCmdToSQLResult ( Cmd )
SELECT ( .ViewName )
ZAP
APPEND FROM DBF([SQLResult])
GO TOP
.Grid1.Refresh
IF RECCOUNT() > 0
   .cmdSelect.Enabled = .T.
   .Grid1.Visible     = .T.
   .Grid1.Column1.Alignment = 0
   .Caption = [Search Form - ] + PROPER(.Name)    ;
           + [  (] + TRANSFORM(RECCOUNT()) + [ matches)]
  ELSE
   .Caption = [Search Form - ] + PROPER(.Name)
```

LISTING 3.6 Continued

```
        MESSAGEBOX( "No records matched" )
      .cmdSelect.Enabled = .F.
  ENDIF
  KEYBOARD [{BackTab}{BackTab}{BackTab}{BackTab}{BackTab}]
  ENDWITH
  ENDPROC


  PROCEDURE cmdClear.Click
  WITH THISFORM
  FOR I = 1 TO .SearchFieldCount
      Fld = [THISFORM.Search] + TRANSFORM(I) + [.Value]
      IF VARTYPE ( &Fld ) <> [U]
          lVal = IIF ( VARTYPE( &Fld) = [C], [],   ;
                  IIF ( VARTYPE( &Fld) = [D], {//}, ;
                  IIF ( VARTYPE( &Fld) = [L], .F.,  ;
                  IIF ( VARTYPE( &Fld) $ [IN], 0, [?]))))
          &Fld = lVal
      ENDIF
  ENDFOR
  ENDWITH
  ENDPROC


  PROCEDURE cmdSelect.Click
  WITH THISFORM
  lcStrValue = TRANSFORM(EVALUATE(.KeyField))
  .ReturnValue = lcStrValue
  .Release
  ENDWITH
  ENDPROC


  PROCEDURE cmdCancel.Click
  WITH THISFORM
  .ReturnValue = []
  .Release
  ENDWITH
  ENDPROC


  ENDDEFINE
```

How to Use the EasySearch **Template**

Here's an example of how to use this template in five easy steps:

1. Type this line in the command window:

    ```
    CREATE FORM FindCust AS EasySearch FROM Pinter
    ```

2. Add two text boxes and a StatesList combo box. Name these three controls Search1, Search2, and Search3.

3. Set the Tab Order to Rows on the search form.

4. Set the MainTable property to Customers, the KeyField property to CustomerID, and the ColumnList property to [CompanyName, ContactName, Phone].

5. Enter **FindCust** as the SearchForm property value in your Customers form.

Figure 3.3 shows the screen for the FindCust form.

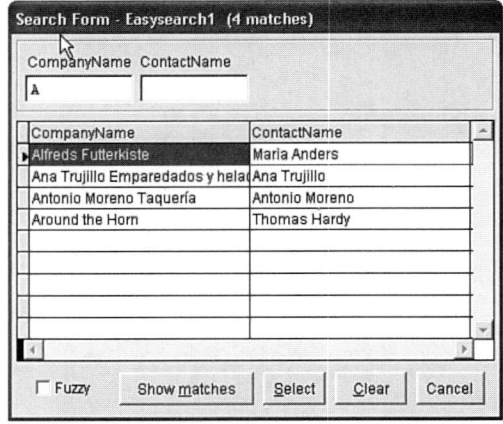

FIGURE 3.3   The FindCust form.

The Data Tier

But there's still a missing piece—the DataTier class library that's the subject of this chapter. Now that you've seen all of the places where its methods are called, you should be able to match up the calls from Listing 3.6 with the methods in Listing 3.7 and see how they fit together.

The data tier is a class used to instantiate an object called oDataTier in MAIN.PRG. Thereafter, any time we need to send data to a data store, we call a method on the oDataTier object.

It's important to note that in this methodology, you either open a DBF or a CURSOR for each table object. If you initiate either an Add or an Edit, you set buffering mode to 3, change something, and then call TableUpdate() and set Buffering back to 1. (If your user cancels, you refresh the screen with whatever was there before—the original, unchanged record. Tablerevert() does that, as long as you add a little code to go back to the record you were pointing to before the APPEND BLANK step.) If you were using FoxPro, you'd be home now.

However, if you're using SQL Server or an XML Web Service, you're only halfway there. You've done the equivalent in .NET of saving changes to a dataset. Now you need to use the saved data to update the data store, which might be on SQL Server or in Timbuktu. So we still need the TableUpdate() and TableRevert() function calls in the Save and Cancel buttons. We just have to add one more call to the DataTier object to see what else to do. If we're using DBFs, as you'll see, it simply excuses itself and returns. Similarly, in the form's Load event, we call the CreateCursor method of this object, which either creates a cursor, or, in the case of DBF access, opens the appropriate table and sets the index tag.

The proper way to read this code is to find the place in the form template code where each routine is being called, and then see what the DataTier routine does after the template code runs. It's the combination of the template code and the DataTier code that works the magic. Listing 3.7 shows the DataTier code.

LISTING 3.7 DataTier.PRG

```
DEFINE CLASS DataTier AS Custom
AccessMethod = []
*   Any attempt to assign a value to this property will be trapped
*                       by the "setter" method AccessMethod_Assign.
ConnectionString = ;
 [Driver={SQL Server};Server=(local);Database=Mydatabase;UID=sa;PWD=;]
Handle      = 0


* Betcha didn't know you could write your own Assign methods...

PROCEDURE AccessMethod_Assign
PARAMETERS AM
DO CASE
    CASE AM = [DBF]
        THIS.AccessMethod = [DBF]     && FoxPro tables
    CASE AM = [SQL]
        THIS.AccessMethod = [SQL]     && MS Sql Server
        THIS.GetHandle
    CASE AM = [XML]
        THIS.AccessMethod = [XML]     && FoxPro XMLAdapter
    CASE AM = [WC]
```

LISTING 3.7 Continued

```
            THIS.AccessMethod = [WC]       && WebConnection server
    OTHERWISE
            MESSAGEBOX( [Incorrect access method ] + AM, 16, [Setter error] )
            THIS.AccessMethod = []
ENDCASE
_VFP.Caption = [Data access method: ] + THIS.AccessMethod
ENDPROC


* CreateCursor actually opens the DBF if AccessMethod is DBF;
* otherwise it uses a structure returned from the data
* store to create a cursor that is bound to the screen controls:

PROCEDURE CreateCursor
LPARAMETERS pTable, pKeyField
IF THIS.AccessMethod = [DBF]
    IF NOT USED ( pTable )
        SELECT 0
        USE ( pTable ) ALIAS ( pTable )
    ENDIF
    SELECT ( pTable )
    IF NOT EMPTY ( pKeyField )
        SET ORDER TO TAG ( pKeyField )
    ENDIF
    RETURN
ENDIF
Cmd = [SELECT * FROM ] + pTable + [ WHERE 1=2]
DO CASE
    CASE THIS.AccessMethod = [SQL]
        SQLEXEC( THIS.Handle, Cmd )
        AFIELDS ( laFlds )
        USE
        CREATE CURSOR ( pTable ) FROM ARRAY laFlds
    CASE THIS.AccessMethod = [XML]
    CASE THIS.AccessMethod = [WC]
ENDCASE


* GetHandle is called in the Assign method of the AccessMethod
* property earlier in this listing (two procedures back).

PROCEDURE GetHandle
IF THIS.AccessMethod = [SQL]
```

LISTING 3.7   Continued

```
    IF THIS.Handle > 0
        RETURN
    ENDIF
    THIS.Handle = SQLSTRINGCONNECT( THIS.ConnectionString )
    IF THIS.Handle < 1
        MESSAGEBOX( [Unable to connect], 16, [SQL Connection error], 2000 )
    ENDIF
  ELSE
    Msg = [A SQL connection was requested, but access method is ] ;
        + THIS.AccessMethod
    MESSAGEBOX( Msg, 16, [SQL Connection error], 2000 )
    THIS.AccessMethod = []
ENDIF
RETURN


PROCEDURE GetMatchingRecords
LPARAMETERS pTable, pFields, pExpr
pFields = IIF ( EMPTY ( pFields ), [*], pFields )
pExpr   = IIF ( EMPTY ( pExpr ), [], ;
            [ WHERE ] + STRTRAN ( UPPER ( ALLTRIM ( pExpr ) ), [WHERE ], [] ) )
cExpr   = [SELECT ] + pFields + [ FROM ] + pTable + pExpr
IF NOT USED ( pTable )
    RetVal = THIS.CreateCursor ( pTable )
ENDIF
DO CASE
    CASE THIS.AccessMethod = [DBF]
        &cExpr
    CASE THIS.AccessMethod = [SQL]
        THIS.GetHandle()
        IF THIS.Handle < 1
            RETURN
        ENDIF
        lr = SQLExec ( THIS.Handle, cExpr )
        IF lr >= 0
            THIS.FillCursor()
          ELSE
            Msg = [Unable to return records] + CHR(13) + cExpr
            MESSAGEBOX( Msg, 16, [SQL error] )
        ENDIF
ENDCASE
ENDPROC
```

In my EasySearch template, I open up a new cursor, the name of which is "View" followed by the name of the table that the data is coming from. So it's not a view, just a cursor name:

```
PROCEDURE CreateView
LPARAMETERS pTable
IF NOT USED( pTable )
   MESSAGEBOX( [Can't find cursor ] + pTable, 16, [Error creating view], 2000 )
   RETURN
ENDIF
SELECT ( pTable )
AFIELDS( laFlds )
SELECT 0
CREATE CURSOR ( [View] + pTable ) FROM ARRAY laFlds
ENDFUNC
```

GetOneRecord is called with all types of data stores. If we're using a DBF, a LOCATE command that refers to the current index tag is Rushmore-optimized and very fast. With SQL, it's also Rushmore-optimized, because SQL 2000 uses Rushmore—with not a single mention of where it came from. But we know...

```
PROCEDURE GetOneRecord
LPARAMETERS pTable, pKeyField, pKeyValue
SELECT ( pTable )
Dlm = IIF ( TYPE ( pKeyField ) = [C], ['], [] )
IF THIS.AccessMethod = [DBF]
   cExpr = [LOCATE FOR ] + pKeyField + [=] + Dlm + TRANSFORM ( pKeyValue ) + Dlm
 ELSE
   cExpr = [SELECT * FROM ] + pTable ;
        + [ WHERE ] + pKeyField + [=] + Dlm + TRANSFORM ( pKeyValue ) + Dlm
ENDIF
DO CASE
   CASE THIS.AccessMethod = [DBF]
        &cExpr
   CASE THIS.AccessMethod = [SQL]
        lr = SQLExec ( THIS.Handle, cExpr )
        IF lr >= 0
           THIS.FillCursor( pTable )
         ELSE
           Msg = [Unable to return record] + CHR(13) + cExpr
           MESSAGEBOX( Msg, 16, [SQL error] )
        ENDIF
   CASE THIS.AccessMethod = [XML]
   CASE THIS.AccessMethod = [WC]
```

```
ENDCASE
ENDFUNC
```

FillCursor is analogous to the Fill method of .NET's DataAdapters. FoxPro's ZAP is like the .NET DataAdapter.Clear method. By appending FROM DBF(*CursorName*) into the named cursor, we don't break the data binding with the form's controls:

```
PROCEDURE FillCursor
LPARAMETERS pTable
IF THIS.AccessMethod = [DBF]
   RETURN
ENDIF
SELECT ( pTable )
ZAP
APPEND FROM DBF ( [SQLResult] )
USE IN SQLResult
GO TOP
ENDPROC
```

I'd like to think that all primary keys were going to be integers, but legacy systems sometimes have character keys. That's what the check for delimiters is in the DeleteRecord routine:

```
PROCEDURE DeleteRecord
LPARAMETERS pTable, pKeyField
IF THIS.AccessMethod = [DBF]
   RETURN
ENDIF
KeyValue = EVALUATE ( pTable + [.] + pKeyField )
Dlm      = IIF ( TYPE ( pKeyField ) = [C], ['], [] )
DO CASE
   CASE THIS.AccessMethod = [SQL]
        cExpr = [DELETE ] + pTable + [ WHERE ] + pKeyField + [=] ;
             + Dlm + TRANSFORM ( m.KeyValue ) + Dlm
        lr = SQLExec ( THIS.Handle, cExpr )
        IF lr < 0
           Msg = [Unable to delete record] + CHR(13) + cExpr
           MESSAGEBOX( Msg, 16, [SQL error] )
        ENDIF
   CASE THIS.AccessMethod = [XML]
   CASE THIS.AccessMethod = [WC]
ENDCASE
ENDFUNC
```

The SaveRecord routine either does an INSERT or an UPDATE depending on whether the user was adding or not:

```
PROCEDURE SaveRecord
PARAMETERS pTable, pKeyField, pAdding
IF THIS.AccessMethod = [DBF]
   RETURN
ENDIF
IF pAdding
    THIS.InsertRecord ( pTable, pKeyField )
 ELSE
    THIS.UpdateRecord ( pTable, pKeyField )
ENDIF
ENDPROC
```

The InsertRecord and UpdateRecord routines call corresponding functions that build SQL INSERT or UPDATE commands, in much the same way that .NET does. I store the resulting string to _ClipText so that I can open up Query Analyzer and execute the command there manually to see what went wrong. It's the fastest way to debug your generated SQL code. Finally, I use SQLExec() to execute the command. SQLExec() returns -1 if there's a problem.

```
PROCEDURE InsertRecord
LPARAMETERS pTable, pKeyField
cExpr = THIS.BuildInsertCommand ( pTable, pKeyField )
_ClipText = cExpr
DO CASE
   CASE THIS.AccessMethod = [SQL]
        lr = SQLExec ( THIS.Handle, cExpr )
        IF lr < 0
           msg = [Unable to insert record; command follows:] + CHR(13) + cExpr
           MESSAGEBOX( Msg, 16, [SQL error] )
        ENDIF
   CASE THIS.AccessMethod = [XML]
   CASE THIS.AccessMethod = [WC]
ENDCASE
ENDFUNC


PROCEDURE UpdateRecord
LPARAMETERS pTable, pKeyField
cExpr = THIS.BuildUpdateCommand ( pTable, pKeyField )
_ClipText = cExpr
DO CASE
   CASE THIS.AccessMethod = [SQL]
```

```
            lr = SQLExec ( THIS.Handle, cExpr )
            IF lr < 0
                msg = [Unable to update record; command follows:] + CHR(13) + cExpr
                MESSAGEBOX( Msg, 16, [SQL error] )
            ENDIF
        CASE THIS.AccessMethod = [XML]
        CASE THIS.AccessMethod = [WC]
    ENDCASE
ENDFUNC


FUNCTION BuildInsertCommand
PARAMETERS pTable, pKeyField
Cmd = [INSERT ] + pTable + [ ( ]
FOR I = 1 TO FCOUNT()
    Fld = UPPER(FIELD(I))
    IF TYPE ( Fld ) = [G]
        LOOP
    ENDIF
    Cmd = Cmd + Fld + [, ]
ENDFOR
Cmd = LEFT(Cmd,LEN(Cmd)-2) + [ } VALUES ( ]
FOR I = 1 TO FCOUNT()
    Fld = FIELD(I)
    IF TYPE ( Fld ) = [G]
        LOOP
    ENDIF
    Dta = ALLTRIM(TRANSFORM ( &Fld ))
    Dta = CHRTRAN ( Dta, CHR(39), CHR(146) )
*    get rid of single quotes in the data
    Dta = IIF ( Dta = [/  /], [], Dta )
    Dta = IIF ( Dta = [.F.], [0], Dta )
    Dta = IIF ( Dta = [.T.], [1], Dta )
    Dlm = IIF ( TYPE ( Fld ) $ [CM],['],;
          IIF ( TYPE ( Fld ) $ [DT],['],;
          IIF ( TYPE ( Fld ) $ [IN],[],    [])))
    Cmd = Cmd + Dlm + Dta + Dlm + [, ]
ENDFOR
Cmd = LEFT ( Cmd, LEN(Cmd) -2) + [ )]   && Remove ", " add " )"
RETURN Cmd
ENDFUNC


FUNCTION BuildUpdateCommand
PARAMETERS pTable, pKeyField
```

```
Cmd = [UPDATE ]   + pTable + [ SET ]
FOR I = 1 TO FCOUNT()
    Fld = UPPER(FIELD(I))
    IF Fld = UPPER(pKeyField)
        LOOP
    ENDIF
    IF TYPE ( Fld ) = [G]
        LOOP
    ENDIF
    Dta = ALLTRIM(TRANSFORM ( &Fld ))
    IF Dta = [.NULL.]
        DO CASE
            CASE TYPE ( Fld ) $ [CMDT]
                Dta = []
            CASE TYPE ( Fld ) $ [INL]
                Dta = [0]
        ENDCASE
    ENDIF
    Dta = CHRTRAN ( Dta, CHR(39), CHR(146) )
*     get rid of single quotes in the data
    Dta = IIF ( Dta = [/  /], [], Dta )
    Dta = IIF ( Dta = [.F.], [0], Dta )
    Dta = IIF ( Dta = [.T.], [1], Dta )
    Dlm = IIF ( TYPE ( Fld ) $ [CM],['],;
           IIF ( TYPE ( Fld ) $ [DT],['],;
           IIF ( TYPE ( Fld ) $ [IN],[],    [])))
    Cmd = Cmd + Fld + [=] + Dlm + Dta + Dlm + [, ]
ENDFOR
Dlm = IIF ( TYPE ( pKeyField ) = [C], ['], [] )
Cmd = LEFT ( Cmd, LEN(Cmd) -2 )              ;
    + [ WHERE ] + pKeyField + [=]           ;
    + + Dlm + TRANSFORM(EVALUATE(pKeyField)) + Dlm
RETURN Cmd
ENDFUNC
```

Sometimes I need to return a cursor that I'll use for my own purposes, for example, to load a combo box. I use the default name SQLResult. I only name it here because if I use FoxPro's SELECT, it returns the cursor into a BROWSE by default, and I need to ensure that the cursor name will be SQLResult when I return from this procedure:

```
PROCEDURE SelectCmdToSQLResult
LPARAMETERS pExpr
DO CASE
    CASE THIS.AccessMethod = [DBF]
```

```
            pExpr = pExpr + [ INTO CURSOR SQLResult]
        &pExpr
    CASE THIS.AccessMethod = [SQL]
        THIS.GetHandle()
        IF THIS.Handle < 1
            RETURN
        ENDIF
        lr = SQLExec ( THIS.Handle, pExpr )
        IF lr < 0
            Msg = [Unable to return records] + CHR(13) + cExpr
            MESSAGEBOX( Msg, 16, [SQL error] )
        ENDIF
    CASE THIS.AccessMethod = [XML]
    CASE THIS.AccessMethod = [WC]
ENDCASE
ENDFUNC
```

When I add a new record, whether I use DBFS or SQL, I'm responsible for inserting a unique value into the table. So I maintain a table of table names and the last key used. If you create this table manually, be sure to update the LastKeyVal field manually before going live, or you'll get *thousands* of duplicate keys.

```
FUNCTION GetNextKeyValue
LPARAMETERS pTable
EXTERNAL ARRAY laVal
pTable = UPPER ( pTable )
DO CASE

    CASE THIS.AccessMethod = [DBF]
        IF NOT FILE ( [Keys.DBF] )
            CREATE TABLE Keys ( TableName Char(20), LastKeyVal Integer )
        ENDIF
        IF NOT USED ( [Keys] )
            USE Keys IN 0
        ENDIF
        SELECT Keys
        LOCATE FOR TableName = pTable
        IF NOT FOUND()
            INSERT INTO Keys VALUES ( pTable, 0 )
        ENDIF
        Cmd = [UPDATE Keys SET LastKeyVal=LastKeyVal + 1 ]     ;
            + [ WHERE TableName='] + pTable + [']
        &Cmd
```

```foxpro
         Cmd = [SELECT LastKeyVal FROM Keys WHERE TableName = '] ;
             + pTable + [' INTO ARRAY laVal]
         &Cmd
         USE IN Keys
         RETURN TRANSFORM(laVal(1))

   CASE THIS.AccessMethod = [SQL]

         Cmd = [SELECT Name FROM SysObjects WHERE Name='KEYS' AND Type='U']
         lr = SQLEXEC( THIS.Handle, Cmd )
         IF lr < 0
            MESSAGEBOX( "SQL Error:"+ CHR(13) + Cmd, 16 )
         ENDIF
         IF RECCOUNT([SQLResult]) = 0
            Cmd = [CREATE TABLE Keys ( TableName Char(20), LastKeyVal Integer )]
            SQLEXEC( THIS.Handle, Cmd )
         ENDIF
         Cmd = [SELECT LastKeyVal FROM Keys WHERE TableName='] + pTable + [']
         lr = SQLEXEC( THIS.Handle, Cmd )
         IF lr < 0
            MESSAGEBOX( "SQL Error:"+ CHR(13) + Cmd, 16 )
         ENDIF
         IF RECCOUNT([SQLResult]) = 0
            Cmd = [INSERT INTO Keys VALUES ('] +  pTable + [', 0 )]
            lr = SQLEXEC( THIS.Handle, Cmd )
            IF lr < 0
               MESSAGEBOX( "SQL Error:"+ CHR(13) + Cmd, 16 )
            ENDIF
         ENDIF
         Cmd = [UPDATE Keys SET LastKeyVal=LastKeyVal + 1 WHERE TableName='] ;
             + pTable + [']
         lr = SQLEXEC( THIS.Handle, Cmd )
         IF lr < 0
            MESSAGEBOX( "SQL Error:"+ CHR(13) + Cmd, 16 )
         ENDIF
         Cmd = [SELECT LastKeyVal FROM Keys WHERE TableName='] +  pTable + [']
         lr = SQLEXEC( THIS.Handle, Cmd )
         IF lr < 0
            MESSAGEBOX( "SQL Error:"+ CHR(13) + Cmd, 16 )
         ENDIF
         nLastKeyVal = TRANSFORM(SQLResult.LastKeyVal)
         USE IN SQLResult
         RETURN TRANSFORM(nLastKeyVal)
```

```
    CASE THIS.AccessMethod = [WC]
    CASE THIS.AccessMethod = [XML]

ENDCASE

ENDDEFINE
```

Running the Application

Type

```
BUILD EXE Chapter3 FROM Chapter3
```

or use the Build button in the Project Manager. When you have an executable, run it and try each of the forms, as well as the search screens. It works pretty nicely, as we're used to seeing with DBF tables.

Now, select Change Data Source from the menu and enter SQL, as shown in Figure 3.4.

FIGURE 3.4   Changing the data access method.

Now, open the Customer form. There's no data! That's standard for a SQL application because until the user requests a record, they don't have one yet. So click on Find, enter some search criteria (actually, to return all records, just leave them all blank), click on Show Matches, and select one. The search form disappears, and you've got data! Select Edit, and then change something and save it. Reload the page to verify that it worked. Add a record, save it, and see if the search form finds it.

Nothing special happens, except that you just built a FoxPro application that works with either DBFs or SQL *without writing a single line of code in any of the forms.*

What's Next?

In the next chapter, we'll build the same application in Visual Basic .NET. That way, you'll see for yourself why I suggested earlier that in .NET, local data access is harder than it is in FoxPro, but SQL access is no harder than local data access.

A Visual Basic .NET Framework

In this chapter, we'll build a simple application framework for Visual Basic .NET forms applications that use SQL Server. You'll see how object-oriented techniques can greatly reduce development time and cost, and simplify your job. If you thought Visual Basic .NET was a lot harder than Visual FoxPro, I think you'll be pleasantly surprised.

A small Visual Basic .NET Windows Application project might consist of

- A Main form to contain the application and the menu
- The Menu control in the Main form
- A few forms to add, edit, and delete records from individual tables

We'll base the Add/Edit/Delete forms on a single inheritable form class, so that we only write the common code once and reuse it as needed.

Starting the New Windows Application Project

To start a Visual Basic .NET project, open up the IDE and select File, New from the menu. The resulting dialog lets you pick from a wide range of project types. Unlike FoxPro, where there is only one language and one project type, in Visual Studio .NET you pick both the project type and the development language. This selection determines which namespaces are included in the project references. For example, if we pick Visual Basic Projects and click on the Windows Application project type, the Windows.Forms namespace (among others) will appear in the list of references. If we instead pick a Smart Devices project, the references for Pocket PC and Windows CE are included.

You first have to pick a name for your new project. When you create this project, Visual Studio adds a new directory under your default projects directory, which is initially `Documents and Settings\`*MyUserID*`\Visual Studio Projects\`*YadaYada*. I changed mine to `C:\VBProjects` and recommend that you do likewise. It creates both a solution (a container for several projects) and a project. As you'll see repeatedly in our examples, Visual Basic .NET assumes a different arrangement for projects than does FoxPro. In FoxPro, we build one project, and may include several class libraries. In Visual Basic .NET, each class library is usually built as its own project, and compiled as a DLL, then included as a reference in other projects that use the classes. It doesn't take long to get used to.

The newly created Visual Basic .NET Windows Application project also includes one form, named `Form1.vb` by default. `Form1` is both the filename and an internal class name. You should change both. In this case, because it's the first form that was created, we'll use it as we used `MAIN.PRG` in our FoxPro project. There's no _Screen object in Visual Basic .NET, so this first form will become our background screen. Using F4, open the Properties window, and change the `Name` property to `AppScreen`. (If you open the code window for the form, you'll see that the class name in the first line has been changed to `AppScreen`.) Open the Solution Explorer with Ctrl+Alt+L and select Rename, and change `Form1.vb` to `AppScreen.vb`. Right-click again on the project in the Solution Explorer and select Rebuild.

> **NOTE**
>
> A FoxPro form would consist of two files, an SCX and an SCT.

Next, we'll need a menu. Use Ctrl+Alt+X to open the Toolbox, select Windows Forms, and drag a `MainMenu` control to anywhere on the AppScreen form. When selected, the `MainMenu` control appears in the upper-left corner of the screen. For now, it's the only control, so it will be selected automatically. Later, if you add other controls (for example, a label) to the form, the menu control will disappear when the label is selected. Click on the `MainMenu` control to begin building your menu.

The `MainMenu` control is simple and intuitive. (I believe it was ported directly from Delphi when the lead architect of Delphi was ported over to Microsoft.) As you move down and right, new text boxes appear to let you add menu selections. You should right-click on each of your menu pads and change the name to something meaningful (for example, `mnuExit` for the File, Exit menu pad), so that the `Click` code for the menu option makes sense when you read it. Add a File pad first, and below it add an Exit bar. Right-click on the File pad, select Properties, change the name to `mnuExit`, and then double-click on it and type in the single command **End**. Press F5 to compile and run the application, and you'll see that your form closes when you click on Exit.

The AppScreen Form Properties

The AppScreen form is the container for the rest of the forms in your application, so let's configure it more to our liking. Use F4 to open the Properties window and make the following property settings:

```
StartPosition    - CenterScreen
FormBorderStyle  - Fixed3D
Text             - My First VB.NET Application
```

Remember that I said that some things are harder in .NET? This is one of them: The drop-shadow trick that we used in Chapter 2, "Building Simple Applications in Visual FoxPro and Visual Basic .NET," to put a title on the screen with a "drop shadow" turns out to be unusually difficult in Visual Basic .NET because the Label control can't be transparent on a Windows form.

> **RANT**
>
> <rant>I'm sure it will be changed by the time this book hits the shelves, but at this moment, you can't get there from here. There is a different kind of control that allows drawing text with a shadow, but it's 15 lines of code, doesn't demonstrate inheritance, and is so complicated that it irritates me.</rant>

Adding a Windows Controls Library

The whole idea of object-oriented programming is that you code things once, and then reuse them throughout your application. That applies to everything—even the controls on each of your forms.

For example, I like to make it easy for users to see which control has the focus. So I either change the background color of the active control or enhance its border. It's a small thing, but it wouldn't be a small thing if I had to code each individual control. Believe it or not, kids, back when I was walking six miles to school in a foot of snow, that's what we had to do. We wrote macros to speed up the process, but what a pain!

Now it's much, much easier. Simply right-click on your solution and select Add Class Library, giving it the name MyControls. A new project will be added to your solution, with an empty code window. Name it MyControls.vb. Add the code shown in Listing 4.1. Recompile the project.

LISTING 4.1   The MyControls Class

```
Imports System.Windows.Forms
Imports System.Drawing


Public Class MyControls
```

LISTING 4.1 Continued

```vb
Public Class MyText
    Inherits TextBox
    Public Sub New()
        MyBase.new()
        Text = ""
        Width = 200
        Enabled = False
        BackColor = System.Drawing.SystemColors.ControlLight
    End Sub
    Public Sub EnterHandler( _
     ByVal Sender As Object, ByVal e As EventArgs) _
     Handles MyBase.Enter
        ForeColor = ForeColor.White
        BackColor = BackColor.Blue
    End Sub
    Public Sub LeaveHandler( _
     ByVal Sender As Object, ByVal e As EventArgs) _
     Handles MyBase.Leave
        ForeColor = ForeColor.Black
        BackColor = BackColor.White
    End Sub
    Public Sub DisableHandler( _
     ByVal Sender As Object, ByVal e As EventArgs) _
     Handles MyBase.EnabledChanged
        Sender.BackColor = _
        IIf(Sender.enabled, BackColor.White, _
            System.Drawing.SystemColors.ControlLight)
    End Sub
End Class

Public Class MyEdit
    Inherits TextBox
    Public Sub New()
        MyBase.new()
        Text = ""
        Width = 200
        Multiline = True
        Enabled = False
        BackColor = System.Drawing.SystemColors.ControlLight
    End Sub
    Public Sub EnterHandler( _
     ByVal Sender As Object, ByVal e As EventArgs) _
```

LISTING 4.1   Continued

```
        Handles MyBase.Enter
            ForeColor = ForeColor.White
            BackColor = BackColor.Blue
        End Sub
        Public Sub LeaveHandler( _
         ByVal Sender As Object, ByVal e As EventArgs) _
         Handles MyBase.Leave
            ForeColor = ForeColor.Black
            BackColor = BackColor.White
        End Sub
        Public Sub DisableHandler( _
         ByVal Sender As Object, ByVal e As EventArgs) _
         Handles MyBase.EnabledChanged
            Sender.BackColor = _
             IIf(Sender.enabled, BackColor.White, _
                 System.Drawing.SystemColors.ControlLight)
        End Sub
    End Class

    Public Class MyCombo
        Inherits ComboBox
        Public Sub New()
            MyBase.new()
            Text = ""
            Width = 200
            Enabled = False
            BackColor = System.Drawing.SystemColors.ControlLight
        End Sub

        Public Sub DisableHandler( _
         ByVal Sender As Object, ByVal e As EventArgs) _
         Handles MyBase.EnabledChanged
            Sender.BackColor = _
             IIf(Sender.enabled, BackColor.White,
                 System.Drawing.SystemColors.ControlLight)
        End Sub
    End Class

    Public Class MyCheck
        Inherits CheckBox
        Public Sub New()
            MyBase.new()
```

LISTING 4.1   Continued

```
                Text = ""
                Width = 200
                Enabled = False
            End Sub
        End Class

        Public Class MyRadio
            Inherits RadioButton
            Public Sub New()
                MyBase.new()
                Text = ""
                Width = 200
                Enabled = False
            End Sub
        End Class

        Public Class MyLabel
            Inherits Label
            Public Sub New()
                MyBase.new()
                Text = ""
                TextAlign = ContentAlignment.MiddleRight
                Height = 12
            End Sub
        End Class


End Class
```

Next, open the Toolbox using Ctrl+Alt+X, right-click, and add a new tab called My User Controls. Open the tab, right-click anywhere under it, and select Add/Remove Items. When the Customize Toolbox dialog appears, click on the Browse button, and add the new `MyControls.dll` component from the `MyControls\bin` directory.

Now when you open the Toolbox and select the `MyControls` tab, you'll see the `MyText`, `MyCombo`, `MyCheck`, `MyRadio`, `MyLabel`, and `MyEdit` components.

From now on you'll use these controls on your forms, rather than the VB standard controls. And if you change `MyLabel`'s font to Tahoma Bold and its color to purple, it will change on every single one of your forms. That's a lot of benefit for 15 seconds of work.

The same holds true for forms. In FoxPro, it's common to build a form to add, edit, and delete records in a single table. Most applications have several such tables, and the logic is the same for all of them. In FoxPro, they're called form templates, but they're just form classes. In Visual Basic .NET, they're called inheritable forms. So let's build one and see if the benefits that accrue are as considerable as they are in FoxPro.

Building Your First Inheritable Form

To create an inheritable form class, open the VS IDE and select New Visual Basic .NET Windows Application project. Enter **InheritedForm** as the project name. (I've changed the location where the solution and project will be created to `C:\VBProjects` so as to make my Visual Basic .NET code easy to find.) Fill in the screen as shown in Figure 4.1.

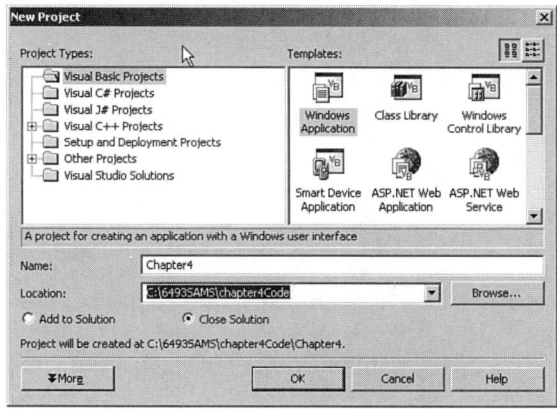

FIGURE 4.1   Starting a new solution and Windows Application project.

Visual Studio will create a solution file named InheritableForm, as well as a project file named InheritableForm containing a form named `Form1.vb`, as shown in Figure 4.2.

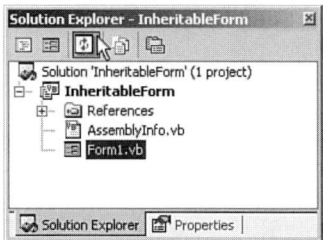

FIGURE 4.2   The solution and project in the Solution Explorer window.

Because we want to create an inheritable form, we need to change the Output type from Windows Application to Class Library. First close the Form Designer because you can't change project properties while the Form Designer has one of its forms open. Make sure the Solution Explorer window (Ctrl+Alt+L) is visible and selected, then right-click on the project name and select Properties. Select Class Library from the Output Type, combo box, change the name to BaseForm, and blank out the Root Namespace text box as shown in Figure 4.3.

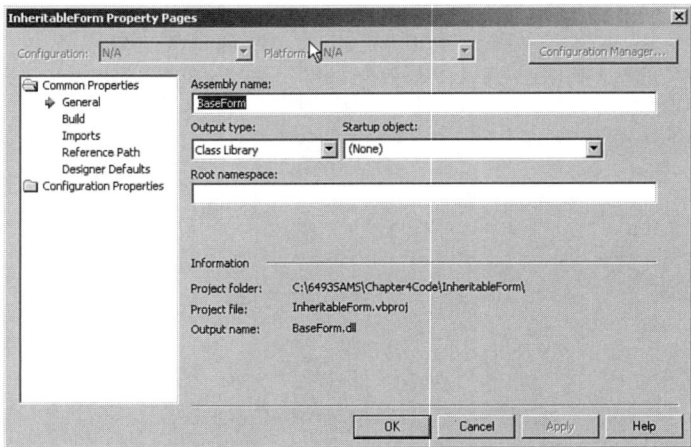

FIGURE 4.3   Changing the inheritable form name in the Inheritable Form Property Page.

Close the Properties page. Finally, right-click on Form1.vb in the Solution Explorer and change the name to BaseForm.vb. The result should look like what's shown in Figure 4.4.

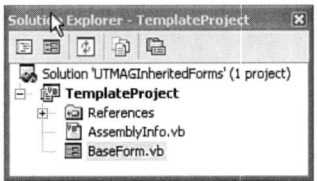

FIGURE 4.4   The renamed form class in the Solution Explorer.

Double-click on baseform.vb to bring up the designer, and then use Ctrl+Alt+X (or select View, Toolbox from the IDE menu) to display the Toolbox. Select Windows Forms. (You can only select it if the Designer is open, so if you don't see the Toolbox tab, that's probably the problem.) I want to have buttons to add, edit, delete, save, cancel, and close the form, so double-click six times on the button control. You can then use the Layout tools to line them up. Select View, Toolbars from the IDE menu and make sure Layout is checked.

Next, change the buttons' Name properties to btnAdd, btnEdit, btnDelete, btnSave, btnCancel, and btnClose, and then change their respective Text values to Add, Edit, Delete, Save, Cancel, and Close. I like to put an ampersand (&) in front of the appropriate capitalized letter of each text caption to enable a hotkey. I use Cl&ose because &Cancel is taken, even though it's not really a conflict because both are never enabled at the same time. Speaking of enabling, I initially disable all buttons except Close, for reasons that will become clear presently. I also changed the form's Text property to Change me! as a reminder to the programmer.

Finally, position all six of the buttons near the bottom left of the screen, and then select all of them and set the Anchor property to Bottom, Left, as shown in Figure 4.5.

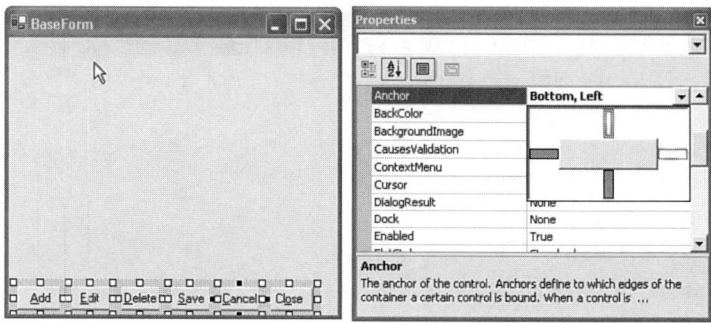

FIGURE 4.5   Anchoring the buttons to the bottom left of the form.

Although some "flat files" are very large, most applications use lots of little tables. So I'm going to make a simplifying assumption that a single level of filtering is sufficient to show a subset of matching records from which a single record can be chosen for viewing or editing. For this purpose, I'll put a text box at the top of the screen so that the user can enter a filtering value for a designated search field, and a button and a list box to show the matching values of said search field. It's not going to work in every case, but if it meets 90% of your needs, it's a good start. Add two labels, a text box, a button, and a list box to make the form look like Figure 4.6.

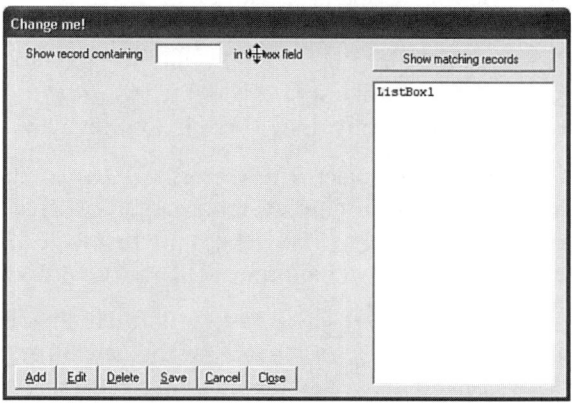

FIGURE 4.6   Adding a search capability to the form.

I anchored the Show Matching Records button at the top and right, and the list box is anchored at the top, right, and bottom. As a result, automatic resizing performs exactly as you would expect. That's better than writing all of that resizing code that used to be required, and it works the same way in the IDE as it does in the final program.

Coding the Form Class

The first thing I code is always the Close button because I'm anxious to see it work. Double-click on the Close button and you'll see that the IDE generates two lines of code. Listing 4.2 shows the code for the `Click` event of the Close button. Note that the `Handles` clause determines which event the routine responds to, not the routine name as is the case in Visual FoxPro.

LISTING 4.2   The Close Button `Click` Event Code

```
Private Sub btnClose_Click( _
  ByVal sender As System.Object, _
  ByVal e As System.EventArgs) _
 Handles btnClose.Click

    Close()
End Sub
```

The `Private Sub` and `End Sub` lines were written by the IDE's code generator. I added the `Close` command. (The ending parentheses were added by the IDE.)

The form displays one record at a time, which makes saving changes simple. That's the reason for this design. But that means we have to have a mechanism for selecting a record for viewing or editing. That's what the text box, the list box, and the Show Matching Record button are for. The user enters a string—one or more letters—into the text box and clicks on the button, and the list is populated with all of the records that match. But match on what? I've decided to specify a single search field, presumably the most important field in the table, as the target for the search. I've also decided to show all records that start with the string entered by the user. As you'll see shortly, matching any part of the expression is equally easy. But it's my design, so I'll do it my way.

To see how this works, compile the project. This creates a DLL named BookInheritedForm.dll, which can contain several inheritable items. Next, add a project called UseTheFormLuke to your current solution. (I did my first FoxBASE project for George Lucas at the Skywalker Ranch.) It will add a form called Form1, which we'll ignore for now.

Next, right-click on the new project and select Add, Add Inherited Form from the context menu. The resulting dialog will first ask for a name for the new form (call it Test), and then it will ask you to select from the available inheritable classes, as shown in Figure 4.7. Select BaseForm, the only one on the list. The resulting form will look just like BaseForm because it inherits from BaseForm.

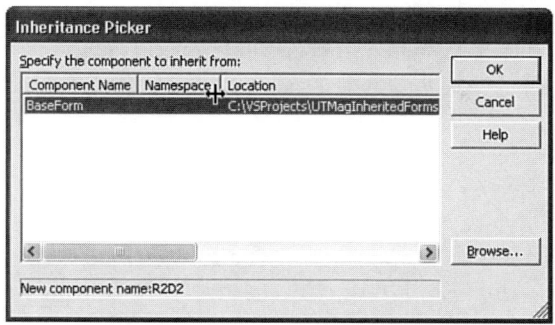

FIGURE 4.7   Selecting an inheritable class for an inherited form.

We'll need a Main Form in order to test our inherited form. You can use Form1, which was created automatically when you added the Windows Application project. Change the file-name to MainForm.vb by right-clicking on the filename and selecting Rename, and then open the form's code and change Class Form1, the first line in the file, to Class MainForm. (You can also open the form in the Form Designer and change the Name prop-erty.)

Next, drag a MainMenu control from the Windows Form toolbox to the form's design surface. Type **File** in the top left cell, and **Exit** just below it, as shown in Figure 4.8.

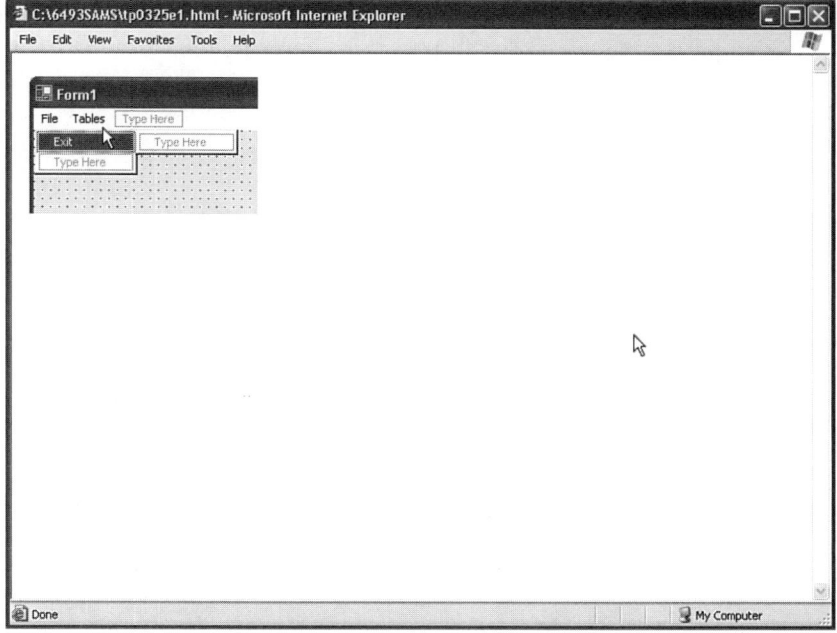

FIGURE 4.8   Adding menu items to the form.

Double-click on `Exit` and enter the single command **End**. Go up and to the right of `File` and type **Tables**, and then go down and type **Test Form**. Double-click on `Test Form` and enter the following three lines of code:

```
Dim frm as Test
frm = New Test
frm.Show()
```

Press F5 to compile and run your application. Then select Tables, Test from the menu, and you'll see your first inherited form. It doesn't do much yet, but it will.

Programming with Class

We want to allow programmers to use this inheritable form simply by filling in some properties. What are properties? In Visual FoxPro, they're something like public variables at the class level. In Visual Basic .NET you can enter a `Public As String` statement in the declarations at the top of a class, and the resulting element (called a **field**) is accessible to classes subclassed from the class. For example, if a class contains `Public MyField as String` in its declarations, then in a subclass of the class, IntelliSense will expose `Me.MyField` (Me is like `THISFORM` in FoxPro). But it's not visible in the class's property sheet, nor is it visible in the property sheet of a subclass of the class.

In order to view and set the property in a subclass of the class, you have to create a private variable and a property procedure to save and retrieve it. And what's exposed is not the private variable, but rather the property procedure containing the Getter and Setter routines. For example, to provide a settable `MainTable` property, you add the code shown in Listing 4.3 to the top of your form class's code, just below the declarations.

LISTING 4.3   Declaring A Property Procedure

```
Private _MainTable As String
Public Property MainTable() As String
    Get
        Return _MainTable
    End Get
    Set(ByVal Value As String)
        _MainTable = Value
    End Set
End Property
```

You really only have to enter four of these lines of code: When you type `Public Property As` and press Enter, the IDE writes all of the code except `Return _MainTable` and `_MainTable = Value`. So you have to create the private variable (by convention the name of the property procedure preceded by an underscore), the procedure name, and the

Return and Value assignment statements. Then, when you subclass the class, MainTable (not _MainTable) appears in the property sheet. It looks unnecessarily complicated, especially to FoxPro developers; but after you do it a few hundred times, you won't even notice it.

Automating Data Access

ADO.NET is the data engine used in .NET applications. It's a disconnected methodology; you request data and close the door. When you want to save it, you reconnect and send the changes. Inside the application, data is stored in a dataset—sort of a miniature data environment, which can contain tables, relations, and some other elements. For our simple application, it will contain a single table, and the programmer will know the table's name. So we'll need a MainTable property. Open up the BaseForm.vb code module and enter the code shown in Listing 4.3. Rebuild the project and then rebuild the solution. Now open the inherited form in the designer, press F4, and look under Misc (see Figure 4.9): Voilà, there's your new MainTable property!

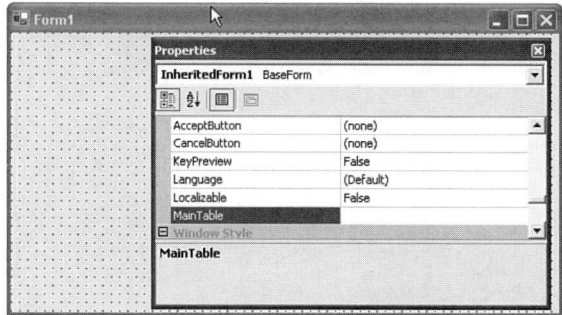

FIGURE 4.9   Exposing a property in a subclass.

How do we use this property? We use it just exactly as we use properties in FoxPro; they're variables that the programmer can set while designing the form. I need two more properties and a constant before I can do what needs to be done, so I'll just fast-forward and list the entire declarations and property procedures code in one fell swoop, as shown in Listing 4.4.

LISTING 4.4   The BaseForm Inheritable Form Class

```
Public Class BaseForm

    Inherits System.Windows.Forms.Form

#Region " My declarations "
    Public Const TurnOn As Boolean = True
```

LISTING 4.4   Contintued

```vb
    Public Const TurnOff As Boolean = False

    Public ConnStr As String = _
      "Provider=SQLOLEDB;server=(local);database=Northwind;uid=sa;pwd=;"
    Public dc As OleDb.OleDbConnection

    Public daFiltered As OleDb.OleDbDataAdapter
    Public dsFiltered As DataSet

    Public daOneRecord As OleDb.OleDbDataAdapter
    Public dsOneRecord As DataSet

    Public _MainTable As String
    Public _keyfield As String
    Public _searchfield As String

    Public spacer As String
#End Region

#Region " My Property procedures "
    Public Property MainTable() As String
        Get
            Return _MainTable
        End Get
        Set(ByVal Value As String)
            _MainTable = Value
        End Set
    End Property

    Public Property KeyField() As String
        Get
            Return _keyfield
        End Get
        Set(ByVal Value As String)
            _keyfield = Value
        End Set
    End Property

    Public Property SearchField() As String
        Get
            Return _searchfield
        End Get
```

LISTING 4.4 Contintued

```
        Set(ByVal Value As String)
            _searchfield = Value
        End Set
    End Property
#End Region
```

The `#Region` directives allow you to hide chunks of code. For example, when I collapse all of my code regions, this is what I see in the code editor for the `BaseForm` (see Figure 4.10). Needless to say, this is a lot easier to navigate than 453 lines of code.

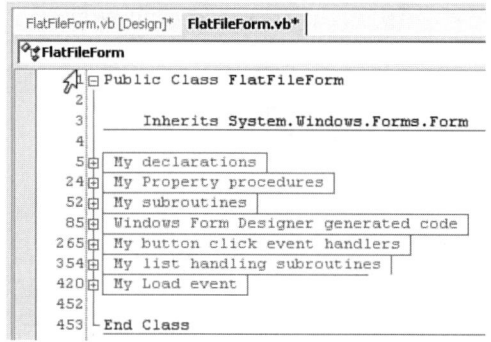

FIGURE 4.10 Collapsed code using `#Region` directives.

The additional public variables declared in the preceding code include constants to provide more meaningful symbols than `True` and `False`; a connection string and `DataConnection` to hook up to SQL Server; a couple of `DataAdapters` and datasets to get a list of candidate records and the single record the user selected, respectively; and public properties for the names of the Main Table, the key field (for retrieving the selected record), and the name of the searchable field to display in the `ListBox`.

The reason that everything has to be declared up front is `Option Strict`. The code won't compile unless we use `DIM`, `PUBLIC`, or `PRIVATE` (or `FRIEND` or whatever) to declare every single variable that we use in the code. IntelliSense uses these declarations to know what to show us when we hit that first period, and the compiler uses them to set aside storage.

ADO.NET uses a connection to build a `DataAdapter`. The `DataAdapter` contains `Select`, `Insert`, `Update`, and `Delete` logic to get the data to and from the data source specified by the connection. The data is stored inside your form in a `DataSet` object, which is like a data environment built of XML. It contains tables, relations, and other stuff that this exercise won't need. For our purposes, it contains a table, and its name is contained in the `MainTable` property. The `KeyField`, the one we'll use to retrieve a single record and to post updates, is another named property, and `SearchField`, the field to search and to display in the list box, is named in the third property. Our code will refer to these three properties, trusting that the programmer has filled them in correctly.

Now we're ready to write some code. The `Load` event fires first in Visual Basic .NET, just as it does in FoxPro. We'll use the connection string to open the connection; then construct a `SELECT` statement and create a `DataAdapter`; then use the `DataAdapter`'s `Fill` method to fill a `DataSet` with a table named using the contents of the `MainTable` property. Listing 4.5 shows the code for the `Load` event.

LISTING 4.5   The BaseForm Load Event Code

```
Private Sub BaseForm_Load( _
  ByVal sender As System.Object, ByVal e As System.EventArgs) _
 Handles MyBase.Load
    Try
        Label2.Text = "in the " + SearchField + " field"
        dc = New OleDb.OleDbConnection
        dc.ConnectionString = ConnStr
        dc.Open()
    Catch oEx As Exception
        MsgBox("Connection failed: " + oEx.Message)
        Close()
    End Try
End Sub
```

How BaseForm Load **Works**
The program puts the name of the search field into the label at the top of the screen so that the display makes sense. Then it uses the connection string from the template form to open a connection to the data source, which could be SQL, ODBC, or anything else.

Loading the List Box and Displaying a Record When Clicked

The user gets a chance to filter the data in the table; if the table contains only a dozen or two records, it may not even be necessary. When the Show Matching Records button is clicked, the list is loaded and the first record in the list is displayed. Subsequently, clicking on any item in the list causes its record to be displayed. The code is shown in Listing 4.6.

LISTING 4.6   The LoadList Button Click Event Code

```
Private Sub LoadList_Click( _
  ByVal sender As System.Object, ByVal e As System.EventArgs) _
 Handles btnLoadList.Click
    LoadTheList()
End Sub
```

LISTING 4.6   Continued

```
Public Sub LoadTheList()
    Dim I As Integer
    Dim NumFound As Integer
    Dim Str As String
    Str = "SELECT * FROM " + MainTable _
        + " WHERE UPPER(" + SearchField + ") LIKE '" _
        + SearchValue.Text.ToUpper.Trim + "%'"
    daFiltered = New OleDb.OleDbDataAdapter(Str, dc)
    dsFiltered = New DataSet
    daFiltered.Fill(dsFiltered, MainTable)
    'Clear the listbox and load it
    With ListBox1
        .Items.Clear()
        NumFound = dsFiltered.Tables(MainTable).Rows.Count - 1
        Dim dr As DataRow
        For I = 0 To NumFound
            dr = dsFiltered.Tables(MainTable).Rows(I)
            Str = dr(SearchField)
            Str = Str.PadRight(40)
            Str = Str + CStr(dr(KeyField))
            .Items.Add(Str)
        Next
    End With
    ListBox1.SelectedIndex = 0
    LoadaRecord()
    Buttons(TurnOn)
End Sub

Private Sub ListBox1_SelectedIndexChanged( _
  ByVal sender As System.Object, ByVal e As System.EventArgs) _
 Handles ListBox1.SelectedIndexChanged
    LoadaRecord()
End Sub

Public Sub LoadaRecord()
    Dim Kv As String
    Kv = ListBox1.SelectedItem
    Kv = Kv.Substring(40)
    Kv = Kv.Trim
    Dim str As String
    str = "SELECT * FROM " + MainTable _
```

4

LISTING 4.6   Continued

```
            + " WHERE " + KeyField + " = '" + Kv + "'"
        daOneRecord = New OleDb.OleDbDataAdapter(str, dc)
        dsOneRecord = New DataSet
        dsOneRecord.Clear()
        daOneRecord.Fill(dsOneRecord, MainTable)
        Dim dr As DataRow
        dr = dsOneRecord.Tables(MainTable).Rows(0)
        ' Load on-screen controls' text properties
        Dim FldName As String
        Dim Ctrl As Control
        For Each Ctrl In Controls
            Try
                If TypeOf Ctrl Is TextBox Or TypeOf Ctrl Is ComboBox Then
                    Ctrl.DataBindings.Clear()
                    FldName = Ctrl.Name.Substring(3)
                ' skip characters "0-2"
                    Ctrl.Text = dr(FldName)
                End If
            Catch   ' ignore fields that don't have a column to bind to
            End Try
        Next
    End Sub
```

How LoadList Click **Works**

Clicking on the Show Matching Records button is handled by the LoadList_Click routine, which simply calls LoadList(). The routine creates a SELECT statement ending in a LIKE condition that matches any string starting with the letters the user typed in (try it with a single letter to start). The field that's searched is the one named in the SearchField property, which is also the field that's loaded into the TextBox item list. The key value for each record, KeyField, is appended to the end of the 40-character SearchField string, so that it's not visible. When the user clicks on the list, the key is extracted from position 41 (40 in VBSpeak) of the selected item and used to return a single record into the dsOneRecord dataset.

The challenge here was to bind the data to the fields on the screen. I used a little trick here; I assume that each field starts with a three-character mnemonic for the control type (txt for text box, cmb for combo box, and so on —a mechanism we're all pretty much used to anyway), and that the remaining characters are precisely the name of a field in the dataset. Datasets don't have field names, but the rows in the tables that they contain do; so I reference a row in the Tables(MainTable) collection, and then use dr(*FieldName*)—

where I just inferred *FieldName* from the control name—to find the data and assign it to the control's `Text` property. The `Try...Catch...End Try` with no code after the `Catch` is a neat trick; if the control doesn't have a matching field in the data row, it's an error, which I throw away.

Utility Routines

There are a few routines that are used by several of the buttons' `Click` events, so I'll show them first. Listing 4.7 shows the code for the `Inputs` subroutine.

LISTING 4.7   The Inputs Subroutine Code

```
Public Sub Inputs(ByVal onoff As Boolean)
    Dim Ctrl As Control
    For Each Ctrl In Controls
        If TypeOf Ctrl Is TextBox _
        Or TypeOf Ctrl Is ComboBox Then
            Ctrl.Enabled = onoff
        End If
    Next
    SearchValue.Enabled = Not onoff
    btnLoadList.Enabled = Not onoff
    Buttons(Not onoff)
End Sub

Public Sub Buttons(ByVal onoff As Boolean)
    btnAdd.Enabled = onoff
    btnEdit.Enabled = onoff
    btnDelete.Enabled = onoff
    btnClose.Enabled = onoff
    btnSave.Enabled = Not onoff
    btnCancel.Enabled = Not onoff
End Sub

Public Sub ClearFields()
    Dim Ctrl As Control
    For Each Ctrl In Controls
        If TypeOf Ctrl Is TextBox _
        Or TypeOf Ctrl Is ComboBox Then
            Ctrl.Text = ""
        End If
    Next
End Sub
```

How the `Inputs` Subroutine Works

Inputs turns the text boxes, combo boxes, and other controls on and off as needed. I can pass it the constant TurnOn (True) to enable them or TurnOff (False) to disable them. Buttons ensures that, when the input fields are enabled, all of the buttons except Save and Cancel are disabled and vice versa. ClearFields blanks the input fields before adding a record.

`Click` **Event Code for the Form's Buttons**

The buttons on the form give the users the options they need. We'll discuss the code one routine at a time. Listing 4.8 shows the code for the Click event of the Add button.

LISTING 4.8   The Add Button `Click` Event Code

```
Private Sub btnAdd_Click( _
  ByVal sender As System.Object, ByVal e As System.EventArgs) _
 Handles btnAdd.Click
    Try
        dsOneRecord.Clear()
        BindingContext(dsOneRecord, MainTable).AddNew()
        ClearFields()
        Inputs(TurnOn)
    Catch oEx As Exception
        MsgBox("Error:  " + oEx.Message)
    End Try
End Sub


Private Sub btnEdit_Click( _
  ByVal sender As System.Object, ByVal e As System.EventArgs) _
 Handles btnEdit.Click
    Inputs(TurnOn)
End Sub

Private Sub btnDelete_Click( _
  ByVal sender As System.Object, ByVal e As System.EventArgs) _
 Handles btnDelete.Click
    Try
        BindingContext(dsOneRecord, MainTable).RemoveAt(0)
        Dim cb As OleDb.OleDbCommandBuilder
        cb = New OleDb.OleDbCommandBuilder
        cb.DataAdapter = daOneRecord
        daOneRecord.UpdateCommand = cb.GetUpdateCommand()
```

LISTING 4.8   Continued

```
        daOneRecord.Update(dsOneRecord, MainTable)
        dsOneRecord.Tables(MainTable).AcceptChanges()
        LoadTheList()
        MsgBox("Record deleted", MsgBoxStyle.Information, "My app")
    Catch oEx As Exception
        MsgBox("Error:   " + oEx.Message)
    End Try
End Sub
```

How the Button Code Works

The Add button clears the text boxes and uses a `BindingContext` object to do the FoxPro equivalent of APPEND BLANK. Because the fields aren't bound to the data row in this exercise, I have to manually blank the onscreen controls, and finally I have to enable them. Edit is much simpler, of course. Listing 4.9 shows the code for the `Click` event of the Delete button.

LISTING 4.9   The Delete Button `Click` Event Code

```
Private Sub btnDelete_Click( _
  ByVal sender As System.Object, ByVal e As System.EventArgs) _
  Handles btnDelete.Click
    Try
        BindingContext(dsOneRecord, MainTable).RemoveAt(0)
        Dim cb As OleDb.OleDbCommandBuilder
        cb = New OleDb.OleDbCommandBuilder
        cb.DataAdapter = daOneRecord
        daOneRecord.UpdateCommand = cb.GetUpdateCommand()
        daOneRecord.Update(dsOneRecord, MainTable)
        dsOneRecord.Tables(MainTable).AcceptChanges()
        LoadTheList()
        MsgBox("Record deleted", MsgBoxStyle.Information, "My app")
    Catch oEx As Exception
        MsgBox("Error:   " + oEx.Message)
    End Try
End Sub
```

How btnDelete Click Works

Because the recordset is disconnected from the data source, I have two separate tasks: First, I mark the record deleted using the `BindingContext` object; then I use a `CommandBuilder` object to construct a `Delete` command object and use the `Update` method of the

DataAdapter object to pass it back to the data source. After updating the data source, I accept the changes to the dataset, clearing it, and reload the list using a call to LoadTheList(). You can't call a .Click method directly in Visual Basic .NET as you can in FoxPro, so that's why LoadTheList is a separate routine called both here and in the LoadList_Click method. Listing 4.10 shows the code for the Click event of the Save button.

LISTING 4.10   The Save Button Click Event Code

```
Private Sub btnSave_Click( _
  ByVal sender As System.Object, ByVal e As System.EventArgs) _
  Handles btnSave.Click
    Try
        BindingContext(dsOneRecord, MainTable).EndCurrentEdit()
        Dim FldName As String
        Dim NewKey As String
        Dim Ctrl As Control
        For Each Ctrl In Controls
            If TypeOf Ctrl Is TextBox And Ctrl.Name <> "SearchValue" Then
                FldName = Ctrl.Name.Substring(3)
                'skip characters 0-2 - thanks, Bill..
                dsOneRecord.Tables(0).Rows(0).Item(FldName) = Ctrl.Text
                If FldName = KeyField Then
                    NewKey = Ctrl.Text
                End If
            End If
        Next
        Dim cb As OleDb.OleDbCommandBuilder
        cb = New OleDb.OleDbCommandBuilder
        cb.DataAdapter = daOneRecord
        daOneRecord.UpdateCommand = cb.GetUpdateCommand()
        daOneRecord.Update(dsOneRecord, MainTable)
        dsOneRecord.Tables(MainTable).AcceptChanges()
        ' Load the list so as to include the new record
        LoadTheList()
        ' Find the new key in the list
        Dim str As String
        Dim I As Integer
        For I = 0 To ListBox1.Items.Count - 1
            str = ListBox1.Items(I)
            If str.ToUpper.Substring(1).IndexOf(NewKey.ToUpper) > 0 Then
                ListBox1.SelectedIndex = I
                Exit For
```

LISTING 4.10 Continued

```
            End If
        Next
        LoadaRecord()
        Inputs(TurnOff)
    Catch oEx As Exception
        MsgBox("Error:  " + oEx.Message)
    End Try
End Sub
```

How btnSave Click Works

Saving the changes was the biggest challenge. First, I must end the current edit using the BindingContext object. Then, I have to put the values stored in the text properties of the onscreen controls back into the dataset. (I've fully qualified the row reference here so that you can see where it's going, but you can also use a DataRow object or even a DataTable object.)

Next I build an Update command and execute it using the Update method. Again, I reload the list to reflect any changes or an added record. Finally, I want the record that I was just editing or adding to be selected when the save is completed, so that's what the last For..Next loop is about. When I find the SelectedIndex, I call LoadARecord and disable all of the input controls. Listing 4.11 shows the code for the Click event of the Cancel button.

LISTING 4.11 The Cancel Button Click Event Code

```
Private Sub btnCancel_Click( _
  ByVal sender As System.Object, ByVal e As System.EventArgs) _
  Handles btnCancel.Click
    Try
        BindingContext(dsOneRecord, MainTable).CancelCurrentEdit()
        LoadaRecord()
        Inputs(TurnOff)
    Catch oEx As Exception
        MsgBox("Error:  " + oEx.Message)
    End Try
End Sub
```

How btnCancel Click Works

The Cancel command only requires that I cancel the current edit using the BindingContext object (which, by the way, also encapsulates the functionality of

TableUpdate(), TableRevert(), DELETE, APPEND BLANK, TOP, BOTTOM, and SKIP), reload the record I was editing, and disable the input fields.

The last bit of code, which we saw at the beginning of this exercise, is shown in Listing 4.12.

LISTING 4.12   The Close Button Click Event Code

```
Private Sub btnClose_Click( _
  ByVal sender As System.Object, ByVal e As System.EventArgs) _
 Handles btnClose.Click
    Close()
End Sub
```

How to Use This Template

To use this template in your projects, either copy it to a directory where you've started a solution, or use Add an Existing Project by right-clicking on the solution in the Solution Explorer and adding it to the solution. All you really need is InheritedForm.dll, but I recommend you copy the code in case you want to make some improvements.

For each inherited form that you want to build, right-click on a project in the Solution Explorer and provide a name (usually the name of one of your data tables), then point to InheritedForm.dll (you may have to browse to it) and click on BaseForm. Fill in the MainTable, KeyField, and SearchField properties with the names of your main data table, key field, and the field you want users to search.

Finally, drag text boxes and/or combo boxes onto the form and name them with three-letter prefixes denoting the control type (for example, txt, cmb, chk) followed by the field names. Be sure to set the tab order using the View, Tab Order menu selection. (Hint: Click the same menu selection again when you're finished. That only took me an hour to discover.) Finally, disable all of the input fields. The user has to click on Add or Edit to change them.

When you've finished your new form, add a menu selection for the table in your Main Form MainMenu control using the pattern described earlier in the chapter, and rebuild the project, and it oughta work. The Customer form shown in Figure 4.11 took me two minutes and 15 seconds to build, from start to finish.

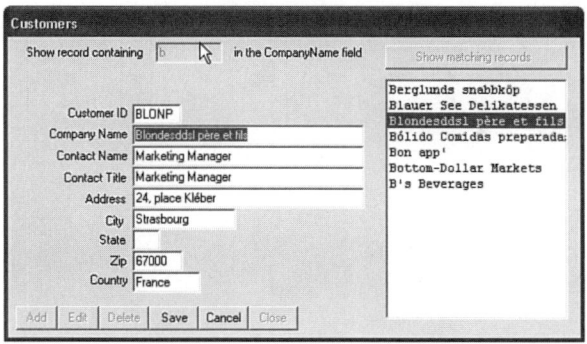

FIGURE 4.11   An Add/Edit/Delete form finished in less than three minutes.

Summary

In this chapter, you saw how you can build inheritable forms, Visual Basic .NET's equivalent of template classes in FoxPro, thereby achieving the same rapid prototyping capability. You've seen how you can support both local tables and SQL Server with no change in the form code.

In Chapter 5, "Adding Internet Access," we'll extend these two models to include support for XML Web Services so that you can offer your clients the ability to run their rich client applications over the Internet.

Adding Internet Access

In the preceding two chapters, we looked at how to build a simple Windows Forms application in Visual FoxPro and in Visual Basic .NET. You learned how to use either local tables or SQL Server in both environments. You saw how FoxPro requires additional coding to use SQL Server, whereas Visual Basic .NET treats local tables and SQL Server tables exactly the same way. Until a few years ago, those were the two technologies we had to offer our clients.

That has changed. Without a doubt, the Internet is the biggest thing that's ever happened to database application development. Using Internet-enabled applications, users can access their data from anywhere that has a telephone connection. With broadband access, the user experience is almost identical to that of a local area network user.

ASP and Database Development

For several years, developers of Windows Forms database applications were at a disadvantage when it came to building Internet-enabled database apps. Active Server Pages (ASP) was easy to learn, easy to use, and free. That's a hard combination to beat.

ASP is a Microsoft technology that generates Web pages containing embedded data. Input fields within forms are used to send data back to the server. Inside a Web page that collects data, a statement like `<form target="xxx.asp">` directs the contents of the page to an ASP program (named `xxx.asp` here) that extracts the contents of any input fields and uses them to update tables in a database.

But ASP and even its successor ASP.NET are not the only answer. In fact, for most applications, they're not even a good answer. Browsers like Internet Explorer and Netscape

Navigator have remarkable capabilities, but they're best for distributing a simple interface to a large number of unknown users. When it comes to complex applications like billing and purchasing systems, sophisticated inventory or payroll applications, and other programs that might accomplish a task in a few seconds or in an hour depending on the capabilities of the user interface, browser clients are a poor choice.

Applications having only a few users who need precise combinations of information and more complex controls such as combo boxes, tree views, and filtered lists are difficult to build for a browser environment. A **smart client application** (the latest name for a database application that connects to a database over the Internet) can allow users to do the same task in seconds instead of minutes. Repeat that task hundreds of times a day, and a smart client application can soon achieve savings that will pay for the cost of development in short order.

Development costs are another saving. Paradoxically, although browser applications tend to be simpler in the sense that a single screen may only do one or two things rather than the entire set of operations that a user needs to do, they also take longer to design and code. And smart clients are cheaper to maintain as the inevitable requests for changes are made.

Finally, besides being slower than their rich client cousins and costing more to develop and maintain, browser applications send their contents as plain text. That's no way to distribute the company's sensitive information; somewhere, some hacker will intercept and read their contents.

For all three of these reasons, many developers feel that thin client application development has been *hugely* oversold. There are several reasons that come to mind.

- IT managers who are tired of the problems inherent in deploying traditional Windows applications to operating systems that may range from Windows 95 through Windows XP and beyond are partly to blame.

- In addition, it can be very difficult to diagnose problems in your own Windows software when someone else's installation overwrites a DLL that your application depends on, and that certainly makes a technology that doesn't need to be deployed appear even more attractive.

- Finally, people who bought a book on ASP and learned it in a week and who are excited by the salaries that database developers earn are also guilty of overestimating the applicability of ASP to database development.

You can't draw a picture of a car and drive it away, but building a Web page that sort of works is pretty easy. However, it will seldom duplicate the performance of an executable. User complaints don't begin until a poorly designed system is deployed, and by then it's too late. Windows Forms applications with well-designed interfaces based on well-designed databases provide the best combination of cost, performance, and features.

Browser applications have their place, but in time users will come to realize that it's a pretty small place. For everything else, there's rich client.

Still, getting access to data has never been easy. Traditional Visual Basic applications used recordsets internally, but recordsets aren't files, but rather in-memory structures that can't easily be sent across the Internet.

XML solves that problem. XML files are text files that express all data fields as strings delimited by tags that reflect the name of the field that the data came from. An inline schema included at the beginning of the file (or named internally and provided in another file) can describe how to reconstruct the table, if it's needed. However, when sending a known record structure to a known client, the table structures are usually known in advance. So XML is a simple way to send data from a server to a client and back again.

However, as you'll see in the examples shown in this chapter, you can send DBFs and FPTs across the Internet, and they work great. When zipped and encrypted, they provide data security in about one-seventh the space required for the equivalent XML. I wonder why Microsoft didn't decide to use them as the basis for Internet data interchange as a complement to XML. You'll have to ask them.

Microsoft and others developed Simple Object Access Protocol (SOAP) to enable remote access to a data server. SOAP provides descriptions of the functions and procedures available on a server in such a way that the client can discover what is available from a Web service and exchange data with it. A Web Services Description Language (WSDL) file is available at the server and can be queried by the client application to discover available services and their required parameters.

The implications for database applications are tremendous. You can open up an empty table structure and go to a Web server for data. After modifying a record, or after entering a new record, you can send it back to the Web server to update the appropriate database table. Deleting records is even simpler; you can just send the table name, a key field name and a key value, and the Web service can create and execute a DELETE command on the data table.

With the inclusion of support for XML Web Services in Visual FoxPro 8, FoxPro applications have begun to look like database applications written in .NET languages. Data acquisition involves creating a proxy for the remote Web Service, data translation to and from XML strings, and learning about diffgrams. It's a little different, but the results are spectacular.

In this chapter we'll add Internet access to the data tier developed in our FoxPro application in Chapter 2, "Building Sample Applications in Visual FoxPro and Visual Basic .NET,"and we'll add XML Web Services to our Visual Basic .NET application developed in Chapter 3, "Building a Visual FoxPro Application for SQL Server." I'm going to describe two methods of building Internet access for FoxPro, one for use with Visual FoxPro 7 and another for use with Visual FoxPro 8. Visual FoxPro 7 has less Web Services support than subsequent versions, and not everyone has upgraded.

I can't talk about Internet-enabled FoxPro applications without mentioning the amazing Web Connection, a product developed by Rick Strahl of West Wind Technologies on Maui. Rick is the pioneer who led the way in showing how to incorporate Web access into FoxPro applications. His shareware product is still the easiest and fastest way to build Internet applications in FoxPro, and in Visual FoxPro 7, it's by far the best way. So the first part of this chapter will describe how to use Web Connection to build an Internet application. In Visual FoxPro 8, Web Services are fully supported, so the Visual FoxPro 8 Web server will be built using native Visual FoxPro 8 capabilities. However, you might still end up concluding that Web Connection is the best way to build Internet support in *any* version of FoxPro. You be the judge.

Internet Access in Visual FoxPro 7

Building a Web-enabled smart client in Visual FoxPro is a lot like building a SQL Server application. You use local cursors, get as little data as possible, and pass it around using HTTP.

Visual FoxPro 8 has great support for Internet access. However, many Visual FoxPro developers haven't upgraded, so I'm going to start by showing you how to use Web Connection to build Web-enabled database applications in Visual FoxPro 7. After that, we'll see how Visual FoxPro 8 has added new features that permit development of the same type of applications without using a third-party tool (although you may decide to stick with Web Connection anyway). Finally, we'll see how completely XML Web Services are integrated into Visual Basic .NET, so that very little needs to be done to Web-enable your application.

The first time I read the sentence "The Internet Is The Network," I thought, with my typical Hungarian cynicism: Right. More marketing BS to sell something. Then I spent a few months with Rick Strahl's Web Connection.

Let me make one thing perfectly clear: *The Internet Is The Network.*

If you haven't yet built your first Web-enabled database application, please, please take the time to implement the code in this chapter. It will change your life—professionally, at least.

For this example, I'll use the shareware version of Web Connection. Go to www.west-wind.com and download it. When you've finished this chapter, you can either send Rick $129 for your shareware, or $399 for the whole enchilada. I'd point out some of the additional features included in the complete package, any one of which would be worth the whole price of Web Connection, but I would just start sounding like a salesman, which I'm not; I'm just a very, very satisfied customer. Go ahead, download it. I'll wait right here.

Good, you're back. Let's get started.

Installing Web Connection

First, install Web Connection. I say this as one might say "slice a tomato," but installing Web Connection and configuring your Web server is undoubtedly the most challenging part of this entire exercise. There are four distinct pieces of software involved here, and the database application we're going to write is only one of them. There's Microsoft Internet Information Server (IIS), which comes with Windows but must be installed separately; there is SQL Server, which is a career in itself; and there are the two programs that you're going to write—one for the workstation and the other for the server.

One odd thing you'll soon notice is that the application doesn't have any data files on the client side. That's right, no DBFs. In fact, the entire application when installed, regardless of the number of screens, usually consists of one executable. It's kind of eerie to fire it up and watch data come over the wire. But that's how it works.

It does so by asking a Web server to go to an application server (a FoxPro program that you'll write) that will ask SQL Server (or FoxPro DBFs) for data. The Web server, application server, and SQL Server can be running either on your development machine, on another computer on your LAN, or anywhere on the Internet. During the development phase you'll run both the client and the server on the same computer and then move the server software to a server that can be accessed from anywhere on the Internet.

You must have installed a Web server on the computer before installing Web Connection. The Web server is either Personal Web Server, Internet Information Server 5 (Win2K/XP), or perhaps another such server.

To install Web Connection, extract it to a directory called wconnect on your C: or D: drive, and then run the SETUP.EXE program in the wconnect directory. (When you install it, it will try to run SETUP itself.) It will install the software and prepare two special directories that are used by Web Connection in addition to the \wconnect directory where the server program is installed.

Three conditions must be met during the setup process: IIS has to be correctly installed and running; you will have to set it up to point to a virtual directory that contains part of your server software; and the computer's administrative account must have execute rights to the virtual directory where a little program called wc.dll is going to be installed. If any of these three conditions isn't met, you will have zero, I repeat, zero success. And, these three conditions have nothing to do with the FoxPro programs you're going to write.

I've spent days, maybe weeks, verifying these conditions. They are the heartbreak of Internet programming. However, if you follow Rick's instructions carefully, it will eventually work—unless you're trying to run under Windows 98, in which it may or may not work. So I strongly urge you to do all of this on a computer that's using either Win2K or XP for an operating system. That's the bad news.

All of the rest is good news.

Building Your Application

The truly peculiar part of writing Internet applications is that part of your program is running on one computer, and part of it is running on another one. Here's how it works.

Let's say you want to populate a grid with customers from the state of California. In a traditional FoxPro LAN application, you would write a SQL query like this:

```
SELECT Cust_ID FROM CUSTOMER WHERE STATE = 'CA' INTO CURSOR C1
```

Execute it and bind the resulting cursor to a grid on a form and voilà, you're looking at California customers.

In an Internet application, you construct something like an email that contains the `SELECT` statement and send it to a URL on another computer. The URL must call a program called `wc.dll`, which is the Web Connection component. It's one of only two programs in Web Connection that are written in C++; the rest are all written in FoxPro.

ASP supports (among other things) a `Request` object to read the URL you send to a server, and a `Response` object to send output back to the requestor. IIS takes care of intercepting the URL, running the program named in it, and returning the output (usually HTML) to the computer that sent the URL.

Wc.dll does the same thing. A Web Connection URL must include the wconnect directory, a reference to `wc.dll` (the connection that knows what IIS is expecting), a class name, a function name, and any parameters needed by the function. When the URL arrives, `wc.dll` activates the named class and passes the parameters to the named function in that class. The function first extracts the parameters passed to it using a `wwRequest` object. (You can't use the traditional `PARAMETERS` statement used in FoxPro.) The function constructs and runs the query, and then uses a `wwResponse` object to send back the data in XML format. Your program, meanwhile, is filing its nails and waiting for the data to come back. It sees it, drops the nail file, grabs the data and slaps it into the grid, and voilà redux.

For our example, we'll use the same form that we built in Chapter 2. The only change, it turns out, is in the Data Access Layer.

The Main Program

There are just a few changes to the MAIN program we saw in Chapter 2. They're highlighted in Listing 5.1.

LISTING 5.1   The Main Program

```
* Program-ID..:  MAIN.PRG
* Purpose.....:  MAIN program for application

CLEAR ALL
CLOSE ALL
CLEAR
CLOSE ALL
SET TALK        OFF
```

LISTING 5.1   Continued

```
SET CONFIRM    ON
SET MULTILOCKS ON
SET CENTURY    ON
SET EXCLUSIVE  ON
SET SAFETY     OFF
SET DELETED    ON
SET STRICTDATE TO 0

WITH _Screen
.AddObject ( [Title1], [Title], 0, 0 )
.AddObject ( [Title2], [Title], 3, 3 )
.Title2.ForeColor = RGB ( 255, 0, 0  )
ENDWITH

Global error handler (called if no TRY...CATCH block
* handles an error, or if THROWn from top TRY..CATCH block.
ON ERROR DO ErrTrap WITH LINENO(), PROGRAM(), MESSAGE(), MESSAGE(1)

DO MENU.MPR

SET PROCEDURE TO DataTier.PRG ADDITIVE
oDataTier = CREATEOBJECT ( [DataTier] )
oDataTier.AccessMethod = [DBF]

* Added for WebConnection support
SET PATH       TO WWIPSTUFF

* The next 5 lines refer to Web Connection files
SET CLASSLIB   TO wwIPStuff ADDITIVE
SET PROCEDURE TO wwHTTP     ADDITIVE
SET PROCEDURE TO wwUtils    ADDITIVE
SET PROCEDURE TO WWPOP3     ADDITIVE
SET CLASSLIB   TO wwXML      ADDITIVE

* The following string was needed because my laptop has a different server name.
* Ordinarily the default "(local)" will be adequate.

*!*    oDataTier.ConnectionString = [Driver={SQL Server};]
          + [Server=VAIO\VAIO;Database=Northwind;UID=sa;PWD=;]
*!*    oDataTier.AccessMethod = [SQL Server]     && Last one will be used
```

5

LISTING 5.1   Continued

```
IF NOT EMPTY ( oDataTier.AccessMethod )
   READ EVENTS
ENDIF

ON ERROR

SET PROCEDURE TO
SET CLASSLIB TO

SET SYSMENU TO DEFAULT

WITH _Screen
.RemoveObject ( [Title1] )
.RemoveObject ( [Title2] )
ENDWITH

DEFINE CLASS Title AS Label
Visible   = .T.
BackStyle = 0
FontName  = [Times New Roman]
FontSize  = 48
Height    = 100
Width     = 800
Left      = 25
Caption   = [My application]
ForeColor = RGB ( 192, 192, 192 )

PROCEDURE Init
LPARAMETERS nTop, nLeft
THIS.Top = _Screen.Height - 100 - nTop
THIS.Left=                  25 - nLeft
ENDPROC

ENDDEFINE

PROCEDURE ErrTrap
LPARAMETERS nLine, cProg, cMessage, cMessage1
OnError = ON("Error")
ON ERROR
IF NOT FILE ( [ERRORS.DBF] )
```

LISTING 5.1 Continued

```
  CREATE TABLE ERRORS (;
  Date      Date,        ;
  Time      Char(5),     ;
  LineNum     Integer,    ;
  ProgName     Char(30),   ;
  Msg    Char(240),    ;
  CodeLine     Char(240)    )
ENDIF
IF NOT USED ( [Errors] )
  USE ERRORS IN 0
ENDIF
SELECT Errors
INSERT INTO Errors VALUES ( ;
  DATE(), LEFT(TIME(),5),  nLine, cProg, cMessage, cMessage1 )
USE IN Errors
cStr = [Error at line ] + TRANSFORM(nLine) + [ of ] + cprog + [:] + CHR(13)    ;
    + cMessage + CHR(13) + [Code that caused the error:] + CHR(13) + cMessage1
IF MESSAGEBOX( cStr, 292, [Continue] ) <> 6
  SET SYSMENU TO DEFAULT
  IF TYPE ( [_Screen.Title1] ) <> [U]
    _Screen.RemoveObject ( [Title2] )
    _Screen.RemoveObject ( [Title1] )
  ENDIF
  CLOSE ALL
  RELEASE ALL
  CANCEL
  ELSE
  ON ERROR &OnError
ENDIF
```

The five lines of code about 45 lines down in Listing 5.1 that are preceded by the comment "Web Connection source code" refer to the Web Connection shareware libraries, which in turn call the functions in WWIPSTUFF.DLL, the heart of the product. I've copied these lines from a startup routine that normally would urge you to send Rick your $129.00 for the shareware each time the program starts. The message has been removed, but please remember that this is shareware. If at the end of this exercise you don't think it's worth the price, I would be very surprised.

The StandardForm Class Template

The StandardForm class template is shown in Figure 5.1.

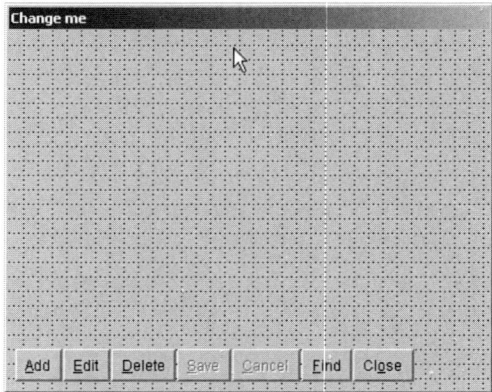

FIGURE 5.1   The StandardForm class template.

I've included in the following snippet the code changes you'll need to make in order to use Internet support:

```
-End-
```

That's right. *There aren't any code changes.*

When we implemented SQL in Chapter 2, we created a cursor to hold the records that we bring back from SQL Server, or the records we add before sending them to SQL Server. These cursors are created in the forms' Load events, before going for data.

An Internet server works exactly the same way, except that now the program goes to the Internet server instead of to SQL Server for the data. It also goes to the Internet server for table structures because that's how cursors are built.

The Internet Server

First let's start building the Internet server. Web Connection installs in a directory structure named \wconnect, typically on the C: drive. If you installed it on another drive, substitute the correct drive letter wherever you see C:. Beneath \wconnect, there are six or seven directories depending on the version. I'm using Web Connection version 4.25 for this book, and at this time the directories are these:

```
Classes
Console
FoxCentral
HTML
Scripts
SoapSamples
Templates
```

```
Tools
Wwdemo
wwDevRegistry
wwIPStuff_Samples
wwReader
wwThreads
```

The shareware version doesn't install all of these; however, the important ones are `Classes` and `wwDemo`. The main directory contains about 15 files, but the one you'll want to look at is called `WCDEMOMAIN.PRG`. Open it up and take a look. About 225 lines down, you'll find a section that looks like Listing 5.2. (I added the last two lines.)

LISTING 5.2   Modifying `WCDEMOMAIN` to Look for Our Web Server Process Class

```
    CASE lcParameter == "WWTHREADS"
        DO wwThreads with THIS

    CASE lcParameter == "WWDEMO"
        DO WWDEMO WITH THIS

    CASE lcParameter == "MYDATASERVER"
        DO MYDATASERVER WITH THIS
```

Web Connection organizes tasks into class libraries written as PRGs. There's a `wwdemo.prg`, a `wwthreads.prg`, and so forth. Each one of them has pretty much the same structure—a `DEFINE CLASS` statement, then some housekeeping, and finally a bunch of `FUNCTION`s and `PROCEDURE`s.

You're required to write a process class that contains your own functions. `wwDemo.PRG` is a sample process class that you can use as a pattern.

How Web Connection works

When a program needs data, it sends an HTTP call to the server using a syntax like this:

```
http://www.lespinter.com/wconnect/wc.dll?wwdemo~Function1~Param1
```

which means "go to `www.lespinter.com`, look in the `wconnect` virtual directory for a program called `wc.dll`, and use it to go to the `wwdemo class library` and run `function1` using the value `Param1` as a parameter."

In a client application, you use an instance of a class called `WWIPSTUFF` to make this call. Within that class, a function named `HTTPGETEX` with three parameters will send the URL and wait for the result. The first parameter is the URL string, the second parameter is the returned string, and the third parameter is a numeric value containing the number of characters in the returned string. It looks like Listing 5.3.

LISTING 5.3   Attempting to Connect to the Server

```
lnReturnCode = oIP.HTTPGetEx ( lcURL, lcReturnedString,lnStrLen)

IF lnReturnCode <> 0
   MessageBox ( [Error connecting to server], 16 )
   RETURN
ENDIF
```

lcURL contains the URL, typically an IP address or Domain Name System (DNS) name (for example, 64.68.235.102 or www.lespinter.com), the wconnect virtual directory name, the wc.dll reference ending with a question mark, the process class library name (a .prg file), a function name, and zero or more parameters. The class library, function name, and parameter names are separated by tildes, and are referred to positionally within the server program. That is, QueryString(1) is the class name, QueryString(2) is the function name, and QueryString(3) is the first parameter. The "http://" prefix is not included. Every single call you make to your Web Connection server will look like this.

The process class library is derived from Rick's wwProcess class. You start with a small skeleton and then add your own functions and procedures. wwDemo.PRG is a sample that ships with Web Connection to show you what a process class is.

How do you set up one of these class libraries? One way is to copy wwdemo.prg to another name, erase most of its contents, and start writing your own using the original wwdemo as a guide. But a utility program that comes with WebConnection will build your empty shell class library for you. Run console.exe and follow the instructions. I named mine MyDataServer, so pick a similarly descriptive name.

After you've added your class library, add two lines to wcDemoMain that direct URLs that reference your process class to the corresponding object by adding the two lines of code shown in Listing 5.2, and you're ready to start writing functions.

I've found two peculiarities in using Web Connection that might also give you a few anxious moments: First, before typing DO WCDEMOMAIN, you need to type the following in the command window:

```
Set path to wwdemo;classes;tools
```

Second, all of Web Connection is quite dependent on wconnect.h, an include file with named constants representing enums (lists of integer codes) used by various Windows components like the WinSock DLL. It has a specific location, and SET PATH doesn't help FoxPro find it. So if you move anything and then start getting messages that HTTP_WHAT-EVER is undefined, try copying WCONNECT.H to wherever you're working. That usually does the trick.

Writing Web Connection Functions

Web Connection server functions typically look in either the `QueryString` or the post buffer for parameters; then they construct a data command (`SELECT`, `INSERT`, `UPDATE`, or `DELETE`) and execute it; finally, if a `SELECT` was issued, the results are sent back.

There are five objects in the ASP model. Web Connection has classes that mimic each of them. One mimics the `Request` object, and another the `Response` object. I like to instantiate these two objects in my Web Connection code with the names `Request` and `Response`, so that I forget which language I'm in and start writing in Visual BasicScript.

Passing Parameters

There are two ways you can send data to a Web page. One is called `GET` and the other is called `POST`. `GET` means you can see the parameters, whereas `POST` means you can't.

GET Parameters

In an ASP program, the following statement

```
lcName = request("Name")
```

will return the value of `Name` in a URL that looks like this:

```
http://www.lespinter.com/subscriptions/login.asp?name=JoeBob
```

Web Connection has a `Request` object, which works a lot like Internet Explorer's `Request` object. However, Web Connection uses the slightly more formal syntax

```
lcEverything = Request.QueryString()
```

for the entire string, or

```
lcName = request.QueryString("Name")
```

for the `Name` value. However, because these are programs talking to programs, we generally simply separate the parameters with tildes ("~") and count them, like this:

```
lcName = request.QueryString(3)
```

That's slightly confusing because the first parameter is the class library name and the function name is the second one, making your first parameter the third one as far as Web Connection is concerned. You'll get used to it.

Here's an example: The following URL sends the name of a table, a key field, and a value from a user who has just picked a name from a drop-down list of customers in Alabama and wants the customer record:

```
http://www.lespinter.com/wconnect/wc.dll?
➥MyDataServer~GetOneRecord~Customers~CustID~3012214
```

The server code to respond to this might be as shown in Listing 5.4.

LISTING 5.4   Web Connection Function to Return a Single Record

```
FUNCTION GetOnerecord
pTable = Request.QueryString(3)
pKeyField = Request.QueryString(4)
pKeyValue = Request.QueryString(5)
cmd = [SELECT * FROM ] + pTable + [ WHERE ] + pKeyField + [=] + pKeyValue
cmd = cmd + [ INTO CURSOR C1]
&Cmd
CursorToXML ( "C1", "lcXML" )
USE IN C1
USE IN ( pTable )
Response.Write ( lcXML )
ENDFUNC
```

However, there are limits to the size of the GET string, which I think is about 128 charac-ters. It's irrelevant, though, because we generally don't want to send our data across the Internet in clear text that absolutely anyone can read, so we'll rarely use GET. Instead, we'll use POST, which stores the variables in a bag called the **post buffer**. They can also be encrypted, which is what you'll eventually want to do with sensitive information.

POST **Variables**

If you instead stuff values into the post buffer, they're hidden. To add a variable and its corresponding value to the post buffer, in your client program you might have this:

```
oIP.AddPostKey ( Value, "key" )
```

The entire URL is then simply

```
http://www.lespinter.com/wconnect/wc.dll?MyDataServer~ShowMeDaData
```

Any parameters, records being sent to be stored, or whatever, are no one's business but your own. There's an AddPostKey function for just that purpose, as you'll see shortly.

GET and POST are only important when sending data or requests to a server. Servers send back whatever you want. It can be an HTML page, of course; but it can also be XML, or a DBF, or an encrypted string.

The next few lines are calls to the WWIPSTUFF class library that's included in Web Connection. It essentially sends a request to the server, waiting for a string containing the results to be returned in the variable lcBuffer.

I've chosen to demonstrate two ways to pass data back: a DBF and an XML string. If a DBF is returned, you just use StrToFile() to turn it back into a DBF and APPEND FROM to read it into the CARRIER cursor. If an XML string is created on the server and returned, it's converted back to a cursor when it's received. In either event it takes about a second (see Listing 5.5).

LISTING 5.5   Using the Post Buffer to Send Parameters to the Web Server

```
lnConnect = o.HTTPConnect ( Server )
  IF lnConnect <> 0
    MessageBox ( ;
      [Couldn't connect to Internet Server], ;
      64, _Screen.Caption )
    .cmdCancel.Click
  ENDIF
  lcBuffer = []
  lnBufLen = 0
  o.AddPostKey  ( [RESET] )
  o.AddPostKey  ( [ParmC], ParmC )
  o.HTTPGetEx   (  FuncC,  @lcBuffer, @lnBufLen  )
  SELECT Carrier
  ZAP
  DO CASE
    CASE gcMethod = [DBF]
   StrToFile    (  lcBuffer, [Carrier.DBF] )
   APPEND FROM Carrier.DBF
   DELETE FILE Carrier.DBF
    OTHERWISE         && must be XML
   lcXML = ALLTRIM( lcBuffer )
   oXML.XMLToCursor ( lcXML,[Carrier] )
  ENDCASE
ENDIF
ENDWITH
WITH THISFORM.List1
IF _Tally > 0
  SCAN
    .AddListItem ( Company      )
    Row = .NewItemID
      .AddListItem ( City,    Row, 2)
       .AddListItem ( Region,  Row, 3)
       .AddListItem ( Cust_ID, Row, 4)
  ENDSCAN
  .ListIndex   = 1
  .Selected[1] = .T.
  THISFORM.cmdSelect.Enabled = .T.
```

5

LISTING 5.5   Continued

```
ELSE
   THISFORM.cmdSelect.Enabled = .F.
ENDIF
ENDWITH
ENDPROC
```

The AddPostKey method stuffs strings into the HTTP transport and sends them over. It's the cleanest way to send strings that contain blanks; otherwise you get all of those funny tildes and pluses.

Show All Customers is even easier; however, it's not advisable in most cases. I'm only doing it here because I know there are just a few records in the table (see Listing 5.6).

LISTING 5.6   Code to Return All Customers

```
PROCEDURE cmdall.Click
SELECT Carrier
ZAP
THISFORM.List1.Clear
FuncC = Prefix +( gcAllCustomers )
lnConnect = o.HTTPConnect ( Server )
IF lnConnect <> 0
   MessageBox ( ;
   [Couldn't connect to Internet Server], ;
   64, _Screen.Caption )
   cmdCancel.Click
ENDIF

lcBuffer = []
lnBufLen = 0
o.HTTPGetEx  ( FuncC,  @lcBuffer, @lnBufLen )
DO CASE
   CASE gcMethod = [DBF]
   StrToFile ( lcBuffer, [Carrier.DBF] )
   SELECT Carrier
   APPEND FROM Carrier.DBF
   DELETE FILE Carrier.DBF
   OTHERWISE        && must be XML
   lcXML = ALLTRIM( lcBuffer )
   oXML.XMLToCursor ( lcXML, [Carrier] )
ENDCASE
WITH THISFORM.List1
```

LISTING 5.6   Continued

```
SCAN
    .AddListItem ( Company        )
     Row = .NewItemID
    .AddListItem ( City,    Row, 2)
    .AddListItem ( Region,  Row, 3)
    .AddListItem ( Cust_ID, Row, 4)
ENDSCAN

.ListIndex    =  1
.Selected[1] = .T.
ENDWITH
ENDPROC
```

Think through the code for a few minutes and you'll see what's going on. You send off a query in the first parameter of HttpGetEx and then wait for the answer to be returned in lcBuffer as a string. You'll then convert it from either a DBF or from XML.

An XML Primer

XML is simplicity itself. (We'll talk about it in detail in Chapter 7, "XML.") If you have a CUSTOMER record with fields NAME, PHONE, and BALANCE, the XML of that record will look like this:

```
<name>Joe Blow</name>
<phone>555-1212</phone>
<balance>123.45</balance>
```

All data is converted to strings for XML transport. The XMLTOCURSOR() method of WWIP-STUFF class converts it back to the correct data types, using the corresponding field names in an open cursor to type the data.

The method call

```
lcXML = oXML.CursorToXML()
```

reads the currently open cursor and stores its XML representation in string lcXML. Its inverse function is

```
oXML.XMLtoCursor ( lcXML )
```

which takes the string and dumps it into the cursor that's open in the current work area, using field names alone to determine what goes where and what data types to use. (It doesn't have to be the current work area, but I'm trying to make this as simple as possible.)

You can also use something called a DTD. There are thick books about XML, and you don't need to know any of it for what we're doing here. If you're one of those anal-retentive types who delights in theoretical purity, you're reading the wrong book.

The Customer Form

The Customer form is based on the StandardForm template. I included some basic capabilities in StandardForm, but a few additional features need to be added for each form that we build. The customer form appears in Figure 5.2.

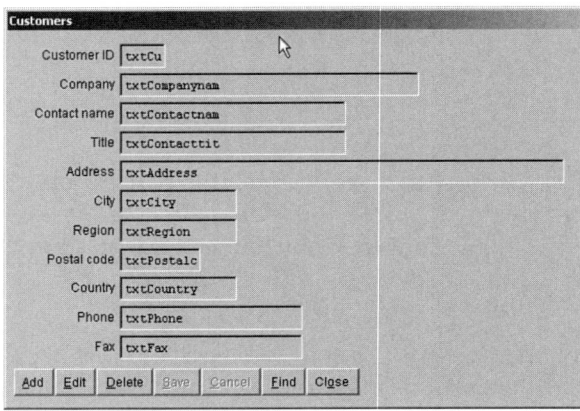

FIGURE 5.2   The Customer form.

The Load event creates a cursor that matches the data source (see Listing 5.7). If you're using SQL Server, the FoxPro data types are slightly different: SQL's Text is our Memo, Money is our Y field, and TinyInt and Smallint are just Int. For SQL VarChar, you can use either Memo or Char.

LISTING 5.7   Load Event for the Form

```
PROCEDURE Load
CREATE CURSOR Customer (;
  CUST_ID    Char( 6), ;
  COMPANY    Char(40), ;
  CONTACT    Char(30), ;
  TITLE        Char(30), ;
  ADDRESS    Char(60), ;
  CITY        Char(15), ;
  REGION        Char(15), ;
  POSTALCODE    Char(10), ;
  COUNTRY    Char(15), ;
  PHONE        Char(24), ;
```

LISTING 5.7   Continued

```
FAX         Char(24), ;
MAXORDAMT    Y        )
ENDPROC
```

The users have to go to the server to pick a record. That's why, unlike what we're used to in the FoxPro world, the screen in most SQL apps is initially empty. The Find function described in Listing 5.8 lets them find a record to display on the form.

LISTING 5.8   Click Event Code for the Find Button

```
PROCEDURE cmdFind.Click

WITH THISFORM

DO FORM GetCust TO CustKey  && GetCust is a MODAL form

IF NOT    EMPTY ( CustKey )
   o.HTTPConnect ( Server )
   lcBuffer = []
   lnBufLen = 0
   o.HTTPGetEx ( Prefix + gcSelectedCustomer + [~] ;
       + CustKey, @lcBuffer, @lnBufLen )
   IF NOT EMPTY ( lcBuffer )
      SELECT CUSTOMER
      ZAP
      DO CASE
        CASE gcMethod = [DBF]
            StrToFile     ( lcBuffer, [Carrier.DBF] )
            APPEND FROM Carrier.DBF
            DELETE FILE Carrier.DBF
        OTHERWISE         && must be XML
            lcXML = ALLTRIM( lcBuffer )
            oXML.XMLToCursor ( lcXML, [Customer])
      ENDCASE
   ENDIF
   .Refresh
   .cmdEdit.Enabled   = .T.
   .cmdDelete.Enabled = .T.
ELSE
   .cmdEdit.Enabled   = .F.
   .cmdDelete.Enabled = .F.
ENDIF
```

LISTING 5.8 Continued

```
.cmdNext.Enabled = .T.
.cmdPrev.Enabled = .T.

ENDWITH
ENDPROC
```

They might just want to add a record. See the template `cmdAdd.click` code shown in Listing 5.9 to see what happens here. Except for our code to ensure that the cursor is zapped before the default `cmdADD.Click` method code runs, there's little difference.

LISTING 5.9 Click Event Code for the Add Button

```
PROCEDURE cmdAdd.Click
SELECT Customer
ZAP
DODEFAULT()
ENDPROC
```

There's no `cmdEdit.Click` code because it's exactly the same as the template code—enable the input fields, then disable all buttons except Save and Cancel. Note that in the template code a form property called `Adding` is set to `True` during an add, because it's very, very important when it comes time to save changes or additions.

Introducing the Server

Depending on what the user's application reads from `CONTROL.TXT`, it's going to ask the app server to run one of three different functions for each of the main tasks—Save, Return a record or records, Delete a record, or skip Forward or Back. To do so, it passes the name of the function to run.

I've included functions to return data in three different ways:

- As a DBF—I don't even zip the file, although it's easy and advisable to do so

- As an XML string built from a DBF

- As an XML string built from a cursor created from data selected from SQL Server

Because of the way I've written this application, it can use either a DBF or SQL Server tables on the server side with no changes in the user's application software. The middle tier—your function in the `MyCode` class library in the `wwdemo` subdirectory of the `wconnect` directory of your app server—stores and retrieves data based on which functions are called. So you can write FoxPro applications that use either DBFs or SQL Server as the data repository, and the Internet as the network. All you have to do is build an app server that has one function for each thing you want to do. As you will see in Listing 5.10, the average Web Connection function is about 8 or 10 lines long.

When you buy Web Connection, it gives you a Console routine to run, which builds a complete project, including a new shell class library where you'll add your own functions. If your class library is called ZCls, your call to a function called F1 on your server would look like this:

```
http://www.MySite.com/wconnect/wc.dll?Zcls~F1
```

However, because you're building this using the shareware version, let's keep it simple. The shareware install creates a subdirectory called wwdemo, and it already contains a little class file called Mycode.prg that will do just fine. So you can open it up and add your functions, and then call it using

```
http://www.MySite.com/wconnect/wc.dll?Mycode~F1
```

That's why line 70 or so of MAIN.PRG assigned a similar string to the global variable Prefix. Listing 5.10 shows a typical Web Connection class library to take care of your remote data access needs.

LISTING 5.10   My App Server Code

```
*PROCEDURE MyDataServer

LPARAMETER loServer
LOCAL loProcess
#INCLUDE WCONNECT.H
loProcess=CREATE("wwDemo",loServer)
loProcess.lShowRequestData = loServer.lShowRequestData
IF VARTYPE(loProcess)#"O"
   WAIT WINDOW NOWAIT "Unable to create Process object..."
   RETURN .F.
ENDIF
loProcess.Process()
RETURN


#DEFINE HOMEPATH  "/wconnect/"
#DEFINE HOMEPAGE  HOMEPATH+"default.htm"
#DEFINE BACKIMG   ""
#DEFINE PAGEFOOT  [<p><HR>]+CRLF;
               + [<A HREF="http://www.west-wind.com/webconnection/">] ;
               + [<IMG SRC="/wconnect/wcpower.gif" BORDER=0 HSPACE=5 ] ;
               + [ALIGN=LEFT ALT="Powered by Web Connection"></a>];
```

LISTING 5.10   Continued

```
                       + [<FONT SIZE=-1>Query created by ] ;
                        + [<A HREF="mailto:rstrahl@west-wind.com">Rick Strahl</A><BR>];
                       + '[<A HREF="'+HOMEPATH+ 'default.htm">] ;
                       + [Web Connection demo page</A>] ;
                       + [<A HREF="/wconnect/wc.dll?wwdemo] ;
                       + [~ShowCode~'+THIS.oRequest.QueryString(2)+'">] ;
                       + [Show Code</a>]'


********************************
DEFINE CLASS wwDemo AS wwProcess
********************************


cHTMLPagePath = ""
cDataPath = ""


*******************
* wwDemo :: Process
*******************
FUNCTION Process
LOCAL lcParameter, lcOutFile, lcIniFile, lcOldError
THIS.CHTMLPAGEPATH = THIS.oServer.oConfig.owwDemo.cHTMLPagePath
THIS.CDATAPATH = THIS.oServer.oConfig.owwDemo.cDataPath
THIS.oResponse.cStyleSheet = "westwind.css"
Config = THIS.oServer.oConfig.owwDemo
DODEFAULT()
RETURN .T.
ENDFUNC


FUNCTION GetRecords
loXML    = CREATE("wwXML")
* loXML.nCreateDataStructure = 1  && Schema
loXML.cDocRootName = "GetRecords"
lcAccess = UPPER(Request.Form("DataAccess"))
lcCmd    = Request.Form("Cmd")
IF lcAccess = "DBF"
   lcCmd = lcCmd + " INTO CURSOR C1"
  &lcCmd
   lcXML = loXML.CursorToXml ( "C1s", "C1" )
  ELSE
  Handle = SQLSTRINGCONNECT(THIS.Connstring)
  IF Handle > 0
     lr = SQLEXEC( Handle, Cmd, [C1] )
```

LISTING 5.10   Continued

```
      IF lr <= 0 Then
         lcXML = [Error: SQL SELECT error]
        ELSE
         lcXML = loXML.CursorToXml ( "C1s", "C1" )
      ENDIF
    ELSE
         lcXML = [Error: SQL connection error]
   ENDIF
ENDIF
SQLDISCONNECT(0)
Response.ContentType="text/xml"
lcXML = loXML.CursorToXML("Records","Record")
IF USED ( "C1"  )
   USE IN  C1
ENDIF
Response.Write( loXML.EncodeXML(lcXML) )
RELEASE loXML
ENDFUNC


FUNCTION GetStructure
lcAccess = UPPER(Request.QueryString(3))
lcTable  = UPPER(Request.QueryString(4))
lcDBF    = UPPER(Request.QueryString(5))  && if nonblank, return a dbf
DO CASE
   CASE lcAccess = [DBF]
       IF lcDBF == ""
            SELECT 0
            USE ( lcTable )
            COPY STRUCTURE EXTENDED TO C1
            USE C1
            COPY TO x.TXT DELIM
            USE
            lcStru = FILETOSTR( "X.txt" )
            ERASE x.TXT
          ELSE
            SELECT 0
            USE ( lcTable )
            COPY STRUCTURE EXTENDED TO C1
            USE
            SELECT 0
            CREATE TABLE Carrier ( ;
                    field_name char(20), field_type char(1), ;
```

LISTING 5.10   Continued

```
                    field_len numeric(3), field_dec numeric(3) )
            APPEND FROM  C1
            ERASE C1.*
            LOCAL oIP as WWIPSTUFF
            oIP = CREA ( "WWIPSTUFF" )
            USE IN CARRIER
            lcStru = oIP.EncodeDBF ( "CARRIER.DBF", .F. )
            ERASE Carrier.dbf
        ENDIF
        Response.Write( lcStru )

    CASE lcAccess = [SQL]
        Handle = SQLSTRINGCONNECT(THIS.Connstring)
        IF Handle > 0
           lr = SQLEXEC( Handle, Cmd, [C1] )
           IF lr <= 0 Then
              lcXML = [Error: SQL SELECT error]
            ELSE
              lcXML = loXML.CursorToXml ( "C1s", "C1" )
           ENDIF
           SQLDISCONNECT(0)
          ELSE
           lcXML = [Error: SQL connection error]
        ENDIF
ENDCASE
RELEASE loXML
ENDFUNC


FUNCTION GetMatchingRecords
lcAccess = UPPER(Request.QueryString(3))
lcCmd    =        Request.QueryString(4)
lcTable  =        Request.QueryString(5)
lcEncode =        Request.QueryString(6)
DO CASE
   CASE lcAccess = [DBF]
        lcCmd = lcCmd + [ INTO CURSOR C1]
        &lcCmd    && Results are now in cursor C1
        IF lcEncode == ""    && return a comma-delimited list of fields
           COPY TO x.TXT DELIM
           USE
           lcStru = FILETOSTR( "X.txt" )
           ERASE x.TXT
```

LISTING 5.10   Continued

```
            ELSE
             COPY TO CARRIER
             HasMemo = THIS.DoesTableHaveAMemoField()
             USE IN C1
             LOCAL oIP AS  WWIPSTUFF
             oIP = CREA ( "WWIPSTUFF")
             lcStru = oIP.EncodeDBF ( "CARRIER.DBF", HasMemo )
             ERASE Carrier.DBF
          ENDIF
          IF USED   ( lcTable )
             USE IN ( lcTable )
          ENDIF
          Response.Write( lcStru )
ENDCASE
ENDFUNC


FUNCTION GetOneRecord
lcAccess   = UPPER(Request.QueryString(3))
lcTable    =         Request.QueryString(4)
lcKeyField =         Request.QueryString(5)
lcKeyValue =         Request.QueryString(6)
lcEncode   =         Request.QueryString(7)
DO CASE
   CASE lcAccess = [DBF]
        SELECT 0
        USE ( lcTable )
        Dlm = IIF ( TYPE(lcKeyField ) $ [CM], ['], [] )
        *  Either string or numeric
        lcCmd      = [SELECT * FROM ] + lcTable + [ WHERE ] ;
                     + lcKeyField + [=] + Dlm + lcKeyValue + Dlm
        lcCmd = lcCmd + [ INTO CURSOR C1]
        &lcCmd    && Results are now in cursor C1
        IF lcEncode == ""    && return a comma-delimited list of fields
           COPY TO x.TXT DELIM
           USE
           lcStru = FILETOSTR( "X.txt" )
           ERASE x.TXT
        ELSE
           COPY TO CARRIER
           HasMemo = THIS.DoesTableHaveAMemoField()
           USE IN C1
           LOCAL oIP AS  WWIPSTUFF
```

LISTING 5.10   Continued

```
                oIP = CREA ( "WWIPSTUFF")
                lcStru = oIP.EncodeDBF ( "CARRIER.DBF", HasMemo )
                ERASE Carrier.DBF
            ENDIF
            IF USED   ( lcTable )
                USE IN ( lcTable )
            ENDIF
            Response.Write( lcStru )
ENDCASE
ENDFUNC


FUNCTION DoesTableHaveAMemoField
HasMemo = .F.
FOR I = 1 TO FCOUNT()
    IF TYPE ( FIELD(I)) = [M]
        HasMemo = .T.
        Exit       && Only need to find one
    ENDIF
ENDFOR
RETURN HasMemo


PROCEDURE InsertOrUpdateRecord
Use POST buffer variables, since the command string may be quite
* long and sensitive data may be included
lcAccess = UPPER(Request.Form("Access"))
lcCmd    =        Request.Form("Cmd"   )
lcTable  =        Request.Form("Table" )
*!*    _Screen.Print ( CHR(13) + lcCmd )
DO CASE
    CASE lcAccess = [DBF]
        &lcCmd
        IF USED   ( lcTable )
            USE IN ( lcTable )
        ENDIF
    CASE lcAccess = [SQL]
        Handle = SQLSTRINGCONNECT(THIS.Connstring)
        IF Handle > 0
            lr = SQLEXEC( Handle, lcCmd )
            IF lr <= 0 Then
                lcResult = [Error: SQL UPDATE/INSERT error]
             ELSE
                lcResult = [Ok]
```

LISTING 5.10   Continued

```
            ENDIF
          ELSE
              lcResult = [Error: SQL connection error]
        ENDIF
        Response.Write ( lcResult )   && Either "Ok" or "Error"
ENDCASE
ENDPROC

PROCEDURE GetNextKeyValue
lcAccess  = UPPER(Request.QueryString(3))
lcTable   = UPPER(Request.QueryString(4))
EXTERNAL ARRAY laVal
DO CASE

   CASE lcAccess = [DBF]
        IF NOT FILE ( [Keys.DBF] )
           CREATE TABLE Keys ( TableName Char(20), LastKeyVal Integer )
        ENDIF
        IF NOT USED ( [Keys] )
           USE Keys IN 0
        ENDIF
        SELECT Keys
        LOCATE FOR TableName = lcTable
        IF NOT FOUND()
           INSERT INTO Keys VALUES ( lcTable, 0 )
        ENDIF
        Cmd = [UPDATE Keys SET LastKeyVal=LastKeyVal + 1 ]     ;
            + [ WHERE TableName='] + lcTable + [']
        &Cmd
        Cmd = [SELECT LastKeyVal FROM Keys WHERE TableName = '] ;
            + lcTable + [' INTO ARRAY laVal]
        &Cmd
        USE IN Keys
        lcResult = TRANSFORM(laVal(1))
        Response.Write ( lcResult )

   CASE lcAccess = [SQL]

        Cmd = [SELECT Name FROM SysObjects WHERE Name='KEYS' AND Type='U']
        lr = SQLEXEC( THIS.Handle, Cmd )
        IF lr < 0
           lcResult = [Error: ] + CHR(13) + Cmd
```

5

LISTING 5.10 Continued

```
         IF lcResult = [Error]
            Response.Write ( lcResult )
            RETURN
         ENDIF
      ENDIF

   IF RECCOUNT([SQLResult]) = 0
      Cmd = [CREATE TABLE Keys ( TableName Char(20), LastKeyVal Integer )]
      lr = SQLEXEC( THIS.Handle, Cmd )
      IF lr < 0
         lcResult = [Error: ] + CHR(13) + Cmd
      ENDIF
      IF lcResult = [Error]
         Response.Write ( lcResult )
         RETURN
      ENDIF
   ENDIF

   Cmd = [SELECT LastKeyVal FROM Keys WHERE TableName='] + lcTable + [']
   lr = SQLEXEC( THIS.Handle, Cmd )
   IF lr < 0
      IF lr < 0
         lcResult = [Error: ] + CHR(13) + Cmd
      ENDIF
      IF lcResult = [Error]
         Response.Write ( lcResult )
         RETURN
      ENDIF
   ENDIF

   IF RECCOUNT([SQLResult]) = 0
      Cmd = [INSERT INTO Keys VALUES ('] +  lcTable + [', 0 )]
      lr = SQLEXEC( THIS.Handle, Cmd )
      IF lr < 0
         IF lr < 0
            lcResult = [Error: ] + CHR(13) + Cmd
         ENDIF
         IF lcResult = [Error]
            Response.Write ( lcResult )
            RETURN
         ENDIF
      ENDIF
   ENDIF
```

LISTING 5.10   Continued

```
      Cmd = [UPDATE Keys SET LastKeyVal=LastKeyVal + 1] ;
        + [ WHERE TableName='] + lcTable + [']
      lr = SQLEXEC( THIS.Handle, Cmd )
      IF lr < 0
        IF lr < 0
          lcResult = [Error: ] + CHR(13) + Cmd
        ENDIF
        IF lcResult = [Error]
          Response.Write ( lcResult )
          RETURN
        ENDIF
      ENDIF

      Cmd = [SELECT LastKeyVal FROM Keys WHERE TableName='] + lcTable + [']
      lr = SQLEXEC( THIS.Handle, Cmd )
      IF lr < 0
        IF lr < 0
          lcResult = [Error: ] + CHR(13) + Cmd
        ENDIF
        IF lcResult = [Error]
          Response.Write ( lcResult )
          RETURN
        ENDIF
      ENDIF

      lcResult = TRANSFORM(SQLResult.LastKeyVal)
      USE IN SQLResult
      Response.Write ( lcResult )

ENDCASE
ENDPROC

PROCEDURE DeleteRecord
lcAccess   = UPPER(Request.QueryString(3))
lcTable    = UPPER(Request.QueryString(4))
lcKeyField = UPPER(Request.QueryString(5))
lcKeyValue = UPPER(Request.QueryString(6))
lcDelim    = UPPER(Request.QueryString(7))
lcCmd      = [DELETE FROM ] + lcTable       ;
           + [ WHERE ] + lcKeyField + [=]    ;
           + lcDelim + lcKeyValue + lcDelim
DO CASE
```

LISTING 5.10 Continued

```
   CASE lcAccess = [DBF]
        &lcCmd
        IF USED   ( lcTable )
           USE IN ( lcTable )
        ENDIF
        lcResult = [Ok]
   CASE lcAccess = [SQL]
        Handle = SQLSTRINGCONNECT(THIS.Connstring)
        IF Handle > 0
           lr = SQLEXEC( Handle, lcCmd )
           IF lr <= 0 Then
              lcResult = [Error: SQL DELETE error]
            ELSE
              lcResult = [Ok]
           ENDIF
          ELSE
              lcResult = [Error: SQL connection error]
        ENDIF
ENDCASE
Response.Write ( lcResult )  && Either "Ok" or "Error"
ENDPROC


FUNCTION GetTable
lcTable   = UPPER(Request.QueryString(3))
Cmd = [SELECT * FROM ] + lcTable + [ INTO CURSOR C1]
loXML = CREATE("wwXML")
*!*    loXML.cDocRootName = "GetTable"
&Cmd
lcXML = loXML.CursorToXml ( "C1s", "C1" )
Response.Write ( lcXML )
USE IN   C1
USE IN ( lcTable )
ENDFUNC


ENDDEFINE
*EOC MyDataServer.PRG
```

I've written one function to handle each type of data transport. So if CONTROL.TXT
contains

```
Server = P400
Method = DBF
```

the program will look around the LAN for a computer named P400, and then send a request to the app server to perform the requested operation by calling a function that returns a DBF. If I write "Method SQL" in Control.txt, the call to HttpGetEx will send a function call to the equivalent SQL function in my app server class library.

In my class library I have a SQLNextCustomer function and a DBFNextCustomer function. The differences are

- The syntax of the SELECT command

- The way the data string is returned

Change the Method assignment in Control.txt to XML, and it still uses a DBF, but uses XML to send it back and forth. Use SQL+XML, and it looks for data in a SQL Server table.

In wcDemoMain.prg I added a few lines of code to open a connection to SQL Server (see Listing 5.11). I used a DSN-less connection so that you don't have to screw with ODBC.

LISTING 5.11   Opening a Connection to SQL Server or MSDE

```
lstr = [uid=sa;pwd=;server=P400;] ;
   + [ driver={SQL Server};database=Customers;]
lh = SQLStringConnect ( lstr )
IF lh < 0
   MessageBox ( ;
     [Couldn't connect to SQL Server ] + pServerName,;
     64, [UGripe] )
   RETURN
ENDIF
```

P400 is my server. You can also use (local) or an IP address. You may need to include UID and PWD parameters if you don't use a DSN. SQL Server can be on any machine on the same LAN as the app server program. You'll also have to add two lines of code to wcDemoMain's PROCESS class to tell it to look at your library of functions, as shown in Listing 5.12.

LISTING 5.12   Redirecting the Request to the New Process Class

```
    CASE lcParameter == "WWDEMO"
       DO WWDEMO WITH THIS


    CASE lcParameter == "MYCODE"     <<- New
       DO MYCODE WITH THIS           <<- New
...
```

The user application can connect to any computer on the Internet that's running your server. If your server is connected to the Internet, open up the command window and type IPCONFIG, and then write down the IP address that has been assigned to your computer. Then go across the street with your laptop, edit Control.txt and enter the IP address as the Server, and restart the eCustomer application. Ta-da!

The SEND2DBF and SEND2SQL Functions

The two big labor-savers in this application are a pair of generic functions that I wrote a year ago to build SQL UPDATE and INSERT statements on the fly. They can be called with any open cursor selected. The DBF version is shown in Listing 5.13.

LISTING 5.13   Building INSERT and UPDATE Statements for SQL

```
* Program-Id....: Send2DBF.PRG
PARAMETERS ;
  CommandOrProc, CursorName, WhereClause, IdentityField
IF EMPTY ( CommandOrProc )
   RETURN [No command string was sent.]
ENDIF
IF NOT CommandOrProc $ [ADD/EDIT]
   RETURN [Valid commands are ADD and EDIT.]
ENDIF
IF NOT EMPTY ( WhereClause ) AND WhereClause <> [WHERE]
   RETURN [Where clause doesn't start with WHERE.]
ENDIF
Adding = .F.
DO CASE
   CASE CommandOrProc = [ADD]
     Adding = .T.
     BuildInsertString()
   CASE CommandOrProc = [EDIT]
     BuildUpdateString()
   OTHERWISE
* Stored Procedure - just execute it
ENDCASE
&CommandOrProc
RETURN [Ok]

PROCEDURE BuildInsertString
CommandOrProc = [INSERT INTO ]+CursorName+[ VALUES ( ]
* Assumes that a temporary cursor is open
FOR I = 1 TO FCOUNT()
   Fld = FIELD(I)
   IF NOT EMPTY ( IdentityField)
```

LISTING 5.13   Continued

```
      IF Fld = UPPER(IdentityField)
    LOOP
      ENDIF
    ENDIF
    DO CASE
    CASE TYPE ( Fld ) $ [IN]
     Str = ALLTRIM(STR(&fld))
    CASE TYPE ( Fld ) $ [CM]
     Str = [']+STRTR(ALLT(&fld),['],['']) + [']
    CASE TYPE ( Fld ) = [Y]
     Str = ALLTRIM(STR(MTON(&fld),10,2))
    CASE TYPE ( Fld ) = [TD]
        Str=IIF(EMPTY(&Fld),[''],['] + TTOC(&fld) + ['])
    ENDCASE
    CommandOrProc=CommandOrProc+Str+IIF(I=FCOUNT(),[],[,])
ENDFOR
CommandOrProc = CommandOrProc + [ )]
ENDPROC


PROCEDURE BuildUpdateString
CommandOrProc = [UPDATE ] + CursorName + [ SET ]
FOR I = 1 TO FCOUNT() && Assumes temporary cursor is open
   Fld = FIELD(I)
   IF NOT EMPTY ( WhereClause )
    IF Fld $ UPPER(WhereClause)
       LOOP
    ENDIF
   ENDIF
   DO CASE
      CASE TYPE ( Fld ) $ [IN]
       Str = ALLTRIM(STR(&fld))
      CASE TYPE ( Fld ) $ [CM]
       Str = ['] + STRTRAN(ALLTRIM(&fld),['],['']) + [']
      CASE TYPE ( Fld ) = [Y]
       Str = ALLTRIM(STR(MTON(&fld),10,2))
      CASE TYPE ( Fld ) = [TD]
       Str = IIF(EMPTY(&Fld),[''],[']+TTOC(&fld)+['])
   ENDCASE
   Str =  Fld + [=] + Str
   CommandOrProc=CommandOrProc+Str+IIF(I=FCOUNT(),[],[,])
ENDFOR
CommandOrProc = CommandOrProc + [ ] + WhereClause
ENDPROC
```

5

The UPDATE statement requires a WHERE clause, which I pass to the function. If you have a key field that has its own method for generating the next unique value, it's automatic in SQL, but in Visual FoxPro you have to deal with it differently. In SQL you leave it out of the VALUES list, but in a FoxPro DBF you call a function like my AutoIncrement function (see my article #221 at www.LesPinter.com) and include it in the list. So you need two different functions: The source code download has both the DBF and the SQL version.

Database Design Still Matters

The sample file uses a very, very bad idea—a key field (CUST_ID) that's a user-specified string. These originated back in the days when users thought they should be able to construct little mnemonics to use as search keys, so that they would know, for example, that SMITH01 was Joe Smith and SMITH02 was Fred Smith. The way to search for records is the way we do it in our GetCust.SCX; the user never even has to see the key.

Table design matters even more in the Internet environment. Keys should be consecutive integers, period. If users can type in their own keys, you have to make an extra trip to the server to make sure they're not trying to add a key that's already in use. What's the point? Users don't even have to know the primary key. SQL Server will generate the next integer key if you simply define the key like this:

```
Cust_ID Integer IDENTITY(1,1)
```

If you're using a DBF, you can use a modification of our AutoIncrement function in the DBFSaveCustomer function. You can make the necessary modifications yourself. It only takes a few minutes. Email me if you need help in doing so.

The use of a user-supplied character string as a primary key in this table has led to countless clumsy imitations by Microsoft customers who assumed that the samples demonstrated good database techniques. And this poor example, which originated with the Access Northwind database, crept into the FoxPro samples without being strangled by someone on the Fox team who should have known better. Hard to imagine.

Modifying the Data Tier to Add Internet Data Access

Listing 5.14 shows the Data Tier program, modified to include calls to Web Connection (DataAccess = [WC]). This will work with both Visual FoxPro 7 and later versions, although in Listing 5.14 we'll include the code to support Visual FoxPro 8 specifically (DataAccess = [XML]).

LISTING 5.14   Adding Internet Access to the Data Tier

```
DEFINE CLASS DataTier AS Custom
AccessMethod = []
* Any attempt to assign a value to this property will be trapped
* by the "setter" method AccessMethod_Assign.
```

LISTING 5.14   Continued

```
ConnectionString = ;
[Driver={SQL Server};Server=(Local);Database=Northwind;UID=sa;PWD=;]
Handle         = 0

* Added for WebConnection:
MyServerURL    = [localhost/]
Prefix         = [wconnect/wc.dll?MydataServer~]
SvrDataAccess = [DBF]      && Either DBF or SQL (on the Server)

PROCEDURE AccessMethod_Assign
PARAMETERS AM
DO CASE
   CASE AM = [DBF]
        THIS.AccessMethod = [DBF]     && FoxPro tables
   CASE AM = [SQL]
        THIS.AccessMethod = [SQL]     && MS Sql Server
        THIS.GetHandle
   CASE AM = [XML]
        THIS.AccessMethod = [XML]     && FoxPro XMLAdapter
   CASE AM = [WC]
        THIS.AccessMethod = [WC]      && WebConnection server
   OTHERWISE
        MESSAGEBOX( [Incorrect access method ] + AM, 16, [Setter error] )
        THIS.AccessMethod = []
ENDCASE
_VFP.Caption = [Data access method: ] + THIS.AccessMethod
ENDPROC

PROCEDURE GetHandle
IF THIS.AccessMethod = [SQL]
   IF THIS.Handle > 0
      RETURN
   ENDIF
   THIS.Handle = SQLSTRINGCONNECT( THIS.ConnectionString )
   IF THIS.Handle < 1
      MESSAGEBOX( [Unable to connect], 16, [SQL Connection error], 2000 )
   ENDIF
  ELSE
   Msg = [A SQL connection was requested, but access method is ] ;
      + THIS.AccessMethod
   MESSAGEBOX( Msg, 16, [SQL Connection error], 2000 )
   THIS.AccessMethod = []
```

LISTING 5.14   Continued

```
ENDIF
RETURN

PROCEDURE CreateCursor
LPARAMETERS pTable, pKeyField
DO CASE
        CASE THIS.AccessMethod = [DBF]
        IF NOT USED ( pTable )
           SELECT 0
           USE ( pTable ) ALIAS ( pTable )
        ENDIF
        SELECT ( pTable )
        IF NOT EMPTY ( pKeyField )
           SET ORDER TO TAG ( pKeyField )
        ENDIF
        RETURN
    CASE THIS.AccessMethod = [SQL]
        Cmd = [SELECT * FROM ] + pTable + [ WHERE 1=2]
        SQLEXEC( THIS.Handle, Cmd )
        AFIELDS ( laFlds )
        USE
        CREATE CURSOR ( pTable ) FROM ARRAY laFlds

    CASE THIS.AccessMethod = [WC]
        LOCAL oIP AS WWIPSTUFF
        oIP = CREATEOBJECT( "WWIPSTUFF" )
        oIP.HTTPConnect(THIS.MyServerURL)
        lcBuffer = []
        lnBufLen = 0
        Cmd = THIS.Prefix + [GetStructure] + [~] ;
            + THIS.SvrDataAccess + [~] + pTable + [~] + [EncodeDBF]
        oIP.HTTPGetEx ( Cmd,  @lcBuffer, @lnBufLen )
        lcTxt = ALLTRIM( lcBuffer )
        oIP.DecodeDBF ( lcTxt, "Carrier.DBF" )
        SELECT 0
        USE Carrier
        COPY TO ARRAY aStru
        USE
        ERASE Carrier.DBF
        CREATE CURSOR ( pTable ) FROM ARRAY aStru
    CASE THIS.AccessMethod = [XML]
ENDCASE
```

LISTING 5.14 Continued

```
PROCEDURE GetMatchingRecords
LPARAMETERS pTable, pFields, pExpr
pFields = IIF ( EMPTY ( pFields ), [*], pFields )
pExpr   = IIF ( EMPTY ( pExpr ), [], ;
          [ WHERE ] + STRTRAN ( UPPER ( ALLTRIM ( pExpr ) ), [WHERE ], [] ) )
cExpr   = [SELECT ] + pFields + [ FROM ] + pTable + pExpr
pFields = IIF ( EMPTY ( pFields ), [*], pFields )
pExpr   = IIF ( EMPTY ( pExpr ), [], ;
          [ WHERE ] + STRTRAN ( UPPER ( ALLTRIM ( pExpr ) ), [WHERE ], [] ) )
cExpr   = [SELECT ] + pFields + [ FROM ] + pTable + pExpr
DO CASE
   CASE THIS.AccessMethod = [DBF]
        SET FILTER TO &pExpr
        GO TOP
   CASE THIS.AccessMethod = [SQL]
        lr = SQLExec ( THIS.Handle, cExpr )
        IF lr >= 0
          THIS.FillCursor(pTable)
         ELSE
          Msg = [Unable to return records] + CHR(13) + cExpr
          MESSAGEBOX( Msg, 16, [SQL error] )
        ENDIF
        SELECT ( pTable )
        ZAP
        APPEND FROM DBF( [SQLResult] )
        USE IN SQLResult
   CASE THIS.AccessMethod = [WC]
        LOCAL oIP AS WWIPSTUFF
        oIP = CREATEOBJECT( "WWIPSTUFF" )
        oIP.HTTPConnect(THIS.MyServerURL)
        lcBuffer = []
        lnBufLen = 0
        Cmd = THIS.Prefix + [GetMatchingRecords] + [~] ;
                        + THIS.SvrDataAccess   + [~] ;
                        + cExpr                + [~] ;
                        + pTable               + [~] ;
                        + [EncodeDBF]
        oIP.HTTPGetEx ( Cmd,  @lcBuffer, @lnBufLen )
        lcTxt = ALLTRIM( lcBuffer )
        oIP.DecodeDBF ( lcTxt, "SQLResult.DBF" )
        SELECT ( pTable )
        APPEND FROM SQLResult
```

5

LISTING 5.14   Continued

```
        ERASE SQLResult.DBF
ENDCASE
ENDPROC

PROCEDURE GetMatchingRecordsForView
LPARAMETERS pTable, pFields, pExpr
ViewName = [View] + pTable
IF NOT USED   ( ViewName )
   CreateView ( pTable   )
ENDIF
pFields = IIF ( EMPTY ( pFields ), [*], pFields )
pExpr   = IIF ( EMPTY ( pExpr ), [], ;
           [ WHERE ] + STRTRAN ( UPPER ( ALLTRIM ( pExpr ) ), [WHERE ], [] ) )
cExpr   = [SELECT ] + pFields + [ FROM ] + pTable + pExpr
DO CASE
   CASE THIS.AccessMethod = [DBF]
         cExpr = cExpr + [ INTO CURSOR SQLResult]
        &cExpr
         SELECT ( ViewName )
         APPEND FROM DBF( [SQLResult] )
         USE IN SQLResult
   CASE THIS.AccessMethod = [SQL]
        lr = SQLExec ( THIS.Handle, cExpr )
        IF lr >= 0
           THIS.FillCursor(ViewName)
         ELSE
           Msg = [Unable to return records] + CHR(13) + cExpr
           MESSAGEBOX( Msg, 16, [SQL error] )
        ENDIF
   CASE THIS.AccessMethod = [WC]
        LOCAL oIP AS WWIPSTUFF
        oIP = CREATEOBJECT( "WWIPSTUFF" )
        oIP.HTTPConnect(THIS.MyServerURL)
        lcBuffer = []
        lnBufLen = 0
        Cmd = THIS.Prefix + [GetMatchingRecords] + [~] ;
                          + THIS.SvrDataAccess   + [~] ;
                          + cExpr                + [~] ;
                          + pTable               + [~] ;
                          + [EncodeDBF]
        oIP.HTTPGetEx ( Cmd,  @lcBuffer, @lnBufLen )
        lcTxt = ALLTRIM( lcBuffer )
```

LISTING 5.14   Continued

```
            IF LEN(lcTxt) = 0
               MESSAGEBOX( "Empty string returned", 16 )
               SET STEP ON
            ENDIF
            oIP.DecodeDBF ( lcTxt, "SQLResult.DBF" )
            SELECT ( ViewName )
            APPEND FROM SQLResult
            ERASE SQLResult.DBF
ENDCASE
ENDPROC


PROCEDURE CreateView
LPARAMETERS  pTable
IF NOT USED( pTable )
   MESSAGEBOX( [Table ] + pTable + [ isn't open -] ;
   + [ probable programmer error], 16, [Error creating view], 2000 )
   RETURN
ENDIF
SELECT ( pTable )
AFIELDS( laFlds )
SELECT 0
CREATE CURSOR ( [View] + pTable ) FROM ARRAY laFlds
ENDFUNC


PROCEDURE GetOneRecord
LPARAMETERS pTable, pKeyField, pKeyValue
SELECT ( pTable )
Dlm  = IIF ( TYPE ( pKeyField ) = [C], ['], [] )
IF THIS.AccessMethod = [DBF]
   cExpr = [LOCATE FOR ] + pKeyField + [=] + Dlm + TRANSFORM ( pKeyValue ) + Dlm
 ELSE
   cExpr = [SELECT * FROM ] + pTable + [ WHERE ] + pKeyField ;
        + [=] + Dlm + TRANSFORM ( pKeyValue ) + Dlm
ENDIF
DO CASE

   CASE THIS.AccessMethod = [DBF]
        &cExpr

   CASE THIS.AccessMethod = [SQL]
        lr = SQLExec ( THIS.Handle, cExpr )
        IF lr >= 0
```

LISTING 5.14   Continued

```
            THIS.FillCursor( pTable )
        ELSE
         Msg = [Unable to return record] + CHR(13) + cExpr
         MESSAGEBOX( Msg, 16, [SQL error] )
      ENDIF

   CASE THIS.AccessMethod = [WC]
      LOCAL oIP AS WWIPSTUFF
      oIP = CREATEOBJECT( "WWIPSTUFF" )
      oIP.HTTPConnect(THIS.MyServerURL)
      lcBuffer = []
      lnBufLen = 0
      Cmd = THIS.Prefix + [GetOneRecord] + [~] ;
         + THIS.SvrDataAccess         + [~] ;
         + pTable                     + [~] ;
         + pKeyField                  + [~] ;
         + TRANSFORM(pKeyValue)       + [~] ;
         + [DBFEncode]
      oIP.HTTPGetEx ( Cmd,  @lcBuffer, @lnBufLen )
      lcTxt = ALLTRIM( lcBuffer )
      oIP.DecodeDBF ( lcTxt, "SQLResult.DBF" )
      SELECT ( pTable )
      ZAP
      APPEND FROM SQLResult
      ERASE SQLResult.DBF
      GO TOP


   CASE THIS.AccessMethod = [XML]

ENDCASE
ENDFUNC

PROCEDURE FillCursor
LPARAMETERS pTable
IF THIS.AccessMethod = [DBF]
   RETURN
ENDIF
SELECT ( pTable )
ZAP
APPEND FROM DBF ( [SQLResult] )
USE IN SQLResult
GO TOP
```

LISTING 5.14   Continued

```
ENDPROC

PROCEDURE DeleteRecord
LPARAMETERS pTable, pKeyField
ForExpr  = IIF ( THIS.AccessMethod = [DBF], [ FOR ], [ WHERE ] )
KeyValue = EVALUATE ( pTable + [.] + pKeyField )
Dlm      = IIF ( TYPE ( pKeyField ) = [C], ['], [] )
DO CASE
   CASE THIS.AccessMethod = [DBF]
        cExpr = [DELETE ] + pTable + [ WHERE ] + pKeyField ;
             + [=] + Dlm + TRANSFORM ( m.KeyValue ) + Dlm
        &cExpr
        SET DELETED ON
        GO TOP
   CASE THIS.AccessMethod = [SQL]
        cExpr = [DELETE ] + pTable + [ WHERE ] + pKeyField ;
             + [=] + Dlm + TRANSFORM ( m.KeyValue ) + Dlm
        lr = SQLExec ( THIS.Handle, cExpr )
        IF lr < 0
           Msg = [Unable to delete record] + CHR(13) + cExpr
           MESSAGEBOX( Msg, 16, [SQL error] )
        ENDIF
   CASE THIS.AccessMethod = [WC]
        LOCAL oIP AS WWIPSTUFF
        oIP = CREATEOBJECT( "WWIPSTUFF" )
        oIP.HTTPConnect(THIS.MyServerURL)
        lcBuffer = []
        lnBufLen = 0
        Cmd = THIS.Prefix + [DeleteRecord] + [~] ;
            + THIS.SvrDataAccess        + [~] ;
            + pTable                    + [~] ;
            + pKeyField                 + [~] ;
            + TRANSFORM(KeyValue)       + [~] ;
            + Dlm
        oIP.HTTPGetEx ( Cmd,  @lcBuffer, @lnBufLen )
        IF lcBuffer <> [Ok]
           MESSAGEBOX( lcBuffer )
        ENDIF
   CASE THIS.AccessMethod = [XML]
ENDCASE
ENDFUNC
```

LISTING 5.14   Continued

```
PROCEDURE SaveRecord
PARAMETERS pTable, pKeyField, pAdding
IF THIS.AccessMethod = [DBF]
   RETURN
ENDIF
IF pAdding
    THIS.InsertRecord ( pTable, pKeyField )
 ELSE
    THIS.UpdateRecord ( pTable, pKeyField )
ENDIF
ENDPROC


PROCEDURE InsertRecord
LPARAMETERS pTable, pKeyField
lcCmd = THIS.BuildInsertCommand ( pTable, pKeyField )
_ClipText = lcCmd && Userful for debugging
DO CASE
   CASE THIS.AccessMethod = [SQL]
       lr = SQLExec ( THIS.Handle, lcCmd )
       IF lr < 0
          msg = [Unable to insert record; command follows:] + CHR(13) + lcCmd
          MESSAGEBOX( Msg, 16, [SQL error] )
       ENDIF
   CASE THIS.AccessMethod = [WC]
       LOCAL oIP AS WWIPSTUFF
       oIP = CREATEOBJECT( "WWIPSTUFF" )
       oIP.HTTPConnect(THIS.MyServerURL)
       lcBuffer = []
       lnBufLen = 0
Use POST buffer variables, since the command string may be quite long
*   and sensitive data may be included
       oIP.AddPostKey( [Access], THIS.SvrDataAccess  )
       oIP.AddPostKey( [Cmd],    lcCmd  )
       oIP.AddPostKey( [Table],  pTable )
       oIP.HTTPGetEx ( THIS.Prefix + [InsertOrUpdateRecord],;
                       @lcBuffer, @lnBufLen )
       IF lcBuffer = [Error]
          MESSAGEBOX( lcBuffer, 16, _VFP.Caption )
       ENDIF
   CASE THIS.AccessMethod = [XML]
ENDCASE
ENDFUNC
```

LISTING 5.14 Continued

```
PROCEDURE UpdateRecord
LPARAMETERS pTable, pKeyField
lcCmd = THIS.BuildUpdateCommand ( pTable, pKeyField )
_ClipText = lcCmd && Useful for debugging
DO CASE
   CASE THIS.AccessMethod = [SQL]
        lr = SQLExec ( THIS.Handle, lcCmd )
        IF lr < 0
           msg = [Unable to update record; command follows:] + CHR(13) + cExpr
           MESSAGEBOX( Msg, 16, [SQL error] )
        ENDIF
   CASE THIS.AccessMethod = [WC]
        LOCAL oIP AS WWIPSTUFF
        oIP = CREATEOBJECT( "WWIPSTUFF" )
        oIP.HTTPConnect(THIS.MyServerURL)
        lcBuffer = []
        lnBufLen = 0
        oIP.AddPostKey( [Access], THIS.SvrDataAccess  )
        oIP.AddPostKey( [Cmd],     lcCmd  )
        oIP.AddPostKey( [Table],  pTable )
        oIP.HTTPGetEx ( THIS.Prefix + [InsertOrUpdateRecord], ;
                       @lcBuffer, @lnBufLen )
        IF lcBuffer = [Error]
           MESSAGEBOX( lcBuffer, 16, _VFP.Caption )
        ENDIF
   CASE THIS.AccessMethod = [XML]
ENDCASE
ENDFUNC


FUNCTION BuildInsertCommand
PARAMETERS pTable, pKeyField
Cmd = [INSERT INTO ] + pTable + [ ( ]
FOR I = 1 TO FCOUNT()
   Fld = UPPER(FIELD(I))
   IF TYPE ( Fld ) = [G]
      LOOP
   ENDIF
   Cmd = Cmd + Fld + [, ]
ENDFOR
Cmd = LEFT(Cmd,LEN(Cmd)-2) + [ ) VALUES ( ]
FOR I = 1 TO FCOUNT()
   Fld = FIELD(I)
```

LISTING 5.14   Continued

```
    IF TYPE ( Fld ) = [G]
        LOOP
    ENDIF
    Dta = ALLTRIM(TRANSFORM ( &Fld ))
    Dta = CHRTRAN ( Dta, CHR(39), CHR(146) )
*   get rid of single quotes in the data
    Dta = IIF ( Dta = [/  /], [], Dta )
    Dta = IIF ( Dta = [.F.], [0], Dta )
    Dta = IIF ( Dta = [.T.], [1], Dta )
    Dlm = IIF ( TYPE ( Fld ) $ [CM],['],;
          IIF ( TYPE ( Fld ) $ [DT],['],;
          IIF ( TYPE ( Fld ) $ [IN],[],    [])))
    IF ( THIS.AccessMethod = [DBF] )   ;
    OR ( THIS.AccessMethod = [WC]  AND THIS.SvrDataAccess = [DBF] )
        LDM = IIF ( TYPE ( Fld ) $ [DT], [{], Dlm )
        RDM = IIF ( TYPE ( Fld ) $ [DT], [}], Dlm )
      ELSE
        LDM = Dlm
        RDM = Dlm
    ENDIF
    Cmd = Cmd + LDM + Dta + RDM + [, ]
ENDFOR
Cmd = LEFT ( Cmd, LEN(Cmd) -2) + [ )]   && Remove ", " add " )"
RETURN Cmd
ENDFUNC


FUNCTION BuildUpdateCommand
PARAMETERS pTable, pKeyField
Cmd = [UPDATE ]  + pTable + [ SET ]
FOR I = 1 TO FCOUNT()
    Fld = UPPER(FIELD(I))
    IF Fld = UPPER(pKeyField)
        LOOP
    ENDIF
    IF TYPE ( Fld ) = [G]
        LOOP
    ENDIF
    Dta = ALLTRIM(TRANSFORM ( &Fld ))
    IF Dta = [.NULL.]
        DO CASE
            CASE TYPE ( Fld ) $ [CMDT]
                Dta = []
```

LISTING 5.14   Continued

```
            CASE TYPE ( Fld ) $ [INL]
                Dta = [0]
        ENDCASE
    ENDIF
    Dta = CHRTRAN ( Dta, CHR(39), CHR(146) )
*  get rid of single quotes in the data
    Dta = IIF ( Dta = [/  /], [], Dta )
    Dta = IIF ( Dta = [.F.], [0], Dta )
    Dta = IIF ( Dta = [.T.], [1], Dta )
    Dlm = IIF ( TYPE ( Fld ) $ [CM],['],;
          IIF ( TYPE ( Fld ) $ [DT],['],;
          IIF ( TYPE ( Fld ) $ [IN],[],    [])))
    IF ( THIS.AccessMethod = [DBF] )    ;
    OR ( THIS.AccessMethod = [WC]  AND THIS.SvrDataAccess = [DBF] )
        LDM = IIF ( TYPE ( Fld ) $ [DT], [{], Dlm )
        RDM = IIF ( TYPE ( Fld ) $ [DT], [}], Dlm )
     ELSE
        LDM = Dlm
        RDM = Dlm
    ENDIF
    Cmd = Cmd + Fld + [=] + LDM + Dta + RDM + [, ]
ENDFOR
Dlm = IIF ( TYPE ( pKeyField ) = [C], ['], [] )
Cmd = LEFT ( Cmd, LEN(Cmd) -2 )                ;
    + [ WHERE ] + pKeyField + [=]          ;
    + + Dlm + TRANSFORM(EVALUATE(pKeyField)) + Dlm
RETURN Cmd
ENDFUNC


PROCEDURE SelectCmdToSQLResult
LPARAMETERS pExpr
DO CASE
    CASE THIS.AccessMethod = [DBF]
          pExpr = pExpr + [ INTO CURSOR SQLResult]
          &pExpr
    CASE THIS.AccessMethod = [SQL]
          lr = SQLExec ( THIS.Handle, pExpr )
          IF lr < 0
             Msg = [Unable to return records] + CHR(13) + cExpr
             MESSAGEBOX( Msg, 16, [SQL error] )
          ENDIF
    CASE THIS.AccessMethod = [WC]
```

LISTING 5.14 Continued

```
          LOCAL oIP AS WWIPSTUFF
          oIP = CREATEOBJECT( "WWIPSTUFF" )
          oIP.HTTPConnect(THIS.MyServerURL)
          lcBuffer = []
          lnBufLen = 0
          Cmd = THIS.Prefix + [GetMatchingRecords]
          oIP.AddPostKey ( "ServerAccess", THIS.SvrDataAccess )
          oIP.AddPostKey ( "Expr", pExpr )
          oIP.HTTPGetEx ( Cmd,  @lcBuffer, @lnBufLen )
          lcXML = ALLTRIM( lcBuffer )
          XMLTOCURSOR ( lcXML, "SQLResult" )
          GO TOP
          BROWSE
     CASE THIS.AccessMethod = [XML]
ENDCASE
ENDFUNC

FUNCTION GetNextKeyValue
LPARAMETERS pTable
EXTERNAL ARRAY laVal
pTable = UPPER ( pTable )
DO CASE

     CASE THIS.AccessMethod = [DBF]
          IF NOT FILE ( [Keys.DBF] )
              CREATE TABLE Keys ( TableName Char(20), LastKeyVal Integer )
          ENDIF
          IF NOT USED ( [Keys] )
              USE Keys IN 0
          ENDIF
          SELECT Keys
          LOCATE FOR TableName = pTable
          IF NOT FOUND()
              INSERT INTO Keys VALUES ( pTable, 0 )
          ENDIF
          Cmd = [UPDATE Keys SET LastKeyVal=LastKeyVal + 1 ]     ;
              + [ WHERE TableName='] + pTable + [']
          &Cmd
          Cmd = [SELECT LastKeyVal FROM Keys WHERE TableName = '] ;
              + pTable + [' INTO ARRAY laVal]
          &Cmd
          USE IN Keys
```

LISTING 5.14   Continued

```
        RETURN TRANSFORM(laVal(1))

CASE THIS.AccessMethod = [SQL]

    Cmd = [SELECT Name FROM SysObjects WHERE Name='KEYS' AND Type='U']
    lr = SQLEXEC( THIS.Handle, Cmd )
    IF lr < 0
       MESSAGEBOX( "SQL Error:"+ CHR(13) + Cmd, 16 )
    ENDIF
    IF RECCOUNT([SQLResult]) = 0
       Cmd = [CREATE TABLE Keys ( TableName Char(20), LastKeyVal Integer )]
       SQLEXEC( THIS.Handle, Cmd )
    ENDIF
    Cmd = [SELECT LastKeyVal FROM Keys WHERE TableName='] + pTable + [']
    lr = SQLEXEC( THIS.Handle, Cmd )
    IF lr < 0
       MESSAGEBOX( "SQL Error:"+ CHR(13) + Cmd, 16 )
    ENDIF

    IF RECCOUNT([SQLResult]) = 0
       Cmd = [INSERT INTO Keys VALUES ('] +  pTable + [', 0 )]
       lr = SQLEXEC( THIS.Handle, Cmd )
       IF lr < 0
          MESSAGEBOX( "SQL Error:"+ CHR(13) + Cmd, 16 )
       ENDIF
    ENDIF

    Cmd = [UPDATE Keys SET LastKeyVal=LastKeyVal + 1;
       + [ WHERE TableName='] +  pTable + [']
    lr = SQLEXEC( THIS.Handle, Cmd )
    IF lr < 0
       MESSAGEBOX( "SQL Error:"+ CHR(13) + Cmd, 16 )
    ENDIF

    Cmd = [SELECT LastKeyVal FROM Keys WHERE TableName='] +  pTable + [']
    lr = SQLEXEC( THIS.Handle, Cmd )
    IF lr < 0
       MESSAGEBOX( "SQL Error:"+ CHR(13) + Cmd, 16 )
    ENDIF

    nLastKeyVal = TRANSFORM(SQLResult.LastKeyVal)
    USE IN SQLResult
```

LISTING 5.14   Continued

```
            RETURN TRANSFORM(nLastKeyVal)

    CASE THIS.AccessMethod = [WC]
        LOCAL oIP AS WWIPSTUFF
        oIP = CREATEOBJECT( "WWIPSTUFF" )
        oIP.HTTPConnect(THIS.MyServerURL)
        lcBuffer = []
        lnBufLen = 0
        Cmd = THIS.Prefix + [GetNextKeyValue] + [~] + [DBF] + [~] + pTable
        oIP.HTTPGetEx ( Cmd,  @lcBuffer, @lnBufLen )
        IF LEN(lcBuffer) > 10
           MESSAGEBOX( lcBuffer )
           RETURN []
         ELSE
           RETURN ALLTRIM(lcBuffer)
        ENDIF
    CASE THIS.AccessMethod = [XML]

ENDCASE

ENDDEFINE
```

Building XML Web Services with Visual FoxPro 8

With Visual FoxPro 8, it's quite a bit simpler. You start with a Web service. A Web service is a project with a single .PRG, compiled to a multithreaded DLL. It must start with a DEFINE CLASS <name> AS SESSION OLEPUBLIC declaration. It must declare the type of data to be returned—String in this case because we want to return XML—and it must return the XML string.

Getting the XML string is a snap, thanks to the new XMLAdapter class. We create a connection to SQL Server, execute the SELECT statement, and then instantiate an XMLAdapter and use its ToXML method to create the XML. Listing 5.15 shows the code to return a list of company names and customer IDs for the list box.

LISTING 5.15   An XML Web Service (FoxPro 8)

```
* FoxClass
DEFINE CLASS FoxClass AS Session OLEPUBLIC
ConnectionString = ;
 [Driver={SQL Server};Server=(local);Database=Northwind;UID=sa;PWD=;]
```

LISTING 5.15   Continued

```
FUNCTION AllCustomers AS String
Cmd     = "SELECT CompanyName, CustomerID FROM Customers"
Handle = SQLSTRINGCONNECT( THIS.ConnectionString )
lr      = SQLEXEC( Handle, Cmd, "Customers" )
LOCAL xa AS XMLAdapter
xa      = CREA ( "XMLAdapter" )
WITH xa
    .AddTableSchema("Customers")
    .ToXML("lcXML")
ENDWITH
xa      = NULL
RELEASE xa
USE IN Customers
RETURN lcXML
ENDFUNC


ENDDEFINE
```

The project is called FoxServer, and the class is stored in FoxClass.PRG. I pick the Build option and select the radio button labeled Multithreaded COM Server (dll) in the Build Options dialog, as shown in Figure 5.3.

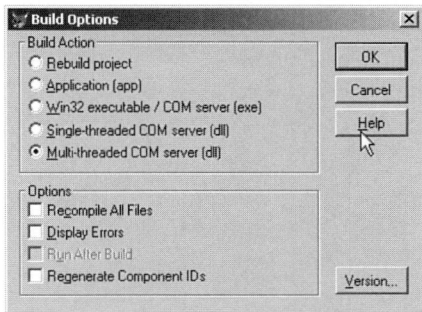

FIGURE 5.3   Building the multithreaded DLL for the XML Web Service.

> **TIP**
>
> You can type BUILD MTDLL FoxServer FROM FoxServer in the command window instead of opening up the project and clicking on the Build button.

To test it, use the following code:

```
o = CREATEOBJECT ( "FoxServer.FoxClass" )
? o.AllCustomers()
```

The first page of the result appears in Listing 5.16.

LISTING 5.16   XML Output from the FoxPro XML Web Service

```
<?xml version = "1.0" encoding="Windows-1252" standalone="yes"?>
<VFPDataSet>
<xsd:schema id="VFPDataSet" xmlns:xsd="http://www.w3.org/2001/XMLSchema"
➥xmlns:msdata="urn:schemas-microsoft-com:xml-msdata">
    <xsd:element name="VFPDataSet" msdata:IsDataSet="true">
      <xsd:complexType>
        <xsd:choice maxOccurs="unbounded">
          <xsd:element name="Customers" minOccurs="0" maxOccurs="unbounded">
            <xsd:complexType>
              <xsd:sequence>
                <xsd:element name="companyname">
                  <xsd:simpleType>
                    <xsd:restriction base="xsd:string">
                      <xsd:maxLength value="40"/>
                    </xsd:restriction>
                  </xsd:simpleType>
                </xsd:element>
                <xsd:element name="customerid">
                  <xsd:simpleType>
                    <xsd:restriction base="xsd:string">
                      <xsd:maxLength value="5"/>
                    </xsd:restriction>
                  </xsd:simpleType>
                </xsd:element>
              </xsd:sequence>
            </xsd:complexType>
          </xsd:element>
        </xsd:choice>
        <xsd:anyAttribute namespace="http://www.w3.org/XML/1998/namespace"
➥processContents="lax"/>
      </xsd:complexType>
    </xsd:element>
  </xsd:schema>
  <Customers>
    <companyname>Ana Trujillo Emparedados y helados</companyname>
```

LISTING 5.16   Continued

```
    <customerid>ANATR</customerid>
  </Customers>
  <Customers>
    <companyname>Antonio Moreno Taquería Terrible</companyname>
    <customerid>ANTON</customerid>
  </Customers>
```

However, it's not a Web service unless it can be called from the Internet. To begin with, the service needs to be located in an IIS virtual directory. If you create a directory under Inetpub\WWWRoot, it's automatically accessible. Otherwise, you can open up the IIS Management Console and add the directory where you created this code, and it will also work.

You must also register the DLL. You can do this with a single line of code. The following will open a DOS command window and register your XML Web Service DLL:

```
! Regsvr32 FoxServer..dll
```

Finally, you need to register your Web service and publish a Web Service Description Language (WSDL, pronounced "wizdil") file so that potential users can see what's available. Open up the Task Pane Manager in Visual FoxPro 8 and click on the XML Web Services tab. Select Publish Your XML Web Service, and follow the dialog to the creation of a WSDL file. If that worked, pick Register an XML Web Service and enter the name of the WSDL file you just created. Yeah, you should have written it down.

You're now ready to consume your Web service in your client application. The code's already written for you. Open the Task Pane in Visual FoxPro and select the Web Services tab. Go down to the next section on the Task Pane, Explore and XML Web Service, and pull down the combo box. Your new Web service will be in the list. Select it, and the edit box below fills with about 15 lines of code. You can copy and paste this code into your consuming application, right where you would otherwise have executed a SQLEXEC() to get your company and customerid cursor. You can also open the toolbox and drag and drop the code from the Web Services tab. You only need to add six lines of code, as shown in Listing 5.17.

LISTING 5.17   Web Service Code Generated by FoxPro

```
LOCAL loFoxClass AS "XML Web Service"
* Do not remove or alter following line. It is used to support IntelliSense
*__VFPWSDef__: loFoxClass = http://localhost/foxws/foxclass.wsdl ,
➥FoxClass , FoxClassSoapPort
LOCAL loException, lcErrorMsg, loWSHandler
TRY
```

LISTING 5.17   Continued

```
  loWSHandler = NEWOBJECT("WSHandler",IIF(VERSION(2)=0,"",;
                          HOME()+"FFC\")+"_ws3client.vcx")
  loFoxClass = loWSHandler.SetupClient(;
  "http://localhost/foxws/foxclass.wsdl", "FoxClass", "FoxClassSoapPort")

  * I inserted the following 6 lines of code:
  lcXML = loFoxClass.AllCustomers()
  XMLTOCURSOR( lcXML, [DataFromWebService] )
  SELECT ( .MainTable )
  ZAP
  APPEND FROM DBF ( [DataFromWebService] )
  USE IN DataFromWebService

CATCH TO loException
  lcErrorMsg="Error: " + TRANSFORM(loException.Errorno) ;
                     + " - "+loException.Message
  DO CASE
     CASE VARTYPE(loFoxClass)#"O"
     CASE !EMPTY(loFoxClass.FaultCode)
          lcErrorMsg=lcErrorMsg+CHR(13)+loFoxClass.Detail
     OTHERWISE
  ENDCASE
  MESSAGEBOX(lcErrorMsg)
FINALLY
ENDTRY
```

Writing a Web Service function to accept a parameter is just as easy. Simply declare the function with parameters—not the PARAMETERS statement used in FoxPro, however. You have to include them in parentheses, with data type declarations, just as you would do in Visual Basic. Add the function shown in Listing 5.18 to the FoxClass.PRG and rebuild the DLL.

LISTING 5.18   Additional Web Service to Return a Single Customer

```
FUNCTION OneCustomer ( CustID as String ) as String
Cmd    = "SELECT * FROM Customers WHERE CustomerID ='" + CustID + "'"
Handle = SQLSTRINGCONNECT( THIS.ConnectionString )
lr     = SQLEXEC( Handle, Cmd, "Customers" )
LOCAL xa AS XMLAdapter
xa     = CREA ( "XMLAdapter" )
WITH xa
```

LISTING 5.18   Continued

```
    .AddTableSchema("Customers")
    .ToXML("lcXML")
ENDWITH
xa      = NULL
RELEASE xa
USE IN Customers
RETURN lcXML
ENDFUNC
```

Finally, you'll need a Web service to send UPDATE, INSERT, and DELETE statements back to the server.

You can also write a Web service to accept a diffgram and apply the changes back to SQL. However, be aware that FoxPro diffgrams are not identical to SQL Server diffgrams, so you will need to do some additional work. For now, sending SQL pass-through statements works fine, and you already know how to write them. The function shown in Listing 5.19 shows how to handle them.

LISTING 5.19   Additional Web Service to Accept a Diffgram

```
FUNCTION SPT ( Cmd as String ) AS String
Handle = SQLSTRINGCONNECT( THIS.ConnectionString )
lr      = SQLEXEC( Handle, Cmd, "Customers" )
Return IIF ( lr < 0, [Error], [Ok] )
ENDFUNC
```

Now that you've made those changes, your FoxPro SQL application needs only to change from calling SQLExec to calling the appropriate WebService function and passing the SQL command built using the SendInsert, SendUpdate, or SendDelete function.

XML Web Services in Visual Basic .NET

To demonstrate how you can add, edit, and delete records that are located on a computer on the other side of the Internet, I'm going to start with a form containing a grid that displays all of the records in a table. It's a simple design and eliminates the need to add a search form. However, you'll be able to see exactly how such a form could be built, using the techniques required for this example. Add, Edit, Delete and Close buttons at the bottom of the screen will provide the necessary functionality.

A Main Form for the Sample Application

My example form is shown in Figure 5.4.

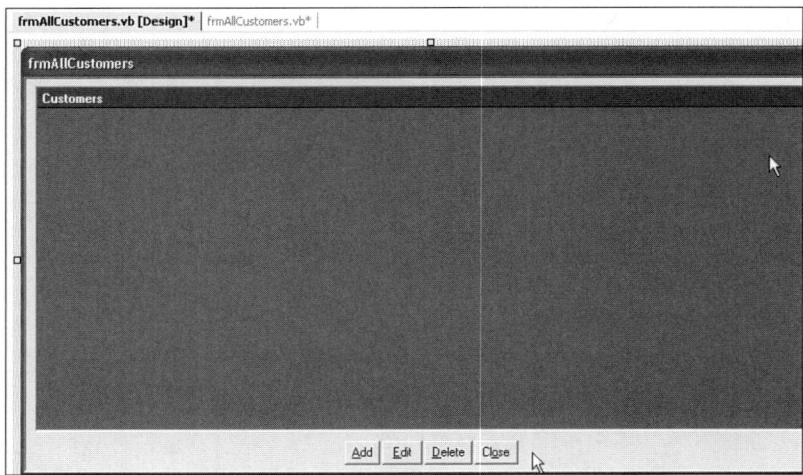

FIGURE 5.4   The Main form for the Web service-based Visual Basic application.

To build it, create a new Windows Application project called UseWS. Both the Solution and the Windows Application Project will be created wherever your default Visual Studio Projects directory is located, based on the default setting in your Tools, Options, Environment, Projects and Solutions default directory. Rename the form frmAllCustomers.vb. Add a DataGrid and four command buttons named cmdAdd, cmdEdit, cmdDelete, and cmdClose, with text captions to match, as shown in Figure 5.4. Double-click on the Close button and enter a single command: End. We'll code the other three buttons shortly.

When you use a local data source, you can add a data adapter and create a dataset from it. But when you're using Web Services, you need to create the Web service first, add a Web reference, and then base the dataset definition on the Web reference. So before going any further, we'll create the Web service.

Building a Web Service for the Sample Application

It's as easy to build a Web service in Visual Basic .NET as it is in Visual FoxPro 8. Add a new project of type Visual Basic ASP.NET Web Service to the solution. Name it Chapter5WebService. This will create a project file named Chapter5WebService.vbproj and a Web service file named Chapter5WebService.asmx. Asmx files aren't Web pages, so there are no visible controls to drop on them. However, data controls are used with XML Web Services, and they make data access very easy. Drag a SQLDataAdapter to the design surface. When the Data Adapter Wizard opens, select the Northwind connection that you created earlier. When asked to type a SELECT command, enter

```
SELECT * FROM CUSTOMERS
```

to return the entire Customer file. The wizard will generate a `DataAdapter`, which you can name daAllCustomers. Right-click on the `DataAdapter` and select Generate Dataset to create a typed dataset. Change the default name of `Dataset1` to `dsAllCustomers`.

Drag a second `DataAdapter` to the Web Service design surface to provide a dataset for a single record. For the SQL statement, enter this:

```
SELECT * FROM CUSTOMERS WHERE (CustomerID = @CustomerID)
```

This creates a parameterized query, which will return one record. You can name the new `DataAdapter` daOneCustomer and the dataset `dsOneCustomer`. You'll be surprised how easy it is to send a parameter to a Web service and retrieve the selected record.

Changes to the `CONFIG.WEB` File

You'll need to open the `Config.Web` file in the project and add the following line immediately after the `<system.web>` tag:

```
<identity impersonate="true" >
```

This provides data requests access to the Web server without requiring a user login. While you're at it, enter the following immediately before the `<system.web>` tag:

```
<appSettings>
  <add key="ConnectionString" value="user id=sa;data source=localhost;persist
➡ security info=False;initial catalog=Northwind" />
</appSettings>
```

This will allow us to read the connection string from a text file that can easily be changed when we deploy the application. We'll add that feature near the end of this topic.

Web Service Functions

Now you're ready to build our Web service. We'll need a function to populate the grid in the main application screen. That's what the `dsAllCustomers` dataset was for. When the user selects a record to edit, the second dataset, `dsOneCustomer`, will be used to return it. The Delete command button will just pass the key of the record to be deleted, to demonstrate the flexibility of Web services. They're called XML Web Services, but you don't have to pass XML back and forth. XML is just the transport mechanism for the parameters and results. You can send rows and columns back as XML, but scalars (strings, integers, dates, and the like) are just scalars.

Double-click on the design surface to open the code window, and enter the code shown in Listing 5.20.

LISTING 5.20   Web Service Functions

```
<WebMethod()> Public Function GetAllCustomers() _
 As dsAllCustomers
    Dim AllCustomers As New dsAllCustomers
    SqlDataAdapter1.Fill(AllCustomers)
    Return AllCustomers
End Function

<WebMethod()> Public Function GetOneCustomer( _
  ByVal RecordKey As String) _
 As dsOneCustomer
    Dim OneCustomer As New dsOneCustomer
    SqlDataAdapter2.SelectCommand.Parameters(0).Value = RecordKey
    SqlDataAdapter2.Fill(OneCustomer)
    Return OneCustomer
End Function

<WebMethod()> Public Function UpdateCustomers( _
  ByVal customerChanges As dsOneCustomer) _
 As dsOneCustomer
    If Not (customerChanges Is Nothing) Then
        SqlDataAdapter2.Update(customerChanges)
        Return customerChanges
    Else
        Return Nothing
    End If
End Function

<WebMethod()> Public Sub DeleteOneCustomer(ByVal RecordKey As String)
    Dim cn As New SqlClient.SqlConnection
    Cn.ConnectionString = ConfigurationSettings.AppSettings("ConnectionString")
    cn.Open()
    Dim sc As New SqlClient.SqlCommand("DELETE CUSTOMERS
➥    WHERE CustomerID='" + RecordKey + "'", cn)
    sc.ExecuteNonQuery()
    cn.Close()
End Sub
```

How It Works

AllCustomers returns all of the records in the Customers table of the Northwind database. For a few hundred records, performance will be adequate, as you'll see when you run this application.

The second line of the `DeleteOneCustomer` method shows you why I added the string to `Web.Config` a few paragraphs earlier. The program can read the `Web.Config` file and find and return the connection string stored in the file. That means you can change the server name, or even the database name, user ID or password, simply by editing a text file on the server.

The function declaration for `GetOneCustomer` says that it has a string parameter named `RecordKey`, which is passed to it. Its return value (the `As` clause at the end of the function declaration) is a dataset—specifically, a `dsOneCustomer` dataset. So this function returns xml. So does `AllCustomers` because its return type is also a dataset.

`UpdateCustomer` accepts a single parameter of type `dsOneCustomer`—a dataset—and returns a dataset. It uses the dataset that is sent to it to call the data adapter's `Update` method, which applies the changes in the dataset (which is actually a `DiffGram`) to the source table.

Finally, `DeleteOneCustomer` takes a string containing a `CustomerID` value, deletes one record, and returns nothing.

Adding References to the Web Service to Your Client

Right-click on the UseWS project's References section and select Add Web Reference. You'll see the Start Browsing for Web Services screen shown in Figure 5.5.

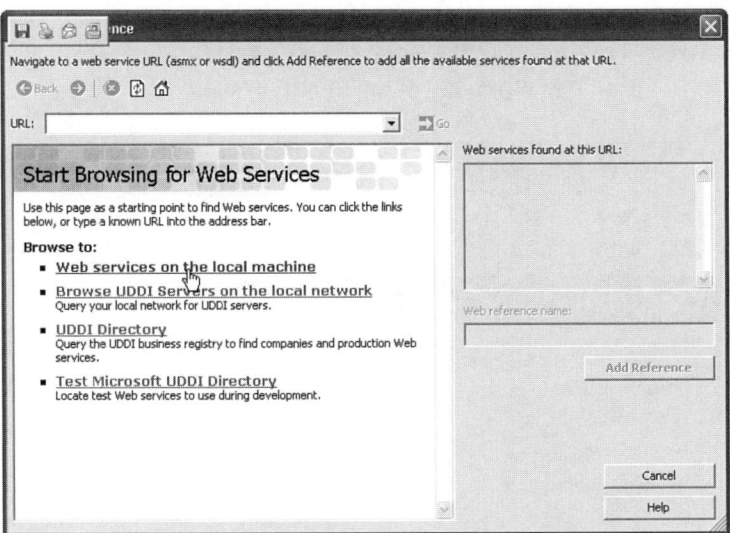

FIGURE 5.5   Browse for Web Services.

This lets you pick a Web service from your development machine or from any computer on the Internet. Select the first link, Web Services on the Local Machine, and you'll be able to pick your new Web service from the Web services that you've built on your development computer, as shown in Figure 5.6. This screen is a welcome addition to Visual Studio 2003. The first release of Visual Studio required you to remember the name of your WSDL file, and it's easy to forget when you're building half a dozen of them a day.

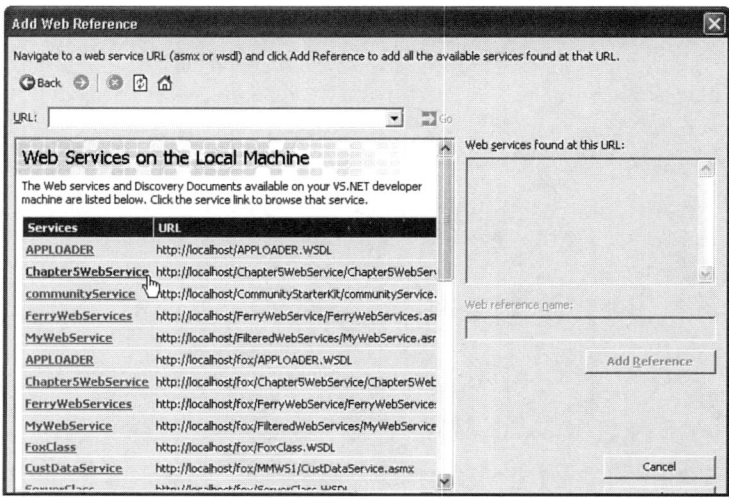

FIGURE 5.6 Web Services on the local machine.

Select Chapter5WebService and you'll see the screen shown in Figure 5.7, which confirms that the functions and subs that we added are indeed available.

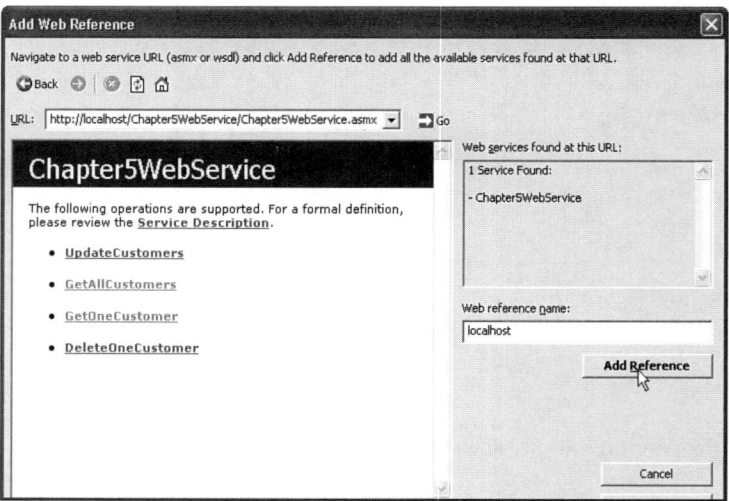

FIGURE 5.7 Add Reference confirmation dialog.

Finally, you'll need to add a dataset to hold the customer records returned from the Web service. Drag a Dataset from the Data tab of the toolbox and drop it on the form. The dialog that appears will offer to base the dataset, not on a `DataAdapter` as in our previous examples, but rather on the Web Reference that we added. Select it and name it `dsAllCustomers`. This creates a typed dataset that's added to the project. You'll still need to fill it, but the code will be a little different.

Code for the Windows Application to Use the Web Service

The code to perform the functions represented by the buttons on the main application form is shown in Listing 5.21.

LISTING 5.21   Code to Interact with the Web Service Functions

```
Private Sub frmAllCustomers_Load( _
  ByVal sender As System.Object, _
  ByVal e As System.EventArgs) _
 Handles MyBase.Load
    LoadData()
End Sub

Public Sub LoadData()
    SuspendLayout()
    Dim ws As New UseWS.localhost.Chapter5WebService
    ws.Credentials = System.Net.CredentialCache.DefaultCredentials
    DsAllCustomers1.Clear()
    DsAllCustomers1.Merge(ws.GetAllCustomers())
    DataGrid1.DataSource = DsAllCustomers1
    DataGrid1.DataMember = "Customers"
    ResumeLayout(False)
End Sub

Private Sub cmdAdd_Click( _
  ByVal sender As System.Object, _
  ByVal e As System.EventArgs) _
 Handles cmdAdd.Click
    Dim frm As New frmEditOneCustomer
    frm.RecordKey = "Add"
    frm.ShowDialog()
    LoadData()
End Sub

Private Sub cmdEdit_Click( _
  ByVal sender As System.Object, _
```

LISTING 5.21 Continued

```
      ByVal e As System.EventArgs) _
   Handles cmdEdit.Click
      Dim Recordkey As String = _
        DsAllCustomers1.Tables(0).Rows(DataGrid1.CurrentRowIndex)(0)
      Dim frm As New frmEditOneCustomer
      frm.RecordKey = Recordkey
      frm.ShowDialog()
      LoadData()
   End Sub

   Private Sub cmdDelete_Click( _
     ByVal sender As System.Object, _
     ByVal e As System.EventArgs) _
   Handles cmdDelete.Click
      Dim Recordkey As String = _
        DsAllCustomers1.Tables(0).Rows(DataGrid1.CurrentRowIndex)(0)
      Dim ws As New UseWS.localhost.Chapter5WebService
      ws.Credentials = System.Net.CredentialCache.DefaultCredentials
      ws.DeleteOneCustomer(Recordkey)
      LoadData()
   End Sub

   Private Sub cmdClose_Click( _
     ByVal sender As System.Object, _
     ByVal e As System.EventArgs) _
   Handles cmdClose.Click
        End
   End Sub
```

How It Works

The form's Load event calls the LoadData method to get the entire Customers table, which is returned as an XML dataset. I call this routine after any sort of change (add, edit, or delete) to the source table, so the routine clears the dataset, creates a proxy to host the Web service's methods, authenticates the proxy (that's what that modification to config.web was for), calls the GetAllCustomers method, and uses the Merge method of the proxy to dump the records into the dataset.

Because an XML dataset is the native data source for a DataGrid, we set the data grid's DataSource to the dataset. We also have to set the DataMember to the precise table name; if we don't, a little "+" appears in the grid for us to expand and pick a table—never mind that there's only one. You can also use DataMember = dsAllCustomers.Tables(0), but any time you can spell out what's happening in .NET you're better off. It's arcane enough as it is.

When the user clicks on either Add or Edit, we create an instance of the `frmEditCustomer` form class, which you'll see in the next section. In the case of an Edit, we pass the value of the key for the currently selected record in the grid, which is returned by the expression

```
DsAllCustomers1.Tables(0).Rows(DataGrid1.CurrentRowIndex)(0)
```

That (0) out at the end means "column 1", for reasons that were the subject of at least one rant in an earlier chapter. This is perhaps the oddest syntax that I've come across in .NET. But it returns the key of the record to edit. Passing the string "Add" instead will be handled by code in the Customer Edit form, which you'll see at the end of this section. In both cases, we use the instance's `ShowDialog()` method, which is like setting a FoxPro form's `WindowType = 1 - Modal` and activating the form. The next line, `LoadData()`, executes when control returns from the modal form.

Delete is accomplished simply by using the value of the key field from the current record to call the Web service proxy's `DeleteOneRecord()` method. I did it a little differently just to demonstrate how Web service functions act almost exactly like methods on local classes. They can't operate on global variables, but they can pass parameters back and forth; and the parameters can be tables, in the form of datasets.

The EditCustomer Form

Figure 5.8 shows the EditCustomer form.

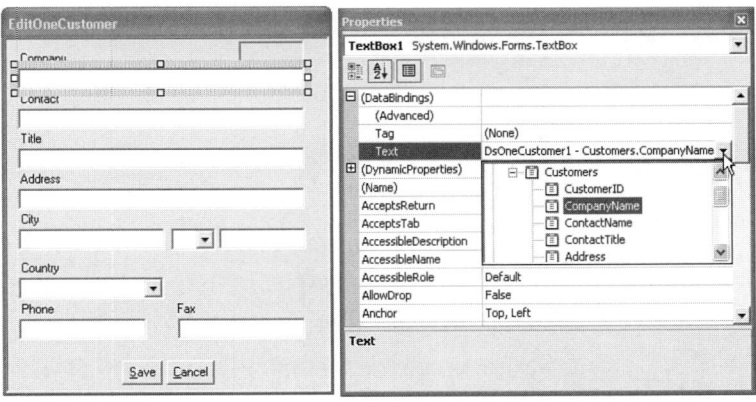

FIGURE 5.8   The Customer Add/Edit form (`frmEditCustomer.vb`).

The form consists of labels and text boxes for each of the fields in the Customer Record. I also included a text box for the record key at the upper-right corner of the screen so that you can see what's happening, although it wouldn't be necessary or desirable in a production environment. In each text box, I set the Databinding for the Text property to the corresponding field in the dsOneCustomer dataset.

The code shown in Listing 5.22 either finds the record to edit and displays it on the screen, or adds a blank record and inserts the first five characters of a GUID (pronounced as two syllables, GOO-id) converted to uppercase.

The approach to passing a parameter is quite different in Visual Basic than in FoxPro. In FoxPro, you include a PARAMETERS statement as the first line in the INIT event code, and you've got parms. In Visual Basic, the easiest way is to create a property procedure and do the record lookup in its Set method, which is just like a FoxPro property's Assign method. The code that triggers this event is the statement frm.RecordKey = RecordKey in cmdEdit_Click method in Listing 5.21, and the statement frm.RecordKey="Add" in the cmdAdd_Click method in the same listing.

LISTING 5.22 Code for the frmEditCustomer Form

```
Public Property RecordKey() As String
    Get
        Return _RecordKey
    End Get
    Set(ByVal Value As String)
        _RecordKey = Value
        If _RecordKey = "Add" Then
            DsOneCustomer1.Clear()
            Dim dr As DataRow
            dr = DsOneCustomer1.Tables(0).NewRow
            Dim I As Integer
            For I = 0 To dr.ItemArray.Length - 1
                dr(I) = ""
            Next
            dr(0) = Guid.NewGuid.ToString.Substring(0, 5).ToUpper
            DsOneCustomer1.Tables(0).Rows.Add(dr)
        Else
            Dim ws As New UseWS.localhost.Chapter5WebService
            ws.Credentials = System.Net.CredentialCache.DefaultCredentials
            DsOneCustomer1.Merge(ws.GetOneCustomer(_RecordKey))
        End If
    End Set
End Property

Private Sub cmdSave_Click( _
  ByVal sender As System.Object, _
  ByVal e As System.EventArgs) _
```

LISTING 5.22   Continued

```
Handles cmdSave.Click
    BindingContext(DsOneCustomer1, "Customers").EndCurrentEdit()
    If DsOneCustomer1.HasChanges Then
        Dim ws As New UseWS.localhost.Chapter5WebService
        ws.Credentials = System.Net.CredentialCache.DefaultCredentials
        Dim diffCustomers As New UseWS.localhost.dsOneCustomer
        diffCustomers.Merge(DsOneCustomer1.GetChanges())
        diffCustomers = ws.UpdateCustomers(diffCustomers)
        DsOneCustomer1.Merge(diffCustomers)
        DsOneCustomer1.AcceptChanges()
        Close()
    End If
End Sub

Private Sub cmdCancel_Click( _
  ByVal sender As System.Object, _
  ByVal e As System.EventArgs) _
 Handles cmdCancel.Click
    Close()
End Sub
```

How It Works

If the record key is Add, it means that the user clicked on the Add button. What follows looks like a lot of code, and compared to FoxPro, it is. But you can't just APPEND BLANK and REFRESH in Visual Basic .NET. You have to Clear the dataset, create a DataRow object based on one of the dataset's rows using the NewRow() method, assign a blank string to all of the fields (that was easy because all of the fields in this table are of type character) so that they won't be DBNulls, and finally add the data row to the empty dataset. If they passed a valid record key, we instead call the Web server proxy's GetOneCustomer method and use the resulting returned XML string to fill the dataset. Databinding takes care of the rest.

The RecordKey property procedure is invoked back in the AllCustomers form in the frm.RecordKey = String statement. The Set method for a property procedure is just like a FoxPro property's Assign method. When you assign the value, the procedure executes. It looks complicated, but it works.

The cmdSave_Click code is also a little more complicated than FoxPro's TableUpdate() function, but not much more involved than the equivalent FoxPro Web Service proxy code generated by dragging your Web service name from the FoxPro toolbox to your code window. You have to end the current edit using the EndCurrentEdit() method, and then call the proxy Web service `UpdateCustomers` method passing it the changes in the record in the form of a `DiffGram` created using the `GetChanges()` method of the dataset. Finally, you have to call the dataset's `AcceptChanges()` method and close the form. The `cmdCancel` `Click` event just closes the form without doing anything.

Using Remoting Instead of Web Services

You should be aware that there is another technology for using remote data services with smart client applications. It's called **remoting**. Remoting sends data in a more compact format, and has many more options, than Web services. It's more complicated than XML Web Services, although I've seen examples that are only 30 or 40 lines of code.

Nonetheless, even the simplest implementation of remoting borders on a level of complexity that stretches the limits of the typical FoxPro developer's skill. .NET is simply a lot harder than FoxPro, and remoting is a pretty good example of that inherently greater complexity. For that reason, it's beyond the scope of this book. However, if you're intent on building a major smart client application and suspect that minimizing data traffic might become important, you should take a look at remoting.

Summary

This chapter has covered a topic that is large, but hopefully straightforward. FoxPro has simple ways to do simple things, but as the task becomes more complicated it takes more code to get the job done. With Visual Basic .NET, the complexity is about the same for all three types of database operations.

If you're using DBFs, you probably figured out that you don't want to send DBFs using Web Connection's Compression methods, because they don't work with long field names. They require a DBC, and you can't send a DBF that's part of a DBC without sending the DBC, DCX, and DTC files as well. And if you think you can just keep all of your field names to 10 characters or less, go look at the field names your users have been using. I've seen field names 30 characters long in SQL databases.

That's why our examples all have short field names. But in the real world they don't, so you may have problems demonstrating the difference between DBF and SQL access if your SQL tables have long field names.

It may look complicated, but it's really pretty easy to do. If you download the source code, you can have it up and running in 30 minutes, and you can probably adapt one of your own forms to use my library of functions (with a few modifications) in an hour or so. And I should point out that the full version of Web Connection contains hundreds of functions, a number of which would make some of the code that I wrote here unnecessary. In fact, there's a function to package a DBF and its associated FPT for transmission in a single command. And there are many, many more.

I don't write purely LAN-based database applications any more, unless users absolutely insist that they don't want Internet access to their data. This kind of app will run just as well on a local area network as it does over the Internet, with no modifications. And if you happen to be on the road and want to hook up with your database, it's just a phone call away.

Visual FoxPro 8 has great new features for building XML Web Services. I hope this doesn't sound like an advertisement. I don't work for West Wind and don't have any interest in the company. However, you may conclude that even though you could save a few hours' pay by building Web Services in Visual FoxPro 8, there's no better combination than FoxPro, Web Connection, and XML for building database applications for the Internet.

5

CHAPTER 6

Data Access

Data is the heart of a FoxPro developer's mission. We design tables and indexes, provide keys for fast data retrieval and updating, and build screens to connect our users to their treasures.

The single most important issue for FoxPro developers contemplating migrating to Visual Basic .NET is this: How hard is it to work with data? .NET has dozens of wonderful capabilities in many other areas. But by and large, we don't care. *How does it do data?* That's our first and most urgent question.

The answer is, as Shakespeare said of love, "not wisely but too well." It does everything we want and more; but *jeez*, why did they do it that way?

If I had never used FoxPro, I wouldn't be nearly so critical. But we know better than any other segment of the database community how simple data access can be. Why can't there be simple defaults that work if you don't specify anything? There are equivalents—sort of; there are things that do a lot of work for us, but often where there was no work to do in FoxPro. And from time to time we'll get a pleasant surprise. But my overall impression as a Fox guy is frankly that *it isn't supposed to be this hard*. And I'm pretty sure that in a not-too-distant future it won't be.

There is a reason for some of the difference. FoxPro data access is *connected*; in Visual Basic .NET, data access is *disconnected*. You connect, get a record, and disconnect. After making modifications, you connect, send the update, and disconnect. The fact that the "connection" is maintained is irrelevant. In your database applications, you can open a connection when the program starts up and then use that same connection until the user closes the program. That would be an expensive *modus operandi*. What is more commonly done is to open a connection, get some data from SQL or send an INSERT, UPDATE, or DELETE command, and immediately close the connection. (In fact, you can build an Internet data server that connects to MSDE with a single connection, and then pool calls to it, so that dozens or hundreds of users can use a single connection. Microsoft will tell you that this violates your license agreement.) The server program is connected to the SQL database, but your client program isn't.

Regardless of the nature of the disconnected access, each new method of access involves a little more work. In Visual Basic .NET, all data access methods are disconnected. That's why it's no harder to work with XML data services in .NET than it is to work with an MDB database.

FoxPro was built for connected data access, which is very simple. As soon as you build a disconnected data access strategy, all of the implications have to be dealt with. .NET, on the other hand, starts with disconnected data access, so the problems have to be dealt with immediately.

Let's look at data issues, first at Visual FoxPro, then at the Visual Basic side. We'll look at the Data Application Blocks, hastily issued after the release of Visual Studio .NET 1.1 to answer the alarmed requests for a simpler way to access data. And we'll speculate (within the bounds of a putative NDA) as to what might be coming from Redmond.

Data Access in Visual FoxPro Before Visual FoxPro 8

In earlier versions of FoxPro, we had a few ways to access data: DBFs, views, remote views, and SQL Pass-Through. The advent of the Internet allowed us to add HTTP and remote data servers to that list, including new HTTP data access to SQL Server.

The DBF Format

Local tables with the extension .dbf are the best-known identifying characteristic of FoxPro applications. The DBF, described in an earlier chapter, is a disk file with a header of 512 bytes if part of a database or 256 bytes if a free table, followed by 32 bytes to describe each field in the table, followed by fixed-length records preceded by a **delete byte**, which contains an asterisk if it has been **marked for deletion** with the DELETE command. (Tables that are members of a database have the name of the database container file [DBC] stored in the additional 256 bytes of the header.) Cursors (described later in this chapter) have the same format as free tables because they can't be created as members of a database. Part of the header information is stored in hexadecimal format, including LSB (least-significant byte first) format, so that reading cursors is a skill in itself. However, it is almost never necessary to do so, unless you're Paul Heiser and you sell a tool to fix them when they get damaged.

Creating a Table

You can create a table either interactively or in code. Usually, when I'm building a system, I simply type

```
CREATE CUSTOMER
```

A Table Designer window opens up and allows me to begin describing the table, as shown in Figure 6.1.

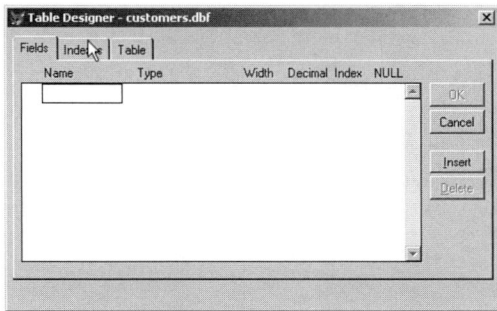

FIGURE 6.1   The MODIFY STRUCTURE dialog.

Field names are limited to 10 characters if the table is not part of a database container. If a database container is open, the table is automatically added to it and can have long field names.

Tables can also be created using the CREATE TABLE command, which has this syntax:

```
CREATE TABLE SUBS (  ;
 SubNumber Integer,  ;
 StartDate Date,     ;
 Cost Numeric(6,2),  ;
 Expires Date,       ;
 CustomerID Char(10) )
```

Typically, you would use some data source, perhaps a table of possible fields to be included in a particular survey, and then generate a string containing the command. Then you would use macro expansion, (for example, &Cmd) to execute the command and create the table.

Using Local Tables (DBFs)

To use a DBF, you, well, USE a DBF:

```
USE ( TableName )
```

This command opens the named DBF in the current work area and moves the record pointer to the first record. In VB, there is no current select area as there is in FoxPro, and the position of the record pointer within a dataset serves as a surrogate for RECNO() (record number). In FoxPro, the current select area (SELECT()) and the current record number (RECNO()) are managed by the FoxPro environment, so that we can use them without resorting to the methods or properties of some data handling class. They're just *there*.

This notion of a current work area is not without its problems, and we've all experienced them. If you already have a table open, say in select area 1, USE (*TableName*) will close it and open the new table in select area 1. So you usually use the following syntax to ensure that you haven't just closed a table that you still needed:

```
SELECT 0    && get the next available work area
USE ( TableName )
```

You can also use abbreviated syntax:

```
USE ( TableName ) IN 0
```

However, this doesn't select the new table; that requires a separate SELECT command. So you would ordinarily use this:

```
USE CUSTOMERS IN 0
SELECT CUSTOMERS
```

Aliases

The USE command can also specify an ALIAS. In a FoxPro program, when you issue the SELECT (*TableName*) command, you actually select the table's ALIAS. The alias is by default the table's name; however, if you're working with a class of tables that might have other names but represent a single type of data, for example timesheets, you can specify an alias, as shown in Listing 6.1.

LISTING 6.1   Specifying an Alias

```
FName = GETFILE ( [DBF], Where is the timesheet to import?]
IF EMPTY ( FName )
   RETURN
  ELSE
   USE ( FName ) IN 0 ALIAS TIMESHEET
   SELECT TIMESHEET
ENDIF
```

When a table is open, the command LIST STRUCTURE provides a list of the fields (columns) in the table. To save the resulting list to a file, use LIST STRUCTURE TO ABC.TXT. You can also use LIST STRUCTURE TO PRINTER NOCONSOLE to send it straight to a printer.

The contents of a field in a table are referred to using the syntax *TABLENAME.FIELDNAME*, for example, CLIENTS.PHONE. You can also SELECT a table, and then refer simply to the PHONE field because the alias of the current work area is assumed by default.

Visual Basic .NET doesn't have the concept of a default alias. You can't type Phone and assume that it will know what table to look in. In fact, it won't look in any table.

TIP

Here's a little preview: The only way that an expression like CLIENTS.Phone will have any meaning in Visual Basic .NET is if you have a Clients object that has a property named Phone. The Clients object is exactly like any other object; it's based on a class, consisting of a CLASS definition containing PUBLIC PROPERTY declarations that have the same names as the fields in your table. You're responsible for building the class and for moving the data from the XML structure that holds it to the class. More about this later.

Cursors

Cursors are temporary tables. You get a cursor when you issue a SQL SELECT statement to retrieve records from a DBF. You also get a cursor when you return records from SQL Server. And as we've seen, you can use XMLToCursor() to build a cursor from an XML string.

There is also a CREATE CURSOR command, which looks exactly like the CREATE TABLE command. It creates a temporary structure like that of a DBF, typically with the extension .tmp, which you won't see unless you use the DBF (*cursorname*) function to return the name. I've only come up with one use for this, in conjunction with the APPEND FROM (*tablename*) command, which requires a table name rather than a cursor name.

Cursors, unlike tables, can have long field names. This makes them perfect for storing the contents of cursors returned from SQL Server because few SQL database administrators limit themselves to 10-character field names.

Supporting Cast

There are a number of commands and functions that are meaningful while a table is open.

TABLE 6.1   Commands and Functions for Working with Open Tables

Function/Command	Action/Return Value
RECNO()	Returns the record number of the current work area
RECCOUNT()	Returns the total number of records in the current work area
FCOUNT()	Returns the number of fields in the current alias
FIELD(n)	Returns the name of the nth field in the current alias
SKIP (n; default is 1)	Moves forward n records
SKIP (-n; no default)	Moves backward n records

TABLE 6.1   Continued

Function/Command	Action/Return Value
TOP or GO TOP	Moves to the first record in the current index order, or to record 1 if no index is attached
BOTTOM or GO BOTTOM	Moves to the last record in the current index order, or to record (RECCOUNT()) if no index is attached
SCAN...ENDSCAN	Executes the code between these two words once for each record in the current alias
CursorSetProp ("Buffering", n)	Sets the current alias's buffering mode to n (1 = none, 2 = pessimistic record locking, 3 = optimistic record locking, 4 = pessimistic table locking, 5 = optimistic record locking)
APPEND BLANK	Adds a blank record to the current alias; if buffering is on, the record is not permanently added until the TableUpdate() function is called
DELETE	Marks the current record in the current alias for deletion the next time PACK is issued while the current alias is selected
TableUpdate()	Makes permanent any changes made since buffering mode for the current alias was turned on
TableRevert()	Undoes any changes made since buffering mode for the current alias was turned on
CursorToXML(alias, "varname")	Converts the records in the current alias to XML and stores it in the named variable
XMLToCursor(varname, cursor, flags)	Converts the XML in the named variable to records in the named cursor, based on the flag values supplied

Buffering

If buffering mode is set to 2, 3, 4, or 5, two versions of changed records are maintained. If the TableUpdate() function is called, the changes become permanent. If TableRevert() is called, the changes are discarded.

TableUpdate() and TableRevert()

When you've enabled buffering, something strange happens; as you change records, FoxPro maintains two copies of each changed record—one before and one after the change. If you issue the TableUpdate() function, changes are made permanent. If you issue the TableRevert() function, changes are not saved.

After you make changes to a buffered table, you can't close the form that's using it unless you call TableUpdate() or TableRevert(). That's why, in your form templates where you use buffering, you either have to set ControlBox to False to eliminate the possibility of a user trying to close a form with pending changes, or automatically call TableUpdate() or TableRevert() if a form is closed after changes have been made, depending on which you want to be the default behavior. It's a little messy, but it's unavoidable when you begin using buffering.

The Phantom Record

FoxPro has a record pointer, which tells it which is the current record. When you use APPEND BLANK, FoxPro jumps to the end of the alias and adds a blank record. However, it's not actually added until you use TABLEUPDATE(), if buffering is enabled. If you use TABLEREVERT(), where is the record pointer? The answer is, it's one record beyond the number of records in the file. So you would have a RECCOUNT() of, say, 12, and a RECNO() of 13.

One of the consequences of this is that if you cancel an add, you have to tell FoxPro what record you were pointing to before the APPEND. That's why the FoxPro template in Chapter 2, "Building Simple Applications in Visual FoxPro and Visual Basic .NET," had a property named BeforeAdd, so that after a canceled add we could go back to the record that was showing before the APPEND BLANK was issued.

Indexes

Indexes are implemented in FoxPro either as single-index IDX files (compact or not compact) or as tags in CDX (compact multiple index) files. To create a simple index, you use the command

```
INDEX ON ( Expression ) TO ( NameWithoutTheExtension ) COMPACT
```

To create a tag in a CDX file you issue the command

```
INDEX ON ( Expression ) TAG ( TagName )
```

To attach an index, you use the command SET INDEX TO (IdxFileName). You can attach several IDX and CDX files in a single SET INDEX statement. However, when you open a DBF, if a CDX file of the same name exists, it is automatically opened, although no tag order is set. To do that, you issue the command

```
SET ORDER TO TAG ( TagName )
```

or simply

```
SET ORDER TO ( TagName )
```

After an index has been selected, a SEEK command for a value that's in the index will find any matching record. Depending on the SET NEAR and SET EXACT commands, the record pointer can be set to the next record following the place where the record would have been had it existed, or to the end of the alias.

Database Containers

So far we've talked about free tables, which are not contained in a database. Many of the features of FoxPro tables and cursors require the use of a **database container** (DBC), a sort of metatable containing references to tables and their fields and indexes. It also holds transactional information, stored procedures and triggers (including generated relational integrity triggers), and the SELECT statements and connection information needed to build local and remote views. You can't use any of the advanced features without including a database container in your project. And if you do, consider buying Doug Hennig's Stonefield Database Toolkit (SDT) (www.Stonefield.com), which adds a ton of additional functionality to the DBC.

In FoxPro, DBFs can either be free tables or can belong to a database container. In the latter case, the table headers include an additional 254 bytes for the name of the DBC file used as the database container. Additional details of the DBC are stored in a memo file with the extension DCX, and an index file with the extension DCT.

The DBC file is itself a DBF. Its structure is shown in Listing 6.2.

LISTING 6.2   The Structure of the DBC File

```
Structure for table:PINTER.DBC
Field  Field Name  TypeWidthDec   Index    Collate Nulls
1   OBJECTIDInteger 4 No
2   PARENTIDInteger 4 No
3   OBJECTTYPE  Character  10 No
4   OBJECTNAME  Character 128 No
5   PROPERTYMemo (binary)   4 No
6   CODEMemo (binary)   4 No
7   RIINFO  Character   6 No
8   USERMemo4 No
** Total **   165
```

When you create the database, five records are added, containing five records with the following values in the ObjectName field:

```
 OBJECTIDPARENTID OBJECTTYPE OBJECTNAME
1   1 Database   Database
2   1 Database   TransactionLog
3   1 Database   StoredProceduresSource
4   1 Database   StoredProceduresObject
5   1 Database   StoredProceduresDependencies
```

Transactions in progress are stored in the database. When transactions are committed, they are removed from the DBC and put into tables and removed from the DBC; if rolled back, they are simply removed from the DBC. Stored procedures, including relational integrity triggers, are stored here. So if you want to use transactions, stored procedures, and relational integrity constraints, you must use a database. Otherwise, the database may not be necessary or even useful. However, if you intend to use local and/or remote views, you *must* use a DBC.

Local Views

Local views are cursors created based on SQL SELECT statements stored in database containers. They don't have indexes, although if the SQL SELECT statement has an ORDER BY statement, it determines the order of the records. Views can be marked as updateable either in the database container or by using CursorSetProp() settings. When a view is marked as updateable, as the view is changed, the records in the underlying table are updated.

Remote Views

Remote views are the same as local views except that their data sources are not FoxPro tables. The sources can be SQL Server, or any ODBC data source. In fact, you can create a remote view to a FoxPro table using an ODBC driver, although as Nixon once said, it would be wrong. (He did it anyway, as some of us recall.) Remote views can also be updateable.

At one time, many of us hoped that remote views would provide a way to use SQL Server. We were wrong. Remote views work, but barely. So, instead, we use SQL Pass-Through (SPT).

SQL Pass-Through

SQL is supported directly in FoxPro. The name is meant to imply that if for some reason you don't want to use remote views, real men use SQL Pass-Through (SPT). The reason for the clear distinction is that for FoxPro people, having to build an INSERT or UPDATE string seemed incredibly difficult. After all, if we use DBFs, there's nothing to do; leave the record, or issue TableUpdate() if you used buffering, and the change is permanent. Issue APPEND BLANK on an unbuffered DBF, and you have inserted a blank record, a truly unnatural act in SQL.

As long as we're quoting Nixon, let me make one thing perfectly clear: To add a record in SQL, you must create and send a complete, syntactically correct INSERT statement to SQL, using SQL delimiters. SQL's syntax is slightly different than that of FoxPro's twangy dialect, and SQL Server makes no effort to understand its distant cousin. Similarly, the UPDATE and DELETE commands must be expressed in their full glory.

SQL offers several things that DBFs don't provide. BACKUP and RESTORE are easier in every way. User access control is built in, and it's virtually impossible to damage SQL tables or index files. We've all had to build our own mechanisms to deal with these three problems, although the excellent Stonefield Database extensions written by Doug Hennig do a great job in these areas and, therefore, are part of the essential FoxPro toolkit.

The ability to back up and restore a database is essential. A SQL database consists of only two files; the database itself and a log file where transactions are stored. To back up a FoxPro application, you have to get all users to close their applications, and then copy all DBF, FPT, and CDX files to a backup location. In SQL, BACKUP is a single command, and users don't have to exit the application.

When a backup is done, the log file is erased. The theory is that if it is necessary to restore a database from the last good backup, the transactions log that has accumulated since that backup can be used to restore the database up to the moment that the database failed. It is also possible to use the BACKUP command to simply erase the transactions log, and in fact that's how it is often used.

SQL only returns a handle to a user when a valid user ID and password are supplied. You can either provide a single user ID and password for all users of your application, or issue one to each user. In either case, you don't have to write a single line of code to manage database access. That can be the single reason that justifies using SQL Server instead of DBFs.

Finally, SQL Server supports indexes that are remarkably similar to those in FoxPro; in fact, the indexing technology used by Microsoft in the latest versions of SQL Server came from FoxPro, and uses the Rushmore technology first developed years ago by the Fox Software team in Toledo. FoxPro indexes can be corrupted; SQL Server indexes are almost impossible to damage, and can be rebuilt automatically by SQL Server.

If any of these three features are important to your client, SQL Server is well worth the additional cost. However, SQL requires knowing more than is required to use DBFs. If you want to use SQL Server, you're going to have to cozy up to the Query Analyzer and get to know it. Help is available, from the Help, Transact-SQL Help menu pad. Transact-SQL is the actual name of the command language used in SQL Server, just as it was when they bought it from Sybase. (Did I mention that Microsoft bought some of its products from other companies rather than developing them in-house? Even Word.) A quick primer follows.

Connections and Connection Strings

The SQLConnect() command is used to supply the parameters necessary to connect to a connection previously defined in a database container (DBC), including (if desired) a user ID and password. If the UID and PWD are not supplied, SQL asks for them. This is necessary because a SQL connection consists at a minimum of the name of the server and the name of the database, and the SQLConnect() function provides no mechanism for naming them.

My preference is to use the SQLStringConnect command, which requires a complete connection string. If you don't know what connection strings look like, create an empty text file with the extension .udl, and double-click on it in Windows Explorer. The dialog that appears will allow you to build one, and will store it in the .udl file. Don't forget to select Microsoft OLE DB Provider for SQL Server on page 1 of the dialog. The usual server name is "(local)" if you've got SQL Server Developer Edition on your computer, and the default user ID of "sa" and a blank password are still there unless you changed them. Click the Test button to see if it worked. If you choose the Northwind database that is installed for testing purposes, your connection string will look like this:

```
Provider={SQL Server};Server=(local);Database=Northwind;UID=sa;PWD=;
```

To use it, do this:

```
Str = [Provider={SQL Server};Server=(local);Database=Northwind;UID=sa;PWD=;]
Handle = SQLStringConnect( str )
```

Either of these two commands returns an integer called a **Handle**. I used Handle as the variable name here, but use whatever you like.

SQLExec()

SQLExec(Handle, Cmd) executes the string defined in the variable Cmd. The command can be any of the four SQL commands: SELECT, INSERT, UPDATE, or DELETE. It can also be a SQL stored procedure, or one of the built-in SQL stored procedures that begin with the letters *sp*.

If the command is a SELECT, the matching records are returned in a cursor named SQLResult by default. If a third parameter, a string containing a cursor name, is supplied, the result is returned in a cursor of that name.

Finally, SQLDisconnect(Handle) closes the connection. For convenience, SQLDisconnect(0) closes any and all open connections.

As we saw in full detail in Chapter 2, you can't bind the controls on your forms to the cursor returned by SQL because it breaks the data binding. The ControlSource property of each control must be the name of an alias and field that exist at the end of the Load event of the form. That's why we create a cursor in the Load event, and then "pour" the data form that the cursor returned either by a call to SQLEXEC() or by a call to a Web service into the previously defined cursor.

Other SQL Commands

FoxPro also provides a few other SQL functions to return useful information about tables. You can do the same thing by instantiating an object based on the SQLDMO.DLL (SQL Data Management Objects) component that comes with SQL. On my computer, it's located in the following directory:

```
Program files\Microsoft SQL Server\80\Tools\Bin
```

It even comes with a pair of help files. The one called SQLDMO80.hlp is of absolutely no use unless you're already a SQLDMO expert. The other one, SQLDMO.CHM, is pretty cool and contains excellent examples. Look for how-to articles on the Internet, or visit my Web site.

Table 6.2 lists a few FoxPro functions that are available for use with SQL Server.

TABLE 6.2   SQL Functions in FoxPro

SQL Command	Purpose
SQLCANCEL()	Requests cancellation of an executing SQL statement
SQLCOLUMNS()	Stores a list of column names and information about each column for the specified data source table to a Visual FoxPro cursor
SQLCOMMIT()	Commits a transaction
SQLGETPROP()	Returns current or default settings for an active connection
SQLMORERESULTS()	Copies another result set to a Visual FoxPro cursor if more result sets are available
SQLPREPARE()	Prepares a SQL statement for remote execution by SQLEXEC()
SQLROLLBACK()	Cancels any changes made during the current transaction
SQLSETPROP()	Specifies settings for an active connection
SQLTABLES()	Stores the names of tables in a data source to a Visual FoxPro cursor

Some of these merit a few comments. SQLSetProp() can be used to establish asynchronous access to SQL Server, so that the program can request data and allow the user to go on doing other things. SQLMORERESULTS() returns the next N records, where N is the number of records you've specified to be returned in each packet of records in this "progressive fetch" scheme.

> **TIP**
>
> This should give you pause. I've done a query against a million records, and returned the few dozen that matched the query, in a few milliseconds. FoxPro tables are free. SQL Server isn't. Is it possible that a free data storage mechanism is hundreds of times faster than one that, to put it one way, isn't free? Try it yourself.

Transactions are considered by some to be the difference between trivial and serious database applications. I don't agree; I've built applications for some of the most important companies and nonprofit organizations in the world in which transactions were completely irrelevant. However, if you want to be able to commit both the header and the detail records of a purchase order, or commit neither if some problem occurs, transactions are how you do it. SQL Server supports transactions. To begin a transaction, issue the following command:

```
= SQLSETPROP(gnHandle, 'Transactions', 2)  && manual
```

> **TIP**
>
> FoxPro supports transactions on DBF tables that are members of a database container using the BEGIN TRANSACTION command.

The Upsizing Wizard

FoxPro includes an Upsizing Wizard, which will "automatically" create tables in SQL Server corresponding to the DBFs in your application, migrate the data in your DBFs to SQL Server, and create remote views to be used in place of DBFs throughout your application. It sounds great, but it isn't.

SQL Server is a different technology. The data is kept elsewhere, and the supposition is that you'll bring only the record or group of records that are needed for the current form. In FoxPro, you get all of the records all the time. The SQL equivalent of USE CUSTOMERS is SELECT * FROM CUSTOMERS, which brings the entire table to each workstation. The slowdown can be *glacial*. So unless you change the architecture of each and every screen, performance will be awful, and your users will be outraged.

On the other hand, if your queries are properly constructed to minimize data traffic, SQL performance for very large numbers of records and a large number of users will actually improve. Index traffic is the single greatest cause of poor performance in DBF-based applications, and SQL Server completely eliminates it.

New Features in Visual FoxPro 8

FoxPro 8 is in my opinion the most important Visual FoxPro upgrade since FoxPro 2.6 for Windows. It includes the Task Pane, which adds all sorts of new features and makes it easier to use features both new and old. It adds the CursorAdapter and DataAdapter classes, which greatly simplify access to any sort of data store, including SQL Server and XML Web Services.

The CursorAdapter Class

The CursorAdapter class permits us to deal with data of any sort, from DBFs to SQL Server to other ODBC data sources to XML Web Services, in a single way. Two new builders ease the transition, although when you know what's required, you may prefer to write the few required lines of code yourself.

When you open the Data Environment of a form and right-click anywhere on the design surface, the context menu will appear. It contains an option to Add CursorAdapter. When you know what properties are required and how to code them, you'll use this. For the moment, click on the Builder option.

The dialog shown in Figure 6.2 will appear.

On the DataEnvironment Builder dialog screen shown in Figure 6.2, there are four data source types: ADO, Native (DBF), ODBC, and XML. This time, choose ADO. Click on the Use Connection String radio button and fill in the connection string shown. The Build button will walk you through the process. If your server isn't "*(local)*", substitute the correct name; if you've changed the UserID and Password, change them as well. Test the connection, and then select Page 2, Cursors.

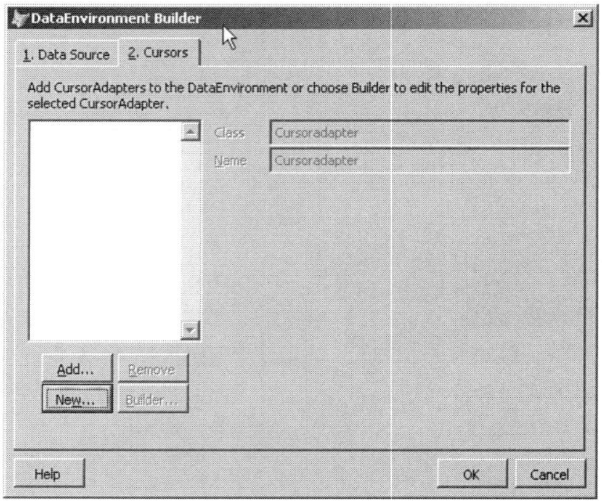

FIGURE 6.2 The DataEnvironment Builder.

Note that the connection strings for ADO and for ODBC are different. The ADO connection string to connect to the Northwind database is this:

```
Provider=SQLOLEDB.1;Persist Security Info=False;User ID=sa;
Initial Catalog=Northwind;Data Source=(local)
```

whereas the ODBC connection string is this:

```
Driver={SQL Server};Server=(local);Database=Northwind;UID=sa;PWD=;
```

Figure 6.3 shows the resulting dialog.

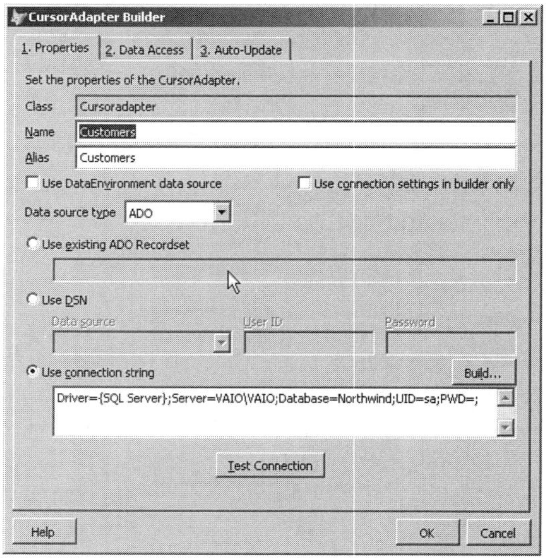

FIGURE 6.3 The Add Cursors page of the CursorAdapter Builder.

Click on New to start up the CursorAdapter Builder. A cursor named Cursor1 with a single field named F1 will be added to the Data Environment in preparation for specifying the fields that we want, and the modal CursorAdapter Builder will appear. I'm going to supply the name Customers for both the Cursor and its Alias. I again specify ADO as the Data Source Type.

I'm going to specify customers from California for this screen, so I select tab 2, Data Access, and enter the following SELECT command:

```
SELECT                  ;
  Customers.CustomerID,  ;
  Customers.CompanyName, ;
  Customers.ContactName, ;
  Customers.Country,     ;
  Customers.Phone        ;
 FROM Customers          ;
 WHERE Region='CA'
```

The Schema edit box is instantly populated with the body of a CREATE CURSOR command:

```
CUSTOMERID C(5), COMPANYNAME C(40), CONTACTNAME C(30), COUNTRY C(15), PHONE C(24)
```

The Data Access page should look like the one shown in Figure 6.4.

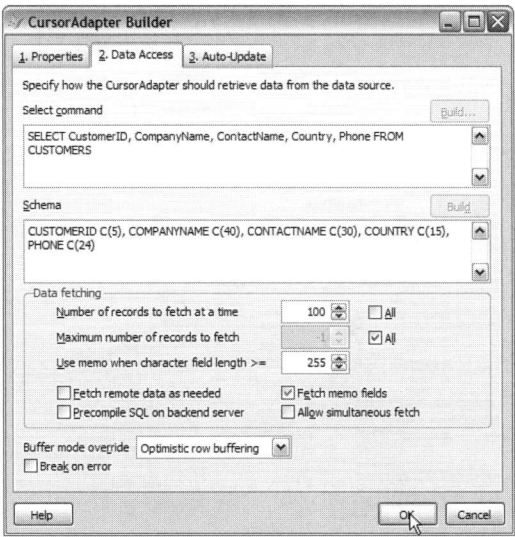

FIGURE 6.4   The Data Access page of the CursorAdapter Builder.

Page 3 of the CursorAdapter Builder allows me to instruct the CursorAdapter to automatically send UPDATE and/or INSERT commands to SQL Server as changes are made. If you're only using the records for display, you can leave this page unchanged. Click OK to save the changes.

Updates can either be done one row at a time, or as a batch for all records in the cursor. The only issue is performance; if sending all changes at once will cause an unacceptable delay, send one each time a row changes. I've selected all fields and specified that CustomerID is the key field, as shown in Figure 6.5.

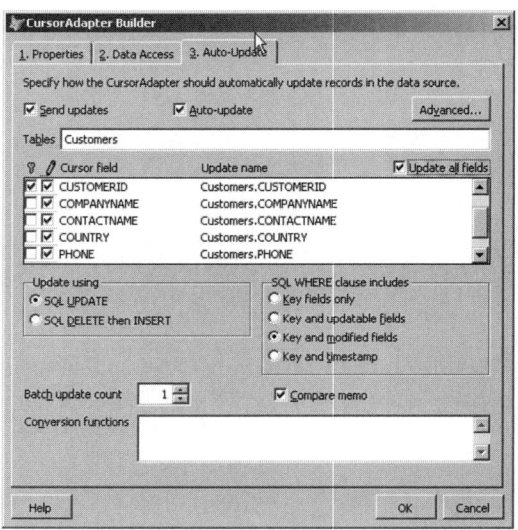

FIGURE 6.5 Specifying the fields to update and the key.

Add a grid, change the RecordSource to Customers, and use Ctrl+E to run the form. Change the ContactName from Jaime Yorres to Joe Smith and close the form. Run the form again to verify that your changes were indeed saved to SQL Server. You can also open the Query Analyzer, select the Northwind database, and enter the same SELECT command we used to populate the CursorAdapter. Sure enough, you just updated a SQL table without using any code.

Recall from Chapter 2 that we can write our own CommandBuilder to create an UPDATE command. The BuildUpdatecommand function shown in Listing 6.3 will build the command string, and SQLExec (Handle, Cmd) will execute it.

LISTING 6.3 The BuildUpdateCommand Function

```
FUNCTION BuildUpdateCommand
PARAMETERS pTable, pKeyField
Cmd = [UPDATE ]  + pTable + [ SET ]
FOR I = 1 TO FCOUNT()
```

LISTING 6.3   Continued

```
    Fld = UPPER(FIELD(I))
    IF Fld = UPPER(pKeyField)
       LOOP
    ENDIF
    IF TYPE ( Fld ) = [G]
       LOOP
    ENDIF
    Dta = ALLTRIM(TRANSFORM ( &Fld ))
    IF Dta = [.NULL.]
       DO CASE
          CASE TYPE ( Fld ) $ [CMDT]
               Dta = []
          CASE TYPE ( Fld ) $ [INL]
               Dta = [0]
       ENDCASE
    ENDIF
    Dta = CHRTRAN ( Dta, CHR(39), CHR(146) )
* get rid of single quotes in the data
    Dta = IIF ( Dta = [/  /], [], Dta )
    Dta = IIF ( Dta = [.F.], [0], Dta )
    Dta = IIF ( Dta = [.T.], [1], Dta )
    Dlm = IIF ( TYPE ( Fld ) $ [CM],['],;
      IIF ( TYPE ( Fld ) $ [DT],['],;
      IIF ( TYPE ( Fld ) $ [IN],[],    [])))
    Cmd = Cmd + Fld + [=] + Dlm + Dta + Dlm + [, ]
ENDFOR
Dlm = IIF ( TYPE ( pKeyField ) = [C], ['], [] )
Cmd = LEFT ( Cmd, LEN(Cmd) -2 )               ;
    + [ WHERE ] + pKeyField + [=]             ;
    + + Dlm + TRANSFORM(EVALUATE(pKeyField)) + Dlm
RETURN Cmd
ENDFUNC
```

Which would you rather use?

If you want to manually code the CursorAdapter class, it's not difficult. Use the Properties sheet to see which properties were set by the builder:

```
Alias = [Customers]
DataSourceType = [ADO]
Name = [Customers]
Tables = [Customers]
```

```
Tag = [Driver={SQL Server};Server=VAIO\VAIO;Database=Northwind;UID=sa;PWD=;]
Flags = 0
```

Three additional properties contain the notation See Init:

```
SelectCmd:  See Init
UpdatableFieldList: See Init
UpdateNameList: See Init
```

The code written by the builder and placed in the Init of the DataEnvironment, shown in Listing 6.4, explains these three entries.

LISTING 6.4   The Init Code Generated by the Builder in Our Example

```
local llReturn
do case
    case not pemstatus(This, '__VFPSetup', 5)
        This.AddProperty('__VFPSetup', 0)
    case This.__VFPSetup = 2
        This.__VFPSetup = 0
        return
endcase
llReturn = dodefault()
*** Setup code: DO NOT REMOVE
***<SelectCmd>
text to This.SelectCmd noshow
SELECT                 ;
  Customers.CustomerID,  ;
  Customers.CompanyName, ;
  Customers.ContactName, ;
  Customers.Country,     ;
  Customers.Phone        ;
 FROM Customers          ;
 WHERE region='CA'
endtext
***</SelectCmd>
***<KeyFieldList>
text to This.KeyFieldList noshow
CUSTOMERID
endtext
***</KeyFieldList>
***<UpdateNameList>
text to This.UpdateNameList noshow
```

LISTING 6.4   Continued

```
CUSTOMERID Customers.CUSTOMERID, COMPANYNAME Customers.COMPANYNAME, CONTACTNAME ;
Customers.CONTACTNAME, COUNTRY Customers.COUNTRY, PHONE Customers.PHONE
endtext
***</UpdateNameList>
***<UpdatableFieldList>
text to This.UpdatableFieldList noshow
CUSTOMERID, COMPANYNAME, CONTACTNAME, COUNTRY, PHONE
endtext
***</UpdatableFieldList>
*** End of Setup code: DO NOT REMOVE
*** Select connection code: DO NOT REMOVE
local loConnDataSource
set multilocks on
loConnDataSource = createobject('ADODB.Connection')
***<DataSource>
loConnDataSource.ConnectionString = ;
 [Driver={SQL Server};Server=VAIO\VAIO;Database=Northwind;UID=sa;PWD=;]
***</DataSource>
loConnDataSource.Open()
This.DataSource = createobject('ADODB.RecordSet')
This.DataSource.CursorLocation   = 3  && adUseClient
This.DataSource.LockType = 3  && adLockOptimistic
This.DataSource.ActiveConnection = loConnDataSource
*** End of Select connection code: DO NOT REMOVE
if This.__VFPSetup = 1
    This.__VFPSetup = 2
endif
return llReturn
```

This looks a little complicated, but it's not bad when you understand what's happening. Note the enhancements to the TEXT TO *<propertyname>* command that allow you to populate properties on the fly.

Finding Your CursorAdapter

If you use a cursor, you can use SELECT (*cursorname*) and you're there. But a CursorAdapter is a class, not a cursor. So how do you find it?

The new GetCursorAdapter function is the answer. To find the CursorAdapter for a cursor and fill the cursor, you can use this:

```
oCA = GetCursorAdapter ( [Customers] )
oCA.CursorFill
```

> **NOTE**
>
> If `GetCursorAdapter` is called without a parameter, it uses the current select area.

Controlling the `CursorAdapter`'s Actions in Code

There are a number of properties that you can set to determine how the `CursorAdapter` operates. As you look at them, you will be reminded of the settings for remote views in FoxPro 7. That's because the `CursorAdapter` *is* the replacement for remote views. Table 6.3 shows the most important `CursorAdapter` properties.

TABLE 6.3   `CursorAdapter` Properties

Property	Use
Alias	The Alias name to use.
BufferModeOverride	The only two permissible values are 3 (optimistic row) or 5 (optimistic table).
CursorSchema	The "between the parentheses" part of a CREATE TABLE or CREATE CURSOR command.
DataSource	Where to get the data from; only valid for ADO or ODBC DataSourceTypes.
DataSourceType	Either ADO or ODBC; values of XML, Native, or an empty string are disregarded.
FetchMemo	.T. | .F.; determines whether Memo fields are included when data is returned. Probably should be set to .T.
KeyFieldList	List of key fields; hopefully, there's only one.
MaxRecords	Maximum number of records to return in any single FillCursor call.
SelectCmd	The text of the SELECT command to use in FillCursor calls and to generate INSERT, UPDATE, and DELETE commands.
SendUpdates	.T. | .F.; determines whether updates to the remote source are permitted.
UpdatableFieldList	Names of fields in the cursor.
UpdateNameList	Pairs of names, first FoxPro then remote data source, in cases where remote table names are invalid FoxPro field names.
AllowDelete	.T. | .F.; determines whether the CursorAdapter is allowed to generate a DELETE statement.
AllowUpdate	.T. | .F.; determines whether the CursorAdapter is allowed to generate an UPDATE statement.
AllowInsert	.T. | .F.; determines whether the CursorAdapter is allowed to generate an INSERT statement.
CursorStatus	0 = no cursor, 1 = CursorFill was used, 2 = CursorAttach was used.
Tables	Tables in the CursorAdapter will appear in this exact order in any generated UPDATE, INSERT, and DELETE statements.
UpdateGram	Contains an UpdateGram of changes.
UpdateType	1=UPDATE, 2=DELETE/INSERT.
WhereType	Indicates whether the WHERE clause includes only the key, or the key and all changed fields to avoid overwriting recent changes by another user.

Table 6.5 shows the most important `CursorAdapter` methods.

TABLE 6.5   `CursorAdapter` Methods

Method	Use
`CursorAttach`	Stores the alias name provided to the `Alias` property of the `CursorAdapter`
`CursorDetach`	Removes the alias name from the `Alias` property
`CursorFill(CreateSchema,GetData)`	Fills the cursor using the `SelectCommand` string; if the first parameter is `True`, the structure is created using the schema in the `CursorSchema` string; if the second parameter is present and `True`, the cursor is created but no data is returned

Final Thoughts on the `CursorAdapter`

It's clear that the new `CursorAdapter` class is reason enough to upgrade to FoxPro 8 if you're using SQL Server. It makes SQL access trivially easy. *But wait, there's more.*

The `XMLAdapter` Class

FoxPro 7 had three functions (`CursorToXML()`, `XMLToCursor()`, and `XMLUpdateGram()`), which constituted collectively the entire toolkit for dealing with XML. The `XMLAdapter` class added in Visual FoxPro 8 greatly enhances FoxPro support for XML.

You can use the `XMLAdapter` to read XML and convert it to a FoxPro cursor. You can also use it to create XML strings. Using an object instantiated from an `XMLAdapter`, you can store one or more table objects and describe XML tables as cursors. The `XMLADapter` is based on MSXML 4.0 Service Pack 1 or later, which is installed in the "Install Prerequisites" phase of the installation of Visual FoxPro 8.

Using the `XMLAdapter`, you can

- Read XDR, ADO recordset, and XSD schemas

- Read XML and related schemas from an XML source using the `LOADXML` or `ATTACH` methods

- Build a `DiffGram` or use one to update a table using the `ApplyDiffgram` method

- Add `XMLTable` objects to the `XMLAdapter Tables` collection, using the `LoadXML`, `Attach`, or `AddTableSchema` methods

- Use the `ToXML` method to create XML

Reading an XDR

You can use an `XMLAdapter` to read an XDR and convert it to an XSD. XDR is the proprietary XML schema developed by Microsoft and used internally. However, it's not used elsewhere, so you usually need to send XML with an XSD schema. The example in Listing 6.5

shows how to do this. In the example, the TEXT command is used to build the sample XDR. If you ever needed to do this, you would probably be reading it from a file sent by an application that was only able to create XDR output.

LISTING 6.5   Converting an XDR Schema to XSD Using an XMLAdapter Object

```
TEXT TO cXML NOSHOW
<xml xmlns:s='uuid:BDC6E3F0-6DA3-11d1-A2A3-00AA00C14882'
   xmlns:dt='uuid:C2F41010-65B3-11d1-A29F-00AA00C14882'
   xmlns:rs='urn:schemas-microsoft-com:rowset'
   xmlns:z='#RowsetSchema'>
<s:Schema id='RowsetSchema'>
   <s:ElementType name='row' content='eltOnly'>
  <s:AttributeType name='xmlfield' rs:number='1'
 rs:writeunknown='true' rs:nullable='true'>
   <s:datatype dt:type='number' rs:dbtype='currency' dt:maxLength='8'
  rs:scale='4' rs:precision='6' />
</s:AttributeType>
  <s:extends type='rs:rowbase'/>
   </s:ElementType>
</s:Schema>
<rs:data>
   <z:row xmlfield='12.12'/>
</rs:data>
</xml>
ENDTEXT


CLOSE DATABASES ALL
CLEAR
LOCAL oXMLAdapter as XMLAdapter
oXMLAdapter = NEWOBJECT('XMLAdapter')
oXMLadapter.LoadXML(cXML)
IF oXMLAdapter.Tables.Item(1).Fields.Item(1).DataType <> "Y" THEN
   ? 'Failed'
ELSE
   oXMLAdapter.Tables.Item(1).ToCursor()
   oXMLAdapter.XMLNamespace=""
   oXMLAdapter.ReleaseXML(.F.)
   oXMLAdapter.XMLSchemaLocation='c:\myxmlfile.xsd'
   oXMLAdapter.ToXML('c:\myxmlfile.xml',,.T.)
   oXMLadapter2 = NEWOBJECT('xmladapter')
   oXMLAdapter2.XMLSchemaLocation='c:\myxmlfile.xsd'
   oXMLAdapter2.LoadXML('c:\myxmlfile.xml',.T.,.T.)
ENDIF
```

Reading XML into a Cursor

The `XMLAdapter` contains a `Tables` collection, which uses an `XMLTable` object to create a cursor. Previously, we used an `MSXML2.DOMDocument` object to load an XML string, and then used the `XMLToCursor()` function to create a cursor (see the example in Chapter 5, "Adding Internet Access"). In Visual FoxPro 8, the corresponding code would be as shown in Listing 6.6.

LISTING 6.6   Creating a Cursor from an XML File

```
oxml.LoadXML("xml1.xml",.T.)   && Read the file (second parm is "is this a file?")
oTable =oxml.Tables.Item(1)    && Get a reference to the XMLTable object
otable.ToCursor(.F.,"ABC")
BROWSE&& Cursor "ABC"
```

Building a Diffgram

FoxPro 7 had an `XMLUpdateGram()` function that got me really excited until I read the documentation. What it says is essentially: If you want to use this to update a table, write the function to do so yourself.

In its online documentation, Microsoft explains the difference between a diffgram and an updategram. In an MSDN article, Rich Rollman explains (and I'm paraphrasing here) that an updategram is an XML string that documents changes made to a SQL Query result. However, updategrams are not supported by ADO, SQL Server, SQLXML, or the XMLDOM. They can't call stored procedures, and there are no ADO or DOM methods that know how to process them. They're just data.

Diffgrams are what we thought updategrams were. The ADO.NET `DataSet` object knows how to apply them, as does XML 4. That's what the `XMLAdapter` implements.

Listing 6.7 demonstrates how to implement a diffgram. In this code, I simulate a client program that changes the data, and a server that receives the changes and applies them. (The code in the following three listings is actually part of a single program, called `DiffgramDemo.PRG` in the source code.)

LISTING 6.7   Client-Side Code to Return a Record and Edit It

```
LOCAL loXMLHTTP AS       [MSXML2.IXMLHTTPRequest]
loXMLHTTP = CREATEOBJECT ( [MSXML2.XMLHTTP.4.0] )
Cmd = [SELECT * FROM CLIENTS WHERE ClID = 1]
Cmd =  CHRTRAN ( Cmd, [ ], [+] )
loXMLHTTP.Open([GET], [http://localhost/Fox/GetClientRecord.asp?cmd=] + Cmd )
loXMLHTTP.Send()
XMLTOCURSOR (loXMLHTTP.ResponseBody)
CursorSetProp([Buffering],5)
BROWSE TITLE [Make changes and press Ctrl+W to save them]
```

This is where the user changes the data. I've used a browse, although a nice edit screen would accomplish the same goal. Pressing Ctrl+W ends the editing phase, and the program continues (see Listing 6.8).

LISTING 6.8   Client-Side Code to Generate a Diffgram and Return It to the Server

```
LOCAL oXML  AS XMLAdapter
oXML = CREA ( "XMLAdapter" )

oXML.AddTableSchema ( "Clientes" )
oXML.IsDiffGram  = .T.
oXML.UTF8Encoded = .T.
oXML.ToXML  ( "lcXML", "", .F., .T., .T. )
LOCAL loXMLHTTP AS        [MSXML2.IXMLHTTPRequest]
loXMLHTTP = CREATEOBJECT ( [MSXML2.XMLHTTP.4.0] )
loXMLHTTP.AddPostVar ( lcXML )
loXMLHTTP.Open([POST], [http://localhost/Fox/ActualizarRegistroCliente.asp] )
loXMLHTTP.Send()
```

At this point, we'll assume that the server has received the contents of the post buffer. You could use an XML Web Service written in FoxPro, or a WebConnection server. In either case, assume that you're now in the server code shown in Listing 6.9.

> **NOTE**
>
> I'm going to use MessageBox to display the data in this example. This is just for instructional purposes; you can't use MessageBox in a Web service.

LISTING 6.9   Server-Side Code to Receive and Process the Diffgram

```
oXML.LoadXML ( lcXML )
MESSAGEBOX( "Diffgram loaded", 48, "Received by Web Service" )

LOCAL oCA AS CursorAdapter
oCA = CREATEOBJECT ( [CursorAdapter] )

oCA.DataSource =   "Native"
oCA.CursorAttach ( "Clients" )

LOCAL oTable AS XMLTable
oTable = CREATEOBJECT ( [XMLTable] )
oTable = oXML.Tables.Item(1)
oField = oTable.Fields.Item(1)
```

LISTING 6.9 Continued

```
oField.KeyField = .T.

oTable.ApplyDiffGram ( "Clients", oCA, .T. )
CLOSE TABLES
CLOSE DATABASE
```

That's all it takes to use diffgrams to update remote tables. This is undoubtedly easier than building an INSERT, DELETE, or UPDATE string at the client and sending it to the server. And notice that we're using FoxPro tables here, which means no royalties for accessing our data.

Of course, you can update a cursor here, then pass the changes on to SQL Server. I personally believe that the combination of a FoxPro middle tier and a SQL Server database is the best way to build Internet-enabled database applications. But if the cost of licensing by the seat is an issue, there are solutions for everyone. Don't tell Microsoft; it might reduce their enthusiasm for FoxPro.

Building an XML String from a FoxPro Cursor

Converting a FoxPro table to XML requires only four lines of code:

```
USE customers
loxml.addTableSchema("Customers")
loxml.ToXML("lcxml")
MESSAGEBOX( lcxml )
```

Building a Web Service in FoxPro 8

You can build a Web service in FoxPro 8 in minutes. Create a project named WebProject in a directory called WebProject. Add a code file called WebClass, and enter the following code:

```
* WebClass.PRG
DEFINE CLASS WebClass AS Custom OLEPUBLIC

Function StateList AS String
SELECT * FROM D:\WebProject\States INTO CURSOR XStates
CURSORTOXML( "XStates", "lcXML" )
USE IN States
USE IN XStates
RETURN lcXML
ENDFUNC

ENDDEFINE
```

Compile it as a multithreaded DLL. Then, open the Task Pane and select Publish Your XML Web Service. Click on the button with the three little dots and select the DLL you just created. The dialog should look like Figure 6.6.

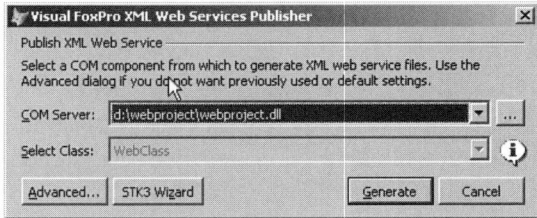

FIGURE 6.6   The XML Web Services Publisher dialog.

TIP

If you're recompiling after trying to use the service, the Internet Information Server will have it in use, and you'll get the message `file access is denied` (*dllname*); open a command window and type IISRESET to free it.

Click on the Advanced button and verify that the only checked methods are the ones you want to expose, and then click on the Generate button. You should see the message box shown in Figure 6.7.

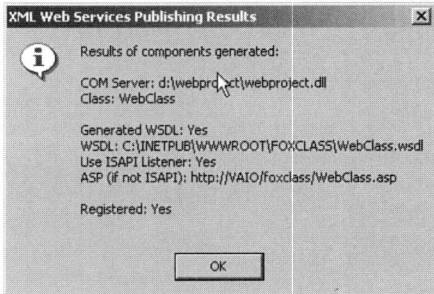

FIGURE 6.7   The XML Web Services Publisher Results dialog.

If you instantiate the DLL directly, you can see the output. This code

```
oWS = CREATEOBJECT ( "WebProject.WebClass" )
? oWS.StateList
```

produces this output (I didn't list all of the states):

```
<?xml version = "1.0" encoding="Windows-1252" standalone="yes"?>
<VFPData>
    <xstates>
        <stateabbr>AL</stateabbr>
        <statename>Alabama</statename>
    </xstates>
    <xstates>
        <stateabbr>CA</stateabbr>
        <statename>California</statename>
    </xstates>
    <xstates>
        <stateabbr>DE</stateabbr>
        <statename>Delaware</statename>
    </xstates>
    <xstates>
</VFPData>
```

Using this code remotely is extraordinarily easy in Visual FoxPro 8. Open a form on another machine, put a grid on the form, and set the RecordSource to States. It doesn't exist yet, but it will. Open the Load event of the form. Now, open the Toolbox, and click on My Web Services. The WebClass service you just registered is there! Drag and drop it into the load event, and you'll only have to add the two shaded lines in the following code:

```
LOCAL loWebClass AS "XML Web Service"
* LOCAL loWebClass AS "MSSOAP.SoapClient30"
* Do not remove or alter following line.
* It is used to support IntelliSense for your XML Web service.
*_VFPWSDef:loWebClass=http://localhost/WebClass.wsdl,WebClass,WebClassSoapPort
LOCAL loException, lcErrorMsg, loWSHandler
TRY
    loWSHandler = NEWOBJECT("WSHandler",IIF(VERSION(2)=0,"",;
                        HOME()+"FFC\")+"_ws3client.vcx")
    loWebClass = loWSHandler.SetupClient("http://localhost/WebClass.wsdl", ;
                        "WebClass", "WebClassSoapPort")
            Call your XML Web service here.
                    * ex: leResult = loWebClass.SomeMethod()
        lcXML = loWebClass.StateList          && ADD THIS LINE
        XMLToCursor ( locXML, "States" )      && ADD THIS LINE
CATCH TO loException
    lcErrorMsg="Error: "+TRANSFORM(loException.Errorno)+" - "+loException.Message
    DO CASE
    CASE VARTYPE(loWebClass)#"O"
```

```
        * Handle SOAP error connecting to web service
    CASE !EMPTY(loWebClass.FaultCode)
        * Handle SOAP error calling method
        lcErrorMsg=lcErrorMsg+CHR(13)+loWebClass.Detail
    OTHERWISE
        * Handle other error
    ENDCASE
    * Use for debugging purposes
    MESSAGEBOX(lcErrorMsg)
FINALLY
ENDTRY
```

Press Ctrl+E, and the form runs as advertised. You can use an `XMLAdapter` to move this data to a cursor, then save changes as a diffgram and send the diffgram back to another function in the Web service, which uses the code shown there to update the original data table.

For me, the ability to quickly and easily build FoxPro Web services is the biggest improvement in version 8.

FoxPro Data Access Notes and Comments

Data access in FoxPro is easy for simple tasks, and not much harder for more complex ones. In .NET, it's also pretty easy. This is partly due to the fact that XML is not just a transport in .NET; XML is how Microsoft spells D-B-F.

Data Access in Visual Basic .NET

In FoxPro, we saw how we could open a DBF and refer to its fields in the `ControlSource` property of controls on a form. This may be called a connected recordset.

Disconnected Data Access

In Visual Basic .NET, all recordsets are disconnected. You must create a cursor, bring the data into the cursor, and show it to the user. After any changes are made, you construct a command to send the data back to the source from whence it came. This is the case regardless of the data source. There are no discounts for local tables in Visual Basic .NET.

Visual Basic .NET uses datasets in the same way that we use cursors in FoxPro. You create a dataset, then call the `Fill` method of the associated `DataAdapter` to pour the data into the dataset. After any changes, you call a `CommandBuilder` object to create an `UPDATE`, `INSERT`, or `DELETE` command to be sent to the driver that actually updates the data source. It's the only way it works.

Connections

Connections are strings that tell the driver how to connect to a data source. Data sources can be OLEDB or ODBC, or they can be managed providers. Managed means "written in .NET," and for this reason they are more efficient (faster) than their OLEDB counterparts. ODBC drivers are just dreadful and are usually used only if there's nothing else available. There's a pretty good third-party market in ODBC drivers, and if you must use a data source supported by ODBC, you should look into them. Microsoft gives away several ODBC drivers for free, and as you might expect, their price is a good indication of their value.

A connection string to the Northwind database on SQL Server accessed from FoxPro was shown earlier in Listing 6.4. It's the same for Visual Basic .NET:

```
Driver={SQL Server};Server=VAIO\VAIO;Database=Northwind;UID=sa;PWD=;
```

However, you can also register a SQL Server database as an ODBC data source by running `ODBCAD32.EXE` from the command line or by clicking on the ODBC Data Sources icon in the Control Panel. The resulting dialog lets you select the driver, specify the database, and optionally provide a user ID and password. If the user ID and password aren't supplied in the connection definition, the user will have to specify them every time a connection is made. Experiment with this a few times and talk to whoever is paying for it before you decide how to proceed. It makes a difference.

In the Visual Studio IDE, there is a Server Explorer. You can open it by selecting View, Server Explorer from the menu, or by pressing Ctrl+Alt+S, whether a project or solution is open or not. The Server Explorer is shown in Figure 6.8.

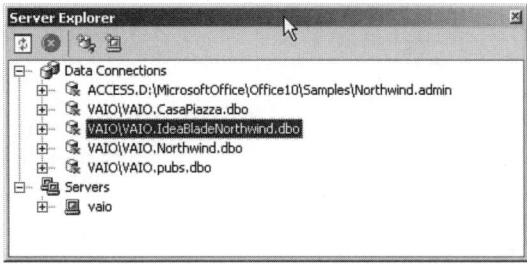

FIGURE 6.8   The Server Explorer.

You can define connections in advance. Because a project will often deal with only two databases, the test version and the production version, this simplifies the process of switching between one and the other.

To create a new connection, right-click on Data Connections and select Add Connection. You'll see the Data Link Properties dialog. This is exactly the same dialog that is produced if you create an empty text file with the extension UDL, as we saw earlier.

Page 1 of the dialog is the Provider page. There are about 20 that have been installed on my laptop by various product installations that I've done. If you buy and install drivers from third parties, there will be a few more. Notice that there is a Microsoft OLE DB Visual FoxPro driver, so if you wondered whether Visual Basic .NET will support your FoxPro tables, now you know. Note that the FoxPro driver option supports either a DBC or a Free Tables Directory. Experiment with both and verify that your choice does what you want it to do.

If you select a provider that has password protection, you'll be asked to supply a password. For most applications, a single user ID and password combination for all users is perfectly adequate. You can go to the Enterprise Manager in the Start, Programs, SQL Server drop-down menu to add a user.

You can also add categories of users and give different rights to each, although the granularity of SQL Server database access may not be adequate for your requirements if you want to control access down to the pageframe or field level. However, if your purpose is to keep users from updating records that they're only supposed to read, producing an error message when they click Save is a pretty blunt instrument compared to simply disabling the Edit button to begin with if they don't have editing rights. Users appreciate subtlety.

Notice on the third page of the Data Link Properties dialog that you can limit access to read-only, read-write, read-write share, read-write exclusive, or write-only. Again, these are probably more than you need in most cases. The default Share Deny None is probably just what you need. It supports optimistic buffering, which means that you're responsible for ensuring that one user's changes don't overwrite another's.

After you save a connection, you can drag and drop it onto a form, and it will be used to connect to the data source. It's used either directly by a command object or by a data adapter.

Data Adapters

A `DataAdapter` is a mechanism that opens a connection and executes a SQL `SELECT` statement. It also automatically creates `UPDATE`, `INSERT`, and `DELETE` statements if a unique key is specified in the `SELECT` statement. That's why it's so terribly important in the SQL world to have a single unique key. Many FoxPro developers have developed the nasty habit of using compound keys, for example, InvoiceNum + LineNum for a detail record of an invoice. That's a spectacularly bad idea even in FoxPro; in SQL Server, it's unthinkable. So before you try to use a `DataAdapter` to connect to your data, add a unique integer key or a GUID to each of your data tables. I'll wait right here.

Good, you're back. Let's continue.

Using a `DataAdapter` with a FoxPro Table

Create a connection to the Customers table. If you didn't download the code, just copy the Customers table that comes with the FoxPro Northwind samples to a directory where you can play with the data without doing any permanent damage. Be sure to use `COPY TO Customers WITH CDX` because without an index, the `DataAdapter` doesn't have a clue, as you'll see. Create a connection to the directory as a Free Table directory in the Solution Explorer.

Next, open the Visual Basic .NET IDE and select File, New Project from the menu. Choose Visual Basic, Windows Application. Make sure that the project is going where you want it to go, and note that the project name is also the name of a new directory that Visual Studio is going to create for you. Visual Studio will create a project with five standard .NET namespace references needed to build a forms project: `System`, `System.Data`, `System.Drawing`, `System.Windows.Forms`, and `System.XML`. Remember that last one. It's there because forms need data, and XML spells data in .NET. It also adds an `AssemblyInfo.vb` file (like a project information file) and `Form1.vb`.

That first form is usually your Main form, which will contain your logo and your application's main menu. However, you can also build an application consisting of just a single form, and that's what we'll do here. Use F4 to open the Properties window and change the `Text` property to `"My customers"`.

Next, open the Solution Explorer and add the connection you just created by dragging and dropping it on the form. Visual Basic .NET will ask you if you want to add a user ID and password. For now, ignore it.

Next, open the Toolbox with Ctrl+Alt+X and add an `OleDBDataAdapter` from the Data toolbox category. The resulting wizard asks what connection to use, and defaults to the one we had added previously Next, the wizard needs to know from which fields, and from which tables you want to generate data (see Figure 6.9).

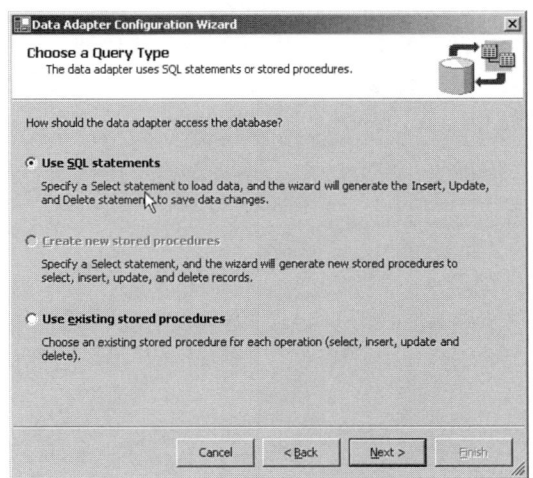

FIGURE 6.9 Adding a `DataAdapter`—specifying a connection.

The wizard will offer to use SQL statements, create new stored procedures, or use existing stored procedures. You'd be surprised how many shops don't build the screens until some database guy has approved the SELECT, INSERT, UPDATE, and DELETE code and written procedures for them in advance. Select Use SQL Statements and click the Next button.

RANT

<rant>The advantage in stored procedures is that after you've built them, migrating to another vendor's SQL is harder. Uh, sorry, that's the advantage for the *vendor*. The advantage for *us* is—uh, sorry, there isn't any.</rant>

In Figure 6.10, the DataAdapter Configuration Wizard is looking for a SELECT statement that returns the records you want.

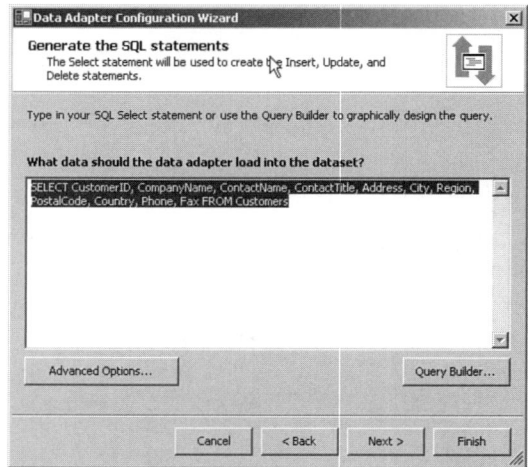

FIGURE 6.10   Enter a SELECT statement for the DataAdapter.

If you want all customers from California, type this:

```
SELECT * FROM Customers WHERE Region = 'CA'
```

SQL can use the SELECT statement and the unique index values to generate the code for the INSERT, UPDATE, and DELETE commands. However, if you only want a SELECT statement, click on the Advanced Options button and uncheck the Generate Insert, Update and Delete Statements check box. Also, if you don't want the code-generated SQL statement to verify that no fields have been changed since the SELECT, uncheck the Use Optimistic Concurrency check box. It improves performance, and in many cases it's not necessary. You be the judge of the probability that two people will try to change the same record on two workstations at the same exact instant. It's usually infinitesimal.

If you want to add a parameter to a query, write the SELECT statement as follows:

```
SELECT * FROM Customers WHERE (CustomerID=?)
```

This will cause the IDE to build a parameterized query. To execute it, you'll need to supply a value for the parameter in code before executing the Fill command:

```
OledbDataAdapter1.SelectCommand.Parameters(0).Value = 1
```

If this looks a lot like a local view in FoxPro, it should. When you open a view in FoxPro, you're executing a SELECT command. When you close the view, the view itself uses the SELECT command and the unique index key to build and execute INSERT, UPDATE, and DELETE commands as needed to update the source table. That's exactly how the DataAdapter works. You just get to see all of the details.

Right-click on the DataAdapter and select Generate Dataset. Select New, and provide the name dsCustomers. This builds an XSD file describing the schema and a .vb file containing property procedures for all fields. We'll look at this in more detail a few pages ahead, under the heading "Datasets." For now, we'll just build one and use it.

Finally, add a grid to the form. Open the Toolbox using Ctrl+Alt+X, click on the Windows Forms controls section heading, and drag a DataGrid to the form. Open the Properties sheet, click on DataSource, and from the pull-down list select dsCustomers1.Customers. You can also use the Properties window to specify the dataset name dsCustomers1 as the DataSource, and the table name Customers as the DataMember, for the data grid.

This is necessary because a dataset can contain several tables, and we just want one for the grid. (If you like, select dsCustomers1 and you'll see a little plus sign, which you have to expand manually to pick the table and display the table in the grid. Grids know how to work with datasets, even if they have multiple tables or hierarchical datasets.)

But we're not done. We have to write some code—one line of code. Double-click anywhere on the form except the grid, and the code window will open with a first and last line of a Form_Load event wired to the Load event of the form via a Handles clause. Type in the following line of code:

```
Me.OleDbDataAdapter1.Fill(DsCustomers1)
```

You don't need the "Me.", but it brings up IntelliSense and saves you some typing. Use the Tab key to select the current suggestion and move to the end of the selected text; or, use a period to do the same thing and add a period at the end. The Fill command of the DataAdapter was built when we constructed the SELECT command, and the dsCustomers1 dataset was constructed from the DataAdapter's SELECT command, so they're guaranteed to be conformable.

Press F5 to run the application. That's one line of code. In FoxPro, it also takes one line of code—a USE statement in the LOAD event of the form. So far, it's a close race.

> **NOTE**
>
> I've had a few problems with the FoxPro OLE DB driver in Visual Basic .NET. During the writing of this chapter, the DataAdapter Configuration Wizard began inserting double quotes around my table name, so that not even the SELECT command would work. And many times it failed to generate UPDATE and DELETE commands for unspecified reasons. I had no such problem with the SQL Server or Access drivers.

Generated Code for the DataAdapter and Dataset

You've probably already done this, but open up the code for the form. You'll see a little box that contains the text

```
Windows Form Designer Generated Code
```

Click on the plus sign to the left of it, and scroll through the code. You'll see a block of code declaring a series of objects named SQLDataAdapter1, SQLSelectCommand1, SQLInsertCommand1, SQLUpdateCommand1, SQLDeleteCommand1, and SQLConnection1. Each of these is defined in the generated code, including the command that SQL Server will need to do its magic. Each field is generated as a parameter, which is filled in when the function is called. Listing 6.10 is an example. The generated code produces long lines, so they look pretty bad on the screen and on the page. Thankfully, we seldom look at this code.

LISTING 6.10   Generated SQLUpdateCommand Code

```
Me.SqlUpdateCommand1.CommandText = "UPDATE Customers SET CustomerID = @Customer
ID, CompanyName = @CompanyName, Contac" & _
"tName = @ContactName, ContactTitle = @ContactTitle, Address = @Address, City =
 @" & _
"City, Region = @Region, PostalCode = @PostalCode, Country = @Country, Phone =
@P" & _
"hone, Fax = @Fax WHERE (CustomerID = @Original_CustomerID) AND (Address = @Ori
gi" & _
"nal_Address OR @Original_Address IS NULL AND Address IS NULL) AND (City = @Ori
gi" & _
"nal_City OR @Original_City IS NULL AND City IS NULL) AND (CompanyName = @Origin
a" & _
"l_CompanyName) AND (ContactName = @Original_ContactName OR @Original_ContactNa
me" & _
" IS NULL AND ContactName IS NULL) AND (ContactTitle = @Original_ContactTitle O
R " & _
"@Original_ContactTitle IS NULL AND ContactTitle IS NULL) AND (Country = @Origi
na" & _
```

LISTING 6.10   Continued

```
"1_Country OR @Original_Country IS NULL AND Country IS NULL) AND (Fax = @Origin
al" & _
"_Fax OR @Original_Fax IS NULL AND Fax IS NULL) AND (Phone = @Original_Phone OR
 @" & _
"Original_Phone IS NULL AND Phone IS NULL) AND (PostalCode = @Original_PostalCo
de" & _
" OR @Original_PostalCode IS NULL AND PostalCode IS NULL) AND (Region = @Origin
al" & _
"_Region OR @Original_Region IS NULL AND Region IS NULL); SELECT CustomerID, Co
mp" & _
"anyName, ContactName, ContactTitle, Address, City, Region, PostalCode, Country
, " & _
"Phone, Fax FROM Customers WHERE (CustomerID = @CustomerID)"
```

That's *one line of code*. I really didn't need to see this. In Visual FoxPro, we're blissfully unaware of what's needed to make things happen; Visual Basic .NET shows you *everything*.

There's also a DSCustomers1 object based on DSCustomers. What is DSCustomers? It's a generated typed dataset, located in another generated code file, as you'll see shortly.

Datasets

A dataset is a cursor. Want to see how it works? Open a new Visual Basic blank project, and then open the Solution Explorer using Ctrl+Alt+L, right-click on the project name, and select Add New Item. Select Dataset from the available selections (others include XML file and XML Schema and others). When the designer opens, use Ctrl+Alt+S to open the Server Explorer, and then pick any connection, expand it to reveal its tables, expand Tables, and drag any table name to the designer surface. You can view the result either as XML or as a table.

Using the DataAdapter to Build a Dataset

To build a dataset, click on the Data tab in the Toolbox and drag an OLEDBDataAdapter (or a SQLDataAdapter) to a form surface. There are small differences, but essentially the SQLDataAdapter works only with SQL Server, whereas the OLEDBDataAdapter works with SQL Server plus many other data sources that have OLEDB drivers. The SQLDataAdapter has less overhead, and is therefore faster and more efficient.

The DataAdapter Configuration wizard asks you to supply a SQL SELECT statement to determine where to get the data. After it's configured, you can use it to add a dataset to your project. This named dataset will be used as a cursor. The DataAdapter will fill it with data using the Fill method and present it to your form; later, when you save data, the changed rows can be sent back through the DataAdapter to the data source to update it.

When the `DataAdapter` has been configured, right-click on it and select Generate Dataset from the context menu. Change the dataset name to the prefix "ds" plus the name of the table and click OK. The resulting wizard will ask you for a `SELECT` statement, and will build the container in which the data will be stored in an XML format with the extension `.xsd`. XSD means "I'm a dataset." It's an empty cursor. Actually, because a dataset can hold multiple tables, it's more like "one or more cursors." But we'll keep it simple for now.

Relationship Between XML, Datasets, and XML Schemas

XML is not a dataset, and a dataset is not a schema. And even though a dataset can start with a schema, the first half-dozen lines of a dataset and an XML schema file created from the same SQL table are quite different. And XML is generic, while a dataset is a particular structure in XML.

Here's how it works: XML is a technology for storing things. A dataset is one or more tables stored in XML format, with (optionally) one or more schemas. A schema describes a data table in an XML file, either inline or in a separate XML file. A dataset can contain multiple schemas and multiple tables. I hope that proves easy to remember. Each piece of the puzzle has its purpose.

Typed Datasets

Typed datasets in Visual Basic .NET are defined by

- An XML schema that describes the tables, columns, keys, and relationships in the dataset

- A class file (written as a Visual Basic class) that inherits from `System.Data.DataSet` and implements properties and methods that provide access to a dataset with the specified schema

Use Ctrl+Alt+L to open the Solution Explorer, and then click on the Show All Files icon at the top of the window. Notice that the dataset you just created has a plus sign, indicating that there's more below it. Click on the plus sign to expand the tree, and you'll see a file with the same name and a `.vb` extension. Double-click on it to open the file. It's a Visual Basic class that describes the tables in the dataset.

Exploring the Typed Dataset

Use the View, Class View menu option to open the Class View window. Select the `DsCustomers.vb` class that was generated automatically by the Generate Dataset Wizard from the `DataAdapter` object, and you're in for a shock. There are dozens and dozens of properties, events, and methods in the generated code.

Most of them are prototypes; that is, you can add code wherever you want to. For example, for each field there's a `SetFaxNull` subroutine. The Customers table has a Fax column. In the database, Nulls are permitted in this column. VB hates nulls. In fact, it will crash if you return one. So, the typed dataset has provided a routine where you can write code to specify what you want to return as a value if you add a record and don't specify a value for the Fax column. The generated routine inserts `DBNull`, but you might want to insert "N/A". The `SetFaxNull` subroutine is where you would do so.

Go a little further and you begin to see how this works. The IDE has generated a class definition called a `CustomersDataTable`, which inherits from the .NET `DataTable` class. That means that it comes with all of the properties, events, and methods of the `DataTable` class, which you probably should learn about. The declaration is followed by a declaration of a private variable called `column&ColumnName` (to use FoxPro syntax—`columnFax` would be created for the Fax column in the table, for example) as `DataColumn` for each of the columns in your original data table. These are called fields, and for the first time, the name makes sense in this context.

A property procedure called `Count` is added, which returns the value of `Me.Rows.Count`. Then follow a raft of property procedures named `&Field.Column` (again using FoxPro syntax—an example would be `FaxColumn`), which is supplied by returning the value stored in `Classname.ColumnFax`, the class's corresponding field name. Visual Basic .NET creates one field (that is, one local variable) for each column, then uses these fields to store the values that are actually available to the user as properties via property procedures named with the word "Column" as a suffix for the property procedures. Confused yet?

It gets more complicated. The last declaration in this class definition is `tableCustomers`, which is actually an object derived from `CustomersDataTable`. What is returned is the `tableCustomers` object, not the `CustomersDataTable` object. When you refer to `dsCustomers`, you're actually referring to an object based on the `tableCustomers` object, which is in turn based on the `CustomersDataTable` class, which is based on the `DataTable` class.

When I drive to the store to buy a loaf of bread, I'm exploding gasoline thousands of times per minute. I know this is true, and in fact it would be pretty dramatic to be down inside the engine watching all of it happen. But I just want a loaf of bread, and I don't care about the exploding gasoline.

I feel exactly, precisely the same way about all of this stuff. The less I know about it, the better. All you need to know is that if you create a dataset, you can bind the `Text` property of your onscreen controls to `Dataset.FieldName` and it will work.

The Data Form Wizard

When you right-click on the Windows form project and select Add, Add New Item, one of the options is Data Form Wizard, as shown in Figure 6.11.

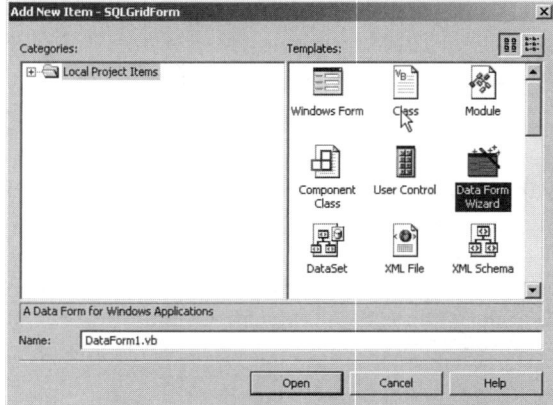

FIGURE 6.11   Double-click to Select the Data Form Wizard project.

When you select Data Form Wizard, the screen shown in Figure 6.12 appears. Click on the Next button to proceed.

FIGURE 6.12   The Data Form Wizard.

If I've already created a typed dataset, I can use it in the form that the Data Form Wizard is building, as shown in Figure 6.13. Typed datasets belong to the project, not to a form, and can be shared by several forms.

The wizard will include a Load and (optionally) an Update button if you check the check box (see Figure 6.14, about halfway down the dialog form).

Finally, the customer table and all of its fields are selected by default. Click the Next button to go to the next step (see Figure 6.15).

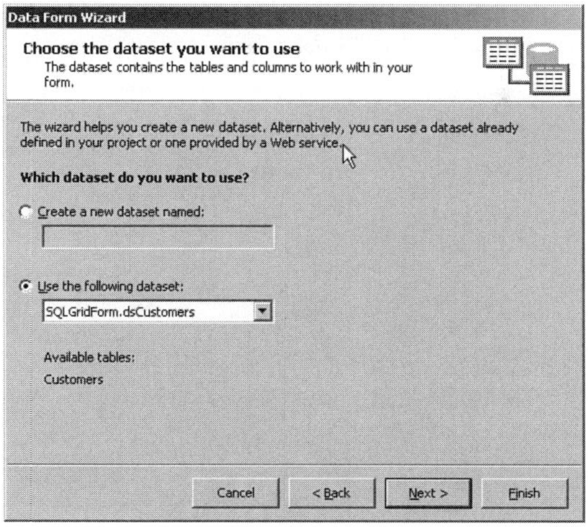

FIGURE 6.13   Selecting an existing typed dataset.

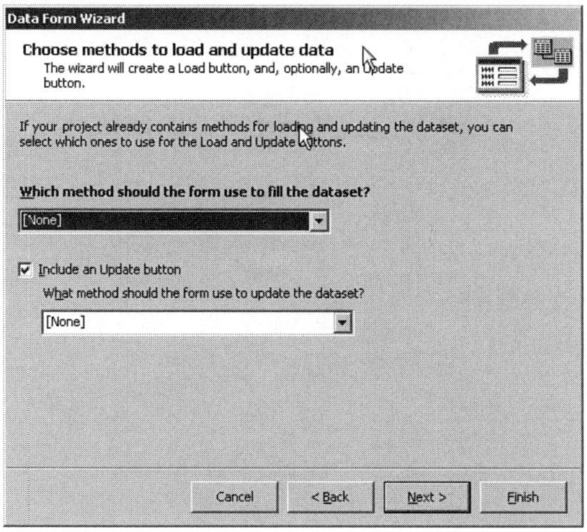

FIGURE 6.14   Setting options for the Data Form Wizard.

The next screen (see Figure 6.16) is the one that I was waiting for. Do I want to present data to my users as a grid (no) or as a record (yes). I don't even know why they offer the first option, although I suppose it's easy to code. But editing records in a grid is almost never a desirable technique. So, pick Single Record in Individual Controls and click Finish. In about three seconds, you've got screen! Forms like the one shown in Figure 6.16 are where I spend most of my day, and this one was written for me in a few seconds. All I have to do is go in and tweak it.

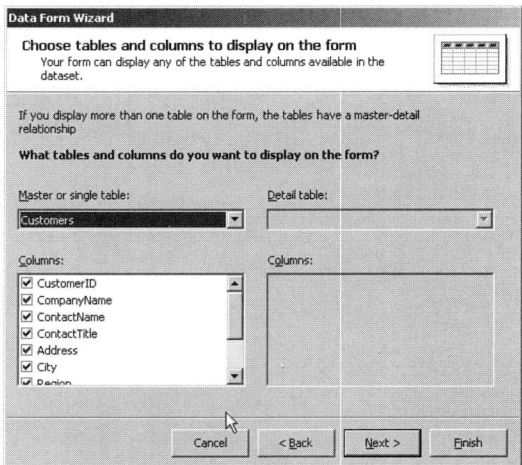

FIGURE 6.15   Selecting the table and all fields.

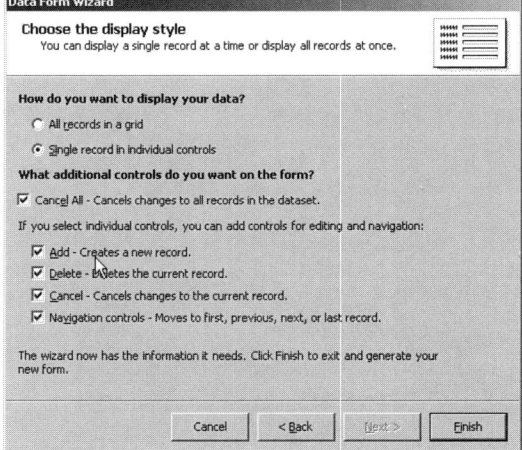

FIGURE 6.16   Specifying the screen type in the Data Form Wizard.

Before we can run this, there's one thing we have to do. I started this project with another form, then added this one. When you press F5 to compile and run a project, you have to tell the project which is the startup form—like FoxPro's SET MAIN selection on the Project menu popup. To do this, click on the solution, then on the project, to make sure it's *selected*. Next, right-click on the project and select Properties from the context menu. You should see the screen shown in Figure 6.17. Pick the form that you want to use as the startup for the executable.

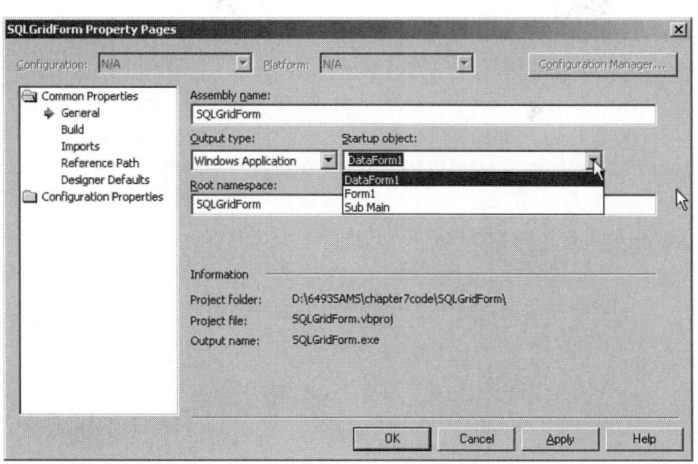

FIGURE 6.17   Setting the Startup form.

Press F5 to run the application. As shown in Figure 6.18, you can indeed move from one record to another, make changes and save them, and add and delete records.

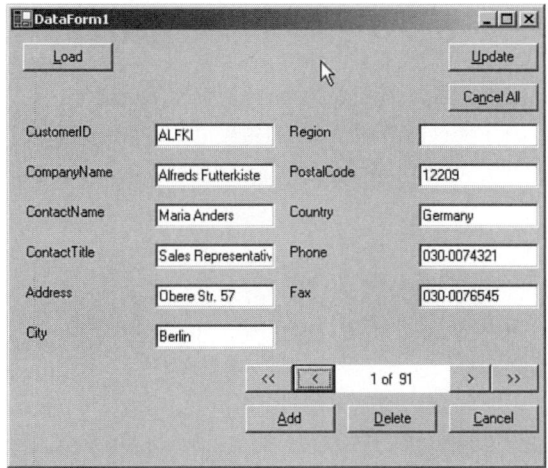

FIGURE 6.18   The generated data form in action.

However, when I click the Load button, nothing happens! It turns out that because I told the wizard to use my existing dataset, it left me with the responsibility of loading the dataset. No big deal, right?

The Generated Code

The code for this generated screen is 360 lines long. It returns all of the records in the table from SQL, then uses the VB equivalent of SKIP to move backward and forward through the tables. It also assumes that my users can just start typing in any field whenever they want, and that they'll know that they need to "update" before they can go to another record—their wrist will be slapped with an error message if they don't. So it has little to commend it as a database application. But it works, and it only took a few seconds.

Here's the code generated by the Data Form Wizard:

```
Private Sub btnCancel_Click( _
 ByVal sender As System.Object, ByVal e As System.EventArgs) _
 Handles btnCancel.Click
  Me.BindingContext(objdsCustomers, "Customers").CancelCurrentEdit()
  Me.objdsCustomers_PositionChanged()
End Sub


Private Sub btnDelete_Click( _
 ByVal sender As System.Object, ByVal e As System.EventArgs) _
 Handles btnDelete.Click

  If (Me.BindingContext(objdsCustomers, "Customers").Count > 0) Then
    Me.BindingContext(objdsCustomers, "Customers").RemoveAt( _
    Me.BindingContext(objdsCustomers, "Customers").Position)
    Me.objdsCustomers_PositionChanged()
  End If
End Sub


Private Sub btnAdd_Click( _
 ByVal sender As System.Object, ByVal e As System.EventArgs) _
 Handles btnAdd.Click
Try
'Clear out the current edits
  Me.BindingContext(objdsCustomers, "Customers").EndCurrentEdit()
  Me.BindingContext(objdsCustomers, "Customers").AddNew()
  Catch eEndEdit As System.Exception
   System.Windows.Forms.MessageBox.Show(eEndEdit.Message)
   End Try
  Me.objdsCustomers_PositionChanged()
End Sub


Private Sub btnNavFirst_Click( _
```

```
  ByVal sender As System.Object, ByVal e As System.EventArgs) _
  Handles btnNavFirst.Click
    Me.BindingContext(objdsCustomers, "Customers").Position = 0
    Me.objdsCustomers_PositionChanged()
End Sub


Private Sub btnLast_Click( +
  ByVal sender As System.Object, ByVal e As System.EventArgs) _
  Handles btnLast.Click
    Me.BindingContext(objdsCustomers, "Customers").Position = _
  (Me.objdsCustomers.Tables("Customers").Rows.Count - 1)
    Me.objdsCustomers_PositionChanged()
End Sub


Private Sub btnNavPrev_Click( +
  ByVal sender As System.Object, ByVal e As System.EventArgs) _
  Handles btnNavPrev.Click

    Me.BindingContext(objdsCustomers, "Customers").Position = _
  (Me.BindingContext(objdsCustomers, "Customers").Position - 1)
    Me.objdsCustomers_PositionChanged()
End Sub


Private Sub btnNavNext_Click( _
  ByVal sender As System.Object, ByVal e As System.EventArgs) _
  Handles btnNavNext.Click
    Me.BindingContext(objdsCustomers, "Customers").Position = _
  (Me.BindingContext(objdsCustomers, "Customers").Position + 1)
    Me.objdsCustomers_PositionChanged()
End Sub


Private Sub objdsCustomers_PositionChanged()
    Me.lblNavLocation.Text = (((Me.BindingContext(objdsCustomers,
    "Customers").Position + 1).ToString _
    + " of  ") + Me.BindingContext(objdsCustomers, "Customers").Count.ToString)
End Sub


Private Sub btnCancelAll_Click( _
  ByVal sender As System.Object, ByVal e As System.EventArgs) _
  Handles btnCancelAll.Click
    Me.objdsCustomers.RejectChanges()
End Sub
```

This is interesting code. There's something called a `BindingContext` that apparently belongs to the form (I didn't instantiate it, so it must be a part of `Windows.Forms.Form`). `BindingContext` takes two parameters, a dataset and a tablename, and contains a count property (like `RECCOUNT()`) and a position (like `RECNO()`). To skip to the next record, all you have to type is

```
Me.BindingContext(objdsCustomers, "Customers").Position = _
(Me.BindingContext(objdsCustomers, "Customers").Position + 1)
```

That's the equivalent of FoxPro's

```
SKIP
```

It looks as if the `BindingContext` is also responsible for deleting records. Here's the command:

```
Me.BindingContext(objdsCustomers, "Customers").RemoveAt( _
Me.BindingContext(objdsCustomers, "Customers").Position)
```

and here's the FoxPro equivalent:

```
DELETE
```

How about adding? I found it. It's this:

```
Me.BindingContext(objdsCustomers, "Customers").AddNew()
```

That's not much harder than FoxPro's equivalent:

```
APPEND BLANK
```

I'm starting to like Visual Basic .NET. But I still like FoxPro better.

Loading the Dataset

But it still isn't loading my table from SQL into my dataset. And it needs to be a table named Customers, because datasets can have multiple tables, and by default the first one is named Table. It took me about 30 seconds to write the following code:

```
Private Sub btnLoad_Click( _
 ByVal sender As System.Object, ByVal e As System.EventArgs) _
 Handles btnLoad.Click
  Dim c As New SqlClient.SqlConnection
  c.ConnectionString = "Server=VAIO\VAIO;Database=Northwind;UID=sa;PWD=;"
  c.Open()
  Dim da As New SqlClient.SqlDataAdapter("SELECT * FROM CUSTOMERS", c)
  da.Fill(Me.objdsCustomers, "Customers")
End Sub
```

Retrieving a dataset requires opening a connection, then defining a `DataAdapter` and giving it a `SELECT` command, and then finally calling the `DataAdapter`'s `Fill` method to fill the dataset and providing the correct name for the table contained in the dataset. It's harder than opening a DBF, but it's easier than creating a cursor in a FoxPro form and dumping a SQL cursor into it. The dataset was declared up at the top of the form, so it has scope throughout the form. The connection and `DataAdapter` do their job and fade away.

I ran the form, and it worked just fine, except that I don't want to load the entire table from SQL or across the Internet into a table in my form. But this will do for now.

Data Binding

In FoxPro, if you open the Data Environment, click on a cursor name, and drag the word Fields onto the surface of the form, you get all of the fields in the table, using your classes, with a label to the left of them with a name for the field to the right of the label. The controls that are used are your own subclassed controls from your own VCX file, based on your settings on the Field Mappings page of the Tools, Options dialog. The labels are the text stored in the corresponding records in the database container, if you used one. The `ControlSource` property of each control is automatically filled in, and when you open the form and navigate through your data, a simple `THISFORM.Refresh` shows you that the record pointer has moved.

In Visual Basic .NET, if you create a dataset from a `DataAdapter`, then drag the dataset onto the form, you get *bupkis*—nothing. No controls are placed on the form.

Open up the form generated by the Data Form Wizard, right-click on any of the text boxes, and look at the `DataBindings` property. You'll have to click on the plus sign to expand the property and see its `Text` property.

TIP

Just to clarify, the `Text` property is the equivalent of the `Value` property of a text box, combo box or check box, or the caption property of a label.

I've opened the drop-down for the `Text` property so that you can see how it has been populated, as shown in Figure 6.19.

Now you know that you can define a dataset, then drop controls on the form and fill in the `Text` `DataBindings` property with individual fields from the dataset, and it will work.

However, if you open up the code, you'll find this:

```
Me.editCustomerID.DataBindings.Add(New System.Windows.Forms.Binding("Text", _
Me.objdsCustomers, "Customers.CustomerID"))
```

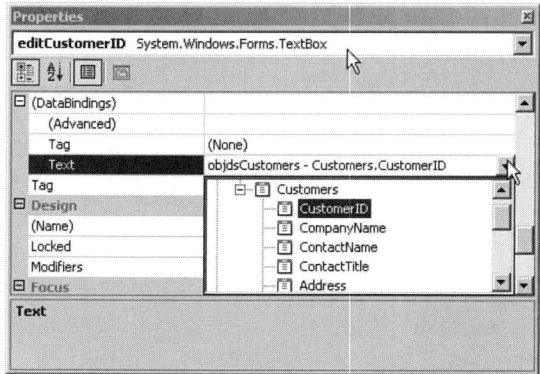

FIGURE 6.19 Populating the Text property of DataBindings.

It seems that data binding is actually the result of a command that we can write ourselves. The syntax in pseudocode is this:

```
Control.DataBindings.Add ( Binding("Text", ds, "table.field"))
```

where ds is our dataset, Control is an object reference to each control on the form, and "table.field" is a string containing the table and field names as part of a typed dataset. It's possible to refer to them in some other way, but this is the easiest.

That's one of the reasons why we'll want to use typed datasets. If I can loop through all of the controls on the form and bind them to my dataset using names from a typed dataset, I don't have to go through dozens of controls on dozens of forms clicking and selecting the field name for each one. This is a *good thing*.

What Else Can You Do with Typed Datasets?

Typed datasets are the tip of the iceberg. At a minimum, a typed dataset contains one property procedure for each column in the corresponding schema, so that, for example, an expression like Customers.Name is meaningful. Otherwise, unlike FoxPro, it has no intrinsic meaning in Visual Studio 1.1.

Many developers have taken the notion of typed datasets far, far further. By adding events that other objects can respond to, it's possible (for example) to detect when data changes, look for "save" and "cancel" command buttons on the form and enable them, without writing any screen-specific code. The DataSet object itself does this. And many very sophisticated extensions are possible. IdeaBlade from ObjectWare, for example, can save data either back to the server, or to a local XML cache for subsequent synchronization with the server whenever a connection can be established. This is done using methods built into a generated DataSet object. There's no limit to what they can be designed to do except our imaginations.

Tables

Datasets contain a tables collection. When you return a dataset, if you want to show it in a grid, you have to specify both the DataSource (the dataset) and DataMember (the table). Otherwise, it shows you a little plus sign, which is your cue that you have to drill down and specify *which* table in the dataset—even though you and I know there's only one. Computers aren't really all that bright.

Technically, you can do this:

```
Dim oTable as DataTable
For each oTable in MyDataset.Tables
    Debug.WriteLine oTable.TableName
End For
```

Of course, the Table object itself has properties, events, and methods. Some of them will be useful. So expect to see code like this:

```
Dim oTable As New DataTable = MyDataSet.Tables(0)
```

followed by calls to methods on the oTable object. If you ever get used to referring to table number zero as the first table, you've outdone me. It just creeps me out.

Rows

By the same token, tables have rows. So we can also write this:

```
For Each oTable In objdsCustomers.Tables
    Dim oRow As DataRow
    For Each oRow In oTable.Rows
        Dim I As Integer
        For I = 0 To oRow.ItemArray.Length - 1
            Debug.WriteLine(oRow.ItemArray(I))
        Next
        Debug.WriteLine(oTable.TableName)
    Next
Next
```

Row objects give you access to their columns via overloading. You can assign a value to the first column in a row, a column named CustomerID, using either the column name or its number (starting with zero, of course):

```
Row("CustomerID") = 1234
```

or

```
Row(0) = 1234
```

Columns

Each row contains a columns collection. The following code prints all of the rows in a table:

```
Private Sub PrintValues(ByVal myTable As DataTable)
    Dim myRow As DataRow
    Dim myColumn As DataColumn
    For Each myRow in myTable.Rows
        For Each myColumn In myTable.Columns
            Console.WriteLine(myRow(myColumn))
        Next
    Next
End Sub
```

XML Web Services

XML Web services in .NET are as easy as they are in Visual FoxPro 8, and a heck of a lot easier than they are in earlier versions of Fox. Create a new project, and pick ASP.NET Web Services from the Visual Basic New Project dialog, as shown in Figure 6.20.

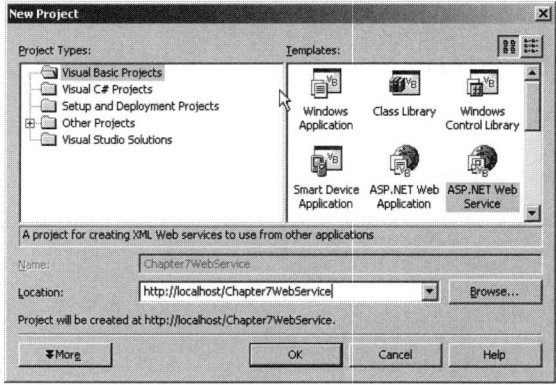

FIGURE 6.20   Creating a Visual Basic New Project.

Notice that the location of the project is `http://localhost/Chapter6WebService`. That means that the location is actually `C:\InetPub\WWWRoot\Chapter6WebService`. IIS is only allowed to see virtual directories that have been expressly added. The only exception is that it can also see any subdirectory under the `C:\InetPub\WWWRoot\` directory that's not hidden from it. So by placing Web service projects there, Visual Studio .NET publishes them in the most logical place. And, because I've probably created 300 Web service projects on my computer since the early beta of .NET, I really appreciate anything that makes them easier to find. Then there's that whole "senior moment" thing.

I also changed both the external filename of `Service1.asmx` and the internal class name of the service to `MyWebService`. Changing the filename is easy; just right-click on `Service1.asmx` in the Solution Explorer, select Rename, and then type the new name. Then select the Web service design surface, then right-click and select Properties, and change the Service1 name to MyWebService as shown in Figure 6.21.

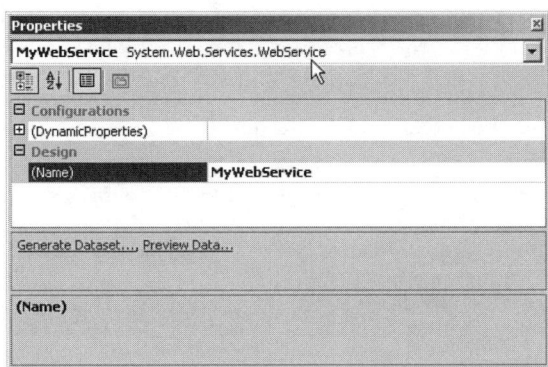

FIGURE 6.21   Naming a Visual Basic .NET XML Web service.

To write the code, double-click on the design surface, or select View, Code from the IDE menu. You'll see some commented code (probably lime green text) with placeholder code that looks like this:

```
'<WebMethod()> _
'Public Function HelloWorld() As String
'    Return "Hello World"
'End Function
```

The `<WebMethod()>` attribute prefix exposes your new Web service for testing on a Web page test bed that's automatically generated by Visual Studio. We'll need that, but everything else has got to go.

But first, we need a connection and a `DataAdapter`. Open the toolbox and drag a `SQLDataAdapter` to the design surface. As before, select the Northwind connection, pick the Customers table with a `SELECT * FROM Customers` statement, and click Finish to end the process.

Next, right-click on the `DataAdapter` and select Generate Dataset. Use `dsCustomers` as the name.

`dsCustomers` is a typed dataset. It's a type, as are integers and dates. Functions return types. So we'll return an XML string of type `dsCustomers`.

Now we're ready. Double-click on the form to open the code window. Replace the entire sample function with this:

```
<WebMethod> Public Function GetCustomers() As dsCustomers
    Dim Customers As New dsCustomers()
    SqlDataAdapter1.Fill(Customers)
    Return Customers
End Function
```

So we instantiate a dsCustomers object named Customers, use the built-in SELECT state-ment in the DataAdapter to fill the Customers dataset (which, as we know, is XML), and return the selected records in an XML string to the requestor.

Press F5 to run this, and the screen shown in Figure 6.22 appears.

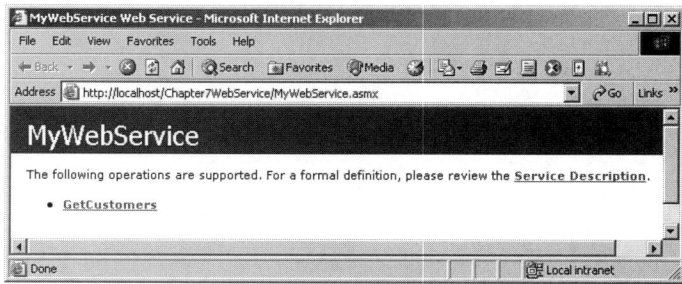

FIGURE 6.22   The generated test bed fir your XML Web Service.

Visual Studio has created a test bed to test our Web service. This test bed page will list all of your Web service's functions, and will allow you to test any of them that have parame-ters that are primitive types and can, therefore, be entered on a Web page for use in testing. Thus any calls that require a dataset as input (such as an update routine) will be listed, but not testable.

Our new function GetCustomers is testable, so click on it. This brings up the next screen, shown in Figure 6.23. This screen appears in case we have parameters to enter. There aren't any in this case, so just click on the Invoke button, and you'll see the results in a browser window shown in Figure 6.24. I scrolled down to a customer in Venezuela, which is where I am at this instant, in a restaurant in Caracas, having cake and eating it too (I've never understood that statement...).

Adding an Update Function

Open the Web service code again and add the following code:

```
<WebMethod> Public Function UpdateCustomers( _
  ByVal CustChanges As dsCustomers) _
  As dsCustomers
    If Not (CustChanges Is Nothing) Then
        SqlDataAdapter1.Update(CustChanges)
        Return CustChanges
```

```
    Else
        Return Nothing
    End If
End Function
```

This function expects a diffgram, which it will call `custChanges`. It will use the `SQLDataAdapter` method `Update` to apply the diffgram to the source table that the `DataAdapter` is charged with updating, then return the diffgram to the caller. If there are no changes, it returns nothing. The reason for this is that if the `Update` method isn't able to process some of the records in the diffgram, it sends the ones it couldn't apply back to the source, presumably to try again later.

How to Use the Web Service

We'll need a Windows form application to test this Web service, so add a Windows Form project to the solution. Call it WinClientCustomers. On the form, add a `DataGrid` and two buttons named `LoadData` and `SaveData`.

To use this Web service, you need one method in your client form to get the records, and a command button to extract any changed records from the dataset and send them back. You'll need a dataset and a data source. But in this case, it's coming from a Web service. We need to write code that goes to the Internet for the data. And that's exactly where we go for the data connection as well.

Right-click on the project and select Add Web Reference from the context menu. You'll see the screen shown in Figure 6.23.

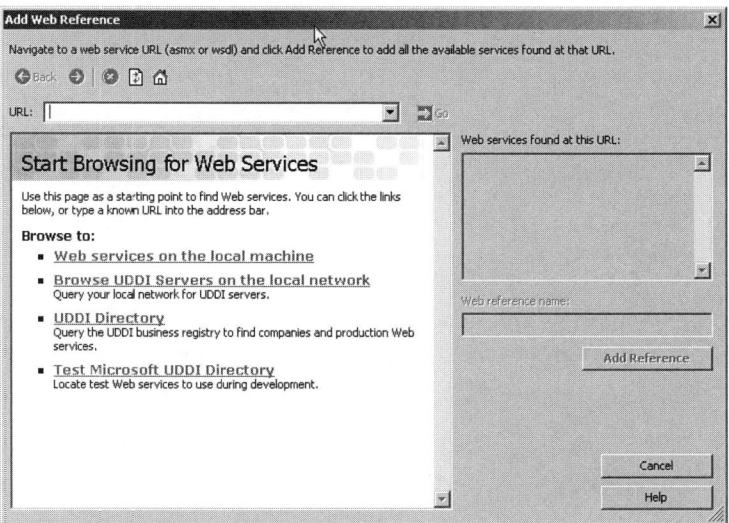

FIGURE 6.23   The Add Web Reference dialog.

Click on the Web Services on Local Machine link. Pick your new Web service from the resulting list. A Web References item will be added to the WinClientCustomer project, right under References.

Next we need to add a dataset. What about the connection and `DataAdapter` components? We don't need them. Add a dataset from the Data tab of the Toolbox, and a dialog will appear asking if you want to use the Typed Dataset with the Web Reference shown in the combo box. Click OK to accept it.

Listing 6.11 has the code for the `Load` event of the form:

LISTING 6.11   Client Form Code to Load Data from a Web Service

```
Private Sub LoadData_Click(ByVal sender As System.Object, _
    ByVal e As System.EventArgs) Handles LoadData.Click
    Dim ws As New WinClientCustomers.localhost.MyWebService
    ws.Credentials = System.Net.CredentialCache.DefaultCredentials
    DsCustomers1.Merge(ws.GetCustomers())
End Sub
```

Listing 6.12 contains the code needed to save changes to the dataset.

LISTING 6.12   Client Form Code to Save Changes to a Web Service

```
Private Sub SaveData_Click(ByVal sender As System.Object, _
    ByVal e As System.EventArgs) Handles SaveData.Click
    If DsCustomers1.HasChanges() Then
        Dim ws As New WinClientCustomers.localhost.MyWebService
        Ws.Credentials = System.Net.CredentialCache.DefaultCredentials
        Dim diffCustomers As New WinClientCustomers.localhost.dsCustomers
        diffCustomers.Merge(DsCustomers1.GetChanges())
        diffCustomers = ws.UpdateCustomers(diffCustomers)
        DsCustomers1.Merge(diffCustomers)
    End If
End Sub
```

The only thing remaining is to enter the `DataSource` for the grid. Open the drop-down and select `DsCustomers1.Customers`, the typed dataset. Now we're ready to give it a try.

Press F5 to run this application. This will bring up the screen shown in Figure 6.24.

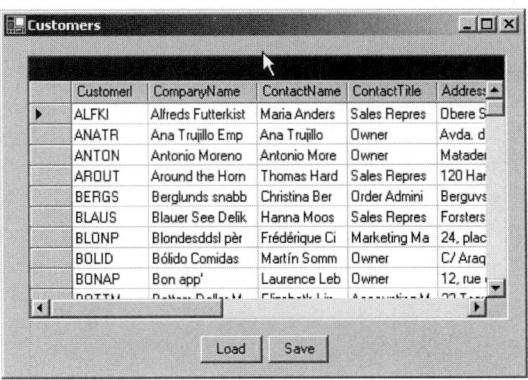

FIGURE 6.24   The CustomersApp form running with a Web service.

Change something and click the Update button, and then close the form and run it again to see if the changes were saved. Worked on mine the first time.

You can hardly beat a Web service that only takes 14 lines of code, and a client form that acquires remote data and saves the changes back to the data source in another 15 lines of code. That's less coding that it takes in FoxPro.

To be fair, there are other issues that need to be addressed in a commercial application. Concurrency, one record per form, data binding, and a nice search screen are all things that take time and code. But with this simple foundation we can build great structures. And if this recession ever ends, we might even get paid for it.

Summary

In this chapter, I've tried to give you a flavor for the difference between data access in FoxPro and in Visual Basic .NET. In the next chapter, we'll look at XML and why it's so important in the new Microsoft order.

XML

As we saw in the previous chapter, XML is instrumental in transmitting data between computers. Visual FoxPro 8 includes robust support for XML. In fact, Ken Levy, head of the FoxPro division at Microsoft, spent the majority of the past year building the XML editor for Whidbey.

In this chapter you'll learn a lot more about XML, and gain an understanding of its advantages in building database applications.

XML is the acronym for *Extensible Markup Language.* XML is Microsoft's replacement for the DBF. It stores tabular data in a text format that can be loaded and displayed as a table in any software. (And it doesn't have indexes, so it's slower than SQL. Hm, I'll bet Microsoft never thought about that. Maybe they'll add them so that you don't have to buy SQL if you don't want to.) But it's much more than that. It stores data in a way that makes it readable by other applications, in other locations, on other operating systems.

XML is the result of a collective effort of a consortium of firms and academic institutions to create a standard mechanism for the sharing of information, including tabular data. For our purposes as database developers, XML is mainly a method for describing the contents of a table in text form so that it can be reconstructed after being sent to a remote computer. In this sense, it does what a DBF does. However, several tables can be included in a single XML file, and hierarchies such as parent-child tables and their data can be represented in XML, neither of which can be done in a single DBF. And because XML works exactly the same way in any language and on any operating system, it's the ideal way to share data.

The Structure of XML

The structure of XML is simple. It always begins with a prologue, thus:

```
<?xml version="1.0" encoding="iso-4459-1" standalone="true" ?>
```

This is optionally followed by a schema, which describes the structure of the data that follows. Although it's optional, we'll shortly see that including the schema is usually a good idea.

Schemas can come in several forms. The most basic is the DTD, which looks like the example in Listing 7.1.

LISTING 7.1   A Document Type Definition

```
<?xml versión="1.0"?>
<!DOCTYPE clientes [
  <!ELEMENT clients    (client)+>
  <!ELEMENT client     (nombre, apellidos)>
  <!ATTLIST client     id CDATA #REQUIRED>
  <!ELEMENT firstname      (#PCDATA)>
  <!ELEMENT lastname   (#PCDATA)>
]>
```

The DTD is like a schema, like what you see in FoxPro if you type

```
USE (filename)
DISPLAY STRUCTURE
```

It lets you reconstruct the structure of the original table that was used to build the XML file.

The DTD is followed by *elements*, which is what XML calls data, and the *element tags* that bracket it. An element is like a field (a table column). It consists of the name of the element between angle brackets (for example, <name>), followed by the data value, followed by the element tag with a forward slash before the element name (for example, </name>). For example

```
<firstname>Les</firstname>
```

would be the XML element representing my first name.

Every record in an XML table has a record descriptor element in the same tagged format, so that a record with two fields might look like this:

```
<record>
<firstname>Les</firstname>
<lastname>Pinter</lastname>
</record>
```

The table itself also has prefix and suffix tags. If an element is empty, a single tag with a forward slash at the end indicates that the attribute is empty, for example, <phone/> means that the phone field is empty. This is not required; you can simply put beginning and ending tags (for example, <phone></phone>) to describe an empty field. But the shorter format occupies less space.

An element can contain *attributes*, which are specified within angle brackets as well. Attributes can represent a record in less space. The fragment shown in Listing 7.2 comes from the Currency.xml table that is widely distributed for use in virtually any software to display the proper symbol for any currency.

LISTING 7.2   An XML File Making Extensive Use of Attributes

```
<?xml version="1.0" encoding="UTF-8" ?>
<!-- _lcid="1033" _version="" -->
<!-- _LocalBinding -->
<currencies>
<currency name="" symbol="" display="Select..." />
- <!-- _locID@display="xdsln_cur_display" _locComment="{StringCategory=TXT}" -->
<currency name="AED" symbol="?.?.?" display="AED (?.?.?)" />
<currency name="ALL" symbol="Lek" display="ALL (Lek)" />
<currency name="AMD" symbol="??." display="AMD (??.)" />
<currency name="ARS" symbol="$" display="ARS ($)" />
<currency name="AUD" symbol="$" display="AUD ($)" />
<currency name="AZM" symbol="???." display="AZM (???.)" />
<currency name="BGL" symbol="??" display="BGL (??)" />
<currency name="BHD" symbol="?.?.?" display="BHD (?.?.?)" />
<currency name="BND" symbol="$" display="BND ($)" />
<currency name="BOB" symbol="$b" display="BOB ($b)" />
<currency name="BRL" symbol="R$" display="BRL (R$)" />
...
<Currencies>
```

XML can also contain XML, because it's just data. But to prevent the XML processor from trying to treat the embedded XML text as XML that needs to be rendered (for example, if the text contains the string "<abc>"), the strings can be enclosed in CDATA sections, which consist of the string "<![CDATA[", followed by the text, followed by "]]" to close the CDATA section. This mechanism is commonly used in memo fields "just in case."

Encoding

The "encoding" notation in the XML prologue (the part of the ?XML line that says encoding="UTF-8") is referred to as a *transformation format*, and can be quite important, especially if you're using a language other than English. Because there are many alphabets, you use the encoding string to specify how the data is encoded.

UTF-8 is the most general. It uses one to six bytes to represent each character. If you ever get a chance to see a Chinese word processor, you can see the operator move down the narrowing tree of choices after each byte until the final tier appears, and you'll have a good understanding of how this works. But the browser just reads bytes until it completes a character, then displays it. How does it know when it's at the end of a character? Easy: The last byte of a character contains a zero in the high-order bit, so the first byte with a hex value of 128 or less is the end of the character. UTF-16 is Unicode, which uses two bytes for every character.

If a transformation format is used, the first two or three bytes of the XML file are used as a Byte Order Mark (BOM) to indicate which code was used to create the content. Documents encoded in UTF-8 start with a BOM of 0xEF 0xBB 0xBF, and those encoded in UTF-16 begin with 0xEF 0Xff or 0Xff 0XFE. The browser knows.

Namespaces

The namespace, if specified (using the xmlns identifier), serves as a prefix to distinguish different XML elements that may have the same element name. And if two different tables happen to have a Phone field, or if two different databases both have a Customers table, this could easily happen. We do something like this already in FoxPro when pulling tables from two different databases:

```
SELECT * FROM Accounting!Invoices A, Sales!Invoices B where A.InvNum = B.InvNum
```

The namespace can be specified before specifying the elements, in which case it can be applied to any of the elements that follow (see Listing 7.3).

LISTING 7.3   XML File with Namespace Reference

```
<?xml versión="1.0" ?>
<clients xmlns:pinter="www.pinter.com <http://www.pinter.com>">
 <client>
  <pinter:name>José</pinter:name>
  <pinter:lastname>García</pinter:lastname>
 </client>
</clients>
```

The only purpose of this is to permit you to qualify each entry with the namespace and a colon, for example, Pinter:name instead of name. This allows you to build XML files in which the same element name may exist in several schema, by prefixing them with the alias for the namespace. It *doesn't have anything to do with your Web site*. The only reason you usually use your Web site is that there's only one, thanks to `Register.com` and the DSN servers. I've never had a name conflict requiring the use of namespaces to resolve conflicts, but the solution is free, so you probably should use it.

Data Models: XDR and XSD

Microsoft created a specification called XDR that was implemented with SQL Server, Office, and BizTalk to validate data structures. However, the World Wide Web Consortium (W3C) has come up with its own specification, the XSD, which does the same thing that the XDR does. Thus XDR is not the preferred type of schema to use; however, you should be able to read XML files containing an XDR schema if you encounter one based on this Microsoft legacy specification.

To implement an XDR schema, you create a DTD file with the extension `.xdr` and include a `<schema></schema>` section that describes the elements by type (for example, integers and dates). Then you implement it by including an `"x-schema"` specification, thusly:

```
<clients xmlns="x-schema:mixdr.xdr">
```

After you've done this, any attempt to load an XML file that doesn't conform to the data definition included in the XDR file will fail. In addition to specifying data types, you can specify minimum and maximum values for certain fields, maximum string lengths, absence of required fields or presence of forbidden ones, and other types of validations.

Later in this chapter we'll see how to create an XSD file in FoxPro and use it to validate XML files. I've never used an XDR to enforce the structure of an XML file. I generally have control over both ends of the process, so I know for sure that the XML is what my program is expecting. I suppose that a browser environment would be the most likely one for using XDR validation. But it's another tool, and at least you'll know what it is when you see it.

Examples of XML

Suppose you have a DBF with the following structure:

```
CLIENTS.DBF:
ClientID    Numeric ( 6)
Company     Char    (20)
Phone       Char    (10)
Balance     Numeric (8,2)
```

And it contains two records:

```
104   Smith Electronics      311-4032      189.00
107   Family Clinic          289-2904      225.12
```

One XML representation is shown in Listing 7.4.

LISTING 7.4   XML Representation of Data in Listing 7.5

```
<clients>
 <client>
  <clientid>104></clientid>
  <company>Smith Electronics</company>
  <phone>311-4032</phone>
  <balance>189.00</balance>
 </client>
 <client>
  <clientid>104></clientid>
  <company>Family Clinic</company>
  <phone>289-2904</phone>
  <balance>225.25</balance>
 </client>
</clients>
```

I say *one* representation because there are several ways to represent this data as XML. For example, you can include a schema at the top of the file, and it could be an XDR or an XSD representation.

You can include or exclude the carriage returns that visually separate the elements and make the file easier for humans to read, although mattering not at all to a parsing program. And you can represent fields as elements or as attributes and thereby reduce the number of tags by half (because the </ends> aren't required when using attributes), so long as the receiving program knows what to look for.

FoxPro can read this kind of XML and turn it into a cursor (a temporary DBF). Use the following syntax:

```
XMLToCursor ( "D:\6493SAMS\Chapter7Code\Simple.XML", "Test", 512 )
BROWSE
```

You can also open this file up and view it as a table in Visual Studio. Select File, Open, File from the menu, and then select Chapter7Code\Simple.XML, and you'll see the screen shown in Figure 7.1. Select the Data tab at the lower-left corner of the screen to display the table.

A console program to read this file in Visual Basic .NET is approximately the same code, given Visual Basic .NET's syntax requirements:

```
Sub Main()
    Dim oXML As New Xml.XmlDocument
    oXML.Load("D:\6493SAMS\Chapter7Code\Simple.xml")
```

```
    Dim oNode As XmlNode
    MsgBox(oXML.InnerXml)
End Sub
```

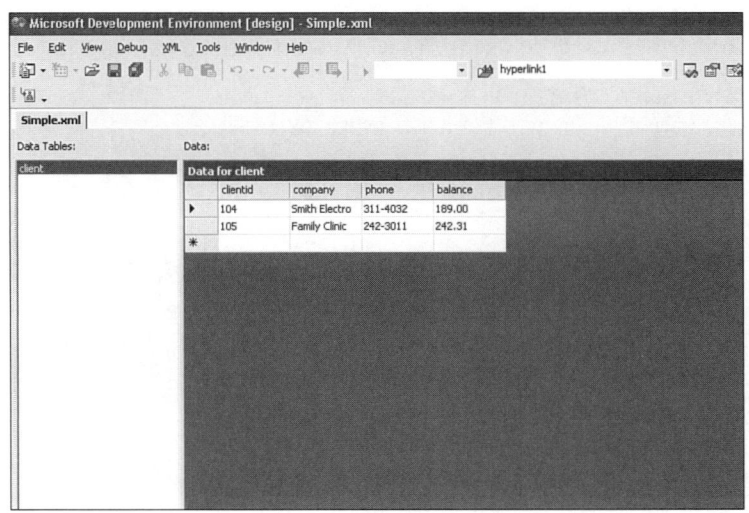

FIGURE 7.1   A simple XML file displayed as a table.

Representation of Complex Structures

XML is capable of representing a hierarchy in a single file, and the resulting representation of the data will occupy even less space compared with what it would require in FoxPro if we tried to use a single table using a JOIN because only one of the pair of matching keys has to be sent. Even if it weren't smaller in terms of space, it's more methodologically elegant.

Let's build a hierarchical XML structure from an invoice header and the corresponding detail file. Assume the following header file:

```
INVOICES.DBF:
InvNum     Integer(4)
ClientID   Integer(4)
Date       Date    (4)
Total      Numeric(8,2)
```

and the following detail file:

```
INVDETL.DBF:
InvNum     Integer(4)
LineNum    Integer(4)
```

```
Quantity    Integer(4)
ProductID   Char(20)
UnitPrice   Numeric(8,2)
Extended    Numeric(8,2)
```

Normally, in order to send these records as XML, we'd need to use a JOIN:

```
SELECT * FROM Invoices, INVDETLS
 WHERE Invoices.INVNUM = INVDETLS.INVNUM ORDER BY Linea
```

The resulting cursor would duplicate the InvNum field in the two tables, which is really not necessary because by definition they have the same value in each joined record. But even more, each record in the resulting cursor would have all of the INVOICE fields as well as all of the INVDETL fields.

If we simply join the two tables, the resulting XML is replete with redundancy, as shown in Listing 7.5.

LISTING 7.5   XML Representation of Joined Tables

```
<?xml version = "1.0" encoding="Windows-1252" standalone="yes"?>
<invoices>
    <invoice>
        <invnum_a>141</invnum_a>
        <clientid>41</clientid>
        <date>2004-04-01</date>
        <total>192.00</total>
        <invnum_b>141</invnum_b>
        <linenum>1</linenum>
        <quantity>3</quantity>
        <productid>303142-A</productid>
        <unitprice>12.95</unitprice>
        <extended>38.85</extended>
    </invoice>
    <invoice>
        <invnum_a>141</invnum_a>
        <clientid>41</clientid>
        <date>2004-04-01</date>
        <total>192.00</total>
        <invnum_b>141</invnum_b>
        <linenum>2</linenum>
        <quantity>4</quantity>
        <productid>1041202</productid>
```

```
        <unitprice>3.15</unitprice>
        <extended>12.60</extended>
    </invoice>
    <invoice>
        <invnum_a>142</invnum_a>
        <clientid>43</clientid>
        <date>2004-04-03</date>
        <total>225.00</total>
        <invnum_b>142</invnum_b>
        <linenum>1</linenum>
        <quantity>1</quantity>
        <productid>2022201</productid>
        <unitprice>25.00</unitprice>
        <extended>25.00</extended>
    </invoice>
    <invoice>
        <invnum_a>142</invnum_a>
        <clientid>43</clientid>
        <date>2004-04-03</date>
        <total>225.00</total>
        <invnum_b>142</invnum_b>
        <linenum>2</linenum>
        <quantity>2</quantity>
        <productid>2016615</productid>
        <unitprice>89.95</unitprice>
        <extended>179.90</extended>
    </invoice>
</invoices>
```

And the fact that there is no longer an element named INVNUM is irritating. Of course, we can write a more specific SQL string to fix the INVNUM element name problem. But it's still a clumsy and redundant solution.

Just in case you doubt whether you've got something here that can describe a table, open Visual Studio, select File, Open, File from the menu, and open Chapter7code\Redundant.XML, the text file containing this text. In the lower-left corner you'll see a Data tab; click it, and you'll see the screen shown in Figure 7.2.

Notice the caption above the table name; it says Data *Tables*, not Data *Table*. That's because a single XML file can contain multiple tables. You'll see how this works shortly.

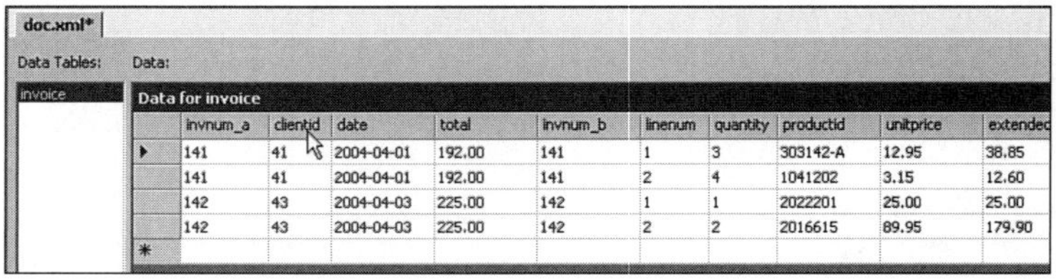

FIGURE 7.2   Data Table View of a Flat File.

Hierarchical XML

The program in Listing 7.6 shows how an XML structure can be built that sends only the data absolutely needed to reconstruct the two tables.

LISTING 7.6   FoxPro Program to Create Hierarchical XML

```
* Program-ID...: BuildXMLHierarchy.PRG
CLOSE ALL
CLEAR ALL
CLEAR
USE InvoiceS IN A
USE INVDETLS IN B
lcXML = ""
Add2XML ( [<?xml version = "1.0" encoding="Windows-1252" standalone="yes"?>] )
SELECT Invoices
Add2XML ( [<Invoices>] )
NoFac = 0
SCAN
  NoFac = NoFac + 1
  Add2XML ( [<Invoice>], 1 )
  FOR I = 1 TO FCOUNT()
    fld = LOWER(FIELD(I))
    Add2XML ( [<]  + fld + [>] + ALLTRIM(TRANSFORM(EVALUATE(fld))) ;
      + [</] + fld + [>], 2)
  ENDFOR
  SELECT INVDETLS
  SET FILTER TO INVNUM = InvoiceS.INVNUM
  NoLine = 0
  SCAN
    NoLine = NoLine + 1
    Add2XML ( [<Line>], 2 )
    FOR I = 1 TO FCOUNT()
      fld = LOWER(FIELD(I))
```

LISTING 7.6   Continued

```
      Add2XML ([<]  + fld + [>] + ALLTRIM(TRANSFORM(EVALUATE(fld))) ;
      + [</] + fld + [>], 3)
   ENDFOR
   Add2XML ( [</Line>], 2 )
 ENDSCAN
 SELECT Invoices
 Add2XML ( [</Invoice>], 1 )
ENDSCAN
Add2XML ( [</Invoices>] )
STRTOFILE( lcXML, "TEST.XML" )
MODIFY FILE TEST.XML NOMODIFY

FUNCTION Add2XML
PARAMETERS Texto, Indent
Indent = IIF ( EMPTY ( Indent ), 0, Indent )
lcXML = lcXML + IIF(EMPTY(lcXML),"",CHR(13)) + REPLICATE(CHR(9),Indent) + Texto
RETURN
```

The resulting XML produced from two invoice headers and four detail lines, two for each invoice, appears in Listing 7.7.

LISTING 7.7   Hierarchical XML

```
<?xml version = "1.0" encoding="Windows-1252" standalone="yes"?>
<Invoices>
    <Invoice>
        <invnum>141</invnum>
        <clientid>41</clientid>
        <date>04/01/2004</date>
        <total>192</total>
        <Line>
            <invnum>141</invnum>
            <linenum>1</linenum>
            <quantity>3</quantity>
            <productid>303142-A</productid>
            <unitprice>12.95</unitprice>
            <extended>38.85</extended>
        </Line>
        <Line>
            <invnum>141</invnum>
            <linenum>2</linenum>
            <quantity>4</quantity>
```

LISTING 7.7   Continued

```
                <productid>1041202</productid>
                <unitprice>3.15</unitprice>
                <extended>12.60</extended>
            </Line>
        </Invoice>
        <Invoice>
            <invnum>142</invnum>
            <clientid>43</clientid>
            <date>04/03/2004</date>
            <total>225</total>
            <Line>
                <invnum>142</invnum>
                <linenum>1</linenum>
                <quantity>1</quantity>
                <productid>2022201</productid>
                <unitprice>25</unitprice>
                <extended>25</extended>
            </Line>
            <Line>
                <invnum>142</invnum>
                <linenum>2</linenum>
                <quantity>2</quantity>
                <productid>2016615</productid>
                <unitprice>89.95</unitprice>
                <extended>179.90</extended>
            </Line>
        </Invoice>
</Invoices>
```

Open Visual Studio and select File, Open, File from the menu to open Hierarchical.XML.
You'll see the screen shown in Figure 7.3.

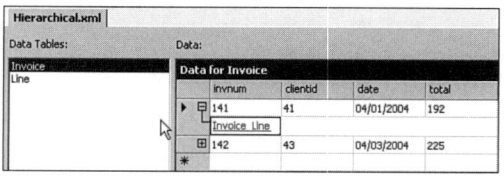

FIGURE 7.3   Data table view of a hierarchical XML file.

It's true that hierarchical XML reduces file size a little, compared to sending the same amount of data as two XML tables. However, the programming required to traverse a hierarchy and load the data into a treeview is more complicated than simply loading the hierarchy from a parent table and a child table (although some day I expect that it will become easier). Until then, broadband is cheaper than programming, so I'd recommend that you just send the two tables and don't bother representing their contents as a hierarchy.

The Document Object Model

The programming object that controls the way we use XML is based on the XML Document Object Model, implemented by Microsoft as a series of DLLs called MSXML.DLL, MSXML2.DLL, and MSXML3.DLL. They are registered as COM objects with the names MSXML.DOMDocument, MSXML2.DOMDocument, and MSXML3.DOMDocument respectively. To use them, use `CreateObject` in FoxPro, or add a reference and create an object from them in Visual Basic .NET:

```
LOCAL loDOM AS "MSXML2.DOMDocument"
loDOM = CREATEOBJECT ("MSXML2.DOMDocument.4.0" )
```

This enables IntelliSense to expose the many properties and methods of the DOM, as shown in Figure 7.4.

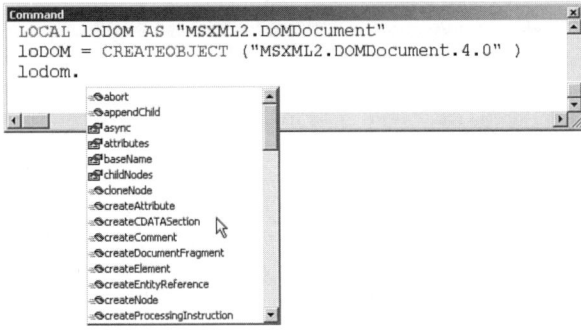

FIGURE 7.4   The XML Document Object Model exposed via IntelliSense.

The `Load` method can read the file directly. It can also read a URL. The result is stored in the object's XML property. You can use `MessageBox` to display `loXML.XML` if you want to see whether it worked. Note that I've occasionally had problems if I didn't turn asynchronous processing off by including the line

```
loDOM.Async = .F.
```

Errors encountered by the DOM will not be trapped either by FoxPro's ON ERROR or by
TRY...ENDTRY. However, the DOM object also reports any errors it encounters. The
program shown in Listing 7.8 will report an error in the named XML file, which is a copy
of Simple.XML with a few extra characters in one of the attributes.

LISTING 7.8   Trapping XML Errors Using the DOM

```
LOCAL loDOM AS "MSXML2.DOMDocument.4.0"
loDOM = CREATEOBJECT ("MSXML2.DOMDocument.4.0" )
loDOM.Async = .F.
loDOM.Load ("D:\6493SAMS\Chapter7Code\XMLWithErrors.xml")
IF loDOM.ParseError.ErrorCode <> 0
  Texto = [There was an error in the document:]       + CHR(13) ;
    + [    Line: ] + TRANSFORM(loDOM.parseError.Line)    + CHR(13) ;
    + [Position: ] + TRANSFORM(loDOM.parseError.LinePos) + CHR(13) ;
    + [  Reason: ] + TRANSFORM(loDOM.parseError.Reason)
  MessageBox ( Texto, 16, [Error leyendo XML] )
ENDIF
loDOM = NULL
RELEASE loDOM
```

You can also build XML directly in code, as shown in Listing 7.9.

LISTING 7.9   Building XML in Code

```
USE CUSTOMERS
LOCATE FOR CustomerID = [AROUT]
PUBLIC lcXML AS String
lcXML = []
TEXT TO lcXML NOSHOW
<clients>
 <client>
  <companyname><<CompanyName>></companyname>
  <contactname><<ContactName>></contactname>
 </client>
</clients>
ENDTEXT
MESSAGEBOX( lcXML )
LOCAL loXML AS MSXML2.DOMDocument
loXML = CREATEOBJECT ( "MSXML2.DOMDocument" )
loXML.LoadXML ( lcXML )
MESSAGEBOX( loXML.xml )
```

Or, you can create elements one at a time, as shown in Listing 7.10.

LISTING 7.10   Building XML in Code by Elements

```
LOCAL loRoot    AS "MXSML2.IXMLDOMElement"
LOCAL loElement AS "MXSML2.IXMLDOMElement"
LOCAL loText    AS "MSXML2.IXMLDOMText"

loRoot = loDOM.documentElement

loElement = loDOM.createElement           ( "client"    )
loRoot.appendChild                        ( loElement   )

loElement = loDOM.createElement           ( "name"      )
loText    = loDOM.createTextNode          ( "Juan"      )
loElement.AppendChild                     ( loText      )
loRoot.ChildNodes.item(1).AppendChild     ( loElement   )

loElement = loDOM.createElement           ( "lastname"    )
loText    = loDOM.createTextNode          ( "Perez"     )
loElement.AppendChild                     ( loTexto     )
loRoot.ChildNodes.item(1).AppendChild     ( loElemento    )

loDOM.Save ( "OneClient.XML" )
```

The code to do this in Visual Basic .NET is virtually identical. You just need to change the LOCAL declarations to DIM.

Commands to Move Data Between a Table and XML

Although you can write your own code to move data between tables and XML, the CursorToXML() and XMLToCursor() functions introduced in FoxPro 7 do a pretty good job in many cases. If that's not enough, the new XMLAdapter and CursorAdapter in Visual FoxPro 8 add many other capabilities, and actually do what you thought you were going to be able to do with XMLUpdateGram() output. I originally assumed that an UpdateGram could be used in some automatic fashion to update the table that the original record came from. I've since been informed that the XMLUpdateGram was never meant to do anything except represent the record before and after changes. We were expected to write our own code to apply the change.

CursorToXML()
The official syntax of FoxPro's CursorToXML() function is as follows:

```
CursorToXML(nWorkArea ¦ cTableAlias,
 cOutput
 [, nOutputFormat
 [, nFlags
 [, nRecords
 [, cSchemaName
 [, cSchemaLocation
 [, cNameSpace ]]]]]])
```

The first parameter can be a work area number, although I always use an alias. You can also use ALIAS() to use the currently selected table.

The second parameter is a little strange for Visual FoxPro developers, because it can be either a filename or a variable name; however, what it expects is either a filename or variable name in quotes, or a filename or variable name stored in a variable.

The third parameter is the output format of the result, and can be one of three values:

1. Elements

2. Attributes

3. Raw (generic)

For a table containing fields Name, Counter, and Date, this is what the XML would look like for these three formats:

```
Elements:

<?xml version = "1.0" encoding="Windows-1252" standalone="yes"?>
<VFPData>
        <test>
                <name>Pinter</name>
                <counter>1234</counter>
                <date>2004-03-12</date>
        </test>
</VFPData>


Attributes:

<?xml version = "1.0" encoding="Windows-1252" standalone="yes"?>
<VFPData>
        <test name="Pinter" counter="1234" date="2004-03-12"/>
</VFPData>


Raw:
```

```
<?xml version = "1.0" encoding="Windows-1252" standalone="yes"?>
<VFPData>
        <row name="Pinter" counter="1234" date="2004-03-12"/>
</VFPData>
```

If we're producing XML for our own use, the first type, which is the default, is okay. External users may need one of the other two formats.

The fourth parameter is the sum of the values of any of the parameters listed in Table 7.1. This is analogous to the way you add values in the `MessageBox()` function (for example, 4 + 32 + 256 means "Display a question mark"; prompts include Yes and No, and default to No, but you can just use 292).

TABLE 7.1 Valid Values of the *Flags* Parameter (the fourth parameter) of the CursorToXML() Function

Value	Description
0	UTF-8 formatting (default)
1	Continuous string
2	Use beginning and ending tags for empty elements (that is, <a></a> instead of <a/>)
4	Conserve white space
8	Enclose memo fields in CDATA sections
16	Use cursor's code page
32	Use UTF-8 without character translation (16+32 = do translation)
512	Create a file instead of a memory variable

For the following examples I'll assume a table named Clients containing a single record.

Example 1:

```
CursorToXML ( "Clients", "lcClients" )
```

This code will store the XML shown in Listing 7.11 in the variable lcClients.

LISTING 7.11 Generated XML

```
<?xml version = "1.0" encoding="Windows-1252" standalone="yes"?>
<VFPData>
    <clients>
        <first>Les</first>
        <last>Pinter</last>
        <phone>650-344-3969</phone>
    </clients>
</VFPData>
```

Example 2:

```
CURSORTOXML ("CLIENTES", "CLIENTES.XML", 1, 512, 0, "1")
```

This code will produce a table containing the results shown in Listing 7.12.

LISTING 7.12   Generated XML

```
<?xml version = "1.0" encoding="Windows-1252" standalone="yes"?>
<VFPData>
    <xsd:schema id="VFPData" xmlns:xsd=http://www.w3.org/2001/XMLSchema
➥xmlns:msdata="urn:schemas-microsoft-com:xml-msdata">
        <xsd:element name="VFPData" msdata:IsDataSet="true">
            <xsd:complexType>
                <xsd:choice maxOccurs="unbounded">
                    <xsd:element name="clients"
                    ➥minOccurs="0" maxOccurs="unbounded">
                        <xsd:complexType>
                            <xsd:sequence>
                                <xsd:element name="first">
                                    <xsd:simpleType>
                                        <xsd:restriction base="xsd:string">
                                            <xsd:maxLength value="15"/>
                                        </xsd:restriction>
                                    </xsd:simpleType>
                                </xsd:element>
                                <xsd:element name="last">
                                    <xsd:simpleType>
                                        <xsd:restriction base="xsd:string">
                                            <xsd:maxLength value="15"/>
                                        </xsd:restriction>
                                    </xsd:simpleType>
                                </xsd:element>
                                <xsd:element name="phone">
                                    <xsd:simpleType>
                                        <xsd:restriction base="xsd:string">
                                            <xsd:maxLength value="13"/>
                                        </xsd:restriction>
                                    </xsd:simpleType>
                                </xsd:element>
                            </xsd:sequence>
                        </xsd:complexType>
                    </xsd:element>
                </xsd:choice>
```

LISTING 7.12   Continued

```
                <xsd:anyAttribute
➥namespace="http://www.w3.org/XML/1998/namespace" processContents="lax"/>
            </xsd:complexType>
        </xsd:element>
    </xsd:schema>
    <clients>
        <first>Les</first>
        <last>Pinter</last>
        <phone>650-344-3969</phone>
    </clients>
</VFPData>
```

XMLToCursor()

The official syntax of the XMLToCursor() command is as follows:

```
XMLTOCURSOR(XMLSource eExpression | cXMLFile
 [, cCursorName
 [, nFlags ]])
```

The first parameter is the name of a memory variable, or the name of a file if the third parameter is 512.

The second parameter is the name of the cursor where the XML will be converted to a table. If the cursor does not already exist, and if the XML contains a schema, the cursor will be created using the schema definition. If no schema definition is included, all fields will be created as type Character, and the length of each field will be the length of the longest string in each data element.

The third parameter is a flag whose value is the sum of any applicable switches, as described in Table 7.2.

TABLE 7.2   XMLToCursor() Flag Values (Third Parameter)

Value	Description
0	The first parameter is the name of a variable containing XML.
4	Conserve white space.
512	The first parameter is a filename (fully qualified).
1024	Don't translate the code page. Produces weird results.
2048	Convert numeric(19,4) to Currency.
4096	Special for binary data.
8192	Don't modify the target table's structure (Visual FoxPro 8!).

The last flag is new in Visual FoxPro 8 and is most welcome. Previously, table structures were always changed to reflect the longest string in each field, and data types occasionally were changed as well. As a result, it was generally necessary to write to a temporary cursor, then append the data from it into the original structure, as shown in Listing 7.13.

LISTING 7.13 How XMLTOCURSOR() Without an XSD Uses Field Lengths to Determine Table Structure

```
<?xml version = "1.0" encoding="Windows-1252" standalone="yes"?>
<VFPData>
    <clients>
        <first>Les</first>
        <last>Pinter</last>
        <phone>650-344-3969</phone>
    </clients>
</VFPData>

XMLToCursor(lcxml,"TEST")
DISP STRU

Structure for table:    TEST
  Field  Field Name    Type           Width   Dec   Index   Collate Nulls
      1  FIRST         Character          3                              No
      2  LAST          Character          6                              No
      3  PHONE         Character         12                              No
** Total **                             22
```

If the XSD is included, the table is rendered properly, as shown in Listing 7.14.

LISTING 7.14 Generated XML

```
<?xml version = "1.0" encoding="Windows-1252" standalone="yes"?>
<VFPData>
  <xsd:schema id="VFPData" xmlns:xsd="http://www.w3.org/2001/XMLSchema"
➥xmlns:msdata="urn:schemas-microsoft-com:xml-msdata">
    <xsd:element name="VFPData" msdata:IsDataSet="true">
      <xsd:complexType>
        <xsd:choice maxOccurs="unbounded">
          <xsd:element name="clients" minOccurs="0" maxOccurs="unbounded">
            <xsd:complexType>
              <xsd:sequence>
                <xsd:element name="first">
                  <xsd:simpleType>
```

LISTING 7.14   Continued

```
                      <xsd:restriction base="xsd:string">
                        <xsd:maxLength value="15"/>
                      </xsd:restriction>
                    </xsd:simpleType>
                </xsd:element>
                <xsd:element name="last">
                  <xsd:simpleType>
                    <xsd:restriction base="xsd:string">
                      <xsd:maxLength value="15"/>
                    </xsd:restriction>
                  </xsd:simpleType>
                </xsd:element>
                <xsd:element name="phone">
                  <xsd:simpleType>
                    <xsd:restriction base="xsd:string">
                      <xsd:maxLength value="13"/>
                    </xsd:restriction>
                  </xsd:simpleType>
                </xsd:element>
              </xsd:sequence>
            </xsd:complexType>
          </xsd:element>
        </xsd:choice>
        <xsd:anyAttribute namespace="http://www.w3.org/XML/1998/namespace"
➥processContents="lax"/>
      </xsd:complexType>
    </xsd:element>
  </xsd:schema>
  <clients>
    <first>Les</first>
    <last>Pinter</last>
    <phone>650-344-3969</phone>
  </clients>
</VFPData>
```

You can use the XMLToCursor() function to convert this XML back into a cursor, and DISPLAY Structure to view the resulting table:

Example: The following two lines of code produce the output that follows the code:

```
XMLTOCURSOR(lcxml,"TEST")
DISPLAY STRUCTURE    && (Output from DISPLAY STRUCTURE follows):
```

```
Structure for table:   TEST
Field  Field Name       Type              Width    Dec    Index    Collate Nulls
    1  FIRST            Character            15                                  No
    2  LAST             Character            15                                  No
    3  PHONE            Character            13                                  No
** Total **                                 44
```

How FoxPro Implements XML

FoxPro's implementation of XML is a wrapper for MSXML, Microsoft's XML DLLs. There are several versions, but when you install FoxPro 7 or 8, the latest version is automatically installed.

There have been six releases of the XML parser as of this writing:

```
MSXML2.DOMDocument.1.0
MSXML2.DOMDocument.2.0
MSXML2.DOMDocument.2.5
MSXML2.DOMDocument.2.6
MSXML2.DOMDocument.3.0
MSXML2.DOMDocument.4.0
```

FoxPro 7 installed 3.0, whereas Visual FoxPro 7 SP1 and Visual FoxPro 8 installed 4.0. That's what determines the version used with the CursorToXML() and XMLToCursor() functions. However, each version is a separate DLL, so if you need to instantiate an earlier version, you can do so using CREATEOBJECT() and fully qualify the ProgID, for example:

```
loXML = CREATEOBJECT ( "MSXML2.DOMDocument.3.0" )
```

That's not a misprint; the MSXML2 prefix is part of the parser ProgID for all of these XML versions. Each version has new features; for example, the addition of the flag parameter value 8192 in the XMLToCursor() function to preserve the structure of an existing cursor was added in version 4.0.

Using XML to Read Other Types of Data

XML can be useful to read other types of data. For example, you can read other types of data using ADODB—Paradox, MDB files, and many others. However, the result is returned as a RecordSet, which FoxPro doesn't know how to read. But RecordSets know how to write their records to disk in XML format, and you can use FoxPro to read the resulting XML file and convert it into a cursor. Try variations on this theme; I'm not going to tell you all the hoops I jumped through to read foreign data before this came along (see Listing 17.15).

LISTING 7.15   Reading Foreign Data Sources with the Help of XMLTOCURSOR()

```
LOCAL Con AS "ADODB.Connection"
LOCAL RS  AS "ADODOB.Recordset"
Con = CREATEOBJECT ( "ADODB.Connection" )
Con.Open ( "Driver={SQL Server};server=(local);UID=sa;PWD=;database=pubs;" )
RS = Con.Execute ( "SELECT * FROM AUTHORS WHERE STATE='CA'" )
RS.Save ( "RS.XML", 1)
* MODI FILE  RS.XML    && remove asterisk to see the XML
XMLTOCURSOR ( "RS.XML", "RSPUBS", 512 )
BROWSE TITLE [Authors table from SQL Server using ADO]
```

Receiving XML Files Directly

Sometimes we receive data directly from branches, main offices, vendors, or clients. If you both have FoxPro, you can send DBFs. But what if they don't have FoxPro? For a while, they sent us comma-delimited or fixed-length records with a written description of the fields, so that we could manually re-create them, and then clean up the data and import it into our production files. It was a lot of work.

This is where XML comes in. After Office '97, just about every Microsoft product (and just about everyone else's product) is capable of creating XML output. If they send us an XML file, we can convert it to XML, and then write a little program to move their field X to our field Y and so on. Or we can simply open the table we created from their XML using XMLToCursor(), change the field names one by one until they match ours, and append their DBF into our own. If we can convince them to create the XML document with the correct field names in the first place, data import is trivially easy, as shown in Listing 17.16.

LISTING 7.16   Importing an XML File into Our Table

```
tempXML = GETFILE("XML")
IF NOT EMPTY (tempXML )
   XMLTOCURSOR (tempXML, "temp" )
   SELECT 0
   USE Invoices
   APPEND FROM DBF("temp")
   USE
   USE IN temp
ENDIF
```

The APPEND FROM DBF("Temp") is necessary because APPEND FROM needs a DBF name, whereas XMLToCursor() creates a cursor, which is usually a temp file with a .tmp extension.

Importing XML into Visual Basic .NET

Just as the DBF is the native data container for Visual FoxPro, XML is the native data container for .NET. In fact, datasets *are* XML. For example, if you have an XML Web Service, the command to create a dataset (the SQLAdapter, the SQLConnection, and the Authors1 dataset have already been defined) and return it as XML is this:

```
<WebMethod> Public Function GetAuthors() As authors1
    Dim authors As New authors1()
    SqlDataAdapter1.Fill(authors)
    Return authors
End Function
```

And the code to receive the output from the Web service and convert it back into a record-set is this:

```
Dim ws As New AuthorsWinClient.localhost.AuthorsService()
ws.Credentials = System.Net.CredentialCache.DefaultCredentials
AuthorData.Merge(ws.GetAuthors())
```

(AuthorData is a dataset on the client.) But don't XML Web Services return XML? Yes, they do. And yet all you see here is references to datasets. *They're the same thing.*

Direct Access to SQL Server with XML

In FoxPro, if a program running on a workstation has access to a server running SQL Server, to pass the result of a query back to a cursor, just call the SQLExec function:

```
Con = SQLStringConnect (;
"Driver={SQL Server};server=(local);UID=sa;PWD=;database=pubs;)"
SQLExec (Con, "select * from authors where state = 'CA'", "SQLResult")
```

This puts the results of the query in a cursor named SQLResult. (In fact, that's the default cursor name if you don't supply that third parameter.)

In the past, it was much more complicated to return data from a remote server. Not any longer. You can configure SQL Server in such a way that query output can be sent directly to your program using HTTP, without any third-party software at all, using just a few lines of code.

In the example in Listing 7.17, the plus signs in the URL are called encoding. URLs can't contain blanks, so either you replace blanks with something like a plus and let IIS remove them, or you call an encoding routine. You can use CHRTRAN(url, " ", "+") to replace blanks with plus signs.

LISTING 7.17   Using the XMLDOM Object to Return XML

```
oXMLDOM = CREATEOBJECT ( "Microsoft.XMLDOM" )
WITH oXMLDOM
.Async = .F.      && might not work without this
.Load ( "http://localhost/xmldir?sql=SELECT ;
 + *+FROM+authors+FOR+XML+AUTO&root=root")
XMLTOCURSOR (.XML, "Authors" )
ENDWITH
```

Before you try this out on your own computer, you'll need to select Start, Programs, SQL Server, Configure SQL XML Support in IIS and specify the name of a directory to be used to hold the results of this type of query.

Figure 7.5 shows the first page of the dialog that you use to configure SQL Server via HTTP. The Virtual Directory name is the name that appears in the URL string; the Actual Directory name is the fully qualified name of the directory on your hard drive. It's easiest if you give them both the same name. If the new physical directory doesn't yet exist, the wizard will create it for you when you close the dialog.

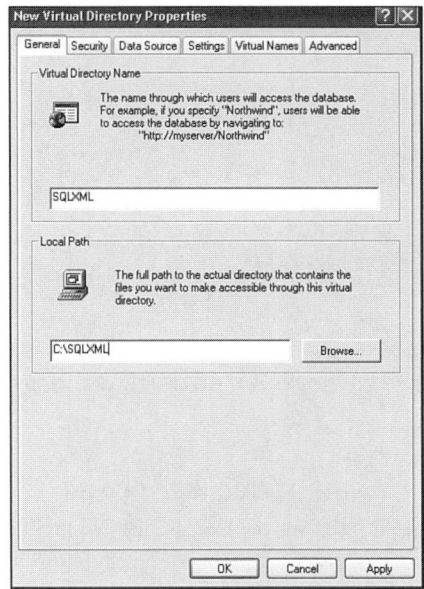

FIGURE 7.5   General settings for XML access to SQL via HTTP.

The password and user ID should be the ones that are used with your database. I've used sa as the username with a blank password as shown in Figure 7.6 because that's what ships with SQL Server and MSDE. You're supposed to remove that combination as soon as you add some other user and password, so use whatever works. Also, my server on my installation of SQL Server on my laptop is called VAIO\VAIO, not (local), so you might have to change your server name as well depending on how you installed SQL or MSDE.

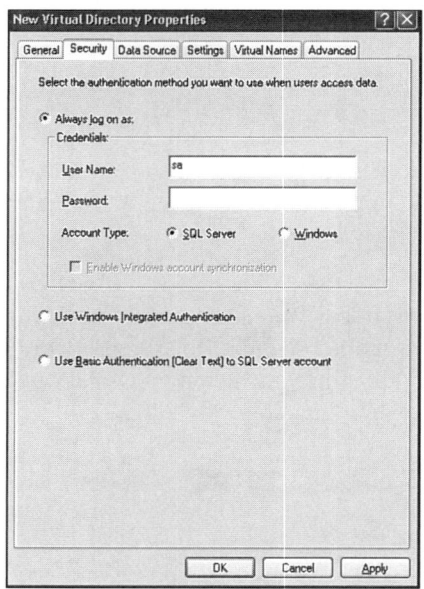

FIGURE 7.6   Security settings for HTTP access to SQL.

The data source is the name of the server—usually (local) or "localhost"—and the name of the database (see Figure 7.7). Note that only one database is supported per virtual SQL directory.

The last page that you have to configure determines which options you want enabled; enable all of them so that you can experiment, as shown in Figure 7.8. You can always turn them off later.

Using the XML DOM to Call a Web Service

Similarly, you can call a Web service written in either FoxPro or in one of the .NET languages. As we'll see below, you can create a Web service in a minute or two. Web services can be of arbitrary complexity, so don't think that there are things you can do in SQL but not with Web services—all it takes is time. And you can use either DBFs or SQL Server (except when using HTTP SQL as described in the preceding section, which obviously only works with SQL).

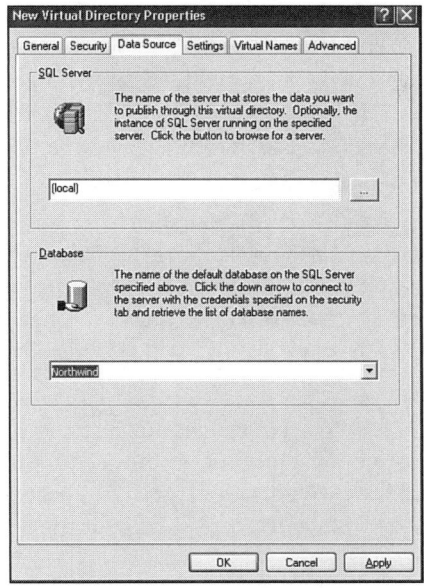

FIGURE 7.7   Data source settings for HTTP access to SQL.

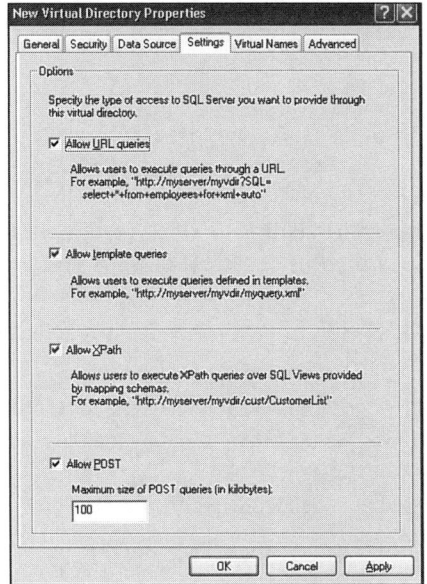

FIGURE 7.8   Miscellaneous settings for HTTP access to SQL.

But there are other MSXML2 components that are also useful. Above we used the `MXSML2.DOMDocument` class to send a query to SQL Server. But we can also use the `MSXML2.XMLHTTP` class to return XML from a URL, as shown in Listing 7.18.

LISTING 7.18   Using the MSXML DOM to Return XML from a URL

```
LOCAL loXMLHTTP         AS "MSXML2.XMLHTTP"
loXMLHTTP = CREATEOBJECT ( "MSXML2.XMLHTTP.4.0" )
loXMLHTTP.Open("GET", "http://localhost/AppName/SendMeSomeXML.ASP")
loXMLHTTP.Send()
WAIT WINDOW [Waiting for data] TIMEOUT 1  && Your response may vary
XMLTOCURSOR (loXMLHTTP.ResponseBody)
```

This will return anything, including a Web page. But because you'd need a browser control to display a Web page, it's not very useful unless you need to do some screen-scraping. Actually, screen-scraping was how we got output from Web sites before XML Web Services were the standard; now you only have to screen-scrape if they don't want you to have their page content.

Using the XML DOM to Validate Documents

We can use the `CursorToXML()` function to create an XSD schema that can be subsequently used to validate the XML that is sent to us. The following code creates an XSD file:

```
USE CLIENTS
CursorToXML ( SELECT(), "lcXML", 1, 0, 0, "clients.xsd" )
MODIFY FILE clients.xsd        && to see what was produced
```

Now we can use the code shown in Listing 17.19 to read XML from a remote source and validate it using the structure stored in `CLIENTS.XSD`.

LISTING 7.19   Using an XSD Schema to Validate XML As It Is Received

```
LOCAL loXMLSchema         AS "MSXML2.XMLSchemaCache.4.0"
loXMLSchema = CREATEOBJECT ( "MSXML2.XMLSchemaCache.4.0" )
loXMLSchema.Add ( "", "clients.xsd" ) && File we created above
LOCAL loXML AS "MSXML2.XMLDOMDocument.4.0"
loXML = CREATEOBJECT ( "MSXML2. XMLDOMDocument.4.0")
loXML.Schemas = loXMLSchema
loXML.Asynch = .F.
loXML.Load (http://www.lespinter.com/SvcsWebXML/Clients.aspx)

IF loXML.ParseError.ErrorCode <> 0
   MessageBox ( ;
```

LISTING 7.19 Continued

```
   [Error: The XML does not match the schema]   + CHR(13) ;
 + [Line:  ] + TRANSFORM(loXML.ParseError.Line) + CHR(13) ;
 + [Cause: ] + loXML.ParseError.Reason )
ENDIF
```

Similarly, the Visual Studio XML Editor can be used to create an XML schema (see Figure 7.9). Create a Windows Forms project, add a `SQLDataAdapter` and configure its connection and `SELECT` statement. Then right-click on the `DataAdapter` and select Generate Dataset, and an XSD file will be added to your project.

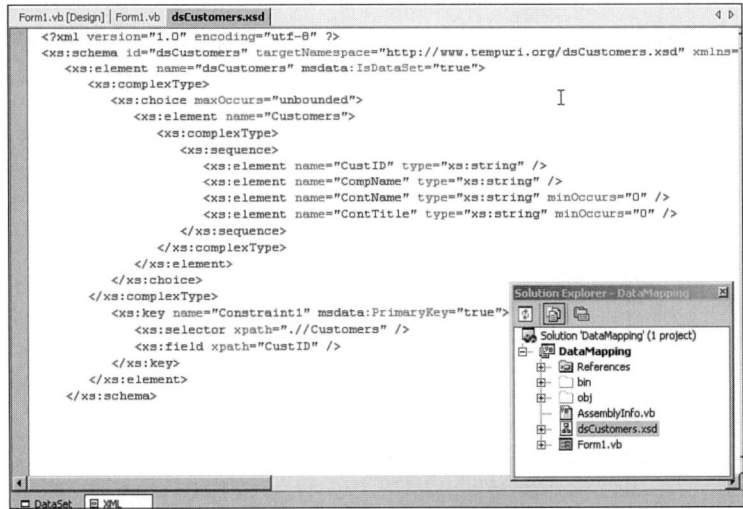

FIGURE 7.9   Using the Visual Studio .NET XML Editor to create a schema file.

XMLUpdateGrams

In FoxPro, we change our tables directly, in a way that is so transparent that we aren't even aware of all of the things that are happening under the surface. It's like a little miracle.

For the rest of the programming world, there's no miracle. It's just code—often *lots of code*.

One way to change records in a table is to send SQL `UPDATE` commands to a server, and let the server engine do what needs to be done. For example, we could copy a record to our workstation application, make some changes in our local cursor, and then generate a SQL `UPDATE` statement to make the same changes to the remote data store that we already made in our FoxPro cursor. But why is this so complicated?

Fortunately, there's something better. When you change a record in a FoxPro app while buffering mode 3 (optimistic table buffering) is in effect, Visual FoxPro remembers the state of all records before and after any changes. (That's why the `CurVal()`, `OldVal()`, and `GetFldState()` functions work.) Using the `XMLUpdateGram()` function, we can get a "snapshot" of the data before and after changes. The server can then use this `UpdateGram` to decide what action to take—sort of.

Do the experiment shown in Listing 7.20.

LISTING 7.20   How to Create an `UpdateGram` Showing an `INSERT`

```
CREATE TABLE TEST ( ContactID Integer, FullName Char(20), Phone Char(15) )
SET MULTILOCKS ON
SELECT TEST
CursorSetProp([Buffering], 5 )
INSERT  INTO TEST VALUES ( 1, [Les Pinter], [324-4321] )
X = XMLUpdateGram()
STRTOFILE( x, "UpdateGram.xml" )
MODIFY FILE UPDATEGRAM.xml
```

Listing 7.21 shows the resulting XML.

LISTING 7.21   `UpdateGram` Resulting from an `INSERT`

```
<?xml version = "1.0" encoding="Windows-1252" standalone="yes"?>
<root xmlns:updg="urn:schemas-microsoft-com:xml-updategram">
    <updg:sync>
        <updg:before/>
        <updg:after>
            <test>
                <contactid>1</contactid>
                <fullname>Les Pinter</fullname>
                <phone>324-4321</phone>
            </test>
        </updg:after>
    </updg:sync>
</root>
```

`<Updg:Before/>` means that the "before" version of the record is empty. Because the "after" has a record, this is an add. Similarly, if you have both a "before" and an "after," it's an update, and if there's a "before" and no "after," it's a delete.

Changes are documented down to the field in an `UpdateGram`, as shown in Listing 7.22.

LISTING 7.22 An UpdateGram Showing an UPDATE

```
CREATE TABLE TEST ( ContactID Integer, FullName Char(20), Phone Char(15) )
SET MULTILOCKS ON
SELECT TEST
INSERT  INTO TEST VALUES ( 1, [Les Pinter], [324-4321] )
CursorSetProp([Buffering], 5 )
CursorSetProp([KeyFieldList],[ContactID])
REPLACE FullName WITH [Juan Carral]
X = XMLUpdateGram()
STRTOFILE( x, "UpdateGram.xml" )
MODIFY FILE UPDATEGRAM.xml
```

The UpdateGram reveals only the changed fields, as shown in Listing 7.23.

LISTING 7.23 UpdateGram Resulting from an UPDATE

```
<?xml version = "1.0" encoding="Windows-1252" standalone="yes"?>
<root xmlns:updg="urn:schemas-microsoft-com:xml-updategram">
    <updg:sync>
        <updg:before>
            <test>
                <contactid>1</contactid>
                <fullname>Les Pinter</fullname>
            </test>
        </updg:before>
        <updg:after>
            <test>
                <contactid>1</contactid>
                <fullname>Juan Carral</fullname>
            </test>
        </updg:after>
    </updg:sync>
</root>
```

Finally, Listing 7.24 shows what a DELETE UpdateGram looks like.

LISTING 7.24 Code to Produce an UpdateGram Showing a DELETE

```
CREATE TABLE TEST ( ContactID Integer, FullName Char(20), Phone Char(15) )
SET MULTILOCKS ON
SET DELETED ON
SELECT TEST
INSERT  INTO TEST VALUES ( 1, [Les Pinter], [324-4321] )
```

LISTING 7.24   Continued

```
CursorSetProp([Buffering], 5 )
DELETE NEXT 1
X = XMLUpdateGram()
STRTOFILE( x, "UpdateGram.xml" )
MODIFY FILE UPDATEGRAM.xml
```

The result is shown in Listing 7.25.

LISTING 7.25   An UpdateGram Showing a DELETE

```
<?xml version = "1.0" encoding="Windows-1252" standalone="yes"?>
<root xmlns:updg="urn:schemas-microsoft-com:xml-updategram">
    <updg:sync>
        <updg:before>
            <test>
                <contactid>1</contactid>
                <fullname>Les Pinter</fullname>
                <phone>324-4321</phone>
            </test>
        </updg:before>
        <updg:after/>
    </updg:sync>
</root>
```

So updategrams are easy to understand and easy to produce. That's the good news.

The bad news is that although SQL Server can read diffgrams, FoxPro 7 can't. And anyway, neither can read updategrams. Visual FoxPro 8 has diffgrams, which are different from updategrams, and Visual FoxPro 8 can read and apply them to add, update, and delete records.

So, unless you write your own UpdateGram parser for receiving and processing these animals, they're interesting but not relevant with working with DBFs.

DiffGrams in Visual FoxPro 8

Visual FoxPro 8 adds the CursorAdapter and the XMLAdapter, the two missing pieces that finally make XML useful to FoxPro developers. Listing 7.26 shows how to create a DiffGram using an XMLAdapter, and how to send it to a Web service that knows what to do with it. You'll have to imagine the search form.

LISTING 7.26 Using Visual FoxPro 8 `DiffGrams` to Update a Record on a Web Server

```
DO SearchForm to lcSelectedRecordKey

LOCAL loXMLHTTP AS        [ MSXML2.IXMLHTTPRequest]
loXMLHTTP = CREATEOBJECT ( [MSXML2.XMLHTTP.4.0] )
lcCmd = [SELECT * FROM CLIENTES WHERE ClID = ] + lcSelectedRecordKey
lcCmd =  CHRTRAN ( Cmd, [ ], [+] )
*  Encode for HTTP, which like nature, abhors a vacuum
loXMLHTTP.AddPostVar ( lcCmd )
loXMLHTTP.Open( [POST], [http://localhost/Fox/GetClientRecord )
loXMLHTTP.Send()
XMLTOCURSOR (loXMLHTTP.ResponseBody)
```

The user clicks on the Edit button:

```
THISFORM.EnableFieldsAndTurnOnSaveAndCancelButtons()
CursorSetProp([Buffering],5)
```

The user modifies the record in the current screen, then clicks on the Save button. This is where we create the `DiffGram` and send it to the server, as shown in Listing 7.27.

LISTING 7.27 The Save Button Click Event Code

```
LOCAL oXML  AS XMLAdapter
oXML = CREA ( "XMLAdapter" )
oXML.AddTableSchema ( "Clientes" )
oXML.IsDiffGram  = .T.
oXML.UTF8Encoded = .T.
oXML.ToXML  ( "lcXML", "", .F., .T., .T. )
LOCAL loXMLHTTP AS        [MSXML2.IXMLHTTPRequest]
loXMLHTTP = CREATEOBJECT ( [MSXML2.XMLHTTP.4.0] )
loXMLHTTP.AddPostVar ( lcXML )
loXMLHTTP.Open([POST], [http://localhost/Fox/UpdateClientsTable] )
loXMLHTTP.Send()
```

When the Server program `UpdateClientsTable` runs, it extracts the diffgram from the post buffer and uses it to update the table, as shown in Listing 7.28.

LISTING 7.28 Updating the Table on the Server

```
oXML.LoadXML ( lcXML )
MESSAGEBOX( "Diffgram loaded", 48, ;
 "Simulating a DiffGram being received on the server" )
```

```
LOCAL oCA AS CursorAdapter
oCA = CREATEOBJECT ( [CursorAdapter] )

oCA.DataSource =   "Native"
oCA.CursorAttach ( "Clients" )

LOCAL oTable AS XMLTable
oTable = CREATEOBJECT ( [XMLTable] )
oTable = oXML.Tables.Item(1)
oField = oTable.Fields.Item(1)
oField.KeyField = .T.

oTable.ApplyDiffGram ( "Clients", oCA, .T. )
CLOSE TABLES
CLOSE DATABASE
```

It's not as simple as updating a FoxPro table on a workstation, and it's not as easy as constructing a SQL UPDATE statement and calling SQLEXEC to execute it. But after you've made it work one time, it's not too difficult the next time.

The Visual FoxPro CursorAdapter

In FoxPro 8, XML has finally received the support that we lacked for communicating with the rest of the world. The new base class CursorAdapter replaces what we used to do with remote views, and to a degree what we did with SQL Pass-Through. And it does so in a homogeneous way, so that only one syntax has to be learned regardless of the data store. It automates the tasks of inserting, updating, and deleting records on remote tables when we make changes locally. What's new is that it also works with XML.

To put this technology to use, you add a CursorAdapter to the form's Data Environment. You set a few properties and call methods to retrieve your data. You can then use the CursorAdapter in conjunction with the new XMLAdapter to construct and send updates. The Server can also use the CursorAdapter and XMLAdapter to apply them.

Let's create a new form called XMLForm1. Open the Data Environment and right-click. You'll see several options, among them Add CursorAdapter and Builder. The first lets you construct the CursorAdapter manually, but the Builder is helpful for learning how it works. For now, we'll use the Builder.

I have a file called XML1.XML, shown in Listing 7.29, which includes an XSD. This is important because the CursorAdapter Wizard in the Data Environment will use it to construct the cursor.

LISTING 7.29   XML1.XML File to Demonstrate Loading XML to a `CursorAdapter`

```xml
<?xml version = "1.0" encoding="Windows-1252" standalone="yes"?>
<Root>
  <xsd:schema id="VFPData" xmlns:xsd="http://www.w3.org/2001/XMLSchema"
➥xmlns:msdata="urn:schemas-microsoft-com:xml-msdata">
    <xsd:element name="VFPData" msdata:IsDataSet="true">
      <xsd:complexType>
        <xsd:choice maxOccurs="unbounded">
          <xsd:element name="clientes" minOccurs="0" maxOccurs="unbounded">
            <xsd:complexType>
              <xsd:sequence>
                <xsd:element name="clave" type="xsd:int"/>
                <xsd:element name="nombre">
                  <xsd:simpleType>
                    <xsd:restriction base="xsd:string">
                      <xsd:maxLength value="20"/>
                    </xsd:restriction>
                  </xsd:simpleType>
                </xsd:element>
                <xsd:element name="apellidos">
                  <xsd:simpleType>
                    <xsd:restriction base="xsd:string">
                      <xsd:maxLength value="30"/>
                    </xsd:restriction>
                  </xsd:simpleType>
                </xsd:element>
                <xsd:element name="telefono">
                  <xsd:simpleType>
                    <xsd:restriction base="xsd:string">
                      <xsd:maxLength value="15"/>
                    </xsd:restriction>
                  </xsd:simpleType>
                </xsd:element>
              </xsd:sequence>
            </xsd:complexType>
          </xsd:element>
        </xsd:choice>
        <xsd:anyAttribute
            ➥namespace="http://www.w3.org/XML/1998/namespace"
➥processContents="lax"/>
      </xsd:complexType>
    </xsd:element>
  </xsd:schema>
```

LISTING 7.29   Continued

```xml
<clientes>
  <clave>1</clave>
  <nombre>Juan</nombre>
  <apellidos>del Pueblo</apellidos>
  <telefono>3312-1234</telefono>
</clientes>
<clientes>
  <clave>2</clave>
  <nombre>Carlos</nombre>
  <apellidos>Estrada</apellidos>
  <telefono>4343-3323</telefono>
</clientes>
<clientes>
  <clave>3</clave>
  <nombre>Jimena</nombre>
  <apellidos>Sánchez</apellidos>
  <telefono>2014-1914</telefono>
</clientes>
</Root>
```

Creating a CursorAdapter to Read XML

Open the Data Environment and right-click somewhere inside it. Select Builder from the context menu. You'll see the screen shown in Figure 7.10.

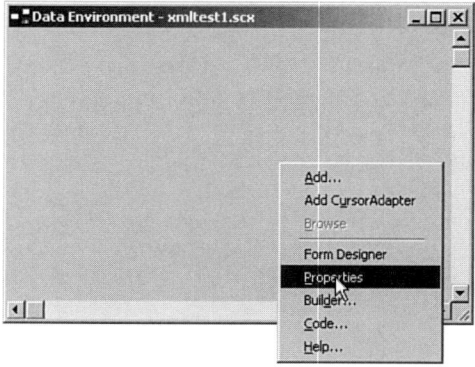

FIGURE 7.10   The DataEnvironment Builder.

The Builder will create almost everything we need to convert this XML file into a cursor, which can be manipulated as if it had come from a DBF, or from SQL Server. Of course we could also select Add CursorAdapter and specify all of the properties; but as is always the case with a new tool, the Builder does it right the first time and we don't. So we'll get trained, and get a working `CursorAdapter` in the bargain.

Since Visual FoxPro 3, the remote view has been the mechanism that permitted us to build a cursor containing the contents of a table from a remote source such as SQL Server, an Access MDB, or any other data source. The `CursorAdapter` lets us use a single syntax for any data source. This lets us migrate the application from DBF to some other data source at any time without changing any code; we simply change the data source from Native (that is, FoxPro DBF) to something else. We also get to practice the use of disconnected recordsets, which are the gospel according to Microsoft.

The first page of the DataEnvironment Builder (see Figure 7.11) lets us select the data source: ADO, Native (DBF), ODBC, and XML. Choose XML for this example. Click on the second tab of the DataEnvironment Builder, "2. Cursors", to continue.

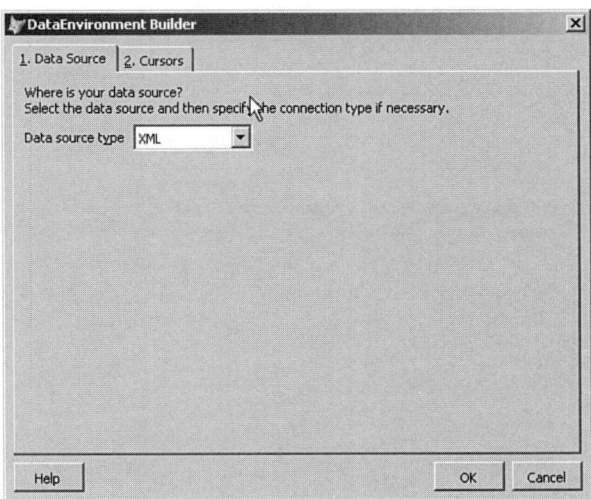

FIGURE 7.11   Select the data source for the DataEnvironment Builder.

After you've selected XML, the Cursors page will launch the CursorAdapter Builder to create a `CursorAdapter`, which will open the XML file, read the XSD, and create the cursor's structure. Click on New to launch the CursorAdapter Builder shown in Figure 7.12.

FoxPro will immediately add a little cursor with a single field named F1. It's a placeholder, and it needs a little more information. Enter XML again as the data source type. (I know we just told it we were going to use XML, but I guess it forgot.) Select page 2, the Data Access tab of the page frame, and click on the Build button to the right of the label caption Schema, as shown in Figure 7.13. The resulting dialog will let you pick the name of the XML file from which you want the schema to be constructed.

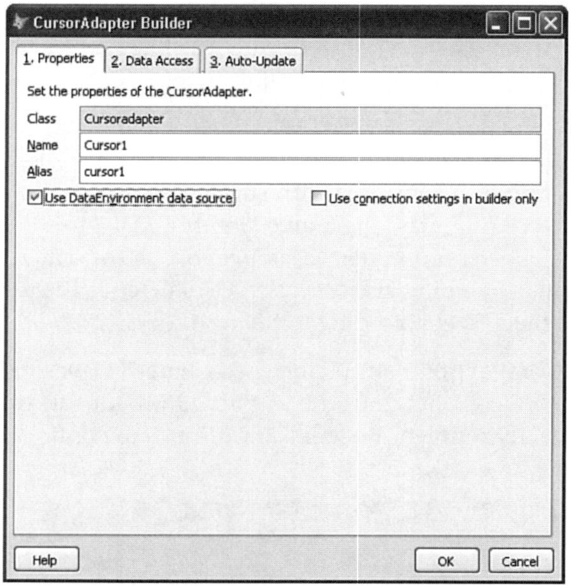

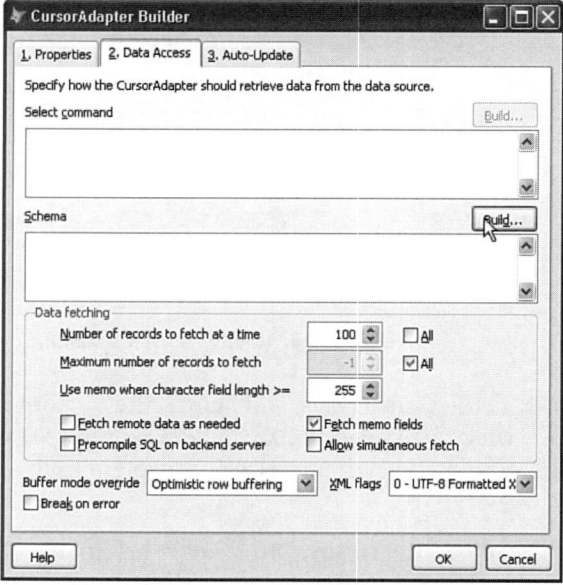

FIGURE 7.12 The Cursors Screen in the DataEnvironment Builder.

FIGURE 7.13 Setting the Data Source Type in the CursorAdapter Builder.

Double-click the name of the file containing the XML. The builder will read the XML file and create the schema that appears in Figure 7.14.

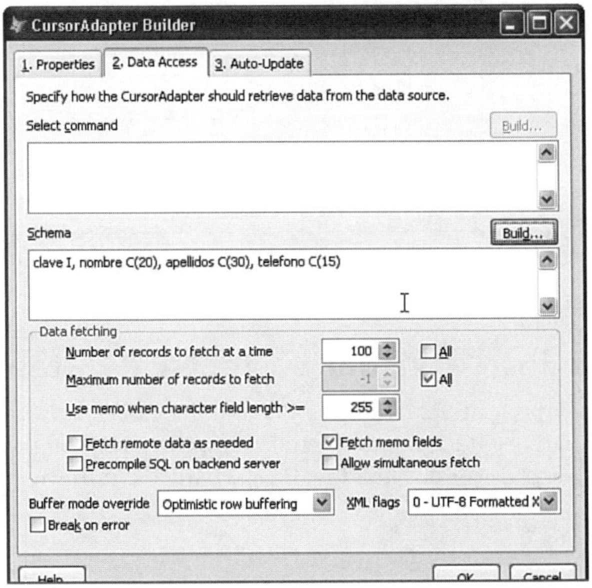

FIGURE 7.14   Creating the schema for the cursor from the XML.

Click OK to close the CursorAdapter Builder and click OK again to close the Data Environment Builder.

Two steps remain to be done in code. First, open the Data Environment, and right-click on Cursor1, select Code. Select the AutoOpen procedure, and you'll see that the CursorAdapter Wizard has added several lines of generated code. At the end of this generated code, add these two lines:

```
THIS.SelectCmd = FILETOSTR( "XML1.XML" )
THIS.CursorFill()
```

Next, add a grid on the form, open the Properties Sheet, and enter the name of the cursor (Cursor1) as the RecordSource. Press Ctrl+E to save the form and run it. The result appears in Figure 7.15.

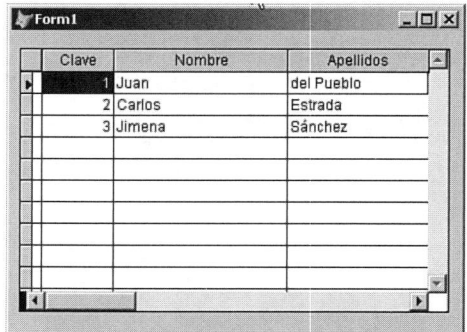

FIGURE 7.15   A Grid Populated with the Contents of an XML File.

Reading XML into a Visual Basic .NET Dataset

Reading XML into a dataset in Visual Basic .NET and displaying it in a grid is even easier because XML is the native data format. The following three lines of code in the `Load` event of a form containing a grid will do the same thing that we did in the preceding FoxPro example:

```
Dim DS As New DataSet
DS.ReadXml("C:\XML1.XML")
DataGrid1.DataSource = DS.Tables(0)
```

That's probably the first time we've seen something that's easier in Visual Basic .NET than it is in FoxPro. But there are a few more as well, as we'll see in later chapters.

TIP

These three lines of Visual Basic .NET code are pretty cryptic, so let me explain what they do: The first line declares a variable of type `DataSet` and creates one in a single line; some purists think that's inelegant, but I don't. The second line uses the `DataSet`'s native `ReadXML` method (or rather, one of about eight *overloads* [versions] of the `ReadXML` method that the `DataSet` has, which can read XML directly from a file). Finally, a grid's data source is not a `DataSet`, but rather one of the Tables in a `DataSet`. `Tables(0)`, according to Bill's weird arithmetic, is the first one. Voilà.

The Visual FoxPro `XMLAdapter`

The `XMLAdapter` class is also new in Visual FoxPro 8. It's similar to the CursorAdapter class, except that it has more methods specifically designed for dealing with XML. It contains most, if not all, of the functions we need in Visual FoxPro to manipulate XML, and this makes the job much easier than it was in Visual FoxPro 7.

In order to use it, you first have to load an XML Document. You can do so using its LoadXML() method to load XML from either a string variable or from a file. Or, you can use Attach() to load an XML document that's already been loaded into an XMLDOMDocument object, or from HTTP. You can also use AddTableSchema to read a FoxPro cursor.

The result is the same: An XML document is loaded into the XMLAdapter object, at which point you can call other XMLAdapter methods. This is a two-way class: Some methods load XML and another writes XML. There are also other utility methods. Table 7.3 contains a preview.

TABLE 7.3   XMLAdapter alternate utility methods

Method	Description
AddTableSchema	Load a schema for a table, as well as its data
Attach	Load an XMLDOM object previously loaded by another object, for example by an XMLHTTP object (see example below)
LoadXML (String/filename)	Loads XML from a string or table
ToXML	Creates a variable of type String or a file and fills it with the XML representation of the currently loaded document

Using XML and Data Islands to Reduce Server Load

If XML had no purpose except to send tables across the Internet, it would be pretty useful. However, it has additional and unexpected benefits. And others will probably be invented that we haven't yet thought about.

Traditionally, if we wanted to send out an attractive page of tabular data, we wrote a program to do a SELECT from a database, generated HTML with TABLE, TR, and TD tags to format the data with nice colors, and sent it out. That required running the same program each time we wanted to display the table, even if the same query was made many times a day.

What if we could send out a file containing data and formatting instructions, and let the user's computer do the formatting? We can do that. We have the technology. It's called *Data Islands*.

Data Islands

Internet Explorer (and probably other browsers as well) support the use of Data Islands, which permit us to output a file containing the instructions for formatting data, and let the user's browser do the work. This is especially attractive because servers have the ability to cache pages as they're served. The next person who requests the same page gets the in-memory copy of the page, which is about a thousand times faster than doing another query and formatting the output.

The HTML page shown in Listing 7.30 contains an example of the use of Data Islands.

LISTING 7.30   An HTML Page Containing XML and a Data Island

```
<html>
<head><title> Example of XML embedded in HTML </title></head>
<body>
<h2><font color="#FF6633">Example of XML embedded in HTML</font></h2>

<XML ID="FantasyIsland">
<clients>
 <client>
  <first>Juan</first>
  <last>Perez</last>
 </client>
 <client>
  <first>Les</first>
  <last>Pinter</last>
 </client>
</clients>
</XML>

<table DATASRC="#FantasyIsland" border="1" bgcolor="#FFFFFF" cellspacing="2">
<tr><td bgcolor="silver" width="100"><div DATAFLD="first"></div></td>
    <td bgcolor="silver" width="200"><div DATAFLD="last"></div></td>
</tr>
</table>

<hr>End
</body>
</html>
```

The resulting Web page is shown in Figure 7.16.

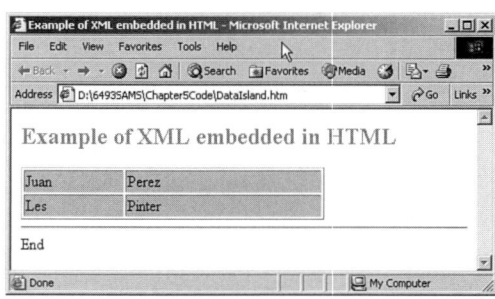

FIGURE 7.16   Formatting an XML data island with HTML.

It's easier to read, and more importantly, all of the rendering is done on the browser. If you already have the XML, you can construct pages like this on the fly, pasting the XML into the middle of the output.

Related Technologies: XPATH and XSLT

There are other ancillary technologies that can be very valuable allies. One is XPATH, and the other is XSLT. Although they are not part of FoxPro or of Visual Basic .NET, they are very useful in building Web pages, a topic that we'll touch on later in this book. So we'll just take a quick look here.

XPATH is a language to manipulate XML. Using its abbreviated syntax, you can loop through an XML document, build a heading based on one type of node, list the child elements of that node in tabular form, and then repeat the pattern for each parent node. And you can do all this in a very cryptic syntax. That means there isn't much code to write, but it's hard.

XPATH expresses the contents of an XML document based on a model containing seven nodes: Root, Element, Attribute, NameSpace, Processing Instruction, Comments, and Text. The content of a document is referred to in terms of some node. Relative references such as parent, child, descendent, and others can also be used to identify a particular element within the document. There are XPATH functions as well. Using XPATH queries, you can do a lot with just a little code.

The example shown in Listing 7.31 reads an XML file, locates a section of text, and produces a list of the related elements using an embedded XPATH query. aaa and bbb are elements in the namespace of the XML that is to be read:

LISTING 7.31 Visual Basic .NET Code to Read XML and List Part of Its Contents Using an Embedded XPATH Query

```
LOCAL loDOM          AS "MSXML2.DOMDocument.4.0"
LOCAL loNodeList     AS "MSXML2.IXMLDOMNodeList"
loDOM = CREATEOBJECT ( "MSXML2.DOMDocument.4.0")
loDOM.Load ( "CLIENTES.XML")


loDOM.SetProperty ( "SelectNameSpaces", "xmlns:y="urn:vfp:mins" )
loNodeList = loDOM.SelectNodes ( "child::y:aaa/child::y:bbb" )


FOR EACH loNode IN loNodeList
    ? loNode.XML
ENDFOR
```

The two lines of code set off in the middle of Listing 7.31 define the selection criteria for the nodes to be included. It's a very compact way to do something that otherwise would have to be required code. *He who codes least codes best.*

Extensible Style Sheet Transformations (XSLT)

XSLT is like a style sheet on steroids. It contains commands to process all of the records in an XML file and generate an XML page displayed as a formatted table. In that sense it's similar to the Data Islands example shown in the preceding section.

The example shown in Listing 7.32 demonstrates how it works.

LISTING 7.32   XSLT for Formatting XML

```
<?xml version="1.0"?>
<xml:stylesheet versión= "1.0" xmlns:xsl=http://www.wc.org/1999/XSL/Transform>
<xsl:template match="/">
 <html>
  <head>
   <title>XSLT used to format an XML file</title>
  </head>
  <body>
    </xsl:apply-templates/>
  </body>
 </html>
</xsl:template>
<xsl:template match="child::clients/child::client">         && use XPATH
 <b>CLient:</b> <xsl:value-of select="client/first"/><br/>
 <hr color="blue"/>
</xsl:template>
</xsl:stylesheet>
```

To use this, simply include a reference to it in the XML file. The server will send the user the XML file and the XSL file, and the client's browser will combine the two. That way, all of the processing is transferred to the computer that requested the document. Multiply this by a few hundred thousand downloads a day, and you've done made some serious scalability improvements.

Summary

XML is a pretty exotic topic, and I hope this chapter has given you some useful insights into what it is and how it's used. Screen design, on the other hand, is the heart of a programmer's daily routine. In the next chapter, we'll look at some ways you can spice up your interfaces and add class to your screens.

CHAPTER **8**

Screen Design

There's a place where I go every day. I spend most of my time there. I know it so well that I can reach for things without looking, and there they are. I feel so at home that I hate to leave it. It's the Screen Designer—the Visual FoxPro Screen Designer, that is.

I'm warming up to the Visual Basic .NET Screen Designer. It certainly has everything you could want, and in fact has more controls, more IDE features, and more ways of doing things than does Visual FoxPro. But somehow, Visual FoxPro is cozy. And you can do *almost* anything with Visual FoxPro that you can with Visual Basic .NET.

In this chapter, we'll compare features more specifically. Screen controls, IDE features, toolbars, and toolboxes lend themselves to comparison at a micro level, unlike big topics like data handling, where the story is that *everything* is different.

I'm going to start with the basic controls and menus, then move up to the design of control classes and screen classes, and then to data binding. Finally, I'll touch on how you can go beyond basics to create really innovative form designs.

The Base Control Classes

FoxPro's base classes appear in the Form Controls toolbar when a form is open. Visual Basic .NET's base controls are found in the Windows Forms toolbar, which also is only visible when a form is open. FoxPro's base class controls are the bare minimum, and I was a little jealous the first time I saw the Visual Basic .NET Form Designer. However, it's really not quite so black-and-white. Some of the FoxPro equivalents of Visual Basic .NET controls (for example, the Color Picker) are exposed as function calls in FoxPro. And in other cases, controls with similar names have different capabilities, or one is harder to use then its counterpart.

With those caveats, Table 8.1 gives the approximate equivalencies of the base control classes. We'll cover important differences as we go through the chapter.

TABLE 8.1   Base Control Classes

FoxPro	Visual Basic .NET
Label	Label
TextBox	TextBox
Editbox	TextBox with Multiline=True
Commandbutton	Button
CommandGroup	Buttons within a Panel
OptionGroup	RadioButton
CheckBox	CheckBox
ComboBox	Combobox
ListBox	ListBox
Spinner	NumericUpDown
Grid	DataGrid
Image, PicClp32.ocx	PictureBox
Timer	Timer
Grid	DataGrid
OLEControl	Various
OLEBoundControl	Various
Line	Label with BorderStyle FixedSingle and Height=1
Shape	Panel
Container	Panel
Separator	N/A
HyperLink	LinkLabel
GetColor()	ColorDialog
CheckBox	CheckedBoxList
Menu Builder Context Menu option	ContextMenu
Visual FoxPro Report Designer Preview	CrystalReportViewer
MSComctl2.ocx	DateTimePicker
Similar to a combo box	DomainUpDown
(Automated valid clauses)	ErrorProvider
GetDir()	FolderBrowserDialog
GetFont()	FontDialog
Built into RadioButtons	GroupBox
SET HELP TO	HelpProvider
Form property	HScrollBar
MSComCtlLib	ImageList
MSComCtlLib	Listview

TABLE 8.1   Continued

FoxPro	Visual Basic .NET
Menu Designer	MainMenu
MSComctl.ocx	MonthCalendar
Puts an icon on the Taskbar (N/A)	NotifyIcon
GetFile()	OpenFileDialog
Report Designer, SYS(1037)	PageSetupDialog
Report Designer, Ctrl+P	PrintDialog
Report Form	PrintDocument
Report Form Preview	PrintPreviewDialog
MSComCtlLib	ProgressBar
RichTextLib	RichTextBox
PutFile()	SaveFileDialog
N/A	Splitter
MSComCtlLib	StatusBar
PageFrame	TabControl
Toolbar Class, MSComctl.ocx	Toolbar
Built into each control	ToolTip
MSComCtlLib	TrackBar
MSComCtlLib	TreeView
Form property	VScrollBar

I'm tempted to say that this list consists of apples and oranges. FoxPro's base control list is actually only 21 controls: Label, TextBox, EditBox, CommandButton, CommandGroup, OptionGroup, CheckBox, ComboBox, ListBox, Spinner, Grid, Image, Timer, PageFrame, ActiveXControl, ActiveXBoundControl, Line, Shape, Container, Separator, and HyperLink. But on my laptop alone I have over 350 ActiveX controls, and every week some vendor sends me another dozen or two. When registered with RegSvr32.exe, these controls appear on the Tools, Options, Controls page, and on the Visual Studio toolbox under each vendor's heading bar. So it's hard to say that one language has something that the other doesn't. Except for the NotifyIcon, HelpProvider, and Splitter controls, each has everything that the other has, although the implementation is sometimes totally different.

Note that many controls listed in Table 8.1 are members of MSComCtlLib. This is a Windows Control Library, which you can easily build yourself in Visual Studio .NET. In fact, they are the equivalent of what we would use a VCX for in building our own subclasses of the standard FoxPro base form controls.

Creating the Startup Screen for Your Application

Most FoxPro developers don't think about the container for their application, because it's automatic in FoxPro. It isn't in Visual Basic .NET; and in fact, we can do the same things in FoxPro that Visual Basic programmers have been doing for years. As usual, it's just a matter of setting a few properties, calling a few methods, and changing some aspects of the main menu.

The Startup Screen for Your Visual FoxPro Application

In FoxPro, there are two ways to build a Windows Forms project. You can either use _Screen (the FoxPro IDE screen) as the container for the rest of your forms, or you can designate your own top-level form by setting the ShowWindow property as follows:

0 - In Screen

1 - In Top-Level form

2 - As Top-Level form

If you use a top-level form, you have to designate the forms that run within it as ShowWindow type 1, In Top-Level form. This is called a **Multiple Document Interface** (MDI). The default is **Single Document Interface (SDI)**, and it's what you've been using for years. You can use either.

If your startup form is a top-level form, you have to select the Top-Level Form Menu option in the Menu Designer. You then have to load the menu inside the form by executing the following command in the form's Load event:

```
DO MENU.MPR WITH THIS, .T.
```

Finally, you have to suppress the appearance of the default _Screen that FoxPro automatically displays. You can make the first command in your application _Screen.WindowsState = 2 to minimize it, but that will still cause the screen to flicker, and it doesn't look professional. The correct way is to specify -T in the command-line invocation of your compiled FoxPro executable application, or to include a Config.VFP file containing the line SCREEN = OFF that's either compiled into your executable or specified following the command-line switch –c. Other than that, there are no other special requirements. It's actually a very crisp interface, and after mastering it, you may prefer it for your applications.

If I use _Screen as the container for my application, I also set a few other main form properties. I set _Screen.ControlBox to .F. so that users don't try to close their application by clicking on the "X" at the upper-right corner of the screen and are forced to use File, Exit from the menu for that purpose. (You can also specify ON SHUTDOWN code, which can be as simple as ON SHUTDOWN QUIT, in your MAIN program to override the default behavior.) I also use _Screen.WindowState = 2 (Maximized) to expand the main screen to fill the available screen.

The Startup Screen for Your Visual Basic .NET Application

In Visual Basic .NET, there is no equivalent to _Screen. When you create a Windows Forms project, the first form that's added is named Form1.vb, and it is assumed that you'll use it as a top-level form that is the container for the rest of your application. I generally change its name both externally (by right-clicking on its name in the Solution Explorer and selecting Rename from the context menu) and internally (by selecting the form in the Designer, then using F4 to open the Properties sheet and changing the (Name) property) to MainForm. Then I select the Solution Explorer again, click on the project to select it, right-click on the project and select Properties, and then open the Startup Object drop-down at the upper-right corner of the dialog and select MainForm.vb as the Main (see Figure 8.1).

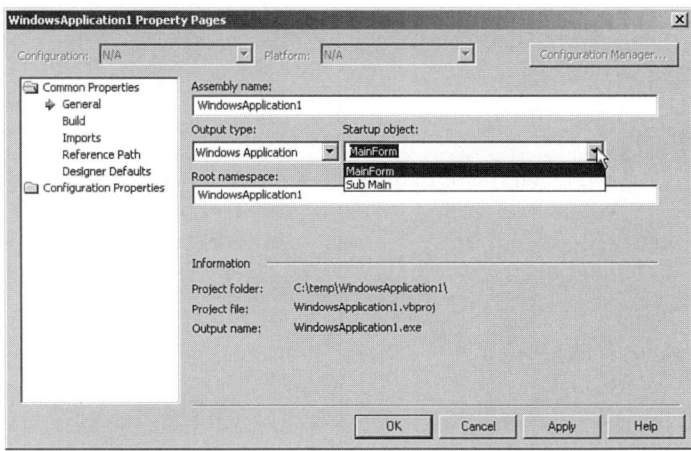

FIGURE 8.1   The Visual Basic .NET equivalent of FoxPro's Set Main option in the Project menu pad.

In this main form, I set the ControlBox property of my MainForm to False, so that the File, Exit command of the MainMenu control is tasked with closing any open forms, saving data, and closing the application.

If I use the FoxPro _Screen, I set the WindowState to 2 programmatically in MAIN.PRG. In Visual Basic .NET, I maximize the form, either in the Properties sheet or in code:

```
_Screen.WindowState = 2  && FoxPro

WindowState = FormWindowState.Maximized
' VB.NET - usually set in the Properties Sheet
```

If I build my own topmost form in FoxPro, I set AutoCenter = .T. in the Properties sheet. In Visual Basic .NET, you can either use the Properties sheet or this code in MainForm.vb:

```
StartPosition = FormStartPosition.CenterScreen
```

In Visual Basic .NET, attempting to set a value for either of these form properties automatically displays the appropriate Enum the instant you type the "=" (see Figure 8.2). So, if you're writing code that someone else might use and there are several options for a property, you might want to create the appropriate Enum in order to take advantage of the way that IntelliSense works.

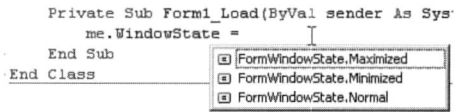

FIGURE 8.2   Maximizing the `MainForm` window.

Creating Menus

Menus are used to provide events for displaying screens, setting options, and informing the user as to what's available. A good menu design makes an application more understandable and can actually determine how many technical support calls you get. The menu designers in FoxPro and in Visual Basic .NET ostensibly do the same thing, but what a difference!

The FoxPro Menu

In Visual FoxPro, we use the Menu Designer to build menus, whether Main or Context. The Menu Designer is, to be charitable, idiosyncratic. When you type MODIFY MENU *name*, you first choose between a menu and a shortcut (a context menu). The first level of the resulting designer creates menu pads, which are displayed horizontally at the top of the screen.

There are four possible types of menu entry: commands, procedures, submenus, and bars. Bars come from a fixed list of possible selections, and specific bar types (for example, Cut, Copy, and Paste) invoke the expected behaviors. Commands are one-line entries, whereas procedures can be multiple lines and result in little generated procedures in the MPR file (the auto-generated menu source code file) with system-supplied names that are the devil to find if you ever need to debug your menu. Submenus consist of menu bars, which will be displayed vertically. When you enter a submenu, visual cues as to their relation to the rest of the menu are minimal.

The design is saved in a table with the extension .mnx (.mnt for the memo fields). When you're done, you must *generate* the source code for the menu by selecting the Generate option from the IDE menu. The resulting code is stored in a text file with the extension .mpr. Therefore, in your MAIN program code, you include the command

```
DO MENU.MPR
```

The resulting menu, named _MSYSMENU, is installed in place of the FoxPro IDE menu.

Menus can be added and removed as needed when the context changes. When you build the menu, you can select View, General Options from the FoxPro IDE menu and use options in the resulting dialog to specify that the menu is to be installed to the left or right of any pad in the current menu or to the right of the current menu. You can use `PUSH MENU _MSYSMENU` before adding a context menu, add it using `DO MENU OtherMenu.MPR`, and then use `POP MENU _MSYSMENU` when done to restore the menu as it was before. There are also shortcut menus, which can be popped up as needed.

Finally, individual menu items can be assigned hotkeys, which allow selections to be invoked without dropping down the menu pop-ups. Pads can also be marked as "selected" with a check or other character, and they can be grayed out to indicate that they are disabled.

All in all, the FoxPro menu is quite functional, but it's a little hard to get used to, and I wouldn't call it intuitive.

The Visual Basic .NET `MainMenu` Control

The Visual Basic .NET menu is a thing of beauty. It's intuitive, easy to understand, and easy to use. Unlike FoxPro's Menu Designer approach, the `MainMenu` control is selected from the Windows Form controls toolbar and dropped on the `MainForm` page. When selected, it appears in the upper-left corner of the screen. You can type directly into the pads and bars. Moving to the right or left of the last available selection produces a new empty box into which you can type the appropriate prompt. Selections can be moved around.

Changes to the menu control produce code in the form itself that is directly viewable—there is no delayed code generation. To make the code more readable, you'll want to right-click on the menu control, turn on the Edit Names option, and type names for each menu selection. For example, I call the File pad `mnuFile`, the File, Exit selection below it `mnuFileExit`, and so forth. It makes it a lot easier to read the code, and it's easy.

To add code for any menu pad or bar, double-click on its name or caption and the corresponding code is displayed in the code window. Visual Basic .NET uses `Handles` clauses to connect the code you write to a particular menu component. The code is actually quite intuitive.

In a FoxPro menu selection to display a form, you'd probably use a `DO FORM (formname)` command. In a Visual Basic .NET menu pad to display a form based on your `CustomerForm` class (all forms in Visual Basic .NET are saved as class files with the `.vb` extension), you need to instantiate the form as an object and call the object's `Show` method, thusly:

```
Dim oFrm as New CustomerForm
oFrm.Show()
```

Similarly you can instantiate and call methods on any other class. The Visual Basic .NET `MainMenu` control is absolutely one of the best things about the Visual Basic .NET Screen

Designer. During a design review, I once irritated the FoxPro design team by alluding to the provenance of this lovely control, which came straight from Delphi (along with the entire Borland programming team).

Traversing the Controls in a Form

At some point, you're going to want to iterate through the controls in a form to do something with them—enable or disable all of them, or perhaps automate binding. In FoxPro, it's done as shown in Listing 8.1.

LISTING 8.1   Disabling All Controls Generically in Code in FoxPro

```
FOR EACH Ctrl in THISFORM.Controls
    Ctrl.Enabled = .F.
ENDFOR
```

In Visual Basic .NET, it's almost identical, as shown in Listing 8.2.

LISTING 8.2   Disabling All Controls Generically in Code in Visual Basic .NET

```
Dim Ctrl As Control

For Each Ctrl in Controls
    Ctrl.Enabled = False
Next
```

Subclassing Controls

The point of object-oriented programming is that what you do to a class is inherited by classes derived from it, and reflected in objects based on it.

You can begin to reap the benefits of object orientation in two minutes by subclassing the base form controls, and then using your subclassed controls on your forms. For example, let's say you create a label control of your own and use it on all of your forms. Shortly thereafter, your client decides to change the font with which labels are displayed on the screen. Instead of changing the FontName property of every label on every label on every screen, you change it in your label class, and the change instantly appears *everywhere* in your application. That's a powerful visual example of what inheritance can do for you.

Subclassing the FoxPro Screen Controls

To subclass the FoxPro screen controls, change to your project directory by typing CD *ProjectDirectory* and type the code shown in Listing 8.3. After each one pops up a designer, close the designer to save the class.

LISTING 8.3   Code to Type in the Command Window to Create a Class Library Containing Subclasses of All of the FoxPro Controls

```
CREATE CLASS MyLabel  OF FormControls AS Label
CREATE CLASS MyText   OF FormControls AS TextBox
CREATE CLASS MyEdit   OF FormControls AS EditBox
CREATE CLASS MyButton OF FormControls AS CommandButton
CREATE CLASS MyGroup  OF FormControls AS CommandGroup

CREATE CLASS MyRadio  OF FormControls AS OptionGroup
CREATE CLASS MyCheck  OF FormControls AS CheckBox
CREATE CLASS MyCombo  OF FormControls AS ComboBox
CREATE CLASS MyList   OF FormControls AS ListBox
CREATE CLASS MySpin   OF FormControls AS Spinner

CREATE CLASS MyGrid   OF FormControls AS Grid
CREATE CLASS MyImage  OF FormControls AS Image
CREATE CLASS MyTimer  OF FormControls AS Timer
CREATE CLASS MyFrame  OF FormControls AS PageFrame

CREATE CLASS MyLine   OF FormControls AS Line
CREATE CLASS MyShape  OF FormControls AS Shape
CREATE CLASS MyPanel  OF FormControls AS Container
CREATE CLASS MyLink   OF FormControls AS HyperLink
```

There are probably a few properties that you'll want to change before using them. For example, change the Enabled property of MyText, MyEdit, MyCheck, MyCombo, MyRadio, and MySpin to .F.. This allows us to display a form with data that users can't edit until they click on the Edit button. I also go into the Click event of the MyButton class and enter this:

```
MessageBox ( "Not yet coded", 64, _VFP.Caption, 1000 )
```

This produces a message that reminds the programmer (that's me) that something isn't done.

Using Your Subclassed FoxPro Controls

Open a form, and then use View, Toolbars from the menu to display the Form Controls toolbar if it isn't already visible. Click on the View Class (the three little books) icon and click on Add (which is very unintuitive, but which actually means "add a new class library to this list") and select FormControls.VCX from the resulting dialog. Voilà, you've got classes! If you use these instead of FoxPro's base classes, you're ready to reap the benefits of OOP with just two minutes' work.

But the best way to begin using your new subclassed controls in FoxPro is to select Tools, Options, Field Mapping, and then enter the name of a control and the `FormControls.vcx` class library for each of the data types you're likely to use in your tables. After you've done this (be sure to click Apply for each selection), you can open the Data Environment of a form, add a table or cursor, click on the word Fields at the top of the cursor icon and drag and drop it on the screen, and you're instantly using your controls, both a label and the appropriate control based on the data type. It's the biggest bang for the buck in FoxPro.

If you want to do something to your controls, say enable or disable them, you can use `FOR EACH Ctrl in THISFORM.CONTROLS...ENDFOR` to iterate through them. Earlier, we saw how that's done. But usually a little more is required.

For example, I often start with all input controls disabled, enable them when the user selects Add or Edit, and then disable them again when they click Save or Cancel. To do this, I add a form class property called `EditableFields`, and populate with the names of the controls that should be enabled or disabled, as shown in Listing 8.4.

LISTING 8.4   Providing a List of Editable Field Classes in Visual FoxPro

```
DEFINE CLASS MyBaseForm AS Form
...
EditableFields = [MyText¦MyEdit¦MyCheck¦MyCombo¦MyRadio¦MySpin]
```

You can also create your form class in the Class Designer, use the Class, Add Property menu selection to add the property, and then open the Properties sheet for the class and type in the "EditableFields = ..." string shown in Listing 8.4. Then, you can enable them in the form class method called `EnableFields` as shown in Listing 8.5.

LISTING 8.5   The EnableFields Form Class Method

```
PARAMETERS OnOff
FOR EACH Ctrl in THISFORM.Controls
    IF UPPER(Ctrl.Class) $ UPPER(THISFORM.EditableFields)
        Ctrl.Enabled = OnOff
    ENDIF
ENDFOR
```

To use this method, include the line `THISFORM.EnableFields(.T.)` in your `cmdAdd` and `cmdEdit` Click event code, and include the line `THISFORM.EnableFields(.F.)` in your `cmdSave` and `cmdCancel` Click event code. Better still, add these lines in the form's Save and Cancel methods that are called by the Edit, Add, Save, and Cancel buttons' `Click` event code.

Subclassing the Screen Controls in Visual Basic .NET

Subclassing the form controls in Visual Basic .NET is as easy as pie, although not as easy as in FoxPro. Visual Basic doesn't have Visual Class Libraries (VCX files). Instead, you build a class file and declare each of the class names you want to use, following each `Public Class` statement with an `Inherits` statement that specifies the base class. It's almost too easy. However, to compensate for that, adding behavior to a class is harder and less obvious.

Let's say you want to create a half-dozen input classes and change the text box background color when it has the focus. In FoxPro you just drag the controls onto the Class Designer, set some properties in the Properties sheet, and then double-click and override the `GotFocus` and `LostFocus` events.

In Visual Basic .NET, you can't set properties visually in a class designer; you have to add a `New` method (a "constructor", like FoxPro's `Init()` method), and then add property assignments in the `New` method after calling the `MyBase.New()` method. Then, if there are base class events where you want to do something, you have to write an "event handler" and add a `Handles` clause to tie it to the original event. Note that the equivalents of `GotFocus` and `LostFocus` are called `Enter` and `Leave` respectively in .NET.

The code shown in Listing 8.6 goes in the `Class1` file that is created automatically when you select File, New, Project from the IDE menu and select Class as the project type. Name the project MyFormControls and change the name of `Class1.vb` to `MyControls.vb`.

> **TIP**
>
> You'll have to add references to `System.Windows.Forms` and to `System.Drawing` to the class library project, and also add the two `Imports` statements at the top of the class listing.

LISTING 8.6   Subclassing the Base Form Control Classes in Visual Basic .NET

```
Imports System.Windows.Forms
Imports System.Drawing

Public Class MyText
    Inherits TextBox

    Public Sub New()
        MyBase.New()
        Text = ""
        Enabled = False
    End Sub

    Public Sub EnterHandler( )
      ByVal o As Object, _
```

LISTING 8.6   Continued

```
      ByVal e As EventArgs) _
     Handles MyBase.Enter
        BackColor = BackColor.Blue
        ForeColor = ForeColor.White
     End Sub

     Public Sub LeaveHandler( _
       ByVal o As Object, _
       ByVal e As EventArgs) _
      Handles MyBase.Leave
        BackColor = BackColor.White
        ForeColor = ForeColor.Black
     End Sub

End Class

Public Class MyCombo
     Inherits ComboBox

     Public Sub New()
        MyBase.New()
        Text = ""
        Enabled = False
     End Sub

     Public Sub EnterHandler( _
       ByVal o As Object, _
       ByVal e As EventArgs) _
      Handles MyBase.Enter
        BackColor = BackColor.Blue
        ForeColor = ForeColor.White
     End Sub

     Public Sub LeaveHandler( _
       ByVal o As Object, _
       ByVal e As EventArgs) _
      Handles MyBase.Leave
        BackColor = BackColor.White
        ForeColor = ForeColor.Black
     End Sub

End Class
```

LISTING 8.6   Continued

```
Public Class MyCheck
    Inherits CheckBox
    Public Sub New()
        MyBase.New()
        Enabled = False
    End Sub
End Class

Public Class MyLabel
    Inherits Label

    Public Sub New()
        MyBase.New()
        Text = "Lbl"
    End Sub

End Class

Public Class MyRightAlignedLabel
    Inherits MyLabel

    Public Sub New()
        MyBase.New()
        TextAlign = ContentAlignment.MiddleRight
    End Sub

End Class

Public Class MyRadio
    Inherits RadioButton
    Public Sub New()
        MyBase.New()
        Enabled = False
    End Sub
End Class
```

Using Your Subclassed .NET Controls

To use these controls, click on the User Controls toolbox heading, and then right-click and select Add/Remove Items. When the dialog appears, use Browse to find and click on *[VSProjDir]*\MyFormControls\bin\MyFormControls.DLL. All of the controls you just created will appear in your User Controls toolbox. You use them, rather than the base control classes, on your forms. Now, just as in FoxPro, if you change the FontName in the subclassed MyLabel class, it changes in all of your forms.

Enabling/Disabling the Controls on a Form

In Listing 8.7, you have an Input procedure that can be called both from here and from click events such as Add and Edit. I look for any control whose name is in the form's list of input fields, and apply the Enabled = True/False logic only to those controls.

LISTING 8.7   Enabling and Disabling All Form Input Controls in Visual Basic .NET

```
Dim UserControls As String = "¦MYTEXT¦MYCOMBO¦MYRADIO¦MYSPIN¦MYCHECK"

Private Sub cmdEnableDisable_Click( _
    ByVal sender As System.Object, _
    ByVal e As System.EventArgs) _
  Handles cmdEnableDisable.Click

    Inputs(Button1.Text = "Enable")
    Button1.Text = IIf(Button1.Text = "Enable", "Disable", "Enable")
End Sub

Public Sub Inputs(ByVal OnOff As Boolean)
    Dim CtrlType As String
    Dim LastPeriod As Integer
    Dim Ctrl As Control
    For Each Ctrl In Controls
    LastPeriod = Ctrl.GetType.ToString.ToUpper.LastIndexOf(".") + 1
    CtrlType = Ctrl.GetType.ToString.ToUpper.Substring(LastPeriod)
    If UserControls.IndexOf(CtrlType) > 0 Then Ctrl.Enabled = OnOff
    Next
End Sub
```

I use the fact that the name of a control's base class is located after the last period in the GetType return value. I convert both search and target to uppercase before looking for the control's base class name in the User Controls string. The initial "¦" character is not optional, by the way; otherwise, MYTEXT is found at location zero (thanks, Bill).

The parameter (Button1.Text = "Enable") uses a shorthand method of coding that sets the value of the Input() call's single parameter to True if the text property of the button is the string "Enable", and to False if it says "Disable" (or anything else, for that matter). The last line changes the caption of the button itself.

Data Binding

Data binding is one of the best things in FoxPro. Curiously, it's one of the *worst* things in Visual Basic .NET. Let's look at them and see what can be done to improve the situation while Microsoft is figuring out how to do data binding more simply in a forthcoming version of Visual Studio .NET.

Data Binding in FoxPro

When you build a screen in FoxPro, you can simply drag the base controls onto a form, and then assign as the ControlSource property the name of a field in a table or cursor, for example, Clients.Name. Thereafter, THISFORM.Refresh will get the current record's value for the Name field, assign it to the Value property of the control, and display it. Nothing could be simpler.

If you subclass the FoxPro form controls, then open the Tools, Options, Field Mapping page and map the data types used in your tables to your subclassed controls, you're in for a real treat. Open a form, open its Data Environment, add a table, and then drag the word Fields to the upper-left corner of the form and let go, and the screen will be autopopulated with all of the fields in the table or cursor, including a label to the left of each using the name of the field. If your table or view is part of a FoxPro Database Container and you've specified additional information, such as the exact spelling of the label caption, any picture clauses, and a few other things, they'll all be used. It's spectacular!

Finally, if you use a FoxPro 8 CursorAdapter to create the cursor, the binding goes all the way from the table or cursor, or from SQL Server, or from an XML Web Service to your screen controls and back again. It's ridiculously easy.

Data Binding in Visual Basic .NET

That last sentence applies to Visual Basic .NET—if you remove the word *easy*. How they could have missed the mark so badly is hard to imagine. They could have walked over to the FoxPro division and asked Randy or Calvin how it's done, but noooooo... So let's see what's required to bind data in Visual Basic .NET, and try to make it better.

Manually Binding Data

To manually bind the base form controls, add a SQLDataAdapter from the Pubs database, and then generate a dataset named dsEmps for the Employee table to the form. Use SELECT * FROM Employee to return all records. (There are only 10 in the sample data.)

Next, open the Properties sheet of each control, expand the Databindings property by clicking on the plus sign, and then open the Text drop-down. You'll see the name of the dataset with a plus sign to the left of the name. Click on it to expand it, and you'll see Employee, the only table contained in the dataset. Expand it in turn, and you can select fname, the employee's first name. Select it, then write the following line of code in the form's Load event:

```
SqlDataAdapter1.Fill(DsEmps)
```

Press F5 to run the form and verify that it loads and displays a record. The first name of our good friend Paolo Accorti should appear.

Using Generic Code to Bind Controls to Data Columns

If you want to write inheritable forms that bind the data automatically, you have two choices: **typed datasets** and **untyped datasets**. A typed dataset is a Visual Basic (or C#) class that has one property procedure for each of the columns in your table. In that way, when you instantiate an object called `Customers` based on your `CustomerRow` class, `Customers.CustomerID` references a property in the class.

You can get a typed dataset by building a `DataAdapter` for the form, then right-clicking on it and selecting Generate Dataset, or by selecting Generate Dataset from the Data menu when a form is open and a `DataAdapter` has been added to the form.

However, you might want to use form properties to specify a connection string, a table name and a `SELECT` statement, and let the inheritable form's generic code do the work for you. The issue is in the `DataBindings.Add` method. If you use a typed dataset, it takes a dataset as the second parameter and `TableName.FieldName` as the third parameter; if you use an untyped dataset, it takes a `DataTable` as the second parameter and a string variable containing the Column name as the third parameter.

If you name the controls on your form with a three-character prefix denoting the control type, and use the name of a table column as the rest of the control name, you can simply iterate through the form controls, make sure they're data controls, and then call the appropriate `databinding.Add()` method.

Listing 8.8 shows how to do databinding with an untyped dataset.

LISTING 8.8   Automatic Data Binding with an Untyped Dataset

```
Private Sub Form1_Load( _
   ByVal sender As System.Object, _
   ByVal e As System.EventArgs) _
  Handles MyBase.Load
   If Not Me.DesignMode Then
      If ConnStr = "" Then
     MsgBox("Connection string is empty", MsgBoxStyle.Critical)
      Else
     CN.ConnectionString = ConnStr
     CN.Open()
      End If
      If CN.State = ConnectionState.Open Then
     DataAccess = DATypes.SQL
     Dim sc As New SqlClient.SqlCommand
     sc.CommandText = SelectCmd
     sc.Connection = CN
```

LISTING 8.8 Continued

```
        DA.SelectCommand = sc
        DA.Fill(DS, MainTable)
        BindInputFields()
         Else
        MsgBox("Could not open data source" + vbCrLf + ConnStr, _
          MsgBoxStyle.Critical)
         End If
    End If
End Sub

Public Sub BindInputFields()
    Dim Ctrl As Control
    Dim FName As String
    Dim DT As DataTable
    DT = DS.Tables(0)
    For Each Ctrl In Controls
        LastPeriod = Ctrl.GetType.ToString.ToUpper.LastIndexOf(".") + 1
        CtrlType = Ctrl.GetType.ToString.ToUpper.Substring(LastPeriod)
        FName = Ctrl.Name.Substring(3)
        If UserControls.IndexOf(CtrlType) > 0 _
            Then Ctrl.DataBindings.Add("Text", DT, FName)
    Next
End Sub
```

If you're using a typed dataset, the BindInputFields() method code is slightly different:

```
Public Sub BindInputFields()
    Dim Ctrl As Control
    Dim FName As String
    For Each Ctrl In Controls
        LastPeriod = Ctrl.GetType.ToString.ToUpper.LastIndexOf(".") + 1
        CtrlType = Ctrl.GetType.ToString.ToUpper.Substring(LastPeriod)
        FName = Ctrl.Name.Substring(3)
        If UserControls.IndexOf(CtrlType) > 0 Then _
            Ctrl.DataBindings.Add("Text", DS, TableNAme + "." + FName)
    Next
End Sub
```

Introducing the BindingContext

This is a good time to introduce something really different. In FoxPro, to move to the next record, you use SKIP. SKIP issued on the last record in the current index order (or on the last record if no index is attached) moves to the phantom record, at which time SKIP will give an error.

The same is true for moving backwards with SKIP -1. The FoxPro environment handles many, many things about records in the current work area, including moving, buffering, application of global settings, and much more.

There are no environmental settings or methods for data in Visual Basic .NET, and it's a shame. Everything about a record is handled by its dataset, or by its data adapter. Everything, that is, except movement within the dataset. That's handled by something called the BindingContext, which is available automatically within a form.

A BindingContext reference uses a single parameter describing the data container in question (for example, Me.BindingContext(dsEmps).*whatever*). The record number within the dataset is both gettable and settable via the Position property, so to move to the first record in the collection would be accomplished by the following code:

```
Me.BindingContext(dsEmps).Position = 0
```

and SKIP would be

```
Me.BindingContext(dsEmps).Position = Me.BindingContext(dsEmps).Position + 1
```

The best way to demonstrate the differences in data binding and navigation is to write the same application in both languages.

A Simple FoxPro Screen to Demonstrate Binding and Navigation

The screen shown in Figure 8.3 was built in Visual FoxPro 7. it uses the same Employee table found in both the SQL Server and the MSDE Northwind databases. There should also be a copy in your Visual FoxPro Solutions directory.

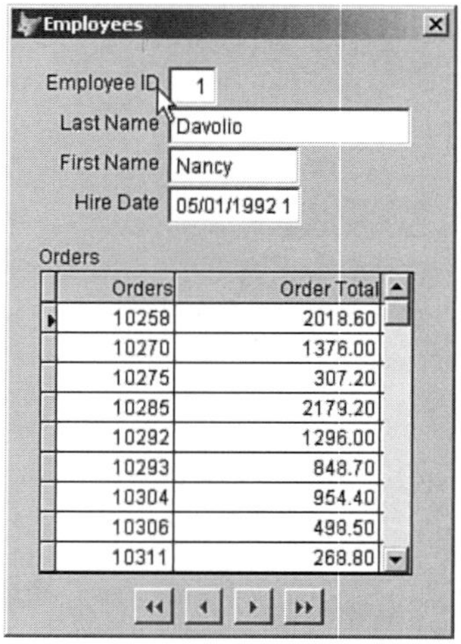

FIGURE 8.3   A FoxPro screen with data binding and navigation buttons.

If you don't have the Northwind!Employee table, you can get a copy from MSDE or SQL. To copy the table to a FoxPro DBF, use the code in Listing 8.9.

LISTING 8.9   Copying the Northwind!Employee Table from MSDE to a DBF

```
h = SQLSTRINGCONNECT( _
 "Driver={SQL Server};Server=(local);Database=Northwind;UID=sa;PWD=;")
SQLEXEC( h, "SELECT * FROM EMPLOYEE")
COPY TO Employee
SQLEXEC( h, "SELECT * FROM Orders")
COPY TO Orders
SQLEXEC( h, "SELECT * FROM OrderDetails")
COPY TO OrderDetails
SQLDisconnect(h)

USE Employees
INDEX ON EmployeeID Tag EmployeeID

USE Orders
INDEX ON OrderID Tag OrderID
INDEX ON EmployeeID Tag EmployeeID

USE OrderDetails
INDEX ON OrderID Tag OrderID
```

There are a few properties that I've set in the Employees form (see Listing 8.10).

LISTING 8.10   Form Properties

```
ShowTips    = .T.
AutoCenter = .T.
Caption     = "Employees"
MaxButton  = .F.
MinButton  = .F.
Width       = 270
Height     = 360
```

In the Data Environment, I open the Employees, Orders, and OrderDetails tables; the Data Environment will automatically close them when the form closes.

In addition, I wrote one line of code each in the Load and Init events of the form, as shown in Listing 8.11.

LISTING 8.11   Load and `Init` event code for the Form

THISFORM::Load
```
CREATE CURSOR RelatedOrders ( OrderID Integer, OrderTotal Numeric(10,2) )
```

Init event:
```
THISFORM.CalculateOrderTotals
```

I added the form method shown in Listing 8.12 to calculate the order subtotal for each order for the current employee.

LISTING 8.12   The `CalculateOrderTotals` Method

```
* CalculateOrderTotals method:

SELECT Employees
RecNo = RECNO()
EmpID = EmployeeID
SELECT                                        ;
   OrderDetails.OrderID,                       ;
   SUM(Quantity*UnitPrice) AS OrderTotal       ;
  FROM Orders, OrderDetails                    ;
 WHERE Orders.EmployeeID = EmpID               ;
   AND Orders.OrderID = OrderDetails.OrderID   ;
 GROUP BY OrderDetails.OrderID                 ;
 ORDER BY OrderDetails.OrderID                 ;
  INTO CURSOR C1
SELECT RelatedOrders
ZAP
APPEND FROM DBF("C1")
USE IN C1
GO TOP
SELECT Employees
GO ( RecNo )
THISFORM.Refresh
```

Most of the remaining code goes in the `Click` event for the four navigation buttons (see Listing 8.13).

LISTING 8.13   Click Event Code for the Buttons

cmdFirst::Click:
```
SELECT Employees
GO TOP
THISFORM.CalculateOrderTotals
```

LISTING 8.13   Continued

```
cmdPrev::Click
SELECT Employees
SKIP -1
IF BOF()
    GO TOP
ENDIF
THISFORM.CalculateOrderTotals

cmdNext::Click
SELECT Employees
SKIP
IF EOF()
    GO BOTTOM
ENDIF
THISFORM.CalculateOrderTotals

cmdLast::Click
SELECT Employees
GO BOTTOM
THISFORM.CalculateOrderTotals
```

Finally, I'm responsible for disposing of the cursor that I created in the Load event:

Unload event:
```
USE IN RelatedOrders
```

That is the sum total of the code required to run this form, which calculates the total of all orders for a given employee and displays them in a grid below the employee information.

The Equivalent Form in Visual Basic .NET

The form shown in Figure 8.4 is the equivalent in Visual Basic .NET to the screen that we created in FoxPro in the preceding section.

Use the Windows Forms toolbox to build this form. After adding the labels and text boxes and the grid, add a SQLDataAdapter from the Data toolbox, selecting the Northwind connection previously created. Then, right-click on the DataAdapter and generate a dataset named dsEmployees. That gives it public scope and creates a typed dataset.

To see the typed dataset, use Ctrl+Alt+L to open the Solution Explorer and verify that dsEmployees has been added to the project. Click on the Show All Files icon at the top of the Solution Explorer, and you'll see a plus sign to the left of the dsEmployees.xsd entry; click it to expand it, and you'll see dsEmployees.vb. That's the typed dataset; it's a class that includes property procedures, one for each column in the table. That's what gives us the ability to do the next step, which is data binding.

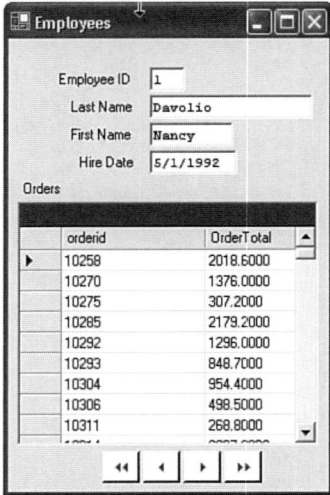

FIGURE 8.4 A Visual Basic .NET screen with data binding and navigation buttons.

Select the form and use F4 to open the Properties sheet. Select the first text box. Then expand the (DataBindings) entry, open the drop-down beside the Text entry, and drill down to the EmployeeID column of the Employees table inside the dsEmployees typed dataset. Do likewise for the FirstName, LastName, and HireDate text boxes.

Coding the Form

The code for the Visual Basic .NET version of this form is pretty informative. You need to add a dataset declaration for the employee orders. Put it at the top of the code, before the Windows Form Generated Code, so that it will have Public scope:

```
Public dsEmployeeOrders As New DataSet
```

Next, add the following code to load the Employees dataset and then load the grid with the first employee's order totals (see Listing 8.14).

LISTING 8.14 The Form's Load Event Code

```
Private Sub Form1_Load( _
  ByVal sender As System.Object, ByVal e As System.EventArgs) _
  Handles MyBase.Load
  Me.SqlDataAdapter1.Fill(DsEmployees1, "Employees")
  LoadGrid()
End Sub
```

The GetData procedure builds and executes the SQL SELECT, statement to subtotal order detail entries. Note that in SQL Server the Order Details table has a space in the name, and so has to be enclosed in square brackets (see Listing 8.15).

LISTING 8.15   The GetData Method

```
Public Sub GetData()
Dim CmdStr As String = _
  "  SELECT " _
+ " [Order Details].OrderID," _
+ " SUM(Quantity*UnitPrice) AS OrderTotal" _
+ " FROM Orders, [Order Details]" _
+ " WHERE Orders.EmployeeID = " + txtEmployeeID.Text.ToString _
+ " AND Orders.OrderID = [Order Details].OrderID " _
+ " GROUP BY [Order Details].OrderID" _
+ " ORDER BY [Order Details].OrderID"

Dim Da As New SqlDataAdapter
Da = New SqlDataAdapter(CmdStr, Me.SqlConnection1.ConnectionString)
dsEmployeeOrders.Clear()
Try
  Da.Fill(dsEmployeeOrders, "Orders")
  Catch oEx As Exception
  MsgBox("Error loading dataset" + vbCrLf + oEx.Message)
  Close()
End Try
End Sub
```

The click events of the four navigation buttons call each of four independent routines. I wrote them that way so that they could also be called elsewhere, as you'll see in Listing 8.16.

LISTING 8.16   The Click Event Code for the Four Navigation Buttons

```
Private Sub cmdTop_Click( _
  ByVal sender As System.Object, ByVal e As System.EventArgs) _
  Handles cmdTop.Click
   FirstRecord()
End Sub

Private Sub cmdBottom_Click( _
 ByVal sender As System.Object, ByVal e As System.EventArgs) _
 Handles  cmdBottom.Click
   LastRecord()
```

LISTING 8.16   Continued

```
End Sub

Private Sub cmdNext_Click( _
  ByVal sender As System.Object, ByVal e As System.EventArgs) _
  Handles cmdNext.Click
    NextRecord()
End Sub

Private Sub cmdPrev_Click( _
  ByVal sender As System.Object, ByVal e As System.EventArgs) _
  Handles cmdPrev.Click
    PreviousRecord()
End Sub
```

The code for the FirstRecord, LastRecord, NextRecord, and PreviousRecord procedures shown in Listing 8.17 will look familiar, although alarmingly verbose. Think of Me.BindingContext(DatasetName,"tablename") as GOTO in FoxPro, or of its Position property as a user-settable RECNO(), and you'll be close. Note that Me.BindingContext(dsEmployees, "Employees").Count is like RECCOUNT().

LISTING 8.17   Code for the Record Positioning Procedures

```
Public Sub FirstRecord()
Me.BindingContext(DsEmployees1, "Employees").Position = 0
LoadGrid()
End Sub

Public Sub PreviousRecord()
Me.BindingContext(DsEmployees1, "Employees").Position -= 1
LoadGrid()
End Sub

Public Sub NextRecord()
Me.BindingContext(DsEmployees1, "Employees").Position += 1
LoadGrid()
End Sub

Public Sub LastRecord()
Me.BindingContext( _
 DsEmployees1, "Employees").Position = _
 DsEmployees1.Tables(0).Rows.Count - 1
LoadGrid()
End Sub
```

Updating the Data Source Tables

The Update button sends changes in the dataset back to SQL. When we built the
DataAdapter, unless you clicked on the Advanced Options button and turned off INSERT,
UPDATE, and DELETE generation, the appropriate UPDATE command object has already been
created and will be executed when the Update method of the SQLDataAdapter is called (see
Listing 8.18).

LISTING 8.18   The Update Button Click Event Code

```
Private Sub cmdUpdate_Click( _
  ByVal sender As System.Object, ByVal e As System.EventArgs) _
  Handles cmdUpdate.Click
Try
  Me.BindingContext("Employees").EndCurrentEdit()
  SqlDataAdapter1.Update(DsEmployees1)
  MessageBox.Show("Database updated.", _
     Me.Text, MessageBoxButtons.OK, _
     MessageBoxIcon.Information)
Catch exp As Exception
  MessageBox.Show("Error updating database: " & exp.Message, _
     Me.Text, MessageBoxButtons.OK, _
     MessageBoxIcon.Error)
End Try
End Sub
```

Adding Functionality with the KeyDown Event

The KeyDown event code shown in Listing 8.19 is a freebie. You can "hook" keystrokes to
the Home, End, left-arrow, and right-arrow keys and navigate using them as well as clicking on the command buttons.

LISTING 8.19   Hooking the Four Navigation Methods to the Home, End, Left-Arrow, and
Right-Arrow Keys in Visual Basic .NET

```
Private Sub frmMain_KeyDown( _
  ByVal sender As Object, ByVal e As System.Windows.Forms.KeyEventArgs) _
  Handles MyBase.KeyDown
   If e.KeyCode = Keys.Right Then NextRecord()
   If e.KeyCode = Keys.Left Then PreviousRecord()
   If e.KeyCode = Keys.Home Then FirstRecord()
   If e.KeyCode = Keys.End Then LastRecord()
End Sub
```

The FoxPro equivalent is shown in Listing 8.20. (Be sure to change the form's KeyPreview
property to .T..)

8

LISTING 8.20   Hooking the Four Navigation Methods to the Home, End, Left-Arrow, and Right-Arrow Keys in FoxPro

```
LPARAMETERS nKeyCode, nShiftAltCtrl
DO CASE
   CASE nKeyCode =  1  && Home
      _Screen.ActiveForm.cmdFirst.Click
   CASE nKeyCode =  6  && End
      _Screen.ActiveForm.cmdLast.Click
   CASE nKeyCode = 19  && LeftArrow
      _Screen.ActiveForm.cmdPrev.Click
   CASE nKeyCode =  4  && RightArrow
      _Screen.ActiveForm.cmdNext.Click
ENDCASE
```

However, it doesn't quite work right. Unfortunately, in FoxPro when you click on a grid, the table that's bound to it gets the focus, and as a result the arrow key interaction is pretty messy. I tried to use ON KEY LABEL for the same purpose in FoxPro, but with even messier results. The problem is fixable in Visual Visual FoxPro 8 thanks to the new MouseEnter and MouseLeave events, which tell me when I'm over the grid; but the code in this book is generally supposed to work with earlier versions of Visual Visual FoxPro as well—certainly Visual FoxPro 7 in most cases. So I didn't support the exact same functionality. Anyway, it's worth noting that *sometimes*, Visual Basic .NET is better than FoxPro....

Loading the Grid

LoadGrid (see Listing 8.21) is where the grid is populated with the calculated subtotals for orders for the selected employee. The GetData part is very similar to its FoxPro counterpart; but *can we talk*?

What is all of this code for configuring the grid? Can't you just lay it out using mouse clicks and the Properties sheet? Not in this version. Microsoft is burning the midnight oil even as I am at this instant, busily fixing this turkey.

LISTING 8.21   The LoadGrid Procedure

```
Sub LoadGrid()

GetData()

With grdOrders
.CaptionText = "Orders"
.DataSource = dsEmployeeOrders
.DataMember = "Orders"
End With
grdOrders.TableStyles.Clear()
```

LISTING 8.21   Continued

```
Dim grdTableStyle1 As New DataGridTableStyle
With grdTableStyle1
.MappingName = "EmployeeOrders"
End With
Dim grdColStyle1 As New DataGridTextBoxColumn
With grdColStyle1
.MappingName = "OrderID"
.HeaderText = "Order ID"
.Width = 75
End With
Dim grdColStyle2 As New DataGridTextBoxColumn
With grdColStyle2
.MappingName = "SubTotal"
.HeaderText = "Sub Total"
.Format = "c"
.Width = 75
End With
grdTableStyle1.GridColumnStyles.AddRange _
(New DataGridColumnStyle() {grdColStyle1, grdColStyle2})
grdOrders.TableStyles.Add(grdTableStyle1)
End Sub
```

Formatting Input in Visual Basic .NET

You might have noticed that you can type "Howdy" into a date field in Visual Basic .NET. That means that you're going to have to write your own custom handlers for each and every date time field. By the time this book hits the street, that nasty oversight should have been repaired in some form or fashion. In the meantime, or in case they haven't fixed it, you can do it yourself.

Say you have a date field and you want dates fixed both coming from the data table and when entered by the user. The following four lines of code will add references to format handlers for the Parse and Format operations of the field, which occur when loading bound data from a table column and when typed in, respectively. This goes in the Load event of your form (see Listing 8.22).

LISTING 8.22   Load Event Code to Manage Data Entry for a Date Field

```
Dim dbnHireDate As New Binding("Text", dsEmployeeInfo, "HireDate")
AddHandler dbnHireDate.Format, AddressOf DateToString
AddHandler dbnHireDate.Parse, AddressOf StringToDate
txtHireDate.DataBindings.Add(dbnHireDate)
```

8

The two procedures in Listing 8.23 are referred to by the `AddHandler` statements shown earlier, so put them somewhere down near the bottom of the form code.

LISTING 8.23   Date Formatting Handlers

```
Protected Sub DateToString(ByVal sender As Object, ByVal e As ConvertEventArgs)
e.Value = CType(e.Value, DateTime).ToShortDateString
End Sub

Protected Sub StringToDate(ByVal sender As Object, ByVal e As ConvertEventArgs)
Try
    e.Value = CDate(e.Value)
Catch exp As Exception
    MessageBox.Show("Bad date format: " & exp.Message, Me.Text, _
                    MessageBoxButtons.OK, MessageBoxIcon.Error)
End Try
End Sub
```

These work like `Valid` clauses in FoxPro, except that this particular `Valid` clause is not needed with date fields in FoxPro. It's kind of a pain in the neck to have to do something that was taken care of automatically back in 1982 in the first version of dBase II, but it's just this same code over and over; so copy it to a code snippet and keep it handy.

Innovative Screen Design

You're not limited to the base controls in either language. There are basic guidelines, but they're only suggestions. If you see a good idea, steal it. Imitation is the sincerest form of flattery. In the sections that follow, I'll explore some variations on the existing base control classes, and experiment with some new ideas imported from the browser environment.

Extending Screen Design in Visual FoxPro

Visual FoxPro permits us to build rich and varied interfaces. The possibilities are limited only by the imagination.

The traditional FoxPro application consists of a background screen (_Screen as MDI form, or an MDI form screen) and the following components:

A FoxPro menu (using the Menu Designer)

One or more "flat file" screens

One or more complex screens (parent-child or one-to-many)

One or more hard-coded reports

There's nothing wrong with this approach. It does everything your users need. But increasingly, we're expected to build more elegant and exciting interfaces. The Internet is one of the motivating factors; users see interesting and intuitive screen designs and ask us for similar approaches. Can we do it? Of course! All we need is ideas.

The Windows Design Guide

A dozen years ago, Microsoft Press published the *Windows Design Guide*, the internal specifications for the Microsoft Office suite spruced up for public consumption. The *Windows Design Guide* describes font usage, distance between controls, and usability recommendations. But it was a guide for designing three products. Database screens are a subset of that set, with considerable additional and more demanding requirements in the data entry dimension. The *Windows Design Guide* gives little guidance with regard to form design for database applications.

But there are several places we can look to get ideas. Successful products are one area, and Web pages are another rich source of design concepts. We'll start with the most successful database application ever designed—Quicken, from Intuit software. (An interesting historical note: Intuit was originally a printing company. The owner designed Quicken and gave it away in order to entice its users to buy preprinted checks.)

The Quicken Interface

Get Quicken 2003, install it, and start it up. You'll see the screen shown in Figure 8.5. The hallmarks of this interface include multiple frames, an icon-based toolbar across the top, links at the top of the target pane, a page frame, and a grid that contains a user control with drop-down combo boxes, links, and calendar buttons. This is the competition.

I'm going to guesstimate that Intuit spent millions of dollars designing this interface. That's a dozen staff designers (or a four-man team from Accenture) working for several years. My clients can't afford that. But the time it took to design this interface is a lot more than the time it will take to borrow and implement its main ideas.

This interface also uses colors to its advantage. The alternating background color in the grid makes it easier for the eye to remember which line we're on. There are at least eight different background colors used on this screen, and nearly as many foreground colors for text. A wonderful little shareware program, GetPixel, described in the Tools section at the end of this chapter, lets you capture screen colors as RGB (Red, Green, Blue) codes.

Can you implement features similar to those on the Quicken 2003 screen in FoxPro? Of course. The toolbar is actually just a series of eight image controls with `Click` event code. Allocate a few hours for each icon. They're really, really labor-intensive. You can capture them from someone's screen and repackage the graphic. (IconTools has an icon extractor tool for those who, like me, have no shame.)

For implementing the page frame, you can use the page frame control that comes with FoxPro. But there are also third-party page frame controls, with more control over the cosmetics of the tabs. We'll see more in the section on OCX controls later.

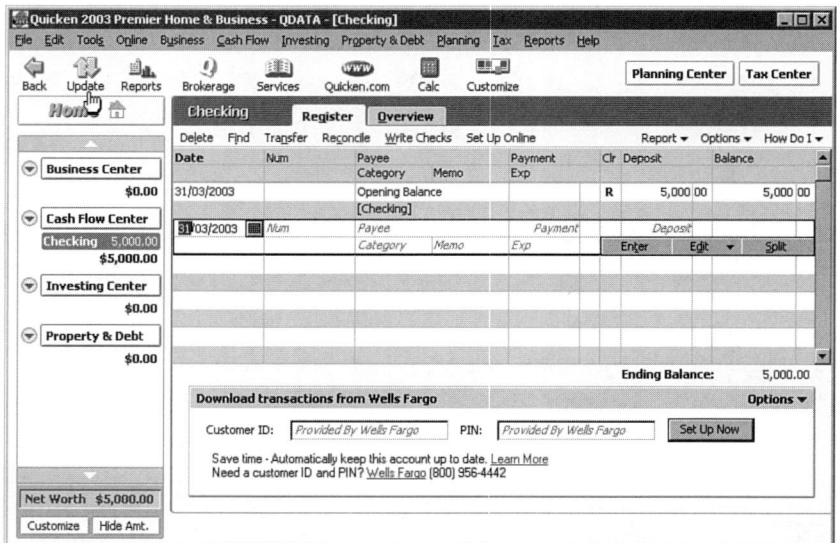

FIGURE 8.5   The Quicken interface.

In Visual FoxPro 7, the links on the Quicken page are easily implemented using Label controls. You could use the "\<" prefix to highlight a "hotkey," but labels don't respond to Alt+Key hotkeys. So you'll probably prefer to use the FontUnderline property to underline the entire link. The MouseEnter and MouseLeave events can be used to change the color of the "link" to red when the mouse enters, and back to black when the mouse leaves. The label's Click event can launch the expected behavior. The LinkLabel control in Visual FoxPro 8 appears in the Form Controls toolbar and acts exactly as you'd expect.

For dates, I built a Calendar.SCX control containing an instance of the Calendar Control 11.0. I call it from my MyDate class, which has DblClick code to call this modal form, passing it the value of the date in the ControlSource field of the object. The Init code in Calendar.SCX displays the passed date (see Listing 8.24).

LISTING 8.24   Validating Date Entry

```
PARAMETERS pdDate
IF EMPTY ( pdDate )
   pdDate = DATE()
ENDIF
WITH THISFORM
.Date = pdDate
.Calendar.Year  = YEAR (pdDate)
.Calendar.Month = MONTH(pdDate)
.Calendar.Day   = DAY  (pdDate)
ENDWITH
```

The `DblClick` code on the `Calendar` control itself passes back the selected value (see Listing 8.25).

LISTING 8.25   Returning the Value Selected by the User in FoxPro Date Format

```
*** ActiveX Control Event ***
THISFORM.Date = DATE ( THIS.Year, THIS.Month, THIS.Day )

THISFORM.Release
```

Finally, the `Calendar` form's `Unload` event passes back the selected value:

```
RETURN THISFORM.Date
```

The `Date` property is then used to set the value of the `MyDate` object that called it (see Listing 8.26).

LISTING 8.26   Popping Up the Calendar Form

```
MyDate::DblClick:
DO FORM Calendar TO Result
IF NOT EMPTY ( Result )
   THIS.Value = Result
ENDIF
```

You can also call the `Calendar` form from a `CommandButton` class that includes a property that is set to name the `MyDate` object that is to be updated if a date is picked from the Calendar screen. This works exactly like the little Calendar button on the Quicken screen.

The use of data as a link, as shown in Figure 8.6, in which the "Min Bal" value that is underlined, is accomplished by displaying a subclassed `Label` control with a `Target` property that can be used in the `Click` event code of the subclass to `DO FORM ShowBalances` or whatever you want to do:

```
MyLinkLabel::Click
IF NOT EMPTY ( THIS.Target )
    Cmd = THIS.Target
    &Cmd
ENDIF
```

The Quicken Interface in Visual Basic .NET

Quicken is pretty easy to simulate in Visual Basic .NET because it was probably written in Visual Basic 6. Refer back to Figure 8.4 as I talk about specific design elements.

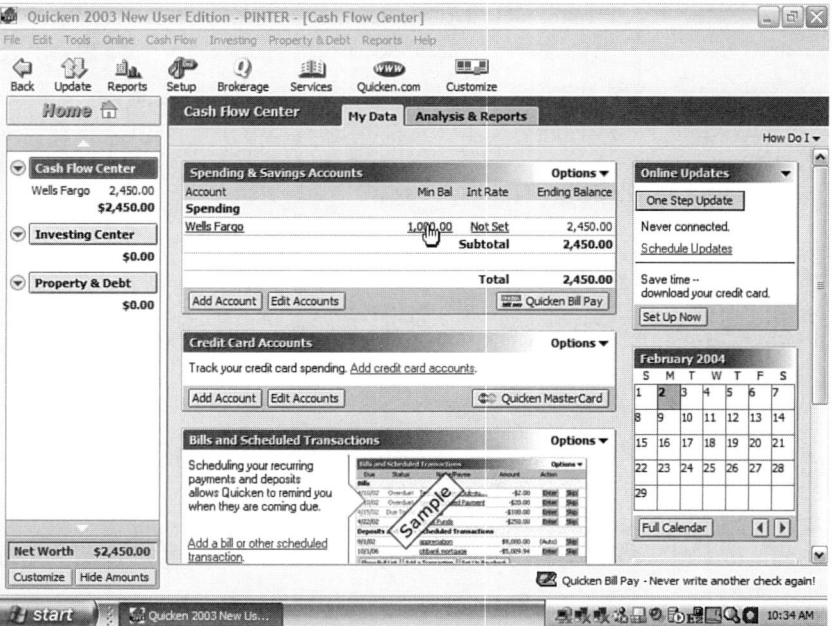

FIGURE 8.6   Use data as a link by displaying a subclassed `Label` control with a `Target` property.

It's important to match screen colors, and I used to guess. Now I use GetPixel, a little utility you can find on the Internet, to exactly duplicate screen colors on screens that I like. You just run it, then position the mouse cursor over any part of the screen, and the color codes are displayed in both RGB and hexadecimal form. You can then type them into the appropriate `BackColor` property in your own control.

The screen background color for the menu bar in Quicken 2003 is RGB(192,192,192). That's our first problem, because as of this writing the `MainMenu` control takes its `BackColor` from the `System` color setting. But the icons just below it have a background color of RGB(255,251,240), and because most of the form is covered by other controls, you can use that for the form's `BackColor`.

The icons below the menu are used to launch other screens, so anything with a `Click` event will do. Buttons, however, have a dark border that you can't get rid of, so I used `PictureBox` controls.

I bought IconCool from Newera Software and was about to draw some of these icons when I noticed an Import option on the File menu. I clicked it and pointed to the Quicken directory, and every time I highlighted a DLL or EXE, a list of icons appeared. Unfortunately there are dozens of DLLs in the directory, so you have to look for quite a while before you find the one containing the icons you want. Sometimes the names help, but not always. This is one time when I long for a single huge `.exe` like we build in FoxPro. You can also use a Capture Region function from any screen capture program—I use HyperSnap DX from Hyperion, and it does a good job with everything.

When I had my image, I dropped eight `PictureBox` controls on the screen, assigned my captured icon images to their Image properties, and put calls to `MsgBox("Run a program here")` code in the `Click` event code.

Similarly, the Home button has soft edges that are just different enough so that a `PictureBox` will give you the exact look. But a `Button` wouldn't be a bad choice. The `Click` event code for this control would bring the user back to the starting screen. The Planning Center and Tax Center "buttons" involve similar cosmetic issues, so their solutions would be the same as the one chosen for the Home button.

The Checking, Register, and Overview tabs suggest a page frame. However, if you add a page frame and try to come anywhere near duplicating the look on the Quicken screen, you'll see that it's not your father's page frame. This is either a third-party tool, a special page frame built at Intuit, or an illusion. Illusion is cheap and easy, so we'll go with that.

Create three graphics by screen-capturing the three tabs on the Quicken screen, add your own text, and use the images for—surprise—three more `PictureBox` controls. After you've done this, displaying the appropriate child form in the area below the "tabs" is easy.

The grid in the Quicken screen has two detail lines. To simulate this, you have to build `UserControls` that mimic the two lines in each cell. Each row is tall enough to hold two "rows." In some columns, there's only a single row. In others, cells have buttons that display other small forms to perform special tasks. This is a very, very busy screen. But you can't argue with success.

But if you click on any column heading, you see something that's very revealing. The balance in the rightmost column is dependent on what has happened in prior rows, so the value that's displayed only "makes sense" if you display transactions in chronological order. So what looks like a grid is actually a display mechanism that lists field contents for as many fields as will fit in the display area, calculating the Balance column as it goes. It's not a grid that's bound to the data; it's just an illusion.

The area at the left of the screen is called a `CoolBar`. If you click on any selection, it expands it. All you have to do to simulate this is have a procedure that uses the name of the clicked button as a parameter, and repaints this part of the screen by adding controls as it goes. Expand the generated code for any screen that has a few controls on it and you'll see what's called for. It's not much harder than just drawing the controls on the screen.

The Download Transactions from Wells Fargo block at the bottom of the screen assumes that your bank has a Web Service, or more likely a Remoting component that you can call. Web Services are very, very easy to build. They're also very, very easy to read as they stream around the Internet. Remoting allows you to encrypt the data and send it to a structure (usually a class) with exactly the same structure as the source, in a process called serialization. The Microsoft download "101 Samples for Visual Basic .NET" contains a directory named `101 VB.NET Samples\VB.NET - Advanced - Remoting - How-To TCP Remoting\`, which contains an example of how to build a remoting host and client. It's not trivial, but if you can make the sample code work, you can make your own version work as well.

As an exercise, you may want to build a screen similar to some application whose look you fancy. The Quicken screen is a good challenge, but I sometimes download vertical market products with expiration dates and see what it takes to copy them.

RANT

<rant>I used to get requests from software developers wanting to know how to copy-protect their FoxPro executables. I'd say that if you can duplicate the look and the menu and the interface in a few hours, and simply infer how the software works from the structure of the tables in the database, copy-protecting your software is a poor way to spend your energy. I think that working hard to stay ahead of the competition is the way to succeed in the software business, and it gives the customer a better deal, too.</rant>

See how close you can come without using any third-party tools. It will take a while, but you'll learn a lot.

The FoxPro Grid

The FoxPro grid has several new features that help spiff up your interface. The most interesting new feature is probably the row highlighting, enabled by setting the `HighlightStyle` to 1 or 2. If you want to use a grid as a drill-down, you'll probably want to set the `ReadOnly` property to `.T.` for all of the grid columns. The `DblClick` method of the grid won't help you, though; it has to be set for each of the columns in the grid. This has inspired some developers to create their own column class and build their grid programmatically when the form instantiates. It takes a little longer to write the first time, but thereafter it's effortless.

The expandable display at the left of the form is built programmatically. It's a `Container` object. When an arrow is clicked, the components corresponding to the arrow that was clicked are added to the container, and their `Top` and `Left` properties are set on the fly. Some or all of the controls can have `Click` event code. So if the user clicks on the first arrow, the first group is expanded in detail; clicking on the second arrow rebuilds the container with the second group of items expanded.

Buttons That Load a Different Form

The Planning Center and Tax Center buttons at the upper right of the Quicken screen bring up these two forms, respectively. This is where we can take a cue from Visual Basic. In Visual Basic .NET, you instantiate all forms at the startup of an application, then `Show()`

them when called for. We can do the same thing in FoxPro. Alternatively we can instantiate only the startup form. Then, when a form is launched using one of the buttons, use

```
DO FORM <FormName> NAME <FormName>
```

This associates the form with an object which can be used to SHOW the form. The existence of the form can be tested using the form's Caption property (set in the property sheet) with WEXIST("FormName"). So if you want to launch the form only if it's not already running, and activate it if it is, the code to do this is shown in Listing 8.27.

LISTING 8.27   Activating a Form That Is Already Running, or Instantiating It If It's Not

```
IF WEXIST("Customer")
   Customer.Show
ELSE
  DO FORM Customer NAME Customer
   Customer.Show
ENDIF
```

Thus, three or four forms having the same size and shape will appear to replace one another seamlessly. It's an alternative to page frames that doesn't require the page tabs, and doesn't require addressing screen objects using THISFORM.PageFrame1.Page1.<ObjectName>.

SDI Forms

Although FoxPro developers and users are used to seeing the _Screen object in the background, and using it as the repository for _MSYSMENU, it's not the only way to do it. You can build applications that look like those written in Delphi or Visual Basic by taking a few simple steps:

1. Designate a main form and assign its ShowWindow property to 2 - As Top Level Form. Set the ShowWindow property of all other form templates and forms to 1 - In Top Level Form (see Figure 8.7).

2. Create your menu with the Top-Level Form option in the General Options checked (select View, General from the FoxPro IDE menu).

3. Include the following line in your main form's Init code:

   ```
   DO MENU.MPR WITH THIS, .T.
   ```

4. Finally, use the -T switch when you start your application to suppress the FoxPro _Screen display. You can also use the -c<configfilename> command-line switch to specify a CONFIG file that includes a SCREEN=OFF directive, or simply compile the CONFIG file into the executable.

8

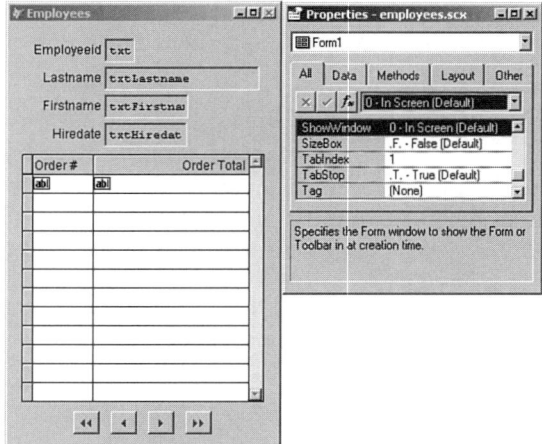

FIGURE 8.7   Setting the ShowWindow property for a Top-Level form.

Colors

Database developers have been slow to adapt to the increasing use of colors in the rest of the design world. Happily, copying is easy, and there are tons of examples. The Internet is a vast source of attractive color combinations. And you don't have to be an expert. If you like it, it's a good color combination.

Colors are usually specified in FoxPro using RGB color specifications; 0 is none and 255 is all there is. So RGB(255,0,0) is red, and RGB(0,0,255) is blue. In between there are about 16 million combinations. Rather than guess until you get close (admit it—you've done it and so have I), you can use a program like GetPixel (described earlier) to move your mouse pointer over a screen element and read off the RGB values. It's so easy, and the results are a thing of beauty. So give the world of color a try.

Colors in Form Controls

The most valuable minute you can spend with FoxPro is the 60 seconds it takes to subclass the FoxPro base classes. The instant you put a few labels and text boxes on a form and decide to change the forecolor of the labels or the color that a text box assumes when it gets focus, your 60-second investment will pay for itself a thousand times.

Changing the color of the active text box makes it easier to see. It takes four lines of code in the class you derive from the TextBox base class. The code is shown in Listing 8.28.

LISTING 8.28   Method Code for the Subclassed TextBox Control

```
TextBox::GotFocus()


THIS.ForeColor = RGB ( 255, 255, 255 )
```

LISTING 8.28 Continued

```
THIS.BackColor = RGB ( 255,   0,   0 )

TextBox::LostFocus()

THIS.ForeColor = RGB (   0,   0,   0 )
THIS.BackColor = RGB ( 255, 255, 255 )
```

Text Color on Command Buttons, Radio Buttons, and Check Boxes

I built the form shown in Figure 8.8 to experiment with text and background colors on these three types of controls. I didn't come to any earthshaking conclusions, though. Download the code and try it for yourself; it's easy to use.

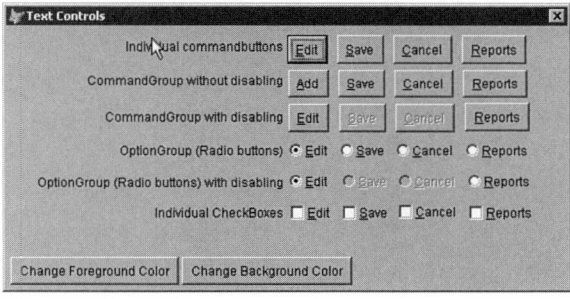

FIGURE 8.8 A form to experiment with text colors and backgrounds on form controls.

Colors on Graphical Style Controls

You can set the Style property of command buttons, radio buttons, and check boxes to Graphical and include a picture. You can either include or exclude a caption. I've seen a lot of applications that used both images and captions, and I think they look hokey. You can use a ToolTip (set the ShowTips property of your form classes to .T.) to display text to elucidate the meaning of a graphic. But good graphics are helpful as well. Tools like IconCool can be used to extract attractive icons from executables, so if you see something you like, imitation is the sincerest form of flattery.

But there's an interesting hybrid: Use graphics that display text. They look a lot better than simple text does, and can make your screen a work of art. For example, I used IconCool to build a set of graphics that consisted simply of the captions I would normally have on my buttons. I created a colored background, then placed two copies of the text on each button. The first instance was black text; the second was white, offset one pixel up and one to the left, on top of the black text. The result is shown in Figure 8.9.

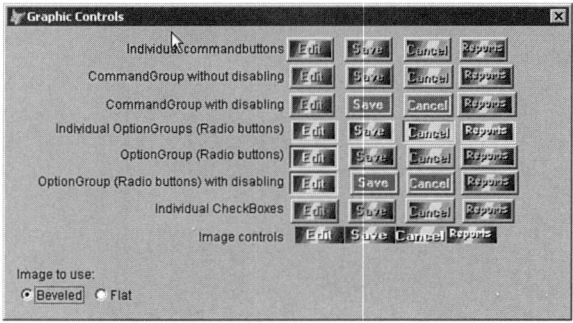

FIGURE 8.9   Graphical controls.

You might not appreciate my delicate color sense, but you must admit they're eye-catching. These buttons took about five minutes, and were my first effort. Figure 8.10 shows my second effort.

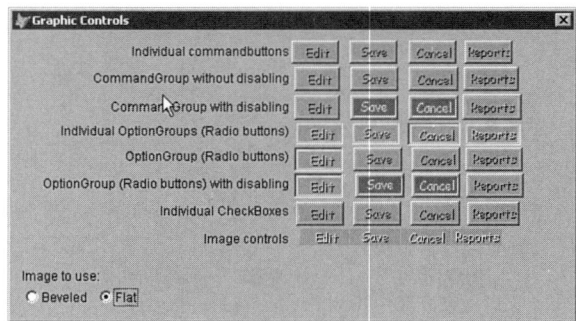

FIGURE 8.10   My second try at designing graphics for my controls.

There are tiny differences that recommend each of these controls for different tasks. For example, when graphical style controls are disabled, they gray out. I usually use individual command buttons; however, if you use a command group (command buttons) or an option group (radio buttons), the selected option remains depressed. It's more obvious when you use a graphical style control. So some types of applications would definitely benefit from the choice of a graphical command group or option group.

For sheer looks, I favor a line of Image controls. After all, they also have a Click event.

User-Settable Form Size and Location

Although it's less common in database applications, in certain instances users can take control of their forms. Figure 8.11 shows a form that demonstrates three user-controlled settings that are written to a file and read back on startup: size, screen location, and the number of user fields that are displayed.

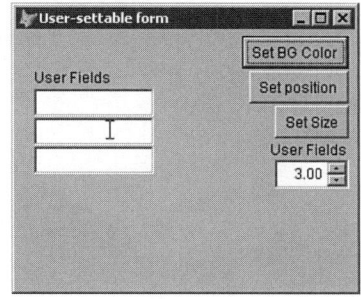

FIGURE 8.11   User-settable options.

The code to control these features is quite small (see Listing 8.29). The structure of FORM-SETTINGS, the table used to store settings, is embedded in comments within the listing.

LISTING 8.29   User-Settable Options

```
PROCEDURE Resize
FOR EACH Ctrl IN THISFORM.Controls
    IF Ctrl.Tag = [Anchor]
        Ctrl.Left = THISFORM.Width - Ctrl.Width - 5
    ENDIF
ENDFOR
ENDPROC


PROCEDURE Init
GetProps ( THISFORM )
THISFORM.Resize
THISFORM.UserFieldsTitle.Visible = ( THISFORM.UserFields > 0 )
FOR I = 1 TO THISFORM.UserFields
    ObjName = [Text] + TRANSFORM(I,[@L ##])
    ClsName = [UserTextBox]
    ClsLib  = [pinter.vcx]
THISFORM.NewObject ( ObjName, ClsName, ClsLib,, I )
THISFORM.&ObjName..Visible = .T.
ENDFOR
ENDPROC


PROCEDURE cmdsetbgcolor.Click
SaveColor = THISFORM.BackColor
THISFORM.BackColor = GETCOLOR()
IF MESSAGEBOX( "Save this color?", 292 ) <> 6
   THISFORM.BackColor = SaveColor
  ELSE
```

LISTING 8.29   Continued

```
   SetProp( THISFORM, [BackColor] )
ENDIF
ENDPROC


PROCEDURE cmdsetposition.Click
SetProp( THISFORM, [Top]  )
SetProp( THISFORM, [Left] )
ENDPROC


PROCEDURE cmdsetsize.Click
SetProp( THISFORM, [Height] )
SetProp( THISFORM, [Width]  )
ENDPROC


PROCEDURE spnuserfieldcounter.Valid
SetProp( THISFORM, [UserFields] )
ENDPROC


PROCEDURE SetProps
* Program-ID...: SetProps.PRG
* Used in User-settable forms
PARAMETERS oForm, cProp
IF NOT USED ( 'FormSettings')
   SELECT 0
   USE FormSettings
ENDIF
SELECT FormSettings

* Structure for FORMSETTINGS.DBF:
* Field  Field Name    Type           Width
*    1   FORMNAME      Character          10
*    2   PROPERTY      Character          20
*    3   PROPTYPE      Character           1
*    4   PROPVALUE     Character          20

GO TOP
LOCATE FOR UPPER(FormName) = UPPER(oForm.Name) AND Property = cProp
IF NOT FOUND()
   APPEND BLANK
   REPLACE FormName WITH oForm.Name, Property WITH cProp
ENDIF
```

LISTING 8.29   Continued

```
REPLACE NEXT 1 PropValue WITH []
Cmd = [REPLACE NEXT 1 PropValue WITH "] ;
    + ALLTRIM(TRANSFORM( oForm.&cProp. )) + ["]
&Cmd
REPLACE NEXT 1 PropType  WITH VARTYPE  ( oForm.&cProp. )
ENDPROC

PROCEDURE GETPROPS
* Program-ID...: GetProps.PRG
* Used in User-settable forms
PARAMETERS oForm
SaveAlias = ALIAS()
IF NOT USED ( 'FormSettings')
   SELECT 0
   USE FormSettings
ENDIF
SELECT FormSettings
SELECT * FROM FormSettings ;
 WHERE UPPER(formname) = UPPER(oForm.Name) ;
 INTO ARRAY aProps
IF _Tally = 0
   RETURN
ENDIF
FOR I = 1 TO    ALEN   (aProps,  1 )
   cProp     = ALLTRIM(aProps(I,2))
   cPropType = ALLTRIM(aProps(I,3))
   cPropVal  = ALLTRIM(aProps(I,4))
   DO CASE
      CASE cPropType $ [IN]
           cPropVal = VAL(cPropVal)
      CASE cPropType = [C]
           cPropVal = VAL(cPropVal)
      CASE cPropType = [L]
           cPropVal = IIF(cPropVal=[.T.],.T.,.F.)
   ENDCASE
   oForm.&Cprop. = cPropVal
ENDFOR
IF NOT EMPTY ( SaveAlias )
   SELECT    ( SaveAlias )
ENDIF
ENDPROC
```

8

Grids Redux

We looked at grid settings earlier, but if you don't like what you see, it's not too hard to write your own. I wrote my own code to build the gorgeous grid shown in Figure 8.12.

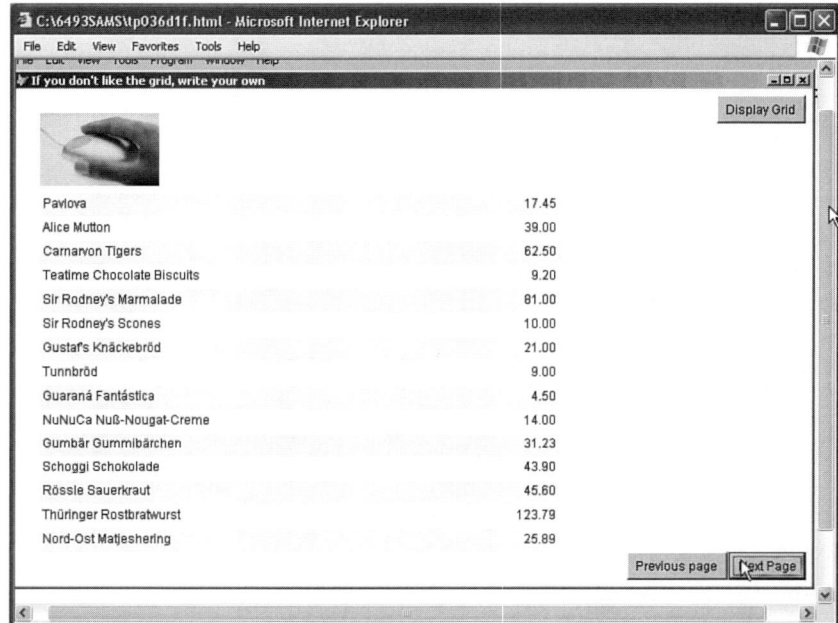

FIGURE 8.12   A home-built grid.

The code to do this is ready to turn into a class that you can use on your own forms (see Listing 8.30).

LISTING 8.30   A Home-Built Grid

```
PROCEDURE ListRecords
WITH THISFORM

* Remove any previously displayed objects:
CellCount = 0
DIMENSION CellList(1)
FOR EACH Ctrl IN THISFORM.Controls
    IF UPPER(Ctrl.Name) = [CELL]
        CellCount = CellCount + 1
        DIMENSION CellList(CellCount)
        CellList(CellCount) = Ctrl.Name
    ENDIF
```

LISTING 8.30 Continued

```
ENDFOR
IF CellCount > 0
    FOR EACH Ctrl IN CellList
        .RemoveObject ( Ctrl )
    ENDFOR
ENDIF
RELEASE CellList, CellCount
Flipper = 1
GO ( .StartTop )
.LastTop = RECNO()
CellTop  = .CellTop
SCAN WHILE CellTop < ( .Height - 50 )
    CellName1 = "Cell1" + TRANSFORM(CellTop)
    CellName2 = "Cell2" + TRANSFORM(CellTop)
    IF MOD(Flipper,2) = 1
        .AddObject ( Cellname1, "Even", CellTop, 25, 400, ;
            "SQLResult.ProductName" )
      .AddObject ( Cellname2, "Even", CellTop, 426,100, ;
            "SQLResult.UnitPrice"   )
     ELSE
    .AddObject ( Cellname1, "Odd",  CellTop, 25, 400, ;
            "SQLResult.ProductName" )
    .AddObject ( Cellname2, "Odd",  CellTop, 426,100, ;
            "SQLResult.UnitPrice"   )
    ENDIF
    .&CellName1..Visible = .T.
    .&CellName2..Visible = .T.
    .&CellName2..InputMask = [#,###.##]
    CellTop = CellTop + 23
    Flipper = IIF ( Flipper = 1, 2, 1 )
ENDSCAN
ENDWITH
ENDPROC


PROCEDURE Load
lcStr = "driver={SQL Server};server=(local);database=northwind;uid=sa;pwd=;"
Handle = SQLSTRINGCONNECT( lcStr )
IF Handle < 1
   MESSAGEBOX( "Couldn't connect to SQL server", 16 )
   RETURN .F.
ENDIF
lr = SQLEXEC( Handle, "SELECT * FROM PRODUCTS" )
```

LISTING 8.30   Continued

```
IF lr < 0
   MESSAGEBOX( "Couldn't return data", 16 )
   RETURN .F.
ENDIF
SQLDISCONNECT(0)
SET CLASSLIB TO FormLib
ENDPROC

PROCEDURE Unload
USE
ENDPROC

PROCEDURE command1.Click
THISFORM.Image1.Visible = .T.
THISFORM.PageTops(1) = 1
THISFORM.cmdNext.Click
ENDPROC

PROCEDURE cmdprevious.Click
WITH THISFORM
.PageCounter = .PageCounter - 1
IF .PageCounter < 2
   .PageCounter = 1
   .cmdPrevious.Enabled = .F.
ENDIF
.StartTop = .Pagetops(.PageCounter)
.ListRecords
.cmdNext.Enabled = .T.
ENDWITH
ENDPROC

PROCEDURE cmdnext.Click
WITH THISFORM
.StartTop = RECNO()
.ListRecords
.PageCounter = .PageCounter + 1
DIMENSION .PageTops ( .PageCounter )
.PageTops(.PageCounter) = .StartTop
IF EOF()
   THIS.Enabled      = .F.
ENDIF
IF .PageCounter > 1
```

LISTING 8.30   Continued

```
   .cmdPrevious.Enabled = .T.
ENDIF
ENDWITH
ENDPROC
```

Figure 8.13 shows a grid that sports incremental searching.

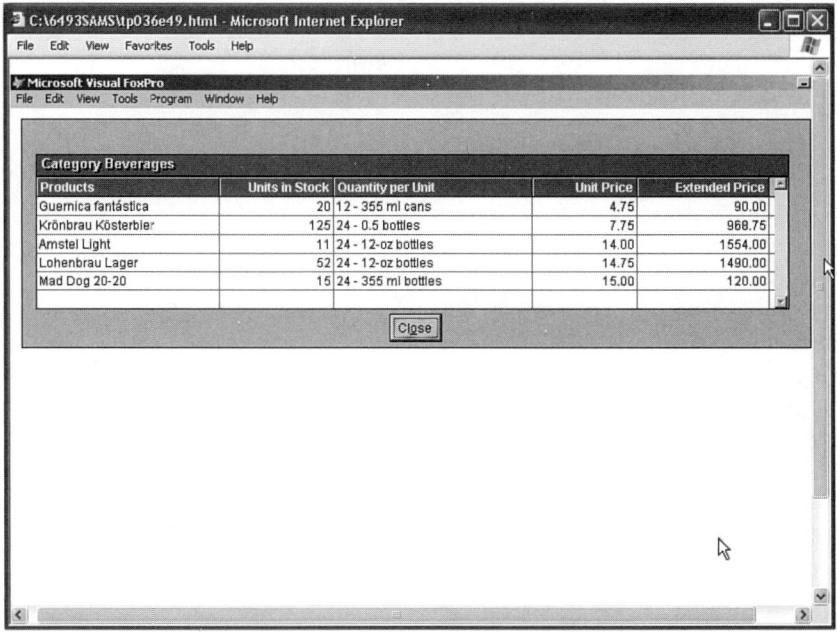

FIGURE 8.13   A grid with incremental searching.

Listing 8.31 shows the code for this grid, all of it in the KeyPress event of the form.

LISTING 8.31   A Grid with Incremental Searching

```
* Form KeyPress event code:
LPARAMETERS nKeyCode, nShiftAltCtrl
WITH THISFORM
IF nKeyCode = 13
   .Grid1.DblClick
   NODEFAULT
   RETURN
ENDIF
```

LISTING 8.31   Continued

```
IF NOT BETWEEN ( nKeyCode, 64, 128 )
   RETURN
ENDIF
.Label3.Visible     = .T.
.SearchLabel.Visible = .T.
THIS.SearchLabel.Caption = UPPER(CHR(nKeyCode))
LOCATE FOR UPPER(EVALUATE(THISFORM.KeyField)) = THIS.SearchLabel.Caption
.Label3.Visible = .T.
IF NOT FOUND()
   Msg = THIS.SearchLabel.Caption + " not found"
   MESSAGEBOX( Msg, 16, [Search], 1000 )
   THIS.Caption = Msg
   RETURN
ENDIF
.Grid1.SetFocus
Start = SECONDS()
DO WHILE SECONDS() - Start < 1
   .KeyPreview= .F.
   a = INKEY()
   THIS.SearchLabel.Caption = THIS.SearchLabel.Caption + UPPER(CHR(a))
   LOCATE FOR UPPER(EVALUATE(THISFORM.KeyField)) = THIS.SearchLabel.Caption
   .Label3.Visible = .T.
   IF NOT FOUND()
      Msg = THIS.SearchLabel.Caption + " not found"
      MESSAGEBOX( Msg, 16, [Search], 1000 )
      THIS.Caption = Msg
      EXIT
   ENDIF
   .Grid1.SetFocus
ENDDO
.KeyPreview          = .T.
.Label3.Visible      = .F.
.SearchLabel.Visible = .F.
ENDWITH
```

Sometimes all you need is color to make a grid work for you. The grid in Figure 8.14 is similar to one that I did for a shipping company a few years ago.

This demo represents a pizza parlor, and shows the times when orders will need to be removed from the oven. As the critical time nears, the row color changes from blue to yellow to orange to red. All it takes is a single line of code in the DynamicBackColor property of each grid column, as shown in Listing 8.32.

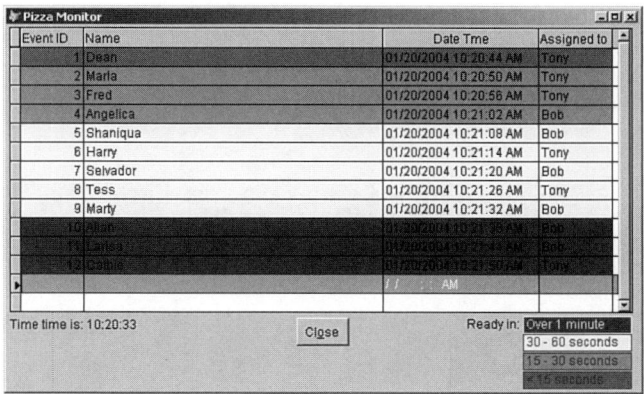

FIGURE 8.14   Color-coded grid using a timer.

LISTING 8.32   A Color-Coded Grid

```
IIF(DateTime-DateTime()>60,RGB(0,0,255), ;
IIF(DateTime-DateTime()>30,RGB(255,255,0), ;
IIF(DateTime-DateTime()>15,RGB(255,128,0), ;
                   RGB(255,0,0))))
```

Tree Views and Lists in FoxPro

For smaller amounts of data, lists offer a clean and simple object. The `DblClick` event fires anywhere on a row, and doesn't require coding a `DblClick` event for each column as grids do. However, don't try this if you have more than a few hundred items to load—maybe a thousand tops. It gets *real* slow....

There are nine ways to load a `ListBox`. However, only one of them really works. Use this paradigm shown in Listing 8.33 to load multicolumn lists.

LISTING 8.33   Loading Multicolumn List Boxes

```
WITH THISFORM.List1
.Clear
SCAN
    .AddListItem ( Column1 )
    Row = .NewItemID
    .AddListItem ( Column2, Row, 2 )
ENDSCAN
ENDWITH
```

8

Tree views are very interesting, and much maligned. Unlike any of the FoxPro controls besides the grid (before the arrival of the `XMLAdapter`, that is), they're the only control that contains a second object inside them (the `Node` object) that you have to instantiate before you can use the container control. As a result, they don't work and you can't look inside them to figure them out.

Luckily, Microsoft has provided us with a simple example, the `BldTree.SCX` solution form in the `Solutions` subdirectory of the FoxPro home directory. It's shown in Figure 8.15, and contains method code to do just about anything you'd want to do.

> **TIP**
>
> The sample code takes whatever you want to load and puts it into a two-column table that you can understand. The data is then loaded from this temporary two-column table. I strongly recommend that you do likewise.

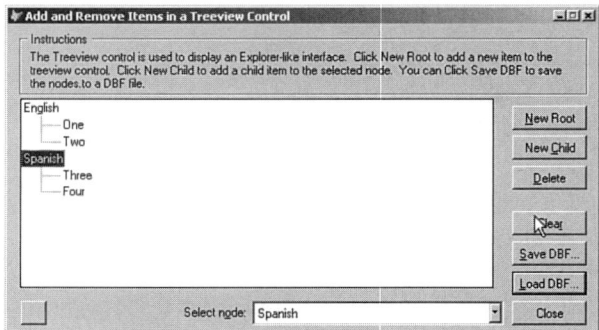

FIGURE 8.15   The `BldTree` form from the Visual FoxPro Solutions examples.

Build Your Own Menu

The Internet has given us some interesting technologies. The best of them is the variety of menuing systems in browser screens. What a coincidence; the worst thing about FoxPro is its menuing system. So can we borrow some of this technology? Figure 8.16 says Yes.

I wrote a little class library that's pretty easy to use. You place the `JavaMenu` class anywhere on the screen, even though it's a nonvisual class, and the code uses its placement on the form to position the first menu element. The rest of the menu pads (the first column) and the menu bars (the selections dependent on the currently selected menu pad) are placed automatically relative to the first element. The menu loads from a table contains the data shown in Figure 8.17.

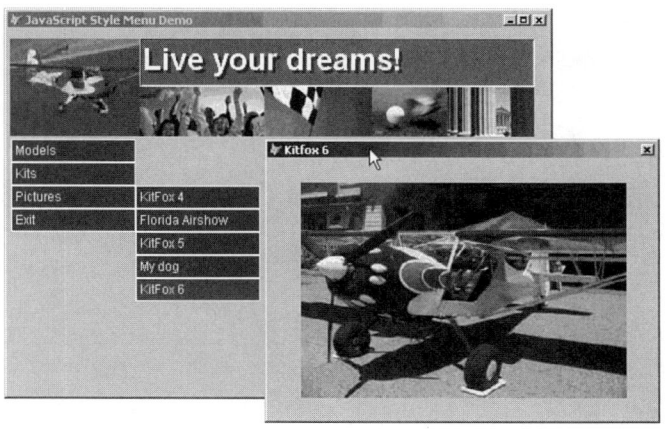

FIGURE 8.16 A JavaScript-style menu in a FoxPro screen.

Menu

Sequence	Menuname	Padnum	Text	Dependson	Action
1	SkyStar	1	Models	0	
2	SkyStar	0	KitFox 4	1	THISFORM.ShowText ([KitFox 4 description])
3	SkyStar	0	KitFox 5	1	THISFORM.ShowText ([KitFox 5 description])
4	SkyStar	0	KitFox 6	1	THISFORM.ShowText ([KitFox 6 description])
5	SkyStar	2	Kits	0	
6	SkyStar	0	Quick Build	2	THISFORM.ShowText ([Quick Build kit details here])
7	SkyStar	0	Slow Build	2	THISFORM.ShowText ([Slow Build kit details here])
8	SkyStar	0	Lifetime Project	2	THISFORM.ShowText ([Cheapest kit details here])
9	SkyStar	3	Pictures	0	
10	SkyStar	0	KitFox 4	3	THISFORM.ShowText ([Picture of KitFox 4 here])
10	SkyStar	0	Florida Airshow	3	THISFORM.ShowText ([Picture of air show here])
11	SkyStar	0	KitFox 5	3	THISFORM.ShowText ([Picture of KitFox 5 here])
11	SkyStar	0	My dog	3	THISFORM.ShowText ([Picture of Pookie here])
12	SkyStar	0	KitFox 6	3	DO FORM KitFox6
13	SkyStar	4	Exit	0	
14	SkyStar	0	Close the form	4	THISFORM.Release

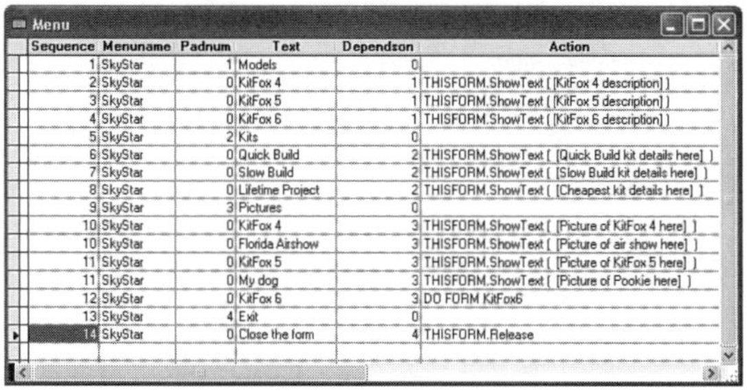

FIGURE 8.17 Contents of MENU.DBF.

Listing 8.34 gives you the code.

LISTING 8.34 JavaMenu Code

```
DEFINE CLASS javamenu AS custom

initialx = 0
x = 0
initialy = 0
y = 0
normalcolor = (RGB(43,85,128))
livecolor = (RGB(192,0,0))
textcolor = (RGB(255,255,255))
```

8

LISTING 8.34 Continued

```
cellheight = 22
cellwidth = 100
Name = "javamenu"

*-- Name of the menu to load from MENU.DBF.
menuname = .F.
DIMENSION menu[1,1]
DIMENSION action[1,1]

PROCEDURE showmenu
PARAMETERS nItemNumber
WITH THISFORM
IF NOT EMPTY ( nItemNumber )
.LockScreen = .T.
DIMENSION oList ( .Objects.Count )
FOR I = 1 TO      .Objects.Count
    oList ( I ) = .Objects(I).Name
ENDFOR
FOR I = 1 TO ALEN ( oList )
    IF oList(I) = [Bar]
        .RemoveObject ( oList(I) )
    ENDIF
ENDFOR
.LockScreen = .F.
ENDIF
ENDWITH
THIS.LoadMenu ( nItemNumber )
IF VARTYPE ( THIS.Menu(1,1) ) <> [C]
   RETURN
ENDIF
FOR I = 1 TO ALEN ( THIS.Menu, 1 )
    THIS.AddCell  ( THISFORM, I, ALLTRIM(THIS.Menu(I,1) ), nItemNumber )
ENDFOR
ENDPROC

PROCEDURE addcell
PARAMETERS oForm, nRow, MenuItemText, nItemNum
WITH oForm
CellName = IIF ( EMPTY(nItemNum), "Pad", "Bar" )
cName    = CellName + TRANSFORM ( nRow )
IF PEMSTATUS ( THISFORM, cName, 5 )
    RETURN
```

LISTING 8.34   Continued

```
ENDIF
.NewObject ( cName, "MenuItem", "pinter.vcx" )
WITH .&cName.
.Top            = THIS.X
.Left           = THIS.Y
.BackColor      = THIS.NormalColor
.ForeColor      = THIS.TextColor
.ActiveColor    = THIS.LiveColor
.InactiveColor  = THIS.NormalColor
.Value          = MenuItemText
.Width          = THIS.CellWidth
.Height         = THIS.CellHeight
THIS.X          = THIS.X + .Height
.Visible        = .T.
ENDWITH
ENDWITH
ENDPROC

PROCEDURE loadmenu
PARAMETERS nItemNum
IF NOT USED ( [MENU] )
   SELECT 0
   USE MENU
ENDIF
DIMENSION THIS.Menu ( 1, 2 )
IF EMPTY ( nItemNum )
   SELECT Text, PadNum            ;
     FROM MENU                    ;
    WHERE MenuName = THIS.MenuName    ;
      AND PadNum > 0              ;
    ORDER BY Sequence            ;
     INTO ARRAY THIS.Menu
  ELSE
   SELECT Text, Action           ;
     FROM MENU                   ;
    WHERE MenuName = THIS.MenuName    ;
      AND DependsOn = nItemNum    ;
    ORDER BY Sequence            ;
     INTO ARRAY THIS.Menu
ENDIF
IF _Tally = 0
   MESSAGEBOX( [No menu defined in MENU.DBF with MenuName "] ;
```

LISTING 8.34   Continued

```
      + THIS.MenuName + ["], 16, [Programmer error], 3000 )
   THIS.Menu(1,1) = .F.
ENDIF
ENDPROC

PROCEDURE bouncingform
PARAMETERS oCell, FormName
oCell.Bounce
DO FORM ( FormName )
ENDPROC

PROCEDURE Init
THIS.X = THIS.Top
THIS.Y = THIS.Left
* If specified, InitialX and InitialY reposition the menu:
IF THIS.InitialX > 0
   THIS.X = THIS.InitialX
ENDIF
IF THIS.InitialY > 0
   THIS.Y = THIS.InitialY
ENDIF
THIS.ShowMenu()
ENDPROC
ENDDEFINE

DEFINE CLASS menuitem AS editbox
Height = 18
ScrollBars = 0
SpecialEffect = 1
Width = 136
BorderColor = RGB(255,255,255)
activecolor = (RGB(255,0,0))
droppable = .F.
Name = "menuitem"
inactivecolor = .F.

PROCEDURE Click
IF THIS.Name <> [Bar]
   RETURN
ENDIF
IF THIS.Droppable
WITH THISFORM
```

LISTING 8.34   Continued

```
DIMENSION oList ( .Objects.Count )
FOR I = 1 TO       .Objects.Count
    oList ( I ) = .Objects(I).Name
ENDFOR
FOR I = 1 TO ALEN ( oList )
        IF oList(I) = [Bar] AND oList(I) <> THIS.Name
    .RemoveObject ( oList(I) )
    ENDIF
ENDFOR
ENDWITH

FOR I = THIS.Top TO THIS.Parent.Height - THIS.Height STEP 10
        a=INKEY(.02)
      THIS.Top = I
    ENDFOR
    A=INKEY(.1)
    THIS.Visible = .F.
ENDIF
ActionNum = VAL ( RIGHT ( THIS.Name, 1 ) )
Cmd = THISFORM.JavaMenu1.Menu ( ActionNum, 2 )
&Cmd
IF THIS.Droppable
   THISFORM.RemoveObject ( THIS.Name )
ENDIF
ENDPROC

PROCEDURE Init
PARAMETERS nTop, nLeft
IF PCOUNT() > 0
   THIS.Top  = nTop
   THIS.Left = nLeft
ENDIF
ENDPROC

PROCEDURE MouseEnter
LPARAMETERS nButton, nShift, nXCoord, nYCoord
THIS.BackColor = THIS.ActiveColor
IF THIS.Name = [Bar]
   RETURN
ENDIF
IF nXCoord <= THIS.Left OR nXCoord >= ( THIS.Left + THIS.Width )
   RETURN
```

LISTING 8.34   Continued

```
ENDIF
WITH THISFORM
.LockScreen = .T.
WITH .JavaMenu1
.X = THIS.Top
.Y = THIS.Left + THIS.Width
.ShowMenu ( VAL ( RIGHT ( THIS.Name, 1 ) ) )
ENDWITH
.LockScreen = .F.
ENDWITH
ENDPROC


PROCEDURE MouseLeave
LPARAMETERS nButton, nShift, nXCoord, nYCoord
THIS.BackColor = THIS.InactiveColor
ENDPROC
```

ActiveX Controls

Visual Basic .NET includes a huge number of controls; I count 49 as of this writing, although some of them (like the Color dialog) are functions or foundation classes in FoxPro. To use them, you drag them from the toolbox and drop them on the design surface. If they're nonvisual, as is the case with data components and dialogs and printing components, or hybrids like the MainMenu control, they appear in the tray at the bottom of the designer. Otherwise, they appear wherever you put them on the screen. In FoxPro, the form controls constitute only the basic visual components.

The form controls that come with FoxPro are not the only ones you can use on your screens. There is a whole universe of OCX and DLL controls that can enhance the appearance and usability of your application. The collective name for this type of control is ActiveX. Some are installed as a part of Windows; others are added when you install FoxPro or other languages. And some are installed as part of other software, like Adobe Acrobat, WinDiff, or other programs. You can use any of them on your FoxPro forms.

Select Tools, Options, Controls from the FoxPro IDE menu. You'll see a long list of installed controls. The names are not always perfectly indicative of their function, but many are recognizable. Figure 8.18 contains a sampling of them.

The Microsoft Date and Time picker is an excellent replacement for FoxPro's TextBox with date formatting. It returns numeric values for Month, Day, and Year. ActiveX controls don't have the ability to bind to FoxPro controls—they don't have a ControlSource property. So, you'll need to add something like the code shown in the LostFocus event of the control in order to convert the date back to FoxPro date format and put it into the field:

```
REPLACE ShipDate DATE ( THIS.Year, THIS.Month, THIS.Day )
```

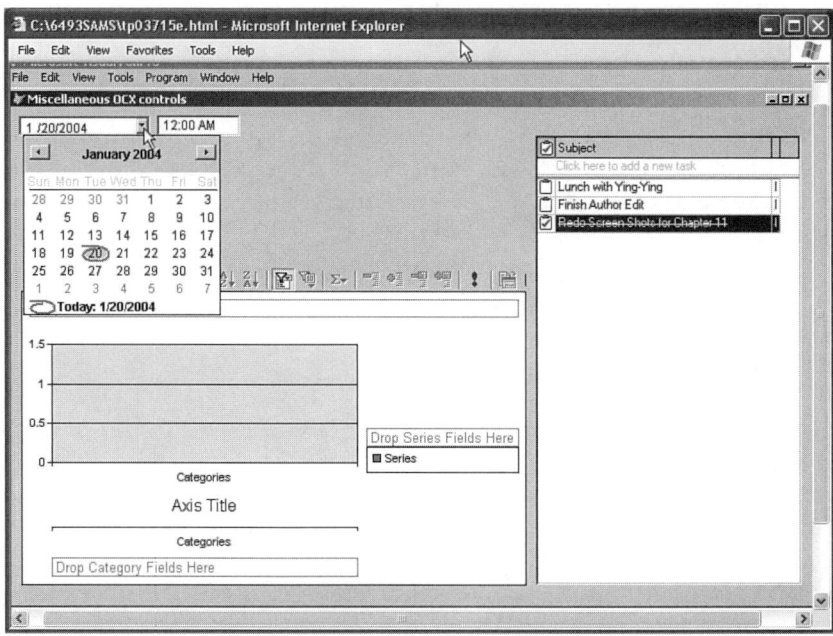

FIGURE 8.18   Miscellaneous OCX controls.

Similarly, controls like the Infragistics ScheduleX DayView and the TaskPad return lists that must be manually loaded from and stored back to your own tables. It usually requires only a SCAN...ENDSCAN to load and a FOR EACH...ENDFOR to save them.

Some ActiveX controls are installed by software that you install. I don't even know where the CurveFitter that appears in my COM objects list came from. And sometimes, you'll simply be amazed. For example, I bought BeyondCompare from ScooterSoftware.com to compare edited source code files. While writing this chapter, I was looking at my ActiveX controls and found one called DiffView. I noticed that it had a method called DiffTwoFiles with two filename parameters. So I dropped it on the OCX testbed form shown in Figure 8.18, and added two text boxes with THIS.Value = GetFile([PRG]) in the DblClick events. Download the source code and try it to see what happens.

There are a number of vendors that are aware of FoxPro developers' needs and cater to them. DBI Technologies (dbi-tech.com) has been FoxPro-friendly for years. HALLoGRAM.com, Infragistics.com, ComponentSource.com, and NewObjects.com are good sources for these valuable tools.

Build Your Own Controls

One of the best ways to enhance your interface is to build controls that do exactly what you want. They also make development easier because you can drop them on any screen with similar requirements. The screen shown in Figure 8.19 contains a Date Range control that lets users pick a starting and ending date for reports. It makes the task quick and easy in several ways:

- I used the Microsoft Date/Time Picker, which is a great way to get a date.

- I enabled the Checked property of the Date/Time controls. If they uncheck a date, it means "whatever." In the case of a start date, that means "Start with January 1, 1900." In the case of the ending date, it assumes 12/31/2089.

FIGURE 8.19   A date range picker.

I used a Container control to build this custom class. I added two labels, two Date/Time Picker ActiveX controls, and a CommandButton. The ActiveX controls have a custom property dialog that you can use to set various properties, such as the Checked property, which sets the date value to NULL if unchecked, allowing the user to say that the date doesn't matter in a simpler way than blanking out the date. We can't build custom property sheets in FoxPro, although you can in Visual Studio .NET. It's a nice touch.

The Init code takes two parameters that are used to pass information back to the form. If we used a modal form, this wouldn't be required, but I wanted to show something a little different (see Listing 8.35).

LISTING 8.35   The Init Code for the DateRange Control

```
PARAMETERS pDateFieldName, pDestination
IF PCOUNT() < 1
   MESSAGEBOX( [You must pass a date field name to this control] )
   RETURN .F.
ENDIF
IF PCOUNT() < 2
   MESSAGEBOX( [You must pass a target property name to this control] )
   RETURN .F.
ENDIF
THIS.DateFieldName = pDateFieldName
THIS.Destination   = pDestination
```

The Done::Click code formats the date and uses macro expansion to fill in the target field:

```
WITH THIS.Parent
* Note: Unchecking changes the date control's value to .NULL.
DateExpr = []
DO CASE
* Both checked, no date entered - assume all dates
   CASE NOT ISNULL ( .FromDate.Object.Value ) ;
    AND NOT ISNULL (    .ToDate.Object.Value ) ;
    AND     EMPTY ( .FromDate.Object.Value ) ;
    AND     EMPTY (    .ToDate.Object.Value )
          DateExpr = [BETWEEN (] + .DateFieldName ;
                 + [, {1/1/1900}, {12/31/2089})]
* First checked, second date not checked; assume single day
   CASE NOT ISNULL ( .FromDate.Object.Value ) ;
    AND     ISNULL (    .ToDate.Object.Value )
        DateExpr = [BETWEEN (] + .DateFieldName + [, {] ;
        +        LEFT(TTOC ( .FromDate.Object.Value ),10) + [},]     ;
        + [{] + LEFT(TTOC ( .FromDate.Object.Value ),10) + [})]
* Both checked, both entered
   CASE NOT ISNULL ( .FromDate.Object.Value ) ;
    AND NOT ISNULL (    .ToDate.Object.Value ) ;
    AND NOT EMPTY ( .FromDate.Object.Value ) ;
    AND NOT EMPTY (    .ToDate.Object.Value )
        DateExpr = [BETWEEN (] + .DateFieldName + [, {] ;
        +        LEFT(TTOC ( .FromDate.Object.Value ),10) + [},]     ;
        + [{] + LEFT(TTOC (    .ToDate.Object.Value ),10) + [})]
ENDCASE
Dest  = .Destination
&Dest = DateExpr
THISFORM.Refresh
FOR EACH oItem IN THIS.Parent.Objects
   oItem.Visible = .F.
ENDFOR
.Visible = .F.
ENDWITH
```

The form shown in Figure 8.20 demonstrates one use of this control. In lieu of displaying the data, I just show the resulting query.

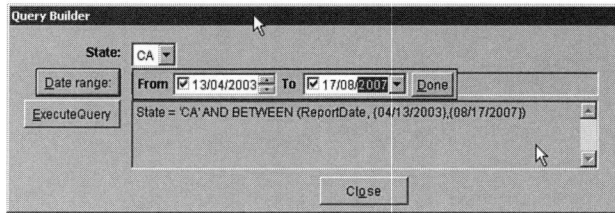

FIGURE 8.20 The date range picker in action.

Listing 8.36 shows the code that makes this control work (`DateRange::Click`).

LISTING 8.36 Implementing the Date Range Picker

```
WITH THISFORM
IF NOT PEMSTATUS ( THISFORM, [DateFilter], 5 )
   .AddProperty ( [DateFilter], [] )
   .DateFilter = [Pending...]
   .Text2.ControlSource = [THISFORM.DateFilter]
   .NewObject ( ;
  [DateRange1],[DateRange],[pinter.vcx],[],[ReportDate],[THISFORM.DateFilter])
ENDIF
WITH .DateRange1
FOR EACH oItem IN .Objects
    oItem.Visible = .T.
ENDFOR
 .Top = THIS.Top
.Left= THIS.Left + THIS.Width + 10
.Visible = .T.
.SetFocus
ENDWITH
ENDWITH
```

Listing 8.37 shows the required implementation code (`ExecuteQuery::Click`).

LISTING 8.37 Implementing the Date Range Picker (Continued)

```
WITH THISFORM
.Edit1.Value = [SELECT * FROM ORDERS]
Cmd1 = []
Cmd2 = []
IF NOT EMPTY ( .Combo1.Value )
   Cmd1 = [ AND State = '] + .Combo1.Value + [']
ENDIF
```

LISTING 8.37   Continued

```
IF NOT EMPTY ( .Text2.Value )
   Cmd2 = [ AND ] + .Text2.Value
ENDIF
Cmd = Cmd1 + Cmd2
IF NOT EMPTY ( Cmd )
   .Edit1.Value = SUBSTR ( Cmd, 6 )
ENDIF
.Edit1.Refresh
ENDWITH
```

Tools

The job of coloring interfaces and adding icons is easier, and in fact fun, if you have good tools. I use HyperSnap from www.Hyperionics.com for screen capture, and IconCool from www.IconCool.com for building or editing icons, bitmaps, and other images for graphic controls. GetPixel, mentioned earlier, allows you to see the RGB values for each color displayed anywhere on your screen. You can download GetPixel from www.aimoo.com/getpixel.

Summary

There are lots of things you can do to spice up the look of a application. You can always learn a little more about the base controls' properties, and discover things they can do that you didn't see before. You can use colors and graphics to unleash the hidden artist within. And you can combine controls to build components that are more than the sum of their parts. I hope this chapter has given you some useful ideas, and some inspiration to experiment.

In the next chapter, we'll look at reporting, the heart of many database applications. If you thought that reporting was easy in FoxPro and hard in Crystal Reports, which is .NET's reporting tool, you might be basing your opinion on outdated information. Let's see if an update improves your attitude toward reporting with Crystal Reports.

8

CHAPTER 9

Searching and Filtering in Visual FoxPro and Visual Basic .NET

What can you understand about a few hundred thousand records? Not much. The difference between data and information is understanding, and searching and filtering the data can provide that understanding.

Record Filtering in FoxPro

In Visual FoxPro, the SET FILTER command provides one mechanism for viewing only certain records. To use it, define the parameters for selecting filter values and issue the command.

To show how little code is required to filter records in Visual FoxPro, I built the form shown in Figure 9.1. The grid's ReadOnly property is set to .T. and the DeleteMark property is set to .F..

The code for the form is located in four places, as shown in Listing 9.1.

LISTING 9.1   Code for the Visual FoxPro Order Filtering Form

```
Form Load event:
SELECT Orders
SET FIELDS TO OrderID, ShipName, ShipCity, ShipCountr

Form Init event
THISFORM.Combo1.SetFocus

cmdClose Click event
THISFORM.Release

Combobox1 InteractiveChange event
SELECT Orders
SET FILTER TO ( ShipCountr = THISFORM.Combo1.Value )
THISFORM.Grid1.Refresh
GO TOP
```

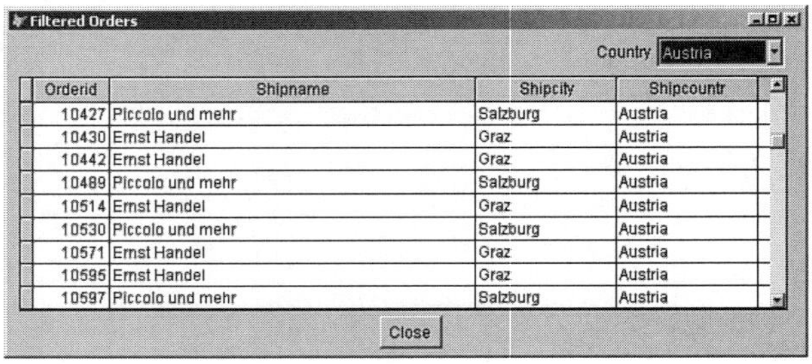

FIGURE 9.1   A simple filtering form.

The RecordSource for the Grid is Orders, and the RecordSource for the ComboBox is Countries. The InteractiveChange event of the ComboBox allows us to apply the filter and display only the records that meet the filtering criteria. The Init event sets the focus to the ComboBox so that the user is made aware of the filtering mechanism as soon as the form instantiates.

Some aspects of data handling are so much easier in FoxPro than they are in any other language that we've become a little spoiled. For example, the form's Data Environment opens the tables, then closes them when the form is closed. The SET FIELDS command in FoxPro limits the fields displayed to the four named fields.

This form shows how powerful FoxPro's SET commands are. As we'll see shortly, there are no SET commands in Visual Basic .NET, so all data management has to be done individually on each dataset or data view.

Record Filtering in Visual Basic .NET

Figure 9.2 shows the equivalent form in Visual Basic .NET.

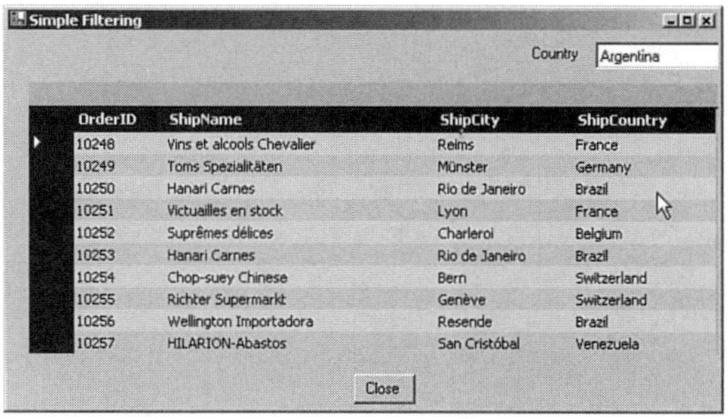

FIGURE 9.2   A simple filtering form in Visual Basic .NET.

I took the liberty of selecting one of the available styles for the grid. It's a nice compensation for only being able to adjust the individual column widths in code. (I expect that to be fixed in the next release of Visual Studio.)

Preparing the data for this example was a little more involved than it was in Visual FoxPro. First, I created a new Windows Forms application called SimpleFiltering, and added a `SQLDataAdapter` to the blank form. The resulting wizard asked for a connection, at which point I added a connection to the database that we've been using for our examples.

For the `DataAdapter` (which you could call daCountries, although I didn't change the default name of `DataAdapter1`), I specified the SQL statement SELECT Country FROM Countries. I also checked the Advanced Options button and unchecked the Generate Insert, Update and Delete Statements option because all we're doing is viewing the records.

For the Orders dataset, I dragged a second `SQLDataAdapter` onto the form, used SELECT OrderID, ShipName, ShipCity, ShipCountry FROM Orders as the SQL statement, unchecked the Generate Insert, Update and Delete Statements option, and specified a new dataset as shown in Figure 9.3.

The `Load` event fills the datasets. Without this, you won't see a thing:

```
SqlDataAdapter1.Fill(DsCountries1, "Countries")
SqlDataAdapter2.Fill(DsOrders1, "Orders")
```

The Grid's `ReadOnly` property is set to `True`. The ComboBox `InteractiveChange` event code is similar to that used in Visual FoxPro. However, note that the filtered records have to be explicitly moved to a `DataView`. I'm not sure whether FoxPro is doing something similar, or if Visual Basic .NET is simply applying a conditional index, as FoxPro does. It's a poorly kept secret that Visual Studio uses many elements of the FoxPro engine to manage datasets and data views:

```
Dim dv As New DataView
dv = DsOrders1.Tables(0).DefaultView
dv.RowFilter = "ShipCountry='" + ComboBox1.Text + "'"
DataGrid1.DataSource = dv
```

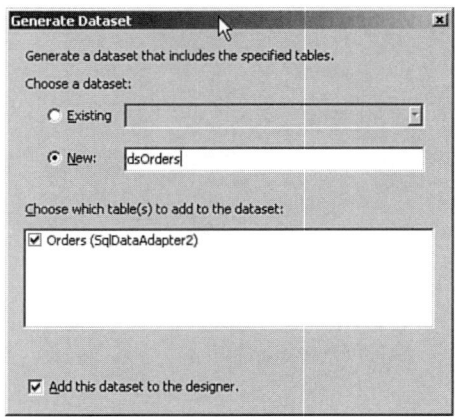

FIGURE 9.3   Adding the dataset for the second data adapter.

A Generic Record Lookup Grid with Column Sorting in Visual FoxPro

As you run the Visual Basic .NET version of this form, you might have noticed that clicking on the column heading not only sorts the grid's contents by the selected column, but toggles between ascending and descending order. This is as good a place as any to show how to do the same thing in FoxPro. We'll also extend the concepts in the simple grid shown earlier in this chapter to make it generic, requiring only the setting of a few properties to handle any table and list of fields.

Programming grids poses a problem in FoxPro. The problem is that the grid adds columns as needed when you assign the RecordSource property. The grid adds as many columns as needed to display the columns in the cursor. But the columns it adds are from the FoxPro Column base class, which has no default behavior to create an index on the selected column. But if you create your own column and add Click event code, you can add your subclassed column to a grid instead.

The unexpected wrinkle was that I couldn't add a class based on either the column class or the header class into a VCX file. It wasn't something I had run into before. But it's a small thing, and easily solved, as you'll see in the following description of creating the form.

I started by creating a form class called SearchForm, with four properties set:

```
CREATE CLASS SearchForm OF Pinter AS FORM

Height = 250
Width  = 375
AutoCenter = .T.
ControlBox = .F.
```

I added form properties named ReturnValue, TableName, FieldList, and KeyField. I then added a grid and two buttons (cmdSelect and cmdCancel), and a Shape to create a wire-frame around the buttons. The code for the two buttons was just this:

```
cmdSelect::Click
WITH THISFORM
    .ReturnValue = TRANSFORM(EVALUATE(.KeyField))
    .Hide
    .Release
ENDWITH

cmdCancel::Click
WITH THISFORM
    .ReturnValue = []
    .Hide
    .Release
ENDWITH
```

The grid has a few settings, mostly for esthetic purposes:

```
Height = 200
Left = 10
Width = 355
Name = Grid1
ScrollBars = 2-Vertical
DeleteMark = .F.
```

I want users to be able to resize this form. Resizing code is easy for a simple form like this:

```
WITH THISFORM
    .LockScreen = .T.
    WITH .Grid1
        .Width  = THIS.Width  - 20
        .Height = THIS.Height - 50
    ENDWITH
    .cmdSelect.Left = .Width/2 - .cmdSelect.Width/2
```

6

```
   .cmdSelect.Top  = .Height - 32
   .cmdCancel.Left = .Width/2 + .cmdCancel.Width/2
   .cmdCancel.Top  = .Height - 32
   .Shape1.Left    = .Width/2 - .Shape1.Width   /2 + 30
   .Shape1.Top     = .Height - 37
   .LockScreen = .F.
ENDWITH
```

So far the form looks like Figure 9.4.

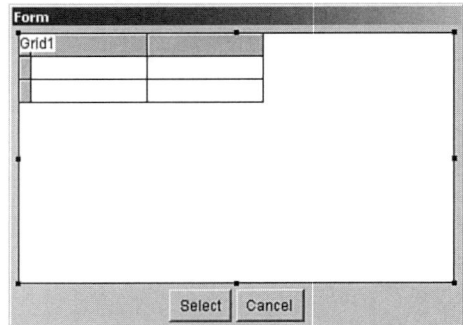

FIGURE 9.4   The grid in Design mode.

The interesting code in this application involves adding columns to the grid corresponding to the fields in the `FieldList` property. (Note: As an exercise, you might want to allow "*" or a blank `FieldList` to expand into a list of all the fields in the table.)

Because the `Init` code in the class references `GRIDLIB.PRG`, which contains the column and header classes, I'll list it first (see Listing 9.2).

LISTING 9.2   `GRIDLIB.PRG`

```
DEFINE CLASS MyCol as Column
   BackColor = RGB(255, 255, 128)
   FontName = "Courier New"
   FontSize = 11
   Width = 150
   Visible = .T.
   Sparse = .F.
   HeaderClass = "MyHeader"
   HeaderClassLibrary = "GridLib.prg"
ENDDEFINE

DEFINE CLASS MyHeader as Header
```

LISTING 9.2 Continued

```
   Caption    = "MyHeader"
   ForeColor = RGB(0, 0, 255)
   FontName  = "Courier New"
   FontSize  = 11
PROCEDURE Click
     WAIT WINDOW [Setting index tag to ] + THIS.Caption NOWAIT
     SET ORDER TO TAG ( THIS.Caption )
     GO TOP
     THIS.Parent.Parent.Refresh
   ENDPROC
ENDDEFINE
```

This is where the new column and header classes change the rules: I've embedded code in the Click event of the column header to set the index tag of the active table to the name used in the caption of each column. This assumes that each column actually corresponds to an index tag; so providing for that tag will be one of the tasks we accomplish in the form's Init method code. So here we go (see Listing 9.3).

LISTING 9.3 Form Init Code to Add a Column for Each Field in the Cursor FieldList

```
* PROCEDURE Init
ErrorStatus = []
WITH THISFORM
TRY
* Make sure that the AddObject method knows where the classes are
   SET PROCEDURE TO GRIDLIB.PRG ADDITIVE
* Don't try to continue if the properties aren't filled in:
   IF EMPTY ( .TableName )
      MESSAGEBOX( "TableName property is empty", 16, "Programmer error", 1000 )
      ErrorStatus = [Empty fieldlist]
   ENDIF
   IF EMPTY ( .FieldList )
      MESSAGEBOX( "FieldList property is empty", 16, "Programmer error", 1000 )
      ErrorStatus = [Empty fieldlist]
   ENDIF
* We only proceed if there were not any errors:
   IF  EMPTY ( ErrorStatus )
      IF NOT USED ( .TableName )
         USE     ( .TableName ) IN 0
      ENDIF
      SELECT    ( .TableName )
```

LISTING 9.3   Continued

```
* If they didn't fill in a key field name, assume it's the first column in
* the FieldList:
    IF EMPTY (    .KeyField  )
        .KeyField = GETWORDNUM(.FieldList,1,",")
    ENDIF
* Later on we'll add the tags that don't exist.
* To avoid an error message, create a little array entry
    ATAGINFO( laTags     )
    IF TYPE ( [laTags(1)] ) > [C]
        DIMENSION laTags(1)
        laTags = ""
    ENDIF
    WITH .Grid1
        .RecordSource = THISFORM.TableName
        .ColumnCount  =  0
        .Visible      = .T.
        FieldCount    = GETWORDCOUNT( THISFORM.FieldList, "," )
        TotalWidth    = 0
        FOR I = 1 TO FieldCount
            cName = "Mycol" + TRANSFORM(I)
            .AddObject ( (cName), "MyCol" )
            cField = ALLTRIM( UPPER( GETWORDNUM( THISFORM.FieldList, I, "," ) ) )
            .&cName..ControlSource    = THISFORM.TableName + "." + cField
            .&cName..MyHeader1.Caption = cField
            IF ASCAN(laTags,cField) = 0
                WAIT WINDOW [Creating index tag ] + cField NOWAIT
                INDEX ON &cField. TAG &cField.
                WAIT CLEAR
            ENDIF
        ENDFOR
* Let FoxPro calculate the column widths:
        .AutoFit()
* Add the column widths to resize the grid and the form:
        FOR EACH Col IN .Columns
            TotalWidth = TotalWidth + Col.Width
        ENDFOR
        .Width = TotalWidth       + 25
    ENDWITH
    THISFORM.Width = .Grid1.Width + 20
    .Refresh()
* Call the resize code to reposition all form elements:
    .Resize()
```

LISTING 9.3 Continued

```
    ENDIF    && End of the "Don't instantiate the form if there were errors" code
CATCH TO oEX
* If there was an error, display it and get the heck out of Dodge:
    MESSAGEBOX( [Error:] + CHR(13) + oEx.Message, 16, ;
                [Initialization error - aborting], 5000 )
    IF USED    ( .TableName )
       USE IN ( .TableName )
    ENDIF
    ErrorStatus = oEx.Message
ENDTRY
ENDWITH


* We couldn't RETURN in the TRY..CATCH block, so do it now.
IF NOT EMPTY ( ErrorStatus )
    RETURN .F.
ENDIF
* Finally, since the form size probably changed, recenter it now:
THISFORM.AutoCenter = .T.
```

The result of this little bit of code is shown in Figure 9.5, where I created an instance of the class, filled in three properties, and ran the form using

```
DO FORM CustSrch TO KeyValue
```

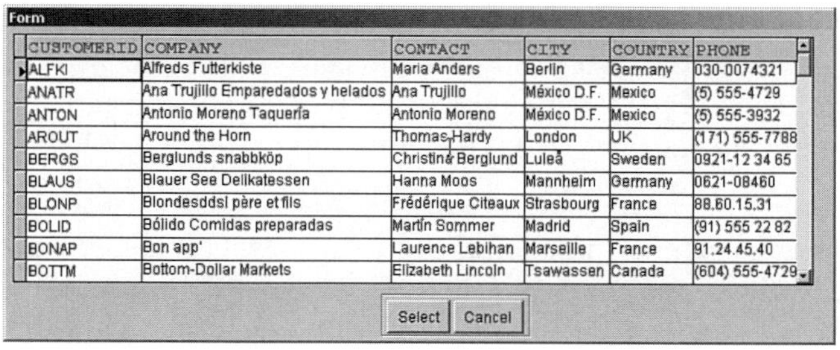

FIGURE 9.5   The sortable grid in action.

You can make several useful modifications to this code. For one, you might want to issue the command USE AGAIN so that if the calling form already has the table open, you don't move the record pointer to the consternation of the user. You might also want to use INDEX TO (*colname*) COMPACT and SET INDEX TO (*colname*) so that you don't arbitrarily add index tags to the table. And you can include code to check for the tag first, so that you only create it once. Of course, you mustn't use this technique if adding index tags would greatly slow down the program. But for a few thousand records, it's pretty cool.

Returning a Value from a Visual Basic .NET Form

The preceding example introduced an additional feature, FoxPro's ability to RETURN a value from the UNLOAD event of a modal form. In Visual Basic .NET, the preferred method is to instantiate the form, but only hide it in the code that closes the search form. To call the form in Visual Basic .NET, you use this:

```
Dim frm as New frmFindCustomer
Frm.ShowDialog()
```

The frmFindCustomer class should have a Public field (recall that what we would call a property or a public variable in Visual FoxPro is called a **field** in a .NET class) in which the search form stores either the value to return, or a null string if the user selected Cancel. Then you simply store the value of the form's field and close the form. Listing 9.4 shows the complete code.

LISTING 9.4   Returning a Value from a Visual Basic. NET Search Form

```
Dim frm as New frmFindCustomer
Frm.ShowDialog()
SelectedValue = Frm.KeyValue
Frm.Close()   ' or Frm.Dispose()
Cmd = "SELECT * FROM Customers WHERE CustomerID="  + SelectedValue
```

Using the `DefaultDataView` for Filtering and Sorting

In FoxPro, we can use SET ORDER TO TAG *IndexTagName* to change the sort order of a table or cursor, and SET FILTER TO *Expr* to limit the records displayed. We can also use LOCATE or SEEK to move the record pointer to a particular record. These commands operate on the current work area, a concept that has no meaning in Visual Basic .NET.

The Visual Basic .NET equivalent is the DataView. The DataView has a Sort property that takes the name of one of the columns in the DataView as its value and changes the display order of the data to the selected column. It also has a RowFilter property to which we can assign an expression like State = 'CA'. Only records matching the filter expression will be displayed.

A DataView can be created from a datatable object using the following assignment:

```
Dim dv as dataview = Dataset.Tables(0).DefaultView
```

However, you can also reference the DefaultView directly. Figure 9.6 shows a form I've built to demonstrate how these features work. In the related code shown in Listing 9.5, the DefaultView of the first table (table 0) in the dataset is the object containing the data displayed in the grid. In my example, you have to type a filter expression that assumes you know the exact spelling of the field name, and the character expression must use single quotes as delimiters. Obviously, you'd want to build this expression in code using the contents of a combo box to select the column name and a text box for the string to search for. If you run the sample code, which is located in the `Chapter9\VB\SearchAndFilter` directory, note that the code looks for an exact match for the name entered in the Search For text box, so if you enter only a first name, the program won't find the record.

FIGURE 9.6   A sort and filter example using the `DefaultDataView`.

LISTING 9.5   Code for the `DefaultDataView` Example

```
Imports System.Data.SqlClient

Public Class Form1
    Inherits System.Windows.Forms.Form

    Dim cn As SqlConnection
    Dim da As SqlDataAdapter
    Dim ds As New DataSet

+ Windows Forms Designer Generated Code omitted

    Private Sub Form1_Load( _
      ByVal sender As System.Object, _
      ByVal e As System.EventArgs) _
    Handles MyBase.Load
        cn = New SqlConnection( _
        "Server=localhost;Database=Northwind;" _
        + "UID=sa;PWD=;")
```

LISTING 9.5   Continued

```
        da = New SqlDataAdapter( _
        "SELECT * FROM CUSTOMERS", cn)
        da.Fill(ds)
        DataGrid1.DataSource = ds.Tables(0)
        ds.Tables(0).DefaultView.Sort = "ContactName"
        Me.Text = "The date is " _
          + Strings.FormatDateTime(Today.Now, DateFormat.ShortDate)
    End Sub

    Private Sub btnFind_Click_1( _
      ByVal sender As System.Object, _
      ByVal e As System.EventArgs) _
     Handles btnFind.Click
        Dim s As String = TextBox1.Text.Trim
        BindingContext(ds.Tables(0)).Position = _
          ds.Tables(0).DefaultView.Find(s)
    End Sub

    Private Sub ComboBox1_SelectedIndexChanged( _
      ByVal sender As System.Object, _
      ByVal e As System.EventArgs) _
     Handles ComboBox1.SelectedIndexChanged
        ds.Tables(0).DefaultView.Sort = _
        ComboBox1.SelectedItem.trim
    End Sub

    Private Sub Button1_Click( _
      ByVal sender As System.Object, _
      ByVal e As System.EventArgs) _
     Handles Button1.Click
        Dim s As String = TextBox2.Text.Trim
        ds.Tables(0).DefaultView.RowFilter = s
    End Sub

End Class
```

A Generic Record Lookup Form in Visual Basic .NET

The preceding Visual Basic .NET example included column sorting, which is built into the
DataGrid control. In FoxPro, adding column sorting turned out to be a little involved, but
the data was easy to get. In Visual Basic .NET, you have to think about data retrieval effi-
ciency.

For small numbers of rows, `DataViews` are okay. But unlike Visual FoxPro, where opening a table of a few hundred thousands of records has no performance implications to speak of, returning a few hundred thousand records into a grid in order to filter the records is not in the cards in the ADO.NET world. Instead, you have to get your data sparingly. That's how we'll design the lookup form.

Create a form with a grid, three command buttons, a text box, and a label, as shown in Figure 9.7.

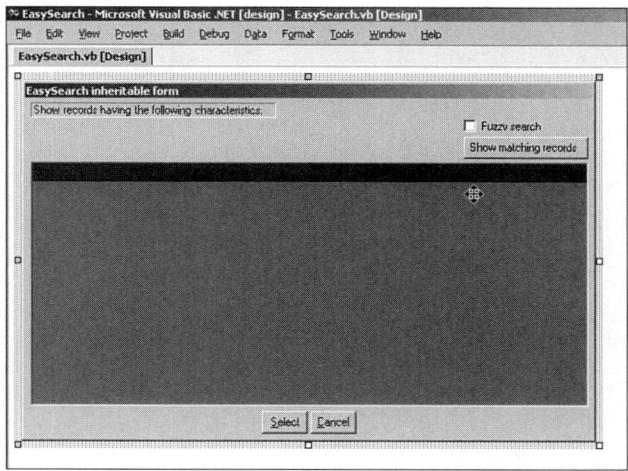

FIGURE 9.7   A generic search form in Visual Basic .NET.

The code in this form creates a `SELECT` statement ending in a `WHERE` clause that matches any string beginning with the letter(s) typed in by the user:

```
Cmd = "SELECT " + FieldList + " FROM " + TableName
    + " WHERE " + SearchField
    + " LIKE '" + TextBox1.Text + "%'"
```

The resulting command might look like this:

```
SELECT CustomerID, CompanyName, ContactName FROM CUSTOMERS
   WHERE CompanyName LIKE 'A%'
```

The code to load the table is trivial, as shown in Listing 9.6.

LISTING 9.6   The Code to Build a `SELECT` String

```
Dim cn As New SqlClient.SqlConnection
cn.ConnectionString = ConnStr
cn.Open()
```

LISTING 9.6   Continued

```
Dim cmd As New SqlClient.SqlCommand
cmd.Connection = cn

cmd.CommandText = "SELECT * FROM " + TableName _
               + " WHERE " + SearchField + " LIKE '" _
               + MyText1.Text.ToUpper.Trim + "%'"

Dim da As New SqlClient.SqlDataAdapter
da.SelectCommand = cmd

ds.Clear()
da.Fill(ds, TableName)
dv = ds.Tables(0).DefaultView

DataGrid1.DataSource = dv
```

This will return only the records that match the filter expression. If you want to match a substring anywhere within the target string, you can include a percent sign at the end of the string " LIKE '", that is, " LIKE '%".

However, users who have been spoiled by using FoxPro may still not be prepared for the consequences of issuing a command like this that returns 25,000 records from SQL, never mind returning records from a Web server. So you can avoid dangerous liaisons by returning a count of the records to be returned, and if it passes some threshold (stored in an integer property called MaxRecords), warn the user (see Listing 9.7).

LISTING 9.7   Visual Basic .NET Code to Count Records and Warn the User If the Records Exceed Some Limit

```
cmd.CommandText = "SELECT Count(*) FROM " + TableName _
    + " WHERE " + SearchField + " LIKE '" + MyText1.Text.ToUpper.Trim + "%'"
Dim HowMany As Integer
HowMany = cmd.ExecuteScalar
If HowMany > MaxRecords Then
   Dim s as string = "This query will return " ;
    + HowMany.ToString + " records. Proceed?"
   If MsgBox(s, _
           MsgBoxStyle.Exclamation, Application.ProductName) _
           = MsgBoxResult.No Then
      Return
   End If
End If
```

The same thing is possible in FoxPro, but not needed for DBFs. For SQL Server, it's easy:

```
ConnStr = "Driver={SQL Server};server=(local);database=Northwind;UID=sa;PWD=;"
handle = SQLSTRINGCONNECT( ConnStr)
SQLEXEC( Handle, "SELECT COUNT(*) AS RecCount FROM Customers" )
```

The command returns a cursor named SQLRESULT. If you don't use an AS clause to rename the result of the COUNT(*) expression, the column is named Exp. So the result of the SQLEXEC call in the preceding code line is SQLResult.Reccount, and

```
SQLEXEC( Handle, "SELECT COUNT(*) FROM Customers" )
```

returns SQLResult.Exp. So you can write the generic code like that shown in Listing 9.8 (again, assume that the form has a property called MaxRecords that's been set to the maximum number of records you want to return without the user's approval).

LISTING 9.8   Visual FoxPro SQL Code to Count Records and Warn the User If the Records Exceed Some Limit

```
WITH THISFORM
FilterExpr = " WHERE " + SearchField + " LIKE '" + .Textbox1.Value + "%'"
Cmd = "SELECT COUNT(*) FROM " + .TableName + " WHERE " + FilterExpr
SQLExec ( Handle, Cmd )

IF SQLResult.Exp > .MaxRecords
   S = "This will return " + TRANSFORM(Exp) + " records; continue?"
   IF MessageBox ( s, 292 ) <> 6
      RETURN
   ENDIF
ENDIF

Cmd = "SELECT " + FieldList + " FROM " + TableName + FilterExpr
SQLExec ( Handle, Cmd )
.Grid1.RecordSource = "SQLResult"
ENDWITH
```

Minimalist Filtering in Visual FoxPro and Visual Basic .NET

Try this: Drop twogrids on a form. Open the Data Environment and add the Orders and OrderDetails tables from the Northwind database. Set the Order property of each of the two tables to OrderID. Finally, drag the OrderID field from the Orders table to the OrderId entry under *Indexes* at the bottom of the OrderDetails cursor icon. The line that appears to connect them documents the relationship. On the form's design surface, set the top grid's

RowSource to Orders and the bottom grid's RowSource to OrderDetails. Run the form. Cool, n'est-ce pas?

The same trick doesn't work in Visual Basic .NET. Build the equivalent two-grid form, as shown in Figure 9.8.

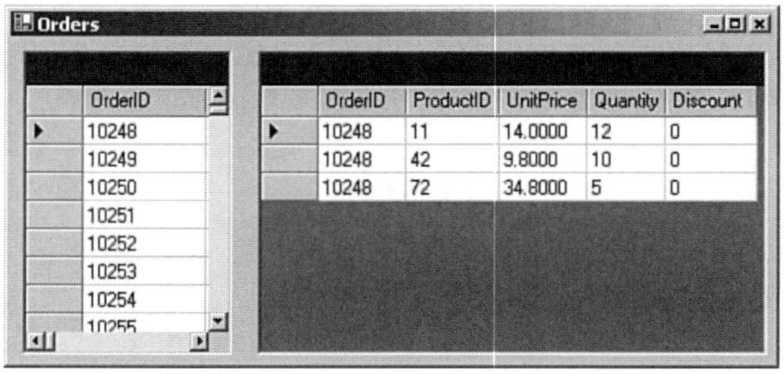

FIGURE 9.8   Scrolling through a grid and displaying related records in a second grid in Visual Basic .NET.

In order for this to work, you have to create two data adapters, using the following SQL statements in their respective wizards:

DataAdapter1:
SELECT * FROM Orders

DataAdapter2:
SELECT * FROM [Order Details] WHERE (OrderID = @OrderID)

We'll do something a little different here. Datasets can contain multiple tables, so we'll use the same dataset for both orders and order details. Right-click on SQLDataAdapter1 and select Generate Dataset to create a dataset named dsOrders1. When you do the same thing with SQLDataAdapter2, *don't change the name of the dataset*; just use the same one (see Listing 9.9).

LISTING 9.9   Code to Display Related Records in a Second Grid

```
Private Sub Form1_Load( _
  ByVal sender As System.Object, _
  ByVal e As System.EventArgs) _
 Handles MyBase.Load
SqlDataAdapter1.Fill(DsOrders1, "Orders")
DataGrid1.DataMember = "Orders"
With SqlDataAdapter2
    .SelectCommand.Parameters(0).Value = _
    DsOrders1.Tables("Orders").Rows(DataGrid1.CurrentRowIndex).Item("OrderID")
```

LISTING 9.9 Continued

```
    .Fill(DsOrders1, "[Order Details]")
End With
DataGrid1_CurrentCellChanged(Me, New System.EventArgs)
End Sub

Private Sub DataGrid1_CurrentCellChanged( _
  ByVal sender As Object, _
  ByVal e As System.EventArgs) _
 Handles DataGrid1.CurrentCellChanged
DsOrders1.Tables("[Order Details]").Clear()
With SqlDataAdapter2
    .SelectCommand.Parameters(0).Value = _
     DsOrders1.Tables("Orders").Rows(DataGrid1.CurrentRowIndex).Item("OrderID")
    .Fill(DsOrders1, "[Order Details]")
End With
With DataGrid2
    .DataSource = DsOrders1
    .DataMember = "[Order Details]"
End With
End Sub
```

This technique is appropriate for relatively small amounts of data. If you're working with huge tables, you should filter the primary table as well.

Search Forms with Additional Fields

How easy is it to allow users to construct a search string from any of several fields? It's easy if you hard-code each form individually.

A Generic Search Form in Visual FoxPro

I've built a generic form class that allows you to create a custom search form in a couple of minutes in FoxPro. The basic form class is shown in Figure 9.9.

Form properties are described in Table 9.1.

TABLE 9.1   Search Form Properties

Properties	Description
TableName	The name of the table to be searched
ColNames	Column names to display from the named table
ColWidths	Relative widths of the displayed table columns
OrderBy	Field(s) by which the returned data should be ordered

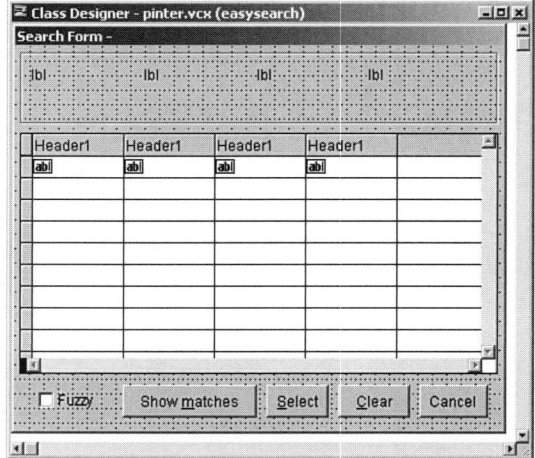

FIGURE 9.9   A generic search form in Visual FoxPro.

You might wonder why the form has no input fields. The reason is that an input field might be a combo box, a text box, or a date picker. All this form requires is that you name the fields Search1, ..., SearchN. I've written the code to allow up to four fields, but you can increase it to any number you want. Listing 9.10 shows the Init code for the class.

LISTING 9.10   The Search Form's Init Code

```
WITH THISFORM
.Caption = [Search form - ] + .Name + [ (Main Table: ] ;
        + TRIM(.TableName)+[)  Data access: ] + .Access
NumWords = GETWORDCOUNT(.ColNames,[,])
IF NumWords > 4
   S = [This class only supports a maximum of 4 fields, sorry]
   MESSAGEBOX( S, 16, _Visual FoxPro.Caption )
   RETURN .F.
ENDIF
FOR I = 1 TO NumWords
        .Field(I)   = GETWORDNUM(.ColNames,   I,[,])
        .Heading(I) = GETWORDNUM(.ColHeadings,I,[,])
        .ColWidth(I)= GETWORDNUM(.ColWidths,  I,[,])
ENDFOR
WITH .Grid1
.ColumnCount                = NumWords
.RecordSource               = THISFORM.ViewName
.RecordSourceType      = 1
GridWidth = 0
```

LISTING 9.10   Continued

```
FOR I = 1 TO NumWords
        .Columns(I).Header1.Caption =              THISFORM.Heading (I)
        GridWidth = GridWidth              +  VAL( THISFORM.ColWidth(I) )
        FldName   = THISFORM.ViewName + [.] + THISFORM.Field   (I)
        .Columns(I).ControlSource       = FldName
ENDFOR
Multiplier = ( THIS.Width / GridWidth ) * .90
FOR I = 1 TO NumWords
        .Columns(I).Width = VAL( THISFORM.ColWidth(I) ) * Multiplier
ENDFOR
.Refresh
ENDWITH
* Look for any controls named SEARCHn (n = 1, 2, ... )
FOR I = 1 TO .ControlCount
        Ctrl = .Controls(I)
        IF UPPER(Ctrl.Name) = [MYLABEL] && That is, if it starts with "MyLabel"
                Sub = RIGHT(Ctrl.Name,1)         && Determine the index
                IF TYPE ( [THISFORM.Search] + Sub ) = [O]
*                   A search field of the same number exists
                   Ctrl.Visible = .T.
                   Ctrl.Enabled = .T.
                   Ctrl.Caption = .Heading(VAL(Sub))
                   .SearchFieldCount = MAX ( VAL(Sub), .SearchFieldCount )
                ENDIF
        ENDIF
ENDFOR
.SetAll ( "Enabled", .T. )
ENDWITH
```

The Load event code verifies that necessary parameters have been supplied, and creates a View to hold returned records (see Listing 9.11). This is necessary because the table that's being queried can't be the carrier for the filtered records used to pick a record from the target table.

LISTING 9.11   The Load Event Code

```
WITH THISFORM

IF EMPTY ( .TableName )
   MESSAGEBOX( [Table name not entered], 16, _Visual FoxPro.Caption )
   RETURN .F.
ENDIF
```

LISTING 9.11   Continued

```
IF EMPTY ( .ColNames )
   Msg = [ColNames property not filled in.]
   MESSAGEBOX( Msg, 16, _Visual FoxPro.Caption )
   RETURN .F.
ENDIF

IF EMPTY ( .ColWidths )
   .ColWidths = [1,1,1,1,1]
ENDIF
IF EMPTY ( .ColHeadings )
   .ColHeadings = .ColNames
ENDIF

.Access = oDataTier.AccessMethod
.ViewName = [View]  +  .TableName
oDataTier.CreateView ( .TableName )


ENDWITH
```

The Show Matches button does the heavy lifting (see Listing 9.12). The `DataTier` object described in Chapter 3, "Building a Visual Fox Pro Application for SQL Server," and expanded in Chapter 5, "Adding Internet Access," creates the `View` cursor and gets the filtered data. Notice how the search can be made "fuzzy", that is, the "%" character is placed both before and after the string entered by the user.

LISTING 9.12   The Show Matches Button `Click` Code

```
WITH THISFORM
Fuzzy = IIF ( THISFORM.Fuzzy.Value = .T., [%], [] )
STORE [] TO Expr1,Expr2,Expr3,Expr4
FOR I = 1 TO .SearchFieldCount
    Fld = [THISFORM.Search] + TRANSFORM(I) + [.Value]
    IF NOT EMPTY ( &Fld )
       LDD = IIF ( VARTYPE( &Fld) = [D], ;
          IIF ( .Access = [DBF],[{],['] ),  ;
          IIF ( VARTYPE( &Fld) = [C], ['],[]) )
       RDD = IIF ( VARTYPE( &Fld) = [D], ;
             IIF ( .Access = [DBF],[}],['] ), ;
             IIF(VARTYPE( &Fld) = [C], ['],[]) )
       Cmp = IIF ( VARTYPE( &Fld) = [C], [ LIKE ],[ = ] )
       Pfx = IIF ( VARTYPE( &Fld) = [C], Fuzzy, [] )
```

LISTING 9.12   Continued

```
          Sfx = IIF ( VARTYPE( &Fld) = [C], [%],[] )
          Exp = [Expr]  + TRANSFORM(I)
          &Exp = [ AND UPPER(] + .Field(I) + [)] + Cmp ;
               + LDD + Pfx + UPPER(ALLTRIM(TRANSFORM(EVALUATE(Fld)))) + Sfx + RDD
          ENDIF
ENDFOR
lcExpr = Expr1 + Expr2 + Expr3 + Expr4
IF NOT EMPTY ( lcExpr )
   lcExpr = [ WHERE ] + SUBSTR ( lcExpr, 6 )
ENDIF
lcOrder = IIF(EMPTY(.OrderBy),[],[ ORDER BY ] ;
        + ALLTRIM(STRTRAN(.OrderBy,[ORDER BY],[])))
Cmd = [SELECT * FROM ] + .TableName + lcExpr + lcOrder
oDataTier.SelectCmdToSQLResult ( Cmd )
SELECT ( .ViewName )
ZAP
APPEND FROM DBF([SQLResult])
GO TOP
.Grid1.Refresh
IF RECCOUNT() > 0
   .cmdSelect.Enabled = .T.
   .Grid1.Visible      = .T.
   .Grid1.Column1.Alignment = 0
   .Caption = [Search Form - ] + PROPER(.Name)         ;
                          + [  (] + TRANSFORM(RECCOUNT()) + [ matches)]
  ELSE
   .Caption = [Search Form - ] + PROPER(.Name)
   MESSAGEBOX( "No records matched" )
   .cmdSelect.Enabled = .F.
ENDIF
KEYBOARD [{BackTab}{BackTab}{BackTab}{BackTab}{BackTab}]
ENDWITH
```

It's useful to be able to clear all of the input fields and start over. The code for this is shown in Listing 9.13.

LISTING 9.13   The Clear Button Click Event Code

```
WITH THISFORM
FOR I = 1 TO .SearchFieldCount
        Fld = [THISFORM.Search] + TRANSFORM(I) + [.Value]
        IF VARTYPE ( &Fld ) <> [U]
```

LISTING 9.13   Continued

```
                 lVal = IIF ( VARTYPE( &Fld) = [C], [],   ;
                          IIF ( VARTYPE( &Fld) = [D], {//}, ;
                          IIF ( VARTYPE( &Fld) = [L], .F.,  ;
                          IIF ( VARTYPE( &Fld) $ [IN], 0, [?])))) 
         &Fld           = lVal
             ENDIF
ENDFOR
ENDWITH
```

The Select button's `Click` code stores the record key to be returned in the class's `ReturnValue` property, as shown in Listing 9.14.

LISTING 9.14   The Select Button `Click` Event Code

```
WITH THISFORM
lcStrValue = TRANSFORM(EVALUATE(.KeyField))
.ReturnValue = lcStrValue
.Release
ENDWITH
```

The `Unload` event closes the view opened in the `Load` event and returns the value from this modal form, as shown in Listing 9.15.

LISTING 9.15   The `Unload` Event Code

```
WITH THISFORM
IF USED   ( .ViewName )
   USE IN ( .ViewName )
ENDIF
RETURN .ReturnValue
ENDWITH
```

To use the `EasySearch` class, type

```
CREATE FORM FindCustomer AS EachSearch FROM Pinter
```

Add a text box, a combo box, and a date picker. Name them `Search1`, `Search2`, and `Search3` because the program uses the control's name to find and match controls to code. Be sure to set the tab order. Enter values for the `TableName`, `KeyField`, and `FieldList` properties. Finally, enter `FindCustomers` as the value of the `SearchForm` property in the Customers form. Recompile and run the application, and it ought to work.

That's a lot of functionality for essentially no code. In the rapid prototyping world that most FoxPro developers inhabit, it doesn't get any better. And we're about to inhabit the .NET world, so let's do the same thing in Visual Basic .NET.

Building the `EasySearch` Form Class in Visual Basic .NET

The same class can be built in Visual Basic .NET, and except for the relatively complicated matter of data access in .NET, the code is quite similar.

Create a new Windows Forms project named EasySearch. Because this will be an inheritable form, change the Output type to Class Library. Add the field declarations shown in Listing 9.16 to the class.

LISTING 9.16   Field Declarations for the `EasySearch` Class

```
#Region " Declarations "
Private _FieldNames As String = ""
Private _TableName As String = ""
Private _KeyField As String = ""
Private _KeyValue As String = ""
Private _OrderBy As String = ""
Public ConnStr As String = ""
Public ds As New DataSet
#End Region
```

Then, add property procedures to allow the developer to supply the few properties that are required, as shown in Listing 9.17.

LISTING 9.17   Property Procedures for the `EasySearch` Class

```
#Region " Property procedures "
Public Property KeyValue() As String
    Get
        Return _KeyValue
    End Get
    Set(ByVal Value As String)
        _KeyValue = Value
    End Set
End Property

Public Property FieldNames() As String
    Get
        Return _FieldNames
    End Get
    Set(ByVal Value As String)
```

LISTING 9.17   Continued

```
        _FieldNames = Value
    End Set
End Property

Public Property TableName() As String
Get
    Return _TableName
End Get
Set(ByVal Value As String)
    _TableName = Value
End Set
End Property

Public Property KeyField() As String
Get
    Return _KeyField
End Get
Set(ByVal Value As String)
    _KeyField = Value
End Set
End Property

Public Property OrderBy() As String
Get
    Return _OrderBy
End Get
Set(ByVal Value As String)
    _OrderBy = Value
End Set
End Property
#End Region
```

The Click events for the various buttons on the form do the important tasks, as shown in
Listing 9.18.

LISTING 9.18   Event Code for the EasySearch Class

```
#Region " My event code "
Private Sub cmdCancel_Click( _
 ByVal sender As System.Object, ByVal e As System.EventArgs) _
 Handles cmdCancel.Click
    KeyValue = ""
```

LISTING 9.18   Continued

```
      Hide()
End Sub

Private Sub cmdSelect_Click( _
 ByVal sender As System.Object, ByVal e As System.EventArgs) _
 Handles cmdSelect.Click
      Dim Recno As Integer = Me.BindingContext(ds, TableName).Position
      KeyValue = ds.Tables(0).Rows(Recno).Item(KeyField).ToString
      Hide()
End Sub

Private Sub cmdShowMatches_Click( _
 ByVal sender As System.Object, ByVal e As System.EventArgs) _
 Handles cmdShowMatches.Click

Dim Cmd As String = ""
Dim Delim As String = ""
Dim Ctrl As Control
Dim Fuzzy As String = ""

If chkFuzzy.Checked Then
      Fuzzy = "%"
Else
      Fuzzy = ""
End If
For Each Ctrl In Controls
      If Ctrl.Name.ToUpper.StartsWith("SEARCH") Then
          If Ctrl.Text.Length > 0 Then
              Cmd = Cmd + " AND " + Ctrl.Name.Substring(6) ;
                  + " LIKE '" + Fuzzy + Ctrl.Text + "%'"
          End If
      End If
Next

If Cmd.Length > 0 Then Cmd = " WHERE " + Cmd.Substring(5)
If FieldNames.Length = 0 Then FieldNames = "*"
Cmd = "SELECT " + FieldNames + " FROM " + TableName + Cmd
If OrderBy <> "" Then Cmd = Cmd + " ORDER BY " + OrderBy

Dim cn As New SqlClient.SqlConnection
cn.ConnectionString = ConnStr
cn.Open()
```

LISTING 9.18   Continued

```vb
Dim cm As New SqlClient.SqlCommand
cm.CommandText = Cmd
cm.Connection = cn

ds.Clear()

Dim da As New SqlClient.SqlDataAdapter
da.SelectCommand = cm
da.Fill(ds, TableName)
If ds.Tables(TableName).Rows.Count = 0 Then
    MsgBox("No records match", MsgBoxStyle.Exclamation, Application.ProductName)
    cmdSelect.Enabled = False
Else
    DataGrid1.DataSource = ds
    DataGrid1.DataMember = TableName
    cmdSelect.Enabled = True
End If

End Sub
```

The `Load` event loads the connection string from `Config.txt` and enables the input controls, as shown in Listing 9.19.

LISTING 9.19   Load Event Code for the `EasySearch` Class

```vb
Private Sub EasySearch_Load( _
  ByVal sender As System.Object, ByVal e As System.EventArgs) _
  Handles MyBase.Load
    Dim DataAccess As New DataAccessManager.DataAccessFileManager
    DataAccess.ReadFile()
    ConnStr = DataAccess.ConnString
    DataAccess = Nothing
    Dim Ctrl As Control
    For Each Ctrl In Controls
        If Ctrl.Name.ToUpper.StartsWith("SEARCH") Then Ctrl.Enabled = True
    Next
End Sub

#End Region
```

Using the Visual Basic .NET EasySearch Form Class

To use this class, add it to a project and compile it. Note that the DLL that's produced is
..\EasySearch\bin\EasySearch.dll. You'll need that when you create an inherited form
based on it.

First, however, be aware that the EasySearch form is meant to be used by a form that is
itself inherited from the BaseForm class. Create a Windows Forms project with a single
form, change its name to MainForm both internally and externally, and add a MainMenu
control. I usually right-click on the MainMenu control and select Edit Names, then enter
names that match the pad's location within the menu. In Figure 9.10, I've entered a mini-
malist menu of four entries, then selected Edit Names to show the names that I've chosen.

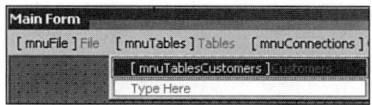

FIGURE 9.10   A MainMenu control.

I created a form called frmCustomers based on the BaseForm class developed in Chapter 4,
"A Visual Basic .NET Framework for SQL Server." To do this, I right-clicked on the project,
then selected Add, Inherited Form from the resulting context menu. The dialog that
appears first asks for a name for the new form (frmCustomers), then asks from where to
inherit the form.

This is where you select Browse and browse to the location of BaseForm.dll, probably
back in the Chapter4\BaseForm\bin directory. If you add the BaseForm project to the
current solution, the selection will appear on page 3 of the dialog under Project
Components. However, BaseForm doesn't have to be part of the current project in order to
inherit from it.

Add a few fields from the Customer table to the form, using the controls that we
subclassed (MyText, MyCombo, and so on). Recall that the names of these controls should be
a three-character prefix (for example, txt, cmb) plus the name of the corresponding table
column.

Similarly, create an inherited form called FindCustomers inherited from EasySearch.dll.
Add two MyText controls and a MyCombo control to the top of the form, labeling them
Customer Name, Contact Name, and Region/State. Name the controls SEARCHCompanyName,
SEARCHContactName, and SEARCHRegion, so that the class code can find them. Be sure to fill
in the TableName, KeyField, and FieldNames properties.

Finally, go back to the frmCustomers and add this one line of code anywhere in the Load
event:

```
SearchForm = New findCustomers
```

Until I come up with a better way to specify this than through Reflection, this gives the most bang for the buck.

Compile and run the application. Inherited forms are a great way to build prototypes for clients. If you decide to add a feature or tweak the way that all of your forms of a given type work, you simply change the class code, and the change is reflected in all of your screens.

What Can Possibly Go Wrong?

While I was building this application, I kept getting an error that I couldn't seem to pin down in the code. I finally stopped to read the error message, and it said something about not having referenced a key field. I had specified `CustomerID`, so I was mystified. Then I went into the Enterprise Manager and looked at the table; I had neglected to set `CustomerID` as the Primary Key for the Customers table.

This highlights one of the peculiarities of our profession. The data is part of the solution. If you don't normalize tables, you make the programming job all that much harder. Similarly, SQL and Visual Studio .NET use the existence of a Primary Key field to make their job easier. In particular, the `CommandBuilder` object uses the Primary Key to construct the UPDATE command. Without the key, it doesn't know where to go. So make sure that your tables are spot on before you start programming against them.

Building Self-Populating Controls

One type of control that's of interest is a combo box that can be placed on a form and will automatically load its data. It can be filtered or unfiltered, but this is a reasonable place to describe how to build them.

Add the code shown in Listing 9.20 to `MyFormControls.vb`.

LISTING 9.20   The `SelfLoadingCombo` Class

```
Public Class MySelfLoadingCombo
    Inherits MyCombo
    Private _TableName As String = ""
    Private _DisplayName As String = ""
    Private _ValueName As String = ""

Public Property TableName() As String
    Get
        Return _TableName
    End Get
    Set(ByVal Value As String)
        _TableName = Value
    End Set
End Property
```

LISTING 9.20 Continued

```vb
Public Property DisplayName() As String
    Get
        Return _DisplayName
    End Get
    Set(ByVal Value As String)
        _DisplayName = Value
    End Set
End Property

Public Property ValueName() As String
    Get
        Return _ValueName
    End Get
    Set(ByVal Value As String)
        _ValueName = Value
    End Set
End Property

Public Sub New()
    MyBase.New()
    Enabled = True
    Tag = "SELFLOADING"
End Sub

Public Sub LoadData()
If TableName <> "" Then
    Dim DataAccess As New DataAccessManager.DataAccessFileManager
    DataAccess.ReadFile()
    Dim ConnStr As String
    ConnStr = DataAccess.ConnString
    DataAccess = Nothing
    Dim SqlCmd As String = "SELECT " + ValueName + "," + DisplayName _
                        + " FROM " + TableName + " ORDER BY " + DisplayName
    Dim sda As New SqlClient.SqlDataAdapter(SqlCmd, ConnStr)
    Dim dt As New DataTable
    sda.Fill(dt)
    DataSource = dt
    DisplayMember = DisplayName
    ValueMember = ValueName
    sda = Nothing
End If
```

LISTING 9.20   Continued

```
End Sub

End Class
```

Recompile the MyControls project, then open the toolbox, right-click and select Add/Remove controls, and add the control to the toolbox.

However, this doesn't run the `LoadData` method. And simply adding a call to the method in the `New()` constructor doesn't do a thing. However, you can use that little `TAG` entry (`Tag = "SELFLOADING"`) to add some code to your form template that makes sure the combo is loaded (see Listing 9.21).

LISTING 9.21   Load Event Code for a Form Containing Self-Loading Controls

```
Dim Ctrl As Control
For Each Ctrl In Controls
    If Ctrl.Tag.ToUpper = "SELFLOADING" Then
        Dim o As Object
        o = Ctrl
        o.LoadData()
    End If
Next
```

How does this tie in with filtering? It allows us to build a combo box that's always desirable when dealing with search screens. We can build a list on the fly of the unique values of any column in a searchable table, by making a small change in the base class:

```
Dim SqlCmd As String = "SELECT DISTINCT " + DisplayName + "," + DisplayName _
                       + " FROM " + TableName + " ORDER BY " + DisplayName
```

Give this class a different name, and you can build a search form that lets users pick from only the values that have been entered into a free-form field in a table.

Cleaning Up Mistakes in Legacy Data to Improve Searching

Speaking of free-form fields, how do you search in fields in which users have been allowed to type in whatever they wanted? I've done a search of a table of 50,000 entries, and found the name of the city in which the client was located (Las Vegas) spelled *75 different ways*. Suffice it to say that you might never find some of your customers if you inherit data that looks like this.

I know that you'd never allow such a thing to happen. However, if you inherit a legacy system, like maybe one that you're migrating to Visual Basic .NET and SQL Server, you might want to clean up the data.

When you inherit a legacy application, you often inherit a lot of really, really sloppy data. As a result, your combo boxes don't work, your reports don't make sense, and you look sloppy, too. Here's a tool to fix the data and your reputation.

Migrating Legacy FoxPro Data to SQL Server

I've done a lot of work upgrading FoxPro 2.6 applications to Visual FoxPro 6.0, Visual FoxPro 7.0, and now Visual FoxPro 8.0. It's a tribute to Visual FoxPro that these applications have been working so well for so long. It's also a tribute to the patience of the users that they've been able to get so much use out of software that wasn't always very well-designed.

After moving a user's data to new tables and building some very nice screens, I noticed that the combo boxes were coming up blank on many records. I thought I had entered all of the values the users said were valid, but because values that aren't in the combo box's list don't appear in the control, something wasn't right. I used

```
SELECT DISTINCT (FieldName) FROM (TableName)
```

to look at the data, and the variety was amazing. I found the name of their city spelled 47 different ways.

This poses real problems. You can't count how many people live in Hoboken, Hooboken, Hobooken, Haboken, and so forth and get an accurate count of what you think you're getting. And it just looks sloppy.

I love FoxPro, but DBFs have problems, especially on Local Area Networks. The main problem lies not in DBFs themselves, but in the CDX files used to enable Rushmore and thereby gain enormous performance enhancements. When you USE a DBF in a networked environment, FoxPro brings part of the index to the workstation. When your user makes a change, it's propagated to all other users. The result can be a slow FoxPro application. (It's hard for me to use the words slow and FoxPro in the same sentence, but it's true.) There goes our competitive advantage.

Add to that the result when you pull the plug on your workstation. The result is often a corrupted index file. And worst of all, the solution is to rebuild the index, an operation that requires exclusive use of the table. So all users have to be logged off—including the ones who went to lunch without exiting the application. You get a lot of exercise walking around the building looking for the offending user. Often it's someone who feels put upon by the requests to close the application, which means that you're soon dealing with a hostile user, a real nightmare for a technician who's also a salesman.

In addition, anyone can get into a DBF and see what's there. In some applications, security is a real issue. DBFs have no protection from prying eyes (there's Cryptor; but I've implemented it, and although it's a technical marvel, implementation is at best a mixed blessing). There's one white paper on implementing security in FoxPro systems published on the Microsoft site, and I wrote it. However, as proud as I am of the techniques described therein, the paper deals with data access issues, but does nothing to solve this fundamental problem. SQL solves it straight out of the box.

Finally, users have actually sued me when they lost their data and didn't back it up. Worse, they won the lawsuit, because the judge was as ignorant as my client. With SQL Server, backup is a one-word command; and what's even better, it's their command.

I don't write applications based on DBFs any more, for all of these reasons. So part of every legacy application rewrite is the migration of their data to SQL Server or to MSDE. And in every single one, I find that the data is a mess. So while migrating it to SQL, I normalize the tables and clean up the data. It's just part of the job.

Migrating to SQL

The migration to SQL requires adding CREATE CURSOR commands to the LOAD event of all of my screens. The actual acquisition of the data and sending back the changes is relatively easy. So's the CREATE CURSOR step. In fact, the migration of a DBF-based application to MSDE or SQL Server is not difficult. The only hard part is cleaning up the data.

Cleaning Up the Data

I built a screen to help the users clean up their data. After all, they have a pretty good idea of what the correct spelling should be. And in the case of client names, they're probably the only people who could clean up their data. Besides, it was a fixed-price job.

The screen appears in Figure 9.11. This screen, called AUDITOR.SCX, runs in the directory where the user's data files are located. I have a list (TabList.DBF) of the tables that need to be audited because there are other tables in the directory that aren't user data.

When I pick a table, the program loads its fields and data types into an array and displays them in the Field picker (see Listing 9.22).

LISTING 9.22   Loading the FieldPicker Combo Box with Text Column Names

```
IF EMPTY ( THIS.Value )
   RETURN
ENDIF
WITH THISFORM.Combo2
.Clear
SELECT 10
USE ( THIS.Value ) ALIAS TheTable
FOR I = 1 TO FCOUNT()
        .AddListItem ( FIELD(I) )
```

LISTING 9.22   Continued

```
       nRow = .NewItemID
       Fld  = FIELD(I)
       .AddListItem ( TYPE (Fld), nRow, 2 )
ENDFOR
USE
ENDWITH
```

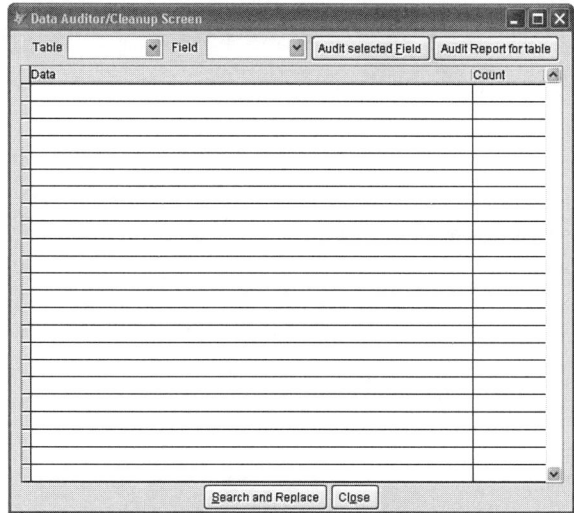

FIGURE 9.11   The Auditor screen.

I can audit other fields, and their names do appear in the list, but generally the character fields are the targets. After I've picked a character field, I can click on Audit Selected Field to see the counts of disparate values found in the named field (see Listing 9.23).

LISTING 9.23   Displaying Unique Values and Counts for the Selected Field

```
IF EMPTY ( THISFORM.Combo2.Value )
   RETURN
ENDIF
IF USED ( "THETABLE" )
   USE IN  THETABLE
ENDIF
SELECT Viewer
ZAP
WITH THISFORM
Cmd = [SELECT TRANSFORM() ;
```

LISTING 9.23   Continued

```
              + .Combo2.Value + [) AS Data, COUNT(*) AS Kount FROM ] ;
              + .Combo1.Value ;
              + [ GROUP BY ] + .Combo2.Value ;
              + [ ORDER BY 2 DESC INTO CURSOR C1]
&Cmd
SELECT Viewer
ZAP
APPEND FROM DBF( [C1] )
GO TOP
USE IN C1
USE IN ALLTRIM( ( .Combo1.Value ) )
.Grid1.Refresh
ENDWITH
```

If the user highlights a value that appears to be incorrect, clicking on the Search and Replace button will bring up a screen that permits specifying the replacement value:

```
DO FORM FixData  WITH   ;
  THISFORM.Combo1.Value,;
  THISFORM.Combo2.Value,;
  Viewer.Data,        ;
  THISFORM.DataType   ;
 TO Result

IF Result = [Changed]
   THISFORM.cmdGo.Click
ENDIF
```

Figure 9.12 shows the screen.

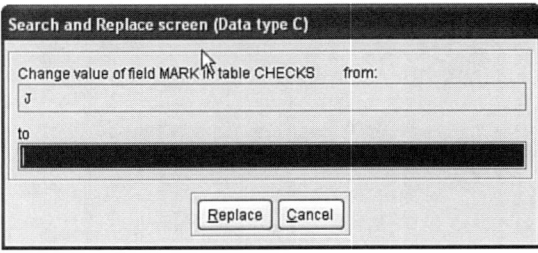

FIGURE 9.12   The Search and Replace screen.

This screen displays the highlighted value and lets the user enter a replacement value. The replacement value is used immediately to replace the offending string with the correct one in the selected field.

The table name, field name, bad value, and replacement value are all written to a table called CHANGES.DBF. This table will be used later to do a batch replacement. Why this is necessary will be made clear shortly.

The program can also print out a summary of all values found in all fields. The program to do this is called AUDIT.PRG (see Listing 9.24). It uses a single SQL SELECT statement to prepare the data, then prints a report of its findings. The SQL statement is simply

```
SELECT (Fld), COUNT(*) FROM (Table) GROUP BY (Fld) ORDER BY 2 DESC
```

It's the quickest way to see what's wrong with your data. It's also interesting to see how many Smiths, for example, are found in a file of a few thousand names. And it's remarkably fast. Nothing runs like a Fox <g>.

LISTING 9.24   The AUDIT Program

```
* Program-ID..: AUDIT.PRG

PARAMETERS Tbl

IF PCOUNT() = 0
   Tbl = GETFILE ( [DBF], [Table name?] )
   IF EMPTY ( Tbl )
         RETURN
   ENDIF
   Tbl = JUSTSTEM( Tbl )
  ELSE
   Tbl = JUSTSTEM( Tbl )
   IF NOT FILE ( Tbl + [.DBF] )
      MESSAGEBOX( [No such table: ] + Tbl + [.DBF], 64,
➥_Visual FoxPro.Caption, 3000 )
      RETURN
   ENDIF
ENDIF

SET TEXTMERGE TO &Tbl..Txt ON NOSHOW
SELECT 10
USE ( Tbl ) ALIAS ( Tbl )
FOR I = 1 TO FCOUNT()
      Fld = FIELD(I)
      IF TYPE ( Fld ) = [M]
```

9

LISTING 9.24   Continued

```
        LOOP
     ENDIF
     \<<REPLICATE([-],10) + [ ] + Fld + REPLICATE([-],10) + CHR(13)>>
     Cmd = [SELECT ]     + Fld + [, COUNT(*) AS Kount FROM ] + Tbl ;
              + [ GROUP BY ] + Fld + [ ORDER BY 2 DESC INTO CURSOR C1]
     &Cmd
     GO TOP
     IF RECCOUNT() > 75
        \<<TRANSFORM(RECCOUNT()) + [ records found - first 5 follow:]>>
           SCAN WHILE RECNO() <= 5
           \<<PADL(TRANSFORM(EVALUATE(Fld)),50) + [ - ] + TRANSFORM(Kount)>>
           ENDSCAN
      ELSE
           SCAN
           \<<PADL(TRANSFORM(EVALUATE(Fld)),50) + [ - ] + TRANSFORM(Kount)>>
           ENDSCAN
     ENDIF
     USE
     SELECT ( Tbl )
ENDFOR
SET TEXTMERGE TO

CREATE CURSOR Reporter ( Line Char(132) )
APPEND FROM &Tbl..Txt SDF
REPORT FORM Reporter PREVIEW
USE
```

REPORTER.FRX is a two-column report (see Figure 9.13) with a table called LINE.DBF, which contains a single field called LINE 80 characters wide. It's just right for dumping the contents of an ASCII file into a report and printing it "two-up."

Running the Data Conversion in Batch Mode

I often build replacement software while the old version is still in use. So every day, more data is being added to the system. And every day, if errors were being allowed into the tables in the past, more erroneous data is being added to those tables. Also, I'm not taking responsibility for the old system—just the new one. So the data that I'm cleaning up is for the new system, not the old one. On conversion day, I've already run the data cleanup dozens of times, so I know it's going to work.

Running the Conversion

The program shown in Listing 9.25 converts the data on the Big Day. I don't want anything to go wrong on that day, so I run this program pretty much every day during the development process. If the users are creating new problems during data entry, this will point them out and give me time to fix them before we go live. And you'd be surprised the number of little details that no one spots until they've been looking at the converted data for a month and finally see a problem. So this ongoing conversion test gives everyone time to think clearly and get it right.

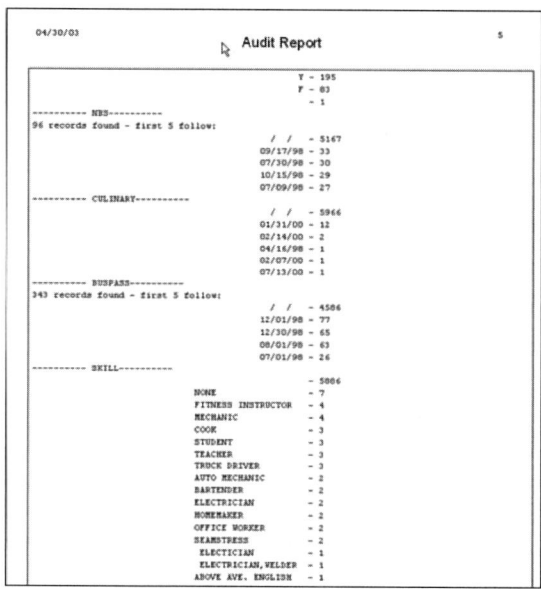

FIGURE 9.13   The Audit Report.

The program, which is shown in Listing 9.25, does more than simply apply the corrections in CHANGES.DBF, so I'll provide a running commentary.

LISTING 9.25   The Convert Program That Actually Cleans the Data

```
* Program-ID....: Convert.prg
* Purpose.......: Convert application tables to new format
*                 and apply cleanup changes
CLOSE ALL
SET EXCLUSIVE ON
SET STRICTDATE TO 0
SET STATUS BAR ON
SET TALK ON
SET SAFETY OFF
SET CPDIALOG OFF

StartTime = TIME()
```

LISTING 9.25   Continued

```
ON KEY LABEL F1 *                    && I don't want to see Help, even accidentally

PUBLIC oDataMgr
oDataMgr = NEWOBJECT ( "DATAMGR", "DATAMGR.PRG" )
USE CONTROL
FOR I = 1 TO FCOUNT()
        Fld = FIELD(I)
        PUBLIC &Fld
ENDFOR
SCATTER MEMVAR
USE
ConnString = ALLTRIM(m.ConnString)

PUBLIC Supervisor AS Integer
PUBLIC DataAccess AS String

Supervisor = 1
DataAccess = [SQL]

=SQLDISCONNECT(0)

ConnString = [Driver={SQLServer};Server=(local);Database=Data;Uid=Les;Pwd=lp;]
oDataMgr.Handle = SQLStringConnect ( m.ConnString )
IF oDataMgr.Handle < 1
   MessageBox ( [Couldn't connect to SQL Server] + CHR(13)           ;
        + [Connection string: ] + CHR(13) + ConnString,              ;
           64, _Visual FoxPro.Caption )
ENDIF

lcPath = [\\UserComputer\c-drive\userdir\]
lcPath = GETDIR([Where are the original tables?])
IF EMPTY ( lcPath )
   RETURN
ENDIF

lcPath = ADDBS ( lcPath )
_Visual FoxPro.Caption = [Migrating data from ] + lcPath

*(1) Remove all entries for the highest key value in each table
SELECT 99
USE KEYFIELDS
ZAP
```

LISTING 9.25 Continued

```
*(2) Remove duplicate cases and create MOVES.DBF
MakeMove()        && detailed after this listing; moves Add1, Add2 to MOVES table
CLOSE TABLES


*(3) Remote duplicate MEMBERS
USE MEMBERS
ZAP
APPEND FROM ( lcPath + [MEMBER] )

GO TOP
REPLACE ALL KEYVALUE WITH RECNO()
GO BOTTOM
INSERT INTO KEYFIELDS VALUES ( [MEMBERS], MEMBERS.KeyValue )

SELECT                    ;
  AlienNum,               ;
  COUNT(*)                  ;
  FROM MEMBERS            ;
 HAVING COUNT(*) > 1       ;
 GROUP BY AlienNum       ;
 ORDER BY 2 DESC            ;
 INTO ARRAY laAliens

FOR I = 1 TO ALEN ( laAliens, 1 )
        IF VAL(laAliens(I,1)) = 0
           LOOP
        ENDIF
        GO TOP
        LOCATE FOR AlienNum = laAliens(I,1)
        FOR J = 1 TO laAliens(I,2) - 1
                CONTINUE
                DELETE NEXT 1
        ENDFOR
ENDFOR

*(4) Convert tables that added a KeyValue field:
USE TABLIST
FldList = [,MOVES, STATUS,]

SCAN FOR ( [,] + TRIM(TableName) + [,] ) $ FldList

        lcFile = TRIM(TableName)
```

LISTING 9.25 Continued

```
        SELECT 0
        USE ( lcFile )
* Don't change MOVES, which is a new file.
        IF lcFile <> [MOVES]
                ZAP
                lcOldFile = lcFile
* Deal with tables whose names have changed here
                IF lcFile    = [CONTACTS]
                    lcOldFile = [CONTACT]
                ENDIF
                APPEND FROM ( lcPath + lcOldFile )
                GO TOP
        ENDIF
* Add key field values here
        REPLACE ALL KEYVALUE WITH RECNO()
        GO BOTTOM
        INSERT INTO KEYFIELDS VALUES ( lcFile, EVAL(lcFile + [.KeyValue]) )
        GO TOP
* Change all check number to seven digits with leading zeroes
        IF ( [,] + lcFile + [,] ) $ [CHECKS,PAYMENTS,]
                REPLACE ALL CHECKNUM WITH TRANSFORM ( VAL(CHECKNUM),[@L #######])
        ENDIF
        USE
ENDSCAN

USE ESL
REPLACE ALL ;
 Class              WITH STRTRAN(Class,'AM','am'),          ;
 Class              WITH STRTRAN(Class,'PM','pm')
USE

*(6) Convert tables with no KeyValue field that changed their name
USE GRANTS
ZAP
APPEND FROM ( lcPath + [GRANT] )
USE

*(7) Convert tables that required a field name change
*    because a reserved word was used as a field name.
USE ALLOCATE
ZAP
SELECT 0
```

LISTING 9.25   Continued

```
CREATE CURSOR CarryAll ( Allocate Char(4), CALLOCATE Char(4), Descrip Char(25) )
APPEND FROM x && ( lcPath +    [Allocate] )
REPLACE ALL CALLOCATE WITH ALLOCATE
SELECT ALLOCATE
APPEND FROM DBF([CarryAll])
USE IN CarryAll
USE

*(8) Convert all other tables
USE TABLIST
ExcludedList = [,NOTES,MOVES,MEMBERS,CASES,ESL,PREMIUM,STATUS,UPGRADE,]

SCAN FOR NOT ( [,] + ALLTRIM(UPPER(TableName)) + [,] ) $ ExcludedList
        *****************************************
        SELECT 0
        USE ( ALLTRIM(TABLIST.TableName) )
        ZAP
        APPEND FROM ( lcPath + ALLTRIM(TABLIST.TableName) )
        USE
        SELECT TABLIST
ENDSCAN
USE

*(9) Fix all data previously corrected by users
SELECT DISTINCT TableName      ;
  FROM CHANGES                      ;
  INTO ARRAY FixerUppers      ;
 ORDER BY TableName

FOR EACH TName IN FixerUppers
        SELECT * FROM Changes WHERE TableName = TName INTO ARRAY laChanges
        SELECT 5
        USE ( TName )
        FOR I = 1 TO  ALEN ( laChanges, 1 )
                F = laChanges[I,2]
                D = VARTYPE  ( F )
                O = ALLTRIM(laChanges[I,3])
                N = ALLTRIM(laChanges[I,4])
                L = []
                R = []
                Cmd = [UPDATE ] + TName + [ SET ] + F + [ = ] + L + N + R ;
```

LISTING 9.25   Continued

```
                        + [ WHERE ] + F + [ = ] + L + O + R
                WAIT WINDOW Cmd NOWAIT
                &Cmd
        ENDFOR
ENDFOR
WAIT CLEAR

*(10) Upload all tables to SQL
USE TABLIST
ExcludedList = [,NOTES,FOXUSER,TABLIST,USERS,]
SCAN FOR NOT ( [,] + UPPER(TableName) + [,] ) $ ExcludedList
        Tbl = ALLTRIM(TABLIST.TableName)
        oDataMgr.CloseIfOpen  ( Tbl )
        oDataMgr.MakeSQLTable ( Tbl )
        oDataMgr.Upload       ( Tbl )
ENDSCAN

oDataMgr.CloseIfOpen  ( [KeyFields] )
oDataMgr.MakeSQLTable ( [KeyFields] )
oDataMgr.Upload                ( [KeyFields] )

*(11) Create the CLASSES table, which doesn't exist in the old system
SQLEXEC ( oDataMgr.Handle, [DROP TABLE    CLASSES] )
SQLEXEC ( oDataMgr.Handle, [CREATE TABLE CLASSES ( Class Character(15) )] )

SQLEXEC ( oDataMgr.Handle, [INSERT INTO CLASSES VALUES ( 'Computer Lab   ')])
SQLEXEC ( oDataMgr.Handle, [INSERT INTO CLASSES VALUES ( 'Level I 11:15am')])
SQLEXEC ( oDataMgr.Handle, [INSERT INTO CLASSES VALUES ( 'Level II 6:00pm')])

* Final data cleanup...
Cmd = [DELETE MEMBERS WHERE CaseNum NOT IN ( SELECT CaseNum FROM Cases )]
lr = SQLEXEC ( oDataMgr.Handle, Cmd )
IF lr < 0
   MESSAGEBOX( [SQL command failed:] + CHR(13) + Cmd, 16 )
ENDIF

* Remove records containing fatal data errors that old system couldn't delete
Cmd = [DELETE MEMBERS WHERE KeyValue IN ( 123,6110,6189 )]
lr = SQLEXEC ( oDataMgr.Handle, Cmd )
```

LISTING 9.25   Continued

```
IF lr < 0
   MESSAGEBOX( [SQL command failed:] + CHR(13) + Cmd, 16 )
ENDIF


* Create a key value for records with a blank value in a required field
* in cases where we couldn't reconstruct the correct value,
* but don't want to discard the data
Cmd = [UPDATE MEMBERS SET AlienNum = LEFT(Last,4) + LEFT(First,4) ;
     WHERE KeyValue IN ( 314,323,1141)]
lr = SQLEXEC ( oDataMgr.Handle, Cmd )
IF lr < 0
   MESSAGEBOX( [SQL command failed:] + CHR(13) + Cmd, 16 )
ENDIF


* Throw away orphans if all attempts to build a relation have failed:
Cmd = [DELETE ESL WHERE aliennum NOT IN ( SELECT aliennum FROM members )]
lr = SQLEXEC ( oDataMgr.Handle, Cmd )
IF lr < 0
   MESSAGEBOX( [SQL command failed:] + CHR(13) + Cmd, 16 )
ENDIF


* Remove ESL records with blank case numbers
Cmd = [DELETE ESL WHERE casenum = '             ']
lr = SQLEXEC ( oDataMgr.Handle, Cmd )
IF lr < 0
   MESSAGEBOX( [SQL command failed:] + CHR(13) + Cmd, 16 )
ENDIF


WAIT CLEAR
Took = [ Took ] + TRANSFORM ( TIME() - StartTime ) + [ seconds]

MESSAGEBOX( [Ta-da!] + CHR(13) + Took, 64, [Done] )

SET TALK OFF
SET STATUS BAR OFF
```

Data Cleanup: Conclusion

Data cleanup is an essential part of the migration of a legacy application to its new home. If you use a tool like the conversion program presented in this section, the data starts out its new life on the right foot.

Getting Filtered Data Across the Web

The advent of simple ways of retrieving data across the Internet has changed what we're able to offer clients. It's easy to build Web services in either Visual FoxPro or Visual Basic .NET, and it's easy to return and display the data.

Building a Parameterized Web Service in Visual FoxPro

Visual FoxPro 7 made it possible to build XML Web Services; Visual FoxPro 8 made it easy. In this example, I'll use only Visual FoxPro 8 or above.

Create a project in Visual FoxPro 8 called XMLProject. Add one program called XMLClass.PRG. Type the contents of Listing 9.26 into that program.

LISTING 9.26   Three Methods for a Simple XML Web Service

```
DEFINE CLASS XMLCLASS AS CUSTOM OLEPUBLIC

FUNCTION CustsByRegion (pRegion AS String ) AS String
S = "Driver={SQL Server};Server=(local);Database=Pinter;UID=sa;PWD=;"
Handle = SQLSTRINGCONNECT(  s )
FieldList = "CustomerID,CompanyName,ContactName,Region"
Cmd = "SELECT " + FieldList + " FROM CUSTOMERS WHERE Region='" + pRegion + "'"
SQLEXEC( Handle, Cmd )
CURSORTOXML("SQLResult","lcXML")
USE
SQLDISCONNECT(0)
RETURN lcXML
ENDFUNC


FUNCTION CustsByCountry (pCountry AS String ) AS String
S = "Driver={SQL Server};Server=(local);Database=Pinter;UID=sa;PWD=;"
Handle = SQLSTRINGCONNECT(  S )
FieldList = "CustomerID,CompanyName,ContactName,Country"
Cmd = "SELECT " + FieldList + " FROM CUSTOMERS WHERE Country='" + pCountry + "'"
SQLEXEC( Handle, Cmd )
CURSORTOXML("SQLResult","lcXML")
USE
SQLDISCONNECT(0)
RETURN lcXML
ENDFUNC


FUNCTION OneCustomer (pCustID AS String ) AS String
S = "Driver={SQL Server};Server=(local);Database=Pinter;UID=sa;PWD=;"
Handle = SQLSTRINGCONNECT(  S )
```

LISTING 9.26   Continued

```
SQLEXEC( Handle, "SELECT * FROM CUSTOMERS WHERE CustomerID='" + pCustID + "'" )
CURSORTOXML("SQLResult","lcXML")
USE
SQLDISCONNECT(0)
RETURN lcXML
ENDFUNC


ENDDEFINE
```

This Web service published three methods: One lists customers by state, another lists customers by country, and the last one returns a customer record. You can present users with a filtered list either by Country or by Region, give them a grid or list box to pick a customer, then return the customer.

Compile this using the Build Multi-Threaded DLL option. If you're compiling again after having tried to use the DLL, it will be in the clutches of IIS, and you'll need to open a DOS window and type

```
IISRESET
```

to stop and restart IIS, thus freeing your DLL.

Using the DLL

Now, if you type

```
! regsvr32 "XMLProject.dll"
```

you'll be able to test this by typing

```
o = CREATEOBJECT ( "XMLProject.XMLClass" )
? o.CustsByRegion("SP")
```

However, that's not how it's supposed to be used. Open the Task Pane and change to the XML Web Services page if it's not already visible. Select Publish Your XML Web Service. Click on the Advanced command button and make sure that only the three functions that you coded are checked. Pick a new virtual directory (which will be created under C:\InetPub\WWWRoot\), and name it FoxWebServices. Click Generate, and you should see the dialog shown in Figure 9.14.

WSDL stands for Web Services Discovery Language, and describes what's available. It's used by IntelliSense to tell prospective users what your Web service can do.

Next, select Register an XML Web Service, and fill in the name of the generated WSDL file, as shown in Figure 9.15.

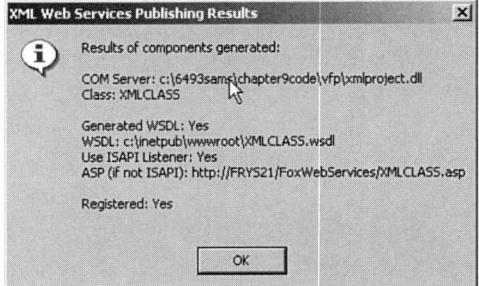

FIGURE 9.14   Generating the WSDL file.

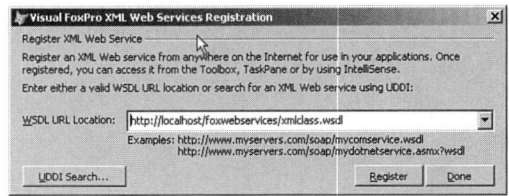

FIGURE 9.15   Registering the WSDL file and the Web service.

The message "Finished generating IntelliSense script" tells you that it worked. Now the fun begins.

Using the Web Service in a Smart Client Application

Now, type **MODIFY COMMAND WSTest**. Open the toolbox and open up the My XML Web Services tab. Click on your Web service entry (and there will probably be two identical entries, so pick either one), hold the left mouse button down, and drag and drop in the open code window. Voilà, you've got code (see Listing 9.27)!

LISTING 9.27   Quick Demonstration of the Use of the Web Service DLL

```
LOCAL loXMLCLASS AS "XML Web Service"
* LOCAL loXMLCLASS AS "MSSOAP.SoapClient30"
* Do not remove or alter following line.
* It is used to support IntelliSense for your XML Web service.

* Note that in our example, I've used Name instead of XMLCLASS,
* the name in our example; the string "Name" will be replaced
* with your class name in the generated code.
* Visual FoxProWSDef__:loName=http://localhost/WSDIR/Name.wsdl,Name,NameSoapPort
LOCAL loException, lcErrorMsg, loWSHandler
TRY
```

LISTING 9.27 Continued

```
    loWSHandler = NEWOBJECT("WSHandler",;
     IIF(VERSION(2)=0,"",HOME()+"FFC\")+"_ws3client.vcx")
    loXMLCLASS = loWSHandler.SetupClient( ;
      "http://FRYS21/FoxWebServices/XMLCLASS.wsdl", "XMLCLASS", ;
        "XMLCLASSSoapPort")
  * Call your XML Web service here.  ex: leResult = loXMLCLASS.SomeMethod()

CATCH TO loException
    lcErrorMsg="Error: "+TRANSFORM(loException.Errorno)+" - "+loException.Message
    DO CASE
    CASE VARTYPE(loXMLCLASS)#"O"
        * Handle SOAP error connecting to web service
    CASE !EMPTY(loXMLCLASS.FaultCode)
        * Handle SOAP error calling method
        lcErrorMsg=lcErrorMsg+CHR(13)+loXMLCLASS.Detail
    OTHERWISE
        * Handle other error
    ENDCASE
    * Use for debugging purposes
    MESSAGEBOX(lcErrorMsg)
FINALLY
ENDTRY
```

There's only one small task left. About nine lines down in the code, you'll see a comment that says "Call your XML Web Service here" or words to that effect. Start a new line, then type the name of the proxy object, loXMLClass, and press the period key (see Figure 9.16).

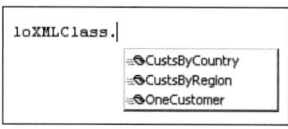

FIGURE 9.16   IntelliSense shows you the available methods.

This lets you know what's available. If you select one of the three choices, just include the proper parameter in parentheses and quotes (because the Customer key is a character field), and you'll get immediate gratification. For example, I included the following code. Try it and see what it does:

```
lcXML = loXMLClass.CustsByCountry("Argentina")
XMLTOCURSOR(lcXML,"TEST")
BROWSE
```

The really remarkable thing about this is that the parameter of the call to the `loWSHandler.SetupClient()` is LOCALHOST here because you're working on your own computer. But if you register this DLL on your Web server, you can change LOCALHOST to `64.86.225.101` and get the data from your Web server.

Note that Internet Information Server is an essential part of this conversation.

Building a Parameterized Web Service in Visual Basic .NET

Open the Visual Studio .NET IDE and create a new VISUAL BASIC .NET project. Select File, New, ASP.NET Web Service. Name it `FilteredWebServices`. Double-click on the design surface to reveal the example code, and type in the code from Listing 9.28.

LISTING 9.28   XML Web Service Code in Visual Basic .NET

```
<WebMethod()> Public Function CustsByRegion( _
  ByVal pRegion As String) As dsByRegion
    Dim data As New dsByRegion
    SqlDataAdapter1.SelectCommand.Parameters(0).Value = pRegion
    SqlDataAdapter1.Fill(data)
    Return data
End Function


<WebMethod()> Public Function CustsByCountry( _
  ByVal pCountry As String) As dsByCountry
    Dim data As New dsByCountry
    SqlDataAdapter2.SelectCommand.Parameters(0).Value = pCountry
    SqlDataAdapter2.Fill(data)
    Return data
End Function


<WebMethod()> Public Function OneCust(ByVal pCustID As String) As dsOne
    Dim data As New dsOne
    SqlDataAdapter3.SelectCommand.Parameters(0).Value = pCustID
    SqlDataAdapter3.Fill(data)
    Return data
End Function
```

I also returned to the design surface and pressed F4, then changed the service name from `Service1` to `MyWebService`. Then I pressed F5, and I got the screen shown in Figure 9.17.

The form I've designed to use these Web services is shown in Figure 9.18. I used a Fixed3D border, CenterScreen StartPosition, Max and Min buttons turned off, and I docked the DataGrid at the bottom of the screen.

FIGURE 9.17   Automatically generated test bed for the Web service.

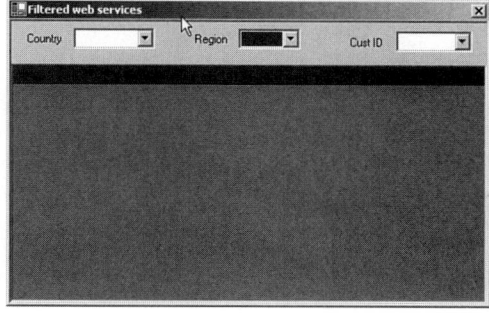

FIGURE 9.18   The form to use the Web service.

The combo boxes are named according to their contents. Although you would probably write code to populate them in a production application, I've done so manually here for simplicity. I opened the SQL Query Analyzer, pressed Ctrl+T to change to Text mode, did a SELECT DISTINCT of each of the fields I needed (Country, Region, and CustomerID) ordered by the selected field in each case, and then pasted them into the Items collection of the respective combo box.

I created a different dataset for each of the three methods available from my Web service. I probably should be changing the SQLDataAdapter names to make it easier to sync up data adapters and datasets, but it's not that hard to keep three methods straight (see Listing 9.29).

LISTING 9.29   Using My XML Web Service Code in a Visual Basic .NET Form

```
Private Sub CountryCombo_SelectedIndexChanged( _
  ByVal sender As System.Object, _
  ByVal e As System.EventArgs) _
Handles CountryCombo.SelectedIndexChanged
    Dim ws As New UseMyWebServices.localhost.MyWebService
    DsByCountry1.Clear()
    DsByCountry1.Merge(ws.CustsByCountry(CountryCombo.Text))
```

LISTING 9.29   Continued

```
    DataGrid1.DataSource = DsByCountry1.Customers
End Sub

Private Sub RegionCombo_SelectedIndexChanged( _
  ByVal sender As System.Object, _
  ByVal e As System.EventArgs) _
Handles RegionCombo.SelectedIndexChanged
    Dim ws As New UseMyWebServices.localhost.MyWebService
    DsByRegion1.Clear()
    DsByRegion1.Merge(ws.CustsByRegion(RegionCombo.Text))
    DataGrid1.DataSource = DsByRegion1.Customers
End Sub

Private Sub CustCombo_SelectedIndexChanged( _
  ByVal sender As System.Object, _
  ByVal e As System.EventArgs) _
Handles CustCombo.SelectedIndexChanged
    Dim ws As New UseMyWebServices.localhost.MyWebService
    DsOne1.Clear()
    DsOne1.Merge(ws.OneCust(CustCombo.Text))
    DataGrid1.DataSource = DsOne1.Customers
End Sub
```

I've put the code in the SelectedIndexChanged event of the respective combo boxes, so as you scroll through the list of available choices, the grid is populated with the matching records.

Summary

I hope you're convinced of the approximate equivalence of Visual FoxPro and Visual Basic .NET for filtering and searching tables. I was initially put off by the strangeness of .NET's data access, but after you do a few queries, you'll know how to get where you want to go today.

In the next chapter we'll see how similar FoxPro and Visual Basic .NET are when it comes to designing and using reports. You've probably been hearing about Crystal Reports for years, and you've probably heard some horror stories. The latest version of Crystal is much, much improved. I believe you'll not only like it, but even be impressed by both its power and its ease of use.

Reporting

In many applications, reporting is the most important feature requested by users. Input is data; reports are information. The ability to sort, filter, and present views of your data can determine whether or not an application is worth building.

FoxPro has long provided an excellent reporting tool. It's easy to use and is completely integrated into the FoxPro IDE. Although it has often been regarded as primitive, clever users have found ways to extend it beyond anything the designers could have imagined.

In the Visual Basic, SQL Server, and other developer communities, reporting has always been done with the help of a third-party tool called Crystal Reports. In Visual Studio .NET, Crystal Decisions has managed to bundle their product with Microsoft while retaining joint marketing rights, a trick that I tried 22 years ago. I wish them well.

Reporting in Visual FoxPro

Reporting in FoxPro is deceptively simple. The FoxPro Report Designer is activated when you type

```
MODIFY REPORT (ReportName)
```

or

```
CREATE REPORT (ReportName)
```

either of which does the same thing. To print a report, you use the command

```
REPORT FORM (name) TO PRINT PREVIEW NOCONSOLE
```

The "official" syntax is shown in Listing 10.1.

LISTING 10.1   The Report Form Command Syntax

```
REPORT FORM FileName1 ¦ ? [ENVIRONMENT] [Scope]
   [FOR lExpression1]
   [WHILE lExpression2]
   [HEADING cHeadingText]
   [NOCONSOLE]
   [NOOPTIMIZE]
   [PLAIN]
   [RANGE nStartPage [, nEndPage]]
   [PREVIEW [[IN] WINDOW WindowName ¦ IN SCREEN] [NOWAIT]]
   [TO PRINTER [PROMPT] ¦ TO FILE FileName2 [ASCII]]
   [NAME ObjectName]
   [SUMMARY]
```

Some of this syntax is obsolete or leads to bad practices. For example, FOR is a filter expression, and WHILE stops the report when the WHILE condition is no longer satisfied. Neither one is the right way to decide how to include data in a report; rather, ordering and filtering should be done before you call the report.

Similarly, the PLAIN and TO FILE *TextFileName* ASCII options that produce a primitive text output have long since been replaced with Excel, HTML, and other types of output; the RANGE command is a command-line device to print only certain pages as a hands-on filtering mechanism. So if you're using most of these options, there's probably a better way to do what you want to do. And if your report is running so slowly that you feel the need to include the NOOPTIMIZE keyword, there's definitely a better way to fix what's wrong.

However, three of these keywords are used almost every time:

- The PREVIEW keyword lets users see their report before they decide to print it.

- NOCONSOLE prevents the output from being duplicated on the _Screen surface, which is never desirable.

- The SUMMARY option prints only the summary lines; detail lines are suppressed.

So you have one command to create the report and one command to display the report. However, don't let the apparent simplicity fool you. For many years, FoxPro has provided an easy and cost-effective way to report on tabular data.

Internal Details

Reports in Visual FoxPro are stored in a pair of tables with the extensions .frx and .frt. Because they're FoxPro tables, you can make changes programmatically or manually to the contents of these tables. Hacking system tables has its risks, but the open nature of FoxPro has long endeared it to developers. So take the usual precautions to back files up first, and you can do just about anything you can imagine. That's the basis of `GenRepoX.PRG`, the amazing pre- and post-processing utility written by Markus Egger. We'll look at GenRepoX later in this chapter to give you some ideas. After that, it's up to you.

Report Layout in FoxPro

The FoxPro Report Designer has bands for Title, Summary, Header, Footer, Group, and Detail bands. To design a report, you create a basic layout, then add bands and grouping to correspond to data ordering or indexing that will be done before the report is run. The resulting interaction between the report file, the FoxPro report processor, and the data is what gives you the end product.

Type **CREATE REPORT SimpleReport1** to open a new, blank report, as shown in Figure 10.1.

FIGURE 10.1   The FoxPro Report Designer.

When you create a new report, the only bands that are added are Page Header, Detail, and Page Footer. A Report menu pad is added to the FoxPro system menu _MSYSMENU, making additional options available. In FoxPro 8 and higher, a Printer Environment selection has been added. Also, two toolbars—Report Controls and Report Designer—are available and meaningful in the context of the Report Designer.

Page Setup

The default page layout of a FoxPro report is a single column, the width of which is determined by the characteristics of your default printer. If you select File, Page Setup from the FoxPro IDE menu to open the Page Setup dialog, you can easily change a report to print two or more columns, or change column margins. You can also tweak printer settings and change the target device if you're building a report that must run on a particular printer, for example, a dot matrix printer with NCR (no carbon required) multicopy forms.

Within the Page Setup dialog, you can also select Print Setup and specify a Landscape report if your printers permit it. If you print more than one column of records, you can choose either **row-major** (left to right, top to bottom) or **column-major** (top to bottom, left to right) order.

10

Printer Problems

FoxPro embeds the name of the printer that you choose, or the name of your default printer if you don't choose one, into your reports. This leads to one of the most annoying problems with the FoxPro Report Designer. When FoxPro builds a report, it embeds the name of the printer for which it was designed into the report layout. The report may not print properly if a user tries to print on a different printer.

As a result, it's necessary to "hack" the report file and remove printer-specific information before delivering it to users. To do that, type `USE` (*Reportname*`.FRX`) and `BROWSE` the file. Then use Ctrl+PgDn to open the `Expr` field in the first line (the one that has `ObjType = 1` and `ObjCode = 53`) and remove the contents of the `Expr`, `Tag1`, and `Tag2` fields. If you open and save the file again in the Report Designer, you'll have to do this again. You might want to write a little program to open all of your reports and search for this problem.

If you want to allow users to specify a printer, use `SET PRINTER TO SYS(1037)`. If you know the exact printer name, you can use `SET PRINTER TO NAME :Name"`. If it's a network printer name, include the `\\ComputerName\` prefix.

Finally, `SET(:PRINTER")` returns "On" or "Off"; `SET(:PRINTER",2)` returns the default Windows printer; and `SET(:PRINTER",3)` returns the default FoxPro printer selected using the SYS(1037) dialog. You don't have to use the command `SET PRINTER ON` to call the `REPORT FORM` (*name*) `TO PRINT NOCONSOLE` command.

Report Controls

In each band, you can drag and drop any of the report controls onto the report. Controls include labels, fields, lines, rectangles, rounded rectangles, and ActiveX (OLE) bound controls (for example, pictures).

Labels are for displaying text that never changes. Report controls are a little different from form controls. On a form, you might use a label to display values of variables—a report title or a group heading. In the Report Designer, labels are constants. When you put one on a form, you immediately start typing the label's caption. You can't assign it a different caption later.

Fields, on the other hand, can be assigned a value either automatically via binding or programmatically. Fields can be bound to columns in a cursor, to memory variables created before you run the report, or to report variables created and managed by processes within the report.

We usually think of fields as the contents of our tables. But a field in a FoxPro report is any data that might change. For example, the date and time of the report can be included by adding fields with `DATE()` and `TIME()` as the contents. (You can restrict the length of these two items best if you use a monospaced font—for example, Courier New—and set their lengths to 10 and 5 characters respectively. You also have to control the nature of the Date display using the `SET CENTURY` and `SET DATE` commands in your code.) Internal variables such as `_PAGENO` (the current report page) can also be used on your report pages.

Fields don't have to have a tablename as a prefix, and in fact, it's often the last thing you want to do. In the past, FoxPro developers had the habit of dragging tables into the Data Environment, then onto the screen. This stored a hard-coded reference to both the table-name and the field name into the ControlSource of each field. If you subsequently wanted to use a SQL SELECT statement to get the data, you'd have to go through the properties of the fields in the report and remove "FieldName." from each ControlSource. Because multiple field properties are stored in a single memo field, there's no really easy way to automate this process. It's easier to avoid the problem than to have to repair it later. So I recommend making a habit of entering expressions without a table prefix.

Lines and rectangles can be used to make a plain report look crisp and professional. If you put a line above each group heading, groups are set off in a way that's clearer for users to understand. Rectangles that start in the Page Header band and end in the Page Footer band, or rectangles that start in the Group Header band and end in the Group Footer band, automatically expand to include detail bands within them. Nested rectangles for pages and groups, separated by three or four pixels, create a very professional look with little effort.

OLE bound controls tied to images in a database provide a very simple mechanism for displaying pictures in reports. Given the widespread availability of inexpensive color print-ers, you can easily print beautiful color catalog pages, until you realize that you're being taken to the cleaners by the toner vendors.

Title and Summary Bands

From the Report menu, select the Title/Summary pad. You'll see the dialog shown in Figure 10.2.

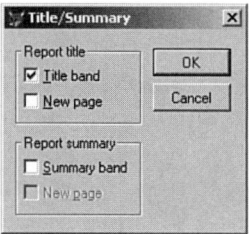

FIGURE 10.2   The Title and Summary band dialog.

The Title and Summary bands, if requested, print only once. As you might surmise, the Title page prints at the beginning of the report, and the Summary prints at the end of the report. The only option for these bands concerns your decision to print title and summary pages as separate pages. If they're small, they probably shouldn't be printed separately. They'll just appear at the top of the first page and the bottom of the last page, respec-tively.

Data Grouping

If you select Data Grouping from the Report menu pad or from the Report Controls toolbar, you can take advantage of any data sorting that might have been done as of the moment the report runs. If you select Data Grouping, you'll see the dialog shown in Figure 10.3.

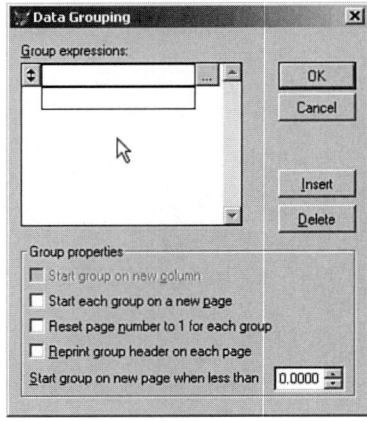

FIGURE 10.3   The Data Grouping dialog.

The Expression Builder browser (the command button with the three little dots on it) opens up a dialog (see Figure 10.4) that lets you type in an expression, which can be a function, a user-defined variable or function, a system variable, or the name of a field from any table that has been opened in the report's Data Environment. Tables that are merely open at design time are not shown in the Fields list.

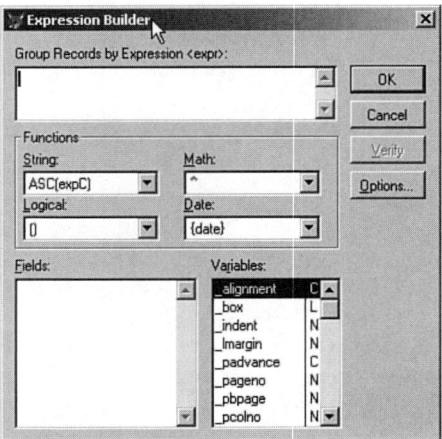

FIGURE 10.4   The Expression Builder dialog.

Notice that the Fields list is empty in this dialog. The Fields list only shows tables that are opened in the report's Data Environment. So if you use a SQL SELECT statement in the BeforeOpenTables event of the report's Data Environment, you'll have to remember, manually enter, and correctly spell all field names. The FoxPro Report Writer has notoriously obscure error messages where misspelled field and variable names are concerned.

Group expressions are presumably fields in the report data that have been used in ORDER BY expressions, or are part of the active index tag(s). Generally, these expressions mirror the current order. For example, if your SELECT statement was

```
SELECT * FROM Customers ORDER BY Country, Region, CompanyName INTO CURSOR C1
```

your GROUP BY expressions would be Country and Region. (The third ORDER BY expression just alphabetizes the data in the report.) You'd have two group bands, a major group based on Country, and a minor group based on Region (state).

However, you can include the name of a report variable that's calculated as the records are processed. For example, suppose you add a variable called StateName and define it using the following expression:

```
IIF ( Country="USA", Region, "" )
```

If you then use StateName as the Group By variable, you won't see any breakdown of departments, provinces, or other subnational groupings except for customers in the United States.

Variables

Report variables in FoxPro are special creatures that are calculated by FoxPro. They are created during the report and still persist after the report has run unless you check the Release After Report check box in the Report Designer. They can be initialized from any source—system variables, memory variables declared before the report is run, values calculated by counting records, a constant, or a calculation based on the contents of a particular field. They can be automatically reset to zero or blank when a given GROUP BY expression changes; thus they're useful in including subtotals and counts in reports. They can also perform other calculations or call user-defined functions (UDFs) to do just about anything.

A Simple Example

For the examples in this chapter, we'll use the tables from the FoxPro sample data directory (HOME() + "Samples\Data\"). Because reports are read-only, you can issue the command

```
SET PATH TO ( HOME() + "Samples\Data\" )
```

to ensure that your programs can find the tables when you USE them.

Start FoxPro and open the Customers table. Type this command:

```
CREATE REPORT Customer FROM Customers COLUMN
```

This creates a primitive report with one column for each field in the current alias until the fields no longer fit. Obviously, it's a pretty primitive approach, but it works. You can specify which fields to include by adding FIELDS *FieldList* where FieldList contains field names to include, separated by commas, after the word COLUMN. Here's an example:

```
CREATE REPORT Customer FROM Customers COLUMN ;
 FIELDS Cust_ID, Company, Contact, Title, Address, City, Region, PostalCode
```

But what you get needs some serious cosmetic attention before it can be used, as can be deduced from the resulting report shown in Figure 10.5.

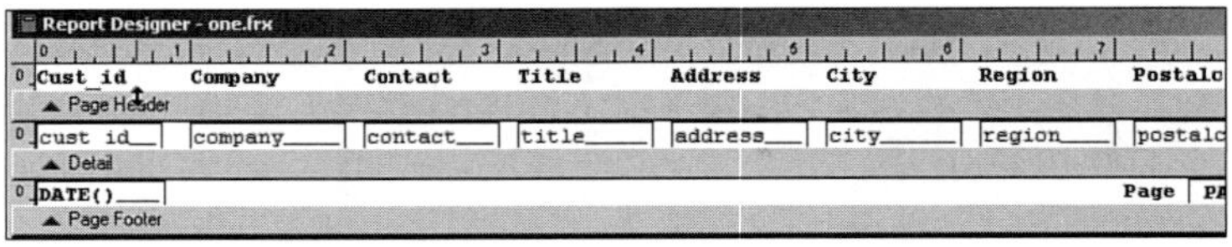

FIGURE 10.5   A QuickReport based on the Customers table.

Adding Groupings

Usually you would create groupings of tabular data that render it more meaningful. For example, let's say you create a cursor of Orders for last month, including customer name from the Customers table, from the Solutions\Data directory in the Samples\Data subdirectory of the FoxPro home directory (see Listing 10.2).

LISTING 10.2   Selecting Data for SimpleReport1.FRX

```
SELECT ORDERS.*, Customer.* ;
FROM ORDERS, CUSTOMER ;
WHERE ORDERS.Cust_ID = CUSTOMER.Cust_ID ;
ORDER BY ;
  Customer.Country, ;
  Customer.Region, ;
  Customer.Company ;
 INTO CURSOR C1
```

This orders the contents of the cursor alphabetically by country, then alphabetically by region (state) within each country, and finally alphabetically by company name within each region. It would probably be interesting to the user to know how many customers there are per state and per country. By creating data groupings corresponding to the ORDER BY clause, you cause the report to include an inner group header and group footer for each region within each country, and a group header and group footer pair outside of the Region group header/footer for the Country group.

Calculated Expressions

Because grouping often goes hand in hand with calculating counts and totals, when you put a field on a summary line, you can right-click on it, select Properties, and select a calculation to be performed on the field that is the object of the control. For example, if the rightmost column in each detail row is the order_amt for each order, it would be useful to copy and paste the order_amt field to the group footer line, placing the copy exactly below the original order_amt field. Open the Calculate Field dialog shown in Figure 10.6 to select the calculation type (sum, count, and so on). Note that you need to reset totals to zero whenever the grouping variable changes in value.

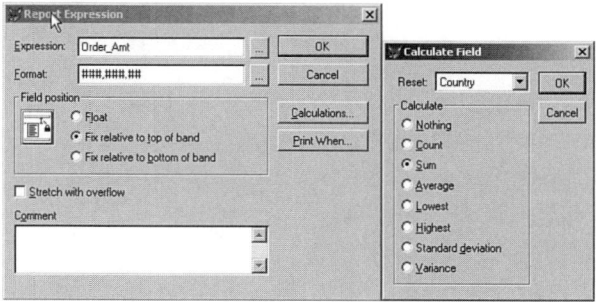

FIGURE 10.6   Calculated data group band fields.

The report layout shown in Figure 10.7 shows a report with subtotals by region within country.

If you select View, Preview from the menu, you can see that the report indeed produces the expected report, shown in Figure 10.8. However, it's not a very attractive report.

To improve this report, we can draw column divider lines and add rectangles around the entire report. Draw the rectangle so that it starts on the Page Header and ends on the Page Footer. In Figure 10.9, I've added a pair of nested rectangles from the page header to the page footer (don't forget to leave a half inch or so at the bottom of the page), and a horizontal line under the text in each of the groupings and under the Grand Total line. I also added a vertical line between the top and bottom of the inner rectangle to separate the two data columns.

The result (see Figure 10.10) is a much more attractive report. And it's not just a cosmetic improvement after all; I find it a lot easier to read.

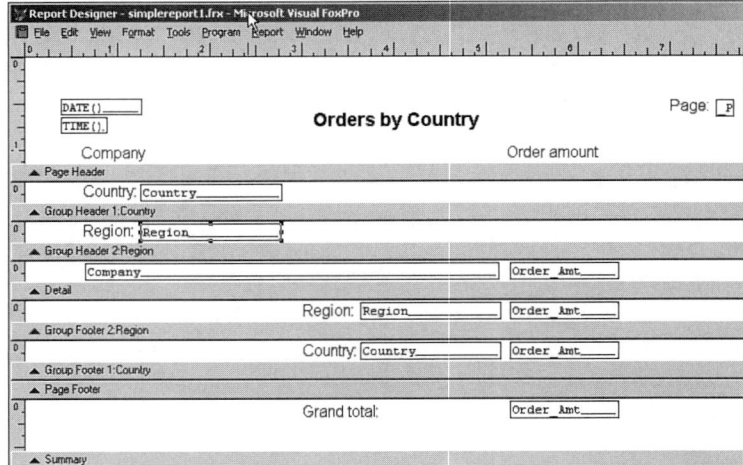

FIGURE 10.7   The Customer Orders report grouped by region within country seen in the Report Designer.

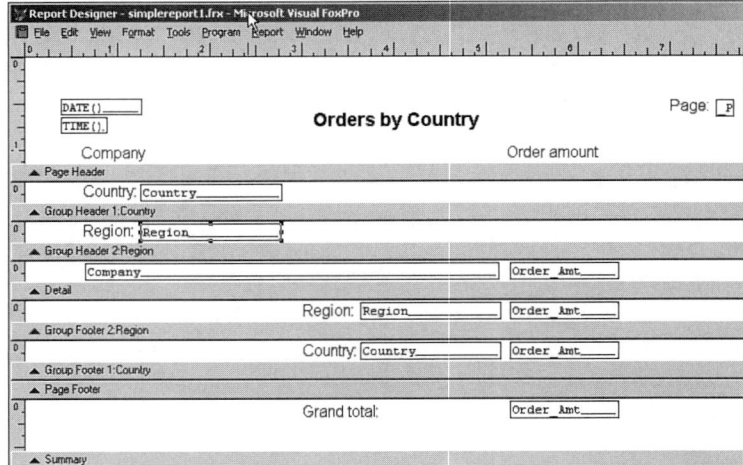

FIGURE 10.8   The Customer Orders report grouped by region within country.

Grouping Using a Report Variable

You're not limited to counts and totals: If you want to display the highest order amount by country, you declare a variable called MaxOrder, set it to MAX(Orders.Order_Amt), and include it on the Group Summary band for Country. The option to reset when Country changes completes the calculation.

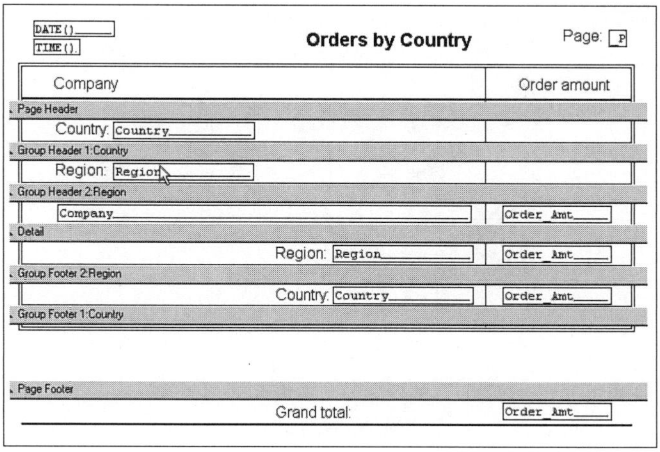

FIGURE 10.9 Making cosmetic improvements to the customer orders report in the Report Designer.

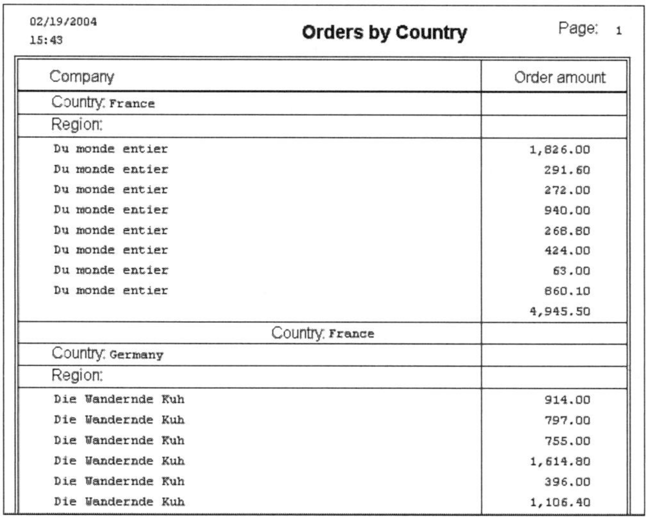

FIGURE 10.10 Previewing the customer orders report after modifications.

I also want to do something about the region totals for countries that don't have a region entry. When we added a second group using the Region variable, we got a group header and a group summary line that has the name of the region. However, the data appears not to have region entries in most cases. Double-click on each of the entries on the Region Header and Region Footer to open the dialog shown in Figure 10.11.

Click on the Print When button, enter `Region <> ""` in the text box with the heading Print Only When Expression Is True, and check the Remove Line If Blank check box. If you do this for all of the fields and labels in the group header and footer for Region, it will indeed disappear except for countries that have named regions.

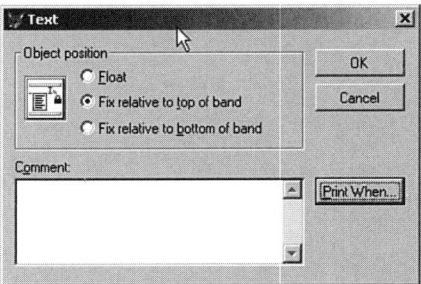

FIGURE 10.11   Suppressing printing of region headers and footers when region is blank.

What if you want to show states only for the United States? If you create a new report variable named, say, m.StateName, specify that it's a blank string if Country is not "USA", and do the group based on it, you won't get a subtotal for countries other than the USA because m.StateName will be blank. The Group Summary line only fires if the value changes.

Report Filtering

The Init event of the Data Environment of a FoxPro report form is the place where data for the report has to be acquired. If at the end of the Init event, your user can't connect to the data source, can't find the tables, or for whatever reason doesn't want to continue, the statement RETURN .F. will cancel the reporting process without printing. For this reason, the Init event of the report's Data Environment is a good place to put a report filtering mechanism.

To do this, build a form like the one shown in Figure 10.12.

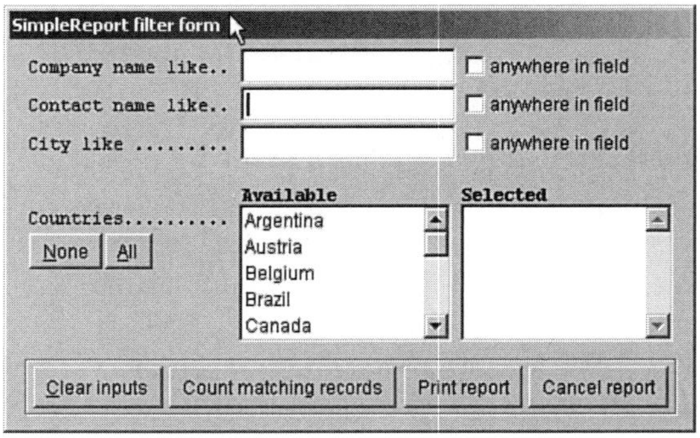

FIGURE 10.12   A report filter form.

The form must be a modal form so that it can return a value. Listing 10.3 shows the Click event code for the Show Matching Records button.

LISTING 10.3   The Click Event Code for the cmdShowMatches Button

```
WITH THISFORM
Exp1 = []
Exp2 = []
Exp3 = []
Exp4 = []
IF NOT EMPTY ( .Text1.Value )
   FuzzyFilter = IIF ( .Check1.Value = 1, [%],[] )
   Exp1 = [ AND LOWER(Company) LIKE '] + FuzzyFilter ;
          + ALLTRIM(LOWER(.Text1.Value)) + [%']
ENDIF
IF NOT EMPTY ( .Text2.Value )
   FuzzyFilter = IIF ( .Check2.Value = 1, [%],[] )
   Exp2 = [ AND LOWER(Contact) LIKE '] + FuzzyFilter ;
          + ALLTRIM(LOWER(.Text2.Value)) + [%']
ENDIF
IF NOT EMPTY ( .Text3.Value )
   FuzzyFilter = IIF ( .Check3.Value = 1, [%],[] )
   Exp3 = [ AND LOWER(City)    LIKE '] + FuzzyFilter ;
          + ALLTRIM(LOWER(.Text3.Value)) + [%']
ENDIF
IF .List2.ListCount <> 0
   Exp4  = [ AND Country IN ( ]
   FOR I = 1 TO .List2.ListCount
       Exp4 = Exp4 + ['] + ALLTRIM(.List2.List(I)) + [',]
   ENDFOR
   Exp4 = LEFT(Exp4,LEN(Exp4)-1) + [)]
ENDIF
Expr = Exp1 + Exp2 + Exp3 + Exp4
Cmd = [SELECT Company, Order_Amt, Region, Country ] ;
    + [ FROM Customer, Orders ]                    ;
    + [ WHERE Customer.Cust_ID = Orders.Cust_ID ]  ;
    + Expr                                         ;
    + [ ORDER BY Country, Region, Company INTO CURSOR C1]
*!*    MESSAGEBOX( Cmd, 64, [Report filter] )
*!*    Uncomment to see the SELECT statement
&Cmd        && This executes the SELECT statement!
ENDWITH
MESSAGEBOX( TRANSFORM ( ;
  RECCOUNT() ) + [ records will be included in the report], ;
  64, [Report filter], 2000 )
```

10

The `cmdSelect` and `cmdCancel` buttons simply determine what value the form returns. In either event, the `Unload` event is going to close the two tables used in the query and return the `ReturnValue`. Listing 10.4 shows the code.

LISTING 10.4   The Rest of the Filter Form Code

```
cmdSelect::Click

WITH THISFORM
.ReturnValue = .T.
.Release
ENDWITH


cmdCancel::Click

WITH THISFORM
.ReturnValue = .F.
.Release
ENDWITH


Unload event code:

IF USED ( [Orders] )
   USE IN  Orders
ENDIF
IF USED ( [Customer] )
   USE IN  Customer
ENDIF
RETURN THISFORM.ReturnValue
```

Build and Execute a `SELECT` Statement in the `Init` Event of the Report's Data Environment

Back in the report, all you have to do is put the code from Listing 10.5 in the form's `Init` code.

LISTING 10.5   The Init Event of the Report's Data Environment

```
DO FORM CustFilter TO Ok
IF NOT Ok
   IF USED ( [ReportCursor] )
      USE IN  ReportCursor
   ENDIF
```

LISTING 10.5 Continued

```
    RETURN .F.
ENDIF
```

Simple, isn't it?

Using a Report Filter with SQL Server

An additional benefit of using a report filter form of this type is that with only a few changes you can use this form with SQL Server or with other data sources. I won't show you any of the others because I've only heard of a very few cases of people using the FoxPro report writer with data sources other than DBFs and SQL Server. But for SQL Server, it's very easy. All you have to do is make the changes shown in Listing 10.6 to the `cmdSelect::Click` event code.

LISTING 10.6 SQL Server Version of the `Click` Event Code for the `cmdShowMatches` Button

```
WITH THISFORM
Exp1 = []
Exp2 = []
Exp3 = []
Exp4 = []
IF NOT EMPTY ( .Text1.Value )
   FuzzyFilter = IIF ( .Check1.Value = 1, [%],[] )
   Exp1 = [ AND LOWER(Company) LIKE '] + FuzzyFilter ;
          + ALLTRIM(LOWER(.Text1.Value)) + [%']
ENDIF
IF NOT EMPTY ( .Text2.Value )
   FuzzyFilter = IIF ( .Check2.Value = 1, [%],[] )
   Exp2 = [ AND LOWER(Contact) LIKE '] + FuzzyFilter ;
          + ALLTRIM(LOWER(.Text2.Value)) + [%']
ENDIF
IF NOT EMPTY ( .Text3.Value )
   FuzzyFilter = IIF ( .Check3.Value = 1, [%],[] )
   Exp3 = [ AND LOWER(City)    LIKE '] + FuzzyFilter ;
          + ALLTRIM(LOWER(.Text3.Value)) + [%']
ENDIF
IF .List2.ListCount <> 0
   Exp4  = [ AND Country IN ( ]
   FOR I = 1 TO .List2.ListCount
       Exp4 = Exp4 + ['] + ALLTRIM(.List2.List(I)) + [',]
   ENDFOR
   Exp4 = LEFT(Exp4,LEN(Exp4)-1) + [)]
ENDIF
```

LISTING 10.6   Continued

```
Expr = Exp1 + Exp2 + Exp3 + Exp4
Cmd = [SELECT Company, Order_Amt, Region, Country ] ;
    + [ FROM Customer, Orders ]                         ;
    + [ WHERE Customer.Cust_ID = Orders.Cust_ID ]    ;
    + Expr                                             ;
    + [ ORDER BY Country, Region, Company]    && Removed this: [ INTO CURSOR C1]
*!*    MESSAGEBOX( Cmd, 64, [Report filter] )
*!*    Uncomment to see the SELECT statement
lr = SQLExec ( THISFORM.Handle, Cmd, [C1] )
*!*    Use this instead of the INTO CURSOR clause
IF lr < 0
   MessageBox ( "SQL Server command failed" )
 ELSE
   MESSAGEBOX( TRANSFORM ( ;
     RECCOUNT() ) + [ records will be included in the report], ;
     64, [Report filter], 2000 )
ENDWITH
```

I had to remove the INTO CURSOR C1 clause because the name of the cursor is supplied as the optional third parameter in the SQLExec() function call.

You could build the form so that it could be used with either SQL or with FoxPro tables, using a form property to determine whether to use macro expansion to run the FoxPro SELECT command, or to call the SQLExec() function. In either case, the result is a cursor, and REPORT FORM *doesn't care*.

There is one other consideration when you work with SQL Server. It's not uncommon to include a date, or a range of dates, in a report filter form. In FoxPro, the date delimiters are braces, like this:

```
ldDate = {03/15/2004}
```

In SQL, dates are delimited with single quotes. So if your filter form includes a pair of date fields, the logic for building an expression based on them would have to delimit the resulting date strings with single quotes instead of with braces.

Finally, the only delimiter allowed for strings in SQL is the single quote. So your expressions must use single quotes to delimit strings. Because of this, if your users type in expressions that contain a single quote, for example, "Frank's Franks", you have to replace the single quote in their entry with either a pair of single quotes or a replacement character. And because you don't know when they might do this, you have to do so every time. CHR(146) is a passable substitute for the offending CHR(39):

```
Exp1 = [ AND LOWER(Company) LIKE '] + FuzzyFilter ;
    + CHRTRAN(ALLTRIM(LOWER(.Text1.Value)),['],CHR(146)) + [%']
```

Printing Tricks

A few of the things you can do with FoxPro reports are less than intuitive. For example, to print "Page 1 of NN," you actually have to run the report twice (see Listing 10.7). The trick is that _PageNo is a system variable; at the end of a report, it still contains the last page number printed. You can then refer to the saved variable in a field expression in your report.

LISTING 10.7   Counting Pages in Order to Include "Page I of N" in a Report Heading

```
nPages = 0
WAIT WINDOW 'Getting page count' NOWAIT
FName = SUBSTR(SYS(3),2,6) + ".txt"
REPORT FORM &ReportName NOCONSOLE TO FILE &FName
nPages = _PAGENO
ERASE (FName)
REPORT FORM &ReportName NOCONSOLE TO PRINTER PREVIEW
```

Generic Reporting

If you open SimpleReport1.frx with a USE statement and BROWSE it, you'll see lots of details, but nothing that's difficult. In fact, using your database container as metadata, you can allow users to build specifications for reports, then generate and execute FRX files just like this, without too much difficulty. In the November 2003 issue of *FoxPro Advisor* magazine, Mike Lewis published an article that shows one solution, thereby relieving me of the need to write said utility here. But if you have the need to provide users with the ability to design their own reports, the fact that the FRX file is a DBF makes it relatively easy to do.

The fact that FoxPro reports are just tables is what made this possible. It also made possible GenRepoX, a fabulous utility written by Markus Egger, which extends the FoxPro report-writing capability considerably.

GenRepoX was written based on the idea of GenScrnX, written by the amazing Ken Levy, head of the FoxPro team at Microsoft. I first met Ken when he was a long-haired teenager, amazing everyone at the early Fox Software conferences with his skill. Markus did a similarly amazing job with GenRepoX. You can download it from the EPS Software Web page, www.eps-software.com.

Reporting on the Internet

When you've designed a nice report, you might want to publish it on the Internet. If the report is one that seldom changes, it's ridiculously easy. Just publish the output of the report as HTML, put the resulting text files into a virtual directory, and send your users links to the filenames.

The Save as HTML feature in FoxPro is unusual. It actually runs the report. Try it using the report we just built with the filter page. In the command window, type **MODIFY REPORT**

10

SimpleReport1 and select File, Save as HTML from the FoxPro IDE menu. The filter page appears and asks you to select records, then publishes the results as an .htm file. But it's not the same as live reporting. Besides, if you open the file as text and look at it, it's way ugly. You can do better. You have the technology.

Listing 10.8 shows the code to build SimpleReport1 as a Web page that is written to a previously determined filename in a virtual directory.

LISTING 10.8   Building Web Pages as Reports

```
SET TALK OFF
SET CONFIRM ON
SET PATH TO ( HOME() + [Samples\data\] )

mCountry = INPUTBOX("Country to include?", ;
   "Leave blank to include all countries, ESC to cancel","")

IF LASTKEY() = 27
   RETURN
ENDIF

mCountry = PROPER( mCountry )

SELECT ;
  ORDERS.Order_Amt,                          ;
  Customer.Company,                      ;
  Customer.Region,                       ;
  Customer.Country                       ;
FROM ORDERS, CUSTOMER                 ;
WHERE ORDERS.Cust_ID = CUSTOMER.Cust_ID ;
AND Country = mCountry                   ;
ORDER BY                               ;
  Customer.Country,                        ;
  Customer.Region,                       ;
  Customer.Company                       ;
 INTO CURSOR C1

IF RECCOUNT() = 0
   MESSAGEBOX( "No records found for " + mCountry, 64, ;
   "No matching records found", 5000 )
   USE IN C1
   RETURN
ENDIF
```

LISTING 10.8 Continued

```
SET TEXTMERGE ON TO C:\inetpub\wwwroot\CustsByCountry.HTM NOSHOW

\<html><head><title>Customers by country</title></head>
\<body>
\<table>
\ <tr><td width="100">
\   <table><tr><td size="1"><<DTOC(DATE())  >></td></tr>
\          <tr><td size="1"><<LEFT(TIME(),5)>></td></tr>
\   </table>
\     <td width="600" size="4" align="center" valign="top">Orders by Country</td>
\     <td width="100" size="1" valign="top">Page 1</td>
\ </tr>
\<table>

LastRegion  = "X"
LastCountry = "X"

\<table>
SCAN

    IF Region <> LastRegion
       \<tr><td>Region: <<Region>></td></tr>
    ENDIF

    IF Country <> LastCountry
       \<tr><td>Country: <<Country>></td></tr>
    ENDIF

* Each row in the table is another small two-column table
    \<tr><td><table><tr><td width="80%"><<Company>></td>
    \                  <td width="20%" align="right">
    \\<<TRANSFORM(Order_Amt,"#,###,###.##")>></td>
    \              </tr>
    \          </table></td>
    \</tr>

    LastCountry = Country
    LastRegion  = Region

ENDSCAN
\</table>
```

LISTING 10.8   Continued

USE

SET TEXTMERGE TO

This is another easy way to build report pages for publication on the Internet, and it gives you additional control over formatting that you can't get with REPORT FORM and SAVE AS HTML.

This would be fine for relatively static information, like a company phone directory. However, it still doesn't do what you usually want to do, which is to format and send output directly to the Internet at the moment the user asks for it. That requires an Internet application. Internet applications have to know how to interact with Internet Information Server (IIS), and that's a little more involved. In the last chapter, we'll explore Internet database application development in more detail.

Exporting to a PDF

Probably the best way to publish a report on the Internet is to create an Adobe Acrobat PDF. PDF is the acronym for Portable Document Format. It was developed by Adobe and really does create portable documents that can be sent to another user and printed on whatever printer they have. It can also be previewed in the free Acrobat Reader. It's an excellent technology that solves many reporting problems. Unfortunately, the cost of a single workstation license is considered prohibitively high by many of my customers. As of this writing, several inexpensive alternatives have appeared. If your project budget permits, you should consider PDF output for some or all of your reports.

Crystal Reports in Visual FoxPro

You can also use Crystal Decisions' product, Crystal Reports, with FoxPro. Crystal Reports does a number of things that FoxPro's native report writer can't do, including

- A "real" zoom capability (any percentage of full size, up to 400%, in 1% increments)

- Data searching

- Summary to detail drill-down capability

- Subreports

- Hyperlinks

- Integrated graphing

- Exporting of the report to Excel, Word, RTF, HTML, or PDF

- Multiline header, detail, and footer bands

If any of these features are important, you can simply use Crystal Reports, which integrates perfectly with FoxPro. It costs about $500, which means that it will probably pay for itself the first day you use it. The runtime that will be needed by users of your application is royalty-free.

> **NOTE**
>
> The ability to include hyperlinks in your reports permits you to add a "drill-down" capability that enormously enhances summary-detail reporting. That feature alone may justify using Crystal Reports for any database application.

Reporting is a huge topic, and I've only scratched the surface. Cathy Pountney has written an excellent book on the subject (*The Visual FoxPro Report Writer*, ISBN 1-930919-25-5, www.Hentzenwerke.com).

Reporting in Visual Studio .NET

Crystal Reports is a third-party product licensed by Microsoft and provided as part of Visual Studio. A separate version (Version 9 as of this writing) is available from Crystal Decisions, and as you might imagine, it has features not included in the Visual Studio version. But the version that's included with Visual Studio has pretty amazing capabilities, and you may never need more than what comes right out of the box.

Building Your First Report with Visual Studio .NET

Crystal Reports provides two mechanisms for building reports. The Report control is the simpler technique. You drop it on a form, set a few values, and you're done. For more complex reports, the Crystal Report object gives you an almost unlimited range of possibilities.

Let's start with a simple report from the Customers table of the Northwind database. Start by creating a Windows application called SimpleReport1. In the code to accompany this book, it's in the Chapter10Code directory. Right-click on the project name in the Solution Explorer, choose Add, Add New Item from the context menu, and then select Crystal Report from the available choices. Call the report SimpleReport1.rpt and click on Open.

From the list of available templates, you'll begin to see the range of possible reports that you can build. The defaults, Use the Report Expert (wizard) and Standard, are fine for now. Click on OK to continue.

For the data source, select OLE DB(ADO), and then pick Microsoft OLE DB Provider for SQL Server. Next, fill in the Connection Information dialog with the server name (local), the user ID (sa), the password (blank), and the Database name (Northwind). (If you need to use a different UserID and password, use them here.) You don't need to change anything in the Advanced Information dialog that follows in most cases. Expand the tree view to show the table names and select Customers.

By this time, the Standard Report Expert dialog will look like Figure 10.13.

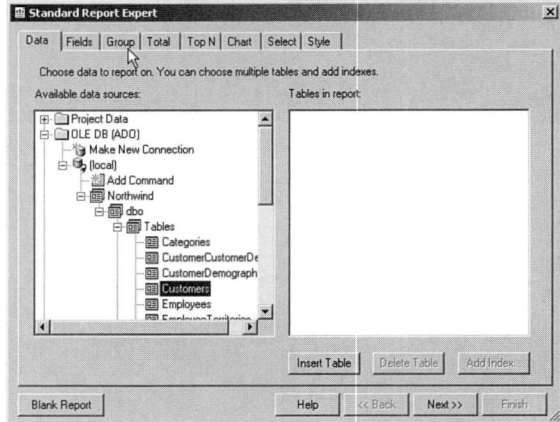

FIGURE 10.13   The Standard Report Expert dialog before you select a table.

Click Insert to select the Customers table, and you'll advance to the next dialog, which lets you pick the fields to be included in the report. Double-click on the CompanyName, ContactName, City, Country, and Phone fields to select them, as shown in Figure 10.14.

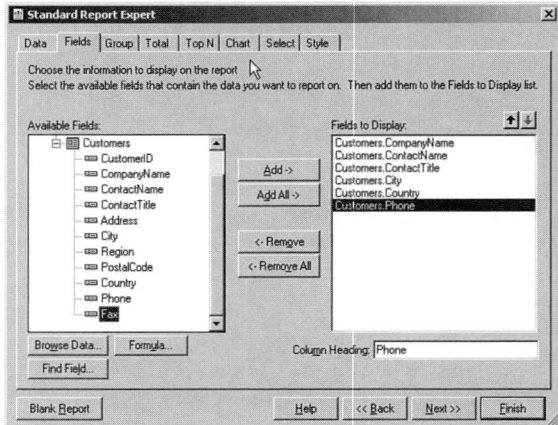

FIGURE 10.14   Selecting fields for your report.

Grouping is a desirable feature in many reports. It's very easy and shows off a few cool Crystal Reports features. Select Country as the Group By field as shown in Figure 10.15 and click Next.

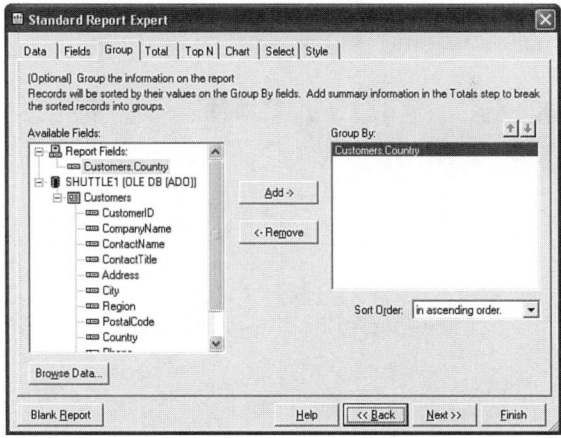

FIGURE 10.15   Selecting a Group By field.

In the subsequent Total (Summary Information) dialog, select Country from the Summarized Fields list, and pick Count from the Summary Type combo box. Don't select any option from the next dialog, which asks whether you want to sort by the subtotals you just selected. As tempting as it is, skip it for now.

Finally, you'll see that a graph has been created based on your selection of subtotals including counts. It's free, although you can suppress it if you want. Finally, when the dialog appears to name the report, enter "Customers by country" as the report title and click Finish.

The designer will display your report at this point, as seen in Figure 10.16.

The mechanism used to display this report is the `CrystalReportViewer`, and it needs to be hosted in a form. So, select a `CrystalReportViewer` from the Windows Forms toolbox (use Ctrl+Shift+X if it's not already visible) and drop it on the default form that was added to the project. Name it Viewer1, set its `Dock` property to `Fill`, and its `ReportSource` property to the name of the report you just created (browse to the name, or just type it in). Press F5 to run the app. Couldn't be simpler. The resulting report is partially shown in Figure 10.17.

If you use Ctrl+Alt+L to open the Solution Explorer and click on the View All Files icon, you'll see that below the `SimpleReport1.rpt` entry there is a `SimpleReport1.vb` class file. The `CrystalReportViewer` allows you to refer to this file, which is called a strongly typed report (because it's a class definition) in a way that's useful for building a generic report preview screen.

`PickAReport.vb` is such a form. It consists of a form, a `CrystalReportViewer` component docked at the bottom of the screen and leaving a half-inch or so at the top, and a combo box at the top of the form. In the Items collection, I've added two entries: "<Pick a report>" and "SimpleReport1". The second entry could also be "Customers by country with graph." The code for the combo box's `SelectedIndexChanged` event is coded with a reference to the class name, as shown in Listing 10.9.

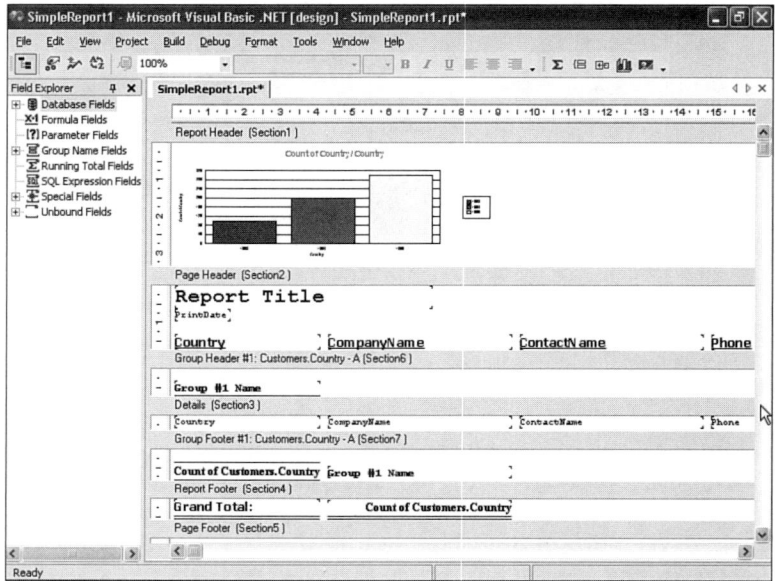

FIGURE 10.16   The Crystal Reports Designer.

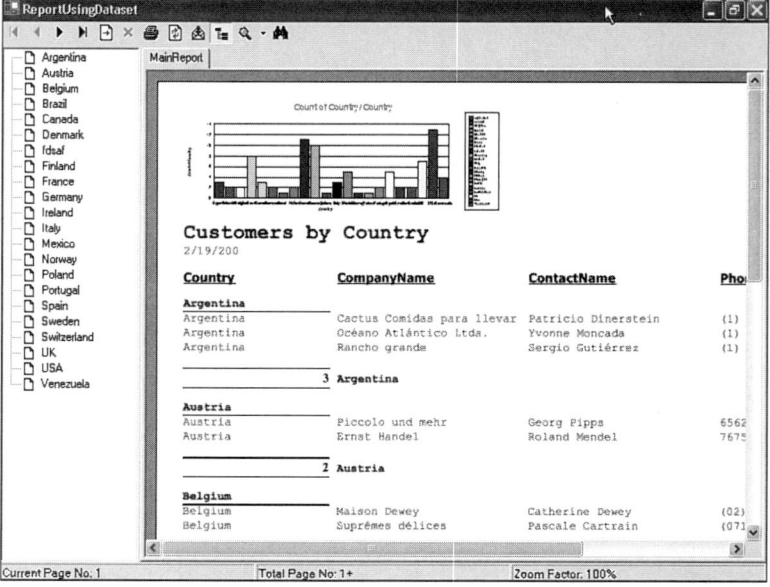

FIGURE 10.17   Previewing the report.

LISTING 10.9   Using a ComboBox to Select the Report to View

```
Private Sub ComboBox1_SelectedIndexChanged( _
 ByVal sender As System.Object, ByVal e As System.EventArgs) _
 Handles ComboBox1.SelectedIndexChanged
    Select Case ComboBox1.Text
        Case "<Pick a report>"
            CrystalReportViewer1.ReportSource = Nothing
        Case "SimpleReport1"
            CrystalReportViewer1.ReportSource = New SimpleReport1
    End Select
End Sub
```

Adding Login Information

If you want to point to a different database, or use a different userID and password combination, include the code in Listing 10.10 before assigning the `ReportSource`.

LISTING 10.10   Logging on to the Database in Code

```
Dim Tab As CrystalDecisions.CrystalReports.Engine.Table
Dim LogonInfo As CrystalDecisions.Shared.TableLogOnInfo
For Each Tab In SimpleReport1.Database.Tables
    LogonInfo = Tab.LogOnInfo
    With LogonInfo.ConnectionInfo
        .ServerName = "localhost"
        .UserID = "sa"
        .Password = ""
        .DatabaseName = "Northwind"
    End With
    Tab.ApplyLogOnInfo(LogonInfo)
Next Tab
```

Putting the User in Control

If you want to offer users options at this point, all you have to do is drag a `ReportDocument` from the Components toolbox onto the form and assign the strongly typed report class to it. Figure 10.18 shows the dialog that appears when you put the `ReportDocument` on your form.

The default name is `ReportDocument1`. Change the name to `rcSimple`, and then comment out the previous assignment of the strongly typed report to the `ReportSource` and add an assignment of the report component instead, as shown in Listing 10.11.

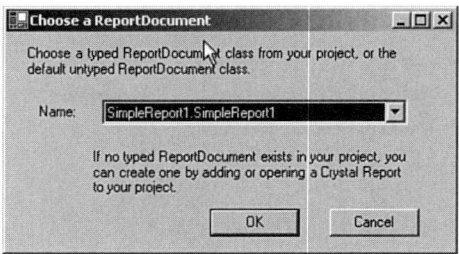

FIGURE 10.18   Adding a `ReportDocument` to the form.

LISTING 10.11   Changing the Report Selection Code to Permit Dynamic Report Selection

```
Private Sub ComboBox1_SelectedIndexChanged( _
 ByVal sender As System.Object, ByVal e As System.EventArgs) _
 Handles ComboBox1.SelectedIndexChanged
    Select Case ComboBox1.Text
        Case "<Pick a report>"
            CrystalReportViewer1.ReportSource = Nothing
        Case "SimpleReport1"
            ' CrystalReportViewer1.ReportSource = New SimpleReport1
            CrystalReportViewer1.ReportSource = rcSimple
    End Select
End Sub
```

This runs exactly as it did before. However, the `ReportViewer` now references an object that can be instanced from anywhere—a class in the application's assembly, an external assembly, or an XML Web Service.

Report Management and Use with the Server Explorer

Use Ctrl+Alt+S to open the Visual Studio Server Explorer. The Server Explorer can be used to create connections, create databases, add tables, and generally do many of the things that we've always been able to do in FoxPro, but which required the Enterprise Manager in SQL Server. MSDE didn't have a user interface, which made using MSDE relatively difficult (a nice way of saying "not worth the trouble"). The Server Explorer fixes that and provides many other features as well.

One of them is something you might have noticed if you've opened the Server Explorer before. If you expand the Servers node, the first entry is Crystal Services. And one of the nodes directly below Crystal Services is Server Files. Server Files shows the contents of a directory in your Visual Studio directory tree; on my computer it's this:

```
Program Files\Microsoft Visual Studio .NET 2003\Crystal Reports\Samples\Reports
```

Any directories under the Reports directory will be shown and their contents displayed in the expandable tree under the directory name. My computer has the two directories (Feature Examples and General Business) that were installed with Visual Studio. Add a My Reports directory and copy SimpleReport1.rpt there, and you'll see it as shown in Figure 10.19. You may have to click the Refresh icon at the top of the Server Explorer window.

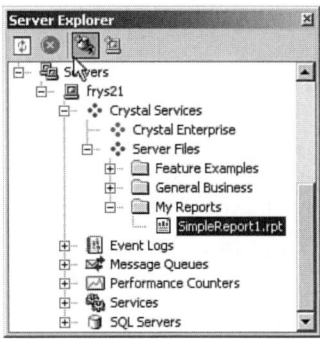

FIGURE 10.19   Displaying your reports in the Server Explorer.

Create a new form called ReportFromServerExplorer and make it the current project Startup form. Use Ctrl+Alt+S to open up the Server Explorer and expand the tree until you see your SimpleReport1.rpt under the My Reports node. Drag it onto the new form. It is given the default name ServerFileReport1. Next, add a CrystalReportViewer control onto the form, change the Dock property to Fill (the big box in the center of the Dock property dialog). Finally, open the ReportSource drop-down in the CrystalReportViewer object and select this:

```
ServerFileReport1 [CrystalDecisions.Shared.ServerFileReport]
```

The reason this is interesting becomes apparent if you add a server. Right-click on the server node and select Add, and a dialog appears asking for the computer name or URL. That means that you can add reports to your application that are located on other servers. That considerably expands what you can offer your users. We'll see more examples shortly.

Using a Dataset as a Data Source

Now that you know how easy it is to populate a dataset, you'll be pleased to know that you can design your report to get its data from an ADO.NET dataset instead of from a database using an OLE DB provider.

To create a strongly typed dataset based on the Customers table in Northwind, add a new empty dataset to the project using the Add New Item dialog. Name it dsCusts.xsd. This puts you into the Dataset Designer, which looks just exactly like an empty Web page or Web service page. Actually, it's more like MODIFY STRUCTURE.

Open the dataset's designer by double-clicking on the dataset's name in the Solution Explorer. Then, drag the Customers table from the Server Explorer (opened with Ctrl+Alt+S) onto the design surface of the dataset, and save it using File, Save All (Ctrl+Shift+S).

If you click on the Show All icon at the top of the Solution Explorer window, you'll see that under the `dsCusts.xsd` file, there are two other files named `dsCusts.vb` and `dsCusts.xsx`. These three files constitute a typed dataset.

First you'll need to create a report using this dataset. Select Add New Item, Crystal Report from the Solution Explorer right-click context menu. In the resulting Standard Report Expert dialog, on the Data page, click on the Database Files node of Available data sources. You'll be given a chance to browse to your new dataset, `dsCusts.xsd`. Click on it and continue with the steps to design the same report layout we designed earlier.

Next, open the new report and right-click on its design surface to get a context menu, then select Database, and then from the submenu select Set Location. In the Set Location dialog, expand the Project Data node, the ADO.NET DataSets node, the node for your dataset, and select the Customers table (see Figure 10.20).

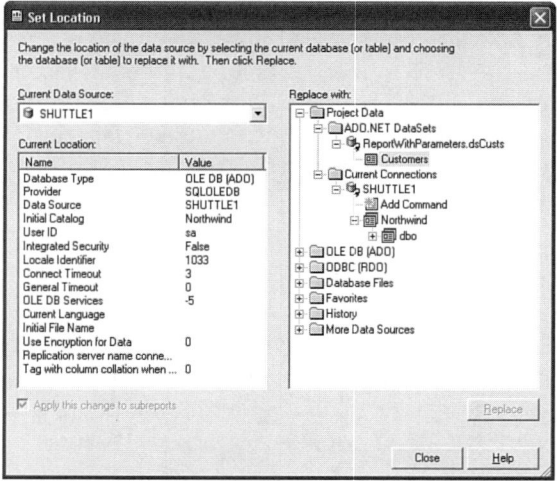

FIGURE 10.20   Adding the Customers dataset.

Your report will now look to your strongly typed dataset for its metadata and will run when bound to an instance of it. Click the Close button to proceed.

Now that we have a report to run against `dsCusts`, drag the Customers table from the Server Explorer onto the designer surface of the form. This will add `SQLConnection` and `SQLDataAdapter` objects to the form that points to the Northwind database and its Customers table, respectively. Rename these objects `scnNorthwind` and `sdaCustomers`, modify the `ConnectionString` property of `scnNorthwind` to include a valid user ID and password, and then right-click `sdaCustomers` and select Generate Dataset. In the Choose a Dataset section, select the Existing radio button, and the class name of your strongly typed dataset from the combo box (see Figure 10.21).

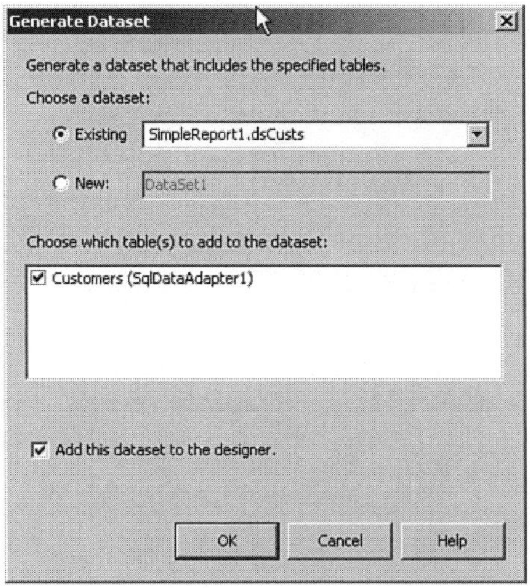

FIGURE 10.21   Pointing to the dataset.

Click the OK button and add the following code to the `Load` event:

```
sdaCustomers.Fill(DsCusts1, "Customers")
datasetReport1.setdatasource(DsCusts1)
CrystalReportViewer1.ReportSource = datasetReport1
```

How It Works

This code first populates `dsCusts1`, an instance of the `dsCusts` strongly typed `DataSet` class. Next, the code sets the `DataSource` property of `DatasetReport1`, which is an instance of the strongly typed report class `SimpleReport1`, to `dsCusts1`. Finally, it points the `ReportSource` of `CrystalReportViewer1` to `DatasetReport1`.

If you change the Startup page of the project to DatasetReport and press F5 to run it, you'll see that the report looks the same as before. However, this time the data doesn't come straight from a database, but rather from a `DataSet` object. The `DataSet` was populated by a `SELECT` statement from the Customers table. The `SELECT` statement and the connection string could have referenced any server and any tablename, as long as the dataset has the same structure. The dataset is like a FoxPro cursor; it's just a container for the data. The `Fill` method of the `DataAdapter` just pours the data into it.

Report Filtering with Parameters

Crystal Reports knows how parameters work and will automatically provide a parameter input form that users can fill in. It's primitive, but it's free. You can also write your own dialog screens and specify the parameters yourself. The description process is going to be very visual, so please forgive all the pictures.

Creating a Parameterized Report

To build a parameterized report, create a new Windows Form project called ReportWithParameters. Right-click on the project and select Add New Item; click on Crystal Reports, name the new report CustomersByCountry, and click OK.

You'll immediately see the Standard Report Expert dialog, which starts by asking you where the data is. Select the OLE DB(ADO) node, as shown in Figure 10.22, and click on the plus sign to the left of it as if to expand it.

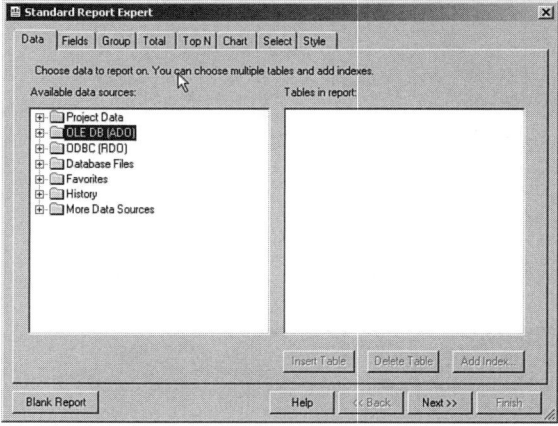

FIGURE 10.22   The Data Selection page of the Standard Report Expert.

Clicking on the plus sign when you haven't yet selected a data source produces the OLE DB Provider Selection Expert (wizard), as shown in Figure 10.23. You'll want to select Microsoft OLE DB Provider for SQL Server, as shown in Figure 10.23.

Click Next and you'll be sent to the next page to fill in the server name, the userID, the password, and the name of the database, as shown in Figure 10.24. Click Finish to complete the process.

When you've done this, you're ready to select one or more tables for your report. Expand the Tables node and double-click on Customers to select it (see Figure 10.25).

On the Fields page, select CompanyName and Country (see Figure 10.26).

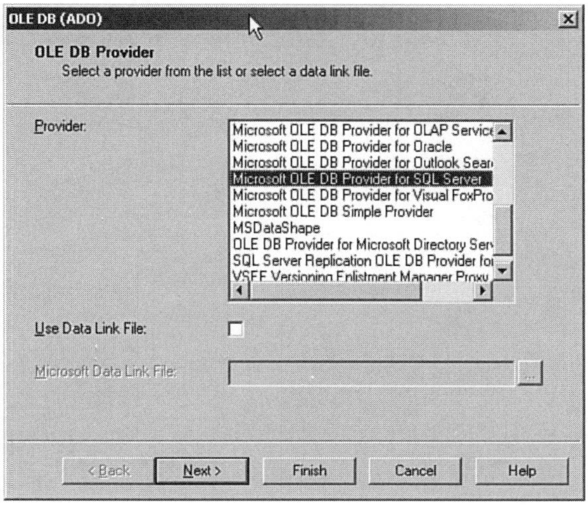

FIGURE 10.23 Selecting the driver to use for the database connection.

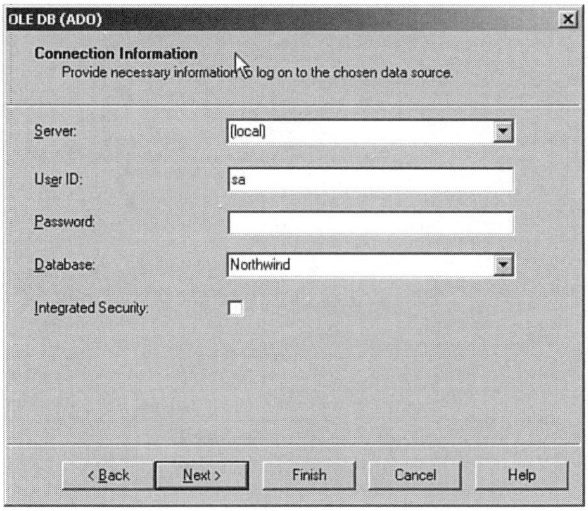

FIGURE 10.24 Specifying the database connection information.

Based on your selections, Crystal then builds the report for you (see Figure 10.27). It's actually a pretty attractive report. You can select from several alternative designs, and the report expert will make the required changes. So far, so good. You can also add or change labels, such as the report heading in the Page Header band.

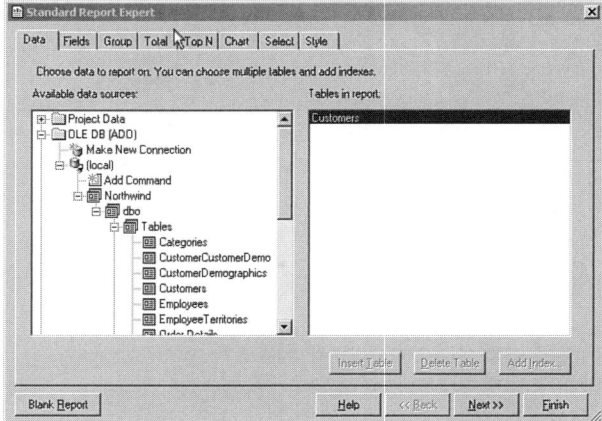

FIGURE 10.25   Selecting the Customers table.

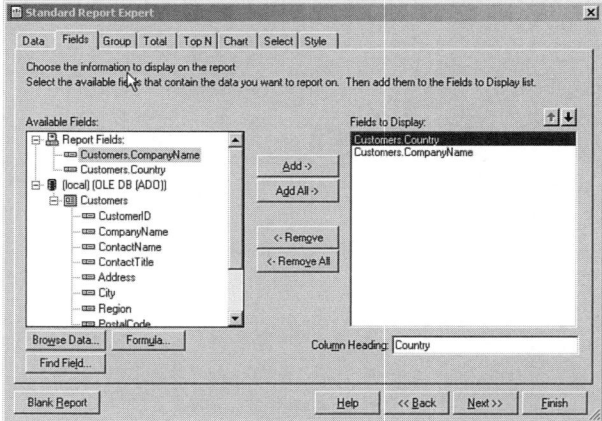

FIGURE 10.26   Selecting fields from the Customers table.

Adding a Parameter

The next step, though, is somewhat unexpected. You might imagine that you would go to the Select tab and enter parameters. The Select tab is used to enter hard-coded selection criteria for building a SELECT statement without any parameters. If you want the user to supply the parameter, there's another way.

Press Ctrl+Alt+T to open the Field Explorer, and right-click on the Parameter Fields node as shown in Figure 10.28, where I've right-clicked on the node to activate the context menu.

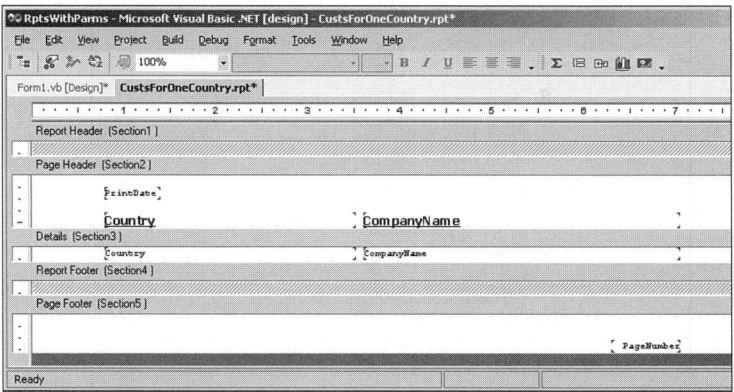

FIGURE 10.27 Viewing and modifying the generated report.

TIP

You can also click on the Toggle Field View icon, the first one in the Crystal Reports toolbar, to show or hide the Field Explorer.

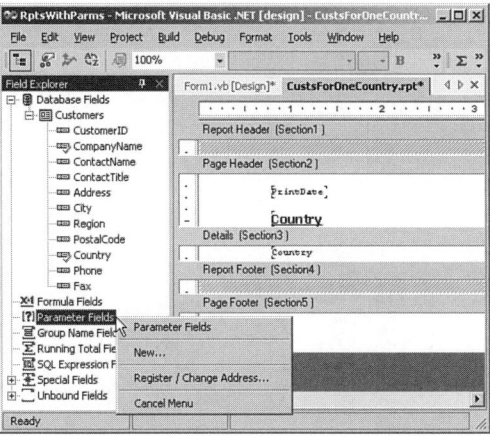

FIGURE 10.28 The Field Explorer.

Select New, and you'll get the dialog shown in Figure 10.29. Enter **mCountry** for the parameter name, **Country to include** as the prompt, and **String** as the type. There are a few more options, but you probably won't use this except for prototyping, so don't get too excited.

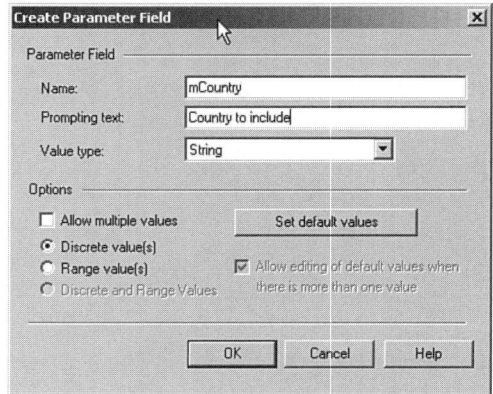

FIGURE 10.29   Specifying the new parameter.

Using the Parameter

The mere fact that you have a parameter doesn't do anything. You have to use it in a selection formula. To do this, right-click anywhere on the form that's not a field or a label, and select Report, Edit Selection Formula, Records from the context menu, as shown in Figure 10.30.

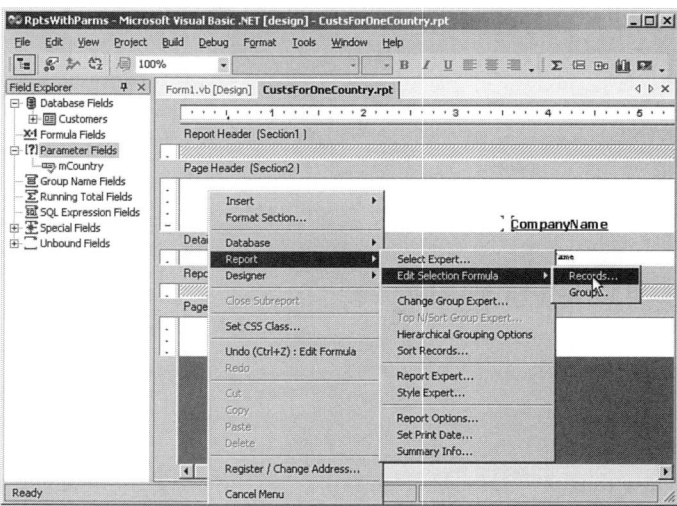

FIGURE 10.30   Adding a selection formula.

Crystal Reports is criticized for having a quirky formula language of its own. In the Edit Selection Formula dialog, you pick a field from the Field Tree window by double-clicking on it. The formula construction process is visible at the bottom of the screen. Double-click on the Operator Tree in the rightmost window and pick the "=" operator, which is added to the selection formula. Finally, go back to the Field Tree and pick the parameter field mCountry by double-clicking on it. As expected, it will be added to the end of the formula. (I've displayed the Function Tree as well, although we don't need it for this example.) The result, (Customers.Country) = (?mCountry), appears at the top of the Edit Selection Formula screen.

Close the dialog, add a `CrystalReportViewer` to the form, dock it with the Fill option, and designate the new report's name in the CrystalReportViewer's `ReportSource` property. Press F5 to run the form. Lo and behold, it prompts you for a country, and displays a report containing only that country's records.

XML Report Web Services

Reports can be published as Web Services and then used as the `ReportSource` for a `CrystalReportViewer` control. This allows you to offer report processing on the server. That doesn't buy you anything if you're printing a complete listing of a file; but if you're building a summary report, it allows you to use the entire database on the server, but send only the summary data over the Internet. Bandwidth savings can be huge.

To make an XML Report Web Service from `SimpleReport1.rpt`, create a new ASP.NET Web Service project named SimpleReportWebService1. Delete the `Service1.asmx` file that is added to the project by default, and add `SimpleReport1.rpt` to the project.

Next, right-click `SimpleReport1.rpt` in the Solution Explorer, and choose Publish as Web Service from the context menu.

This adds a Web Service file, `SimpleReportService.asmx`, to the project.

Now build the project. Open a browser and type the following URL:

`http://localhost/SimpleReportWebService1/SimpleReport1Service.asmx`

You'll get a Web Services testbed like we saw in earlier chapters. Exposed methods include the following:

    DrillGraph

    Refresh

    FindText

    GetPage

    GetTotaller

    TestReport

    GetGroupLevelData

    FindGroup

    GetReportInfo

    Export

You can't test them in the Web page because they're meant to be used from within a Windows form to manipulate and return elements of the report. The `ReportViewer` control knows what to do with them, and that's what matters.

To use this Web service in a form, back in the Windows Forms application, in the `Load` event, set the `CrystalReportViewer` control's `ReportSource` to the URL of the Report Web Service, as shown in Listing 10.12.

LISTING 10.12   Pointing the `ReportSource` to a Web Service

```
Private Sub CrystalReportViewer1_Load( _
 ByVal sender As System.Object, ByVal e As System.EventArgs) _
 Handles CrystalReportViewer1.Load
With CrystalReportViewer1
   .ReportSource = "http://localhost/SimpleReportWebService1/" _
                  + "SimpleReport1Service.asmx"
End With
End Sub
```

You can add a Web reference for this `.asmx` file to the project. Having done this, you can assign a new instance of the Web Service class to the `ReportSource`:

```
CrystalReportViewer1.ReportSource = New localhost. SimpleReport1Service()
```

Try them both. It's really that easy.

In order to make this look easy, however, the folks at Crystal Decisions, or perhaps in Redmond, have done a lot of work. Essentially, two classes have been created in the code-behind file for `SimpleReport1.rpt`:

```
Public Class SimpleReport1
...
Public Class CachedSimpleReport1
```

The first one is the primary class for implementing the strongly typed report. It inherits from `ReportClass` and wraps various members of the `ReportDefinition.Sections` collection. The second one implements the `ICachedReports` interface. It creates a cached report. In its `CreateReport` method it creates an object based on the `SimpleReport1` class. On the Web Service side, there are also two classes, `SimpleReport1Service`, which inherits from `ReportServiceBase`, which exposes the methods that publish the report as a Web service, and `CachedWebSimpleReport1`, the caching counterpart.

When this `.asmx` file has been generated, all you have to do is copy it, together with the related RPT file, to your Web Services directory.

To use these reports, just provide a configuration file (either a TXT or an XML file) that your application can read to determine the IP address of the reports server. You then construct the `ReportSource` URL at runtime.

Building ASP.NET Reporting Clients

Although this book is primarily about Windows application development, I've included a short chapter on building thin client applications because they are part of the competitive environment. Some developers out there are offering thin client as the solution for any type of database application.

The good news is that thin client applications are simple. The bad news is that thin client applications are simple. For simple applications, they're not hard; for complex applications, they're not appropriate. That about covers the controversy.

However, the one area that seems to be an excellent fit for using Internet browsers, either on the Internet or on an intranet, is reporting. Reporting is one-way, which is perfect for use with a browser.

Create a new ASP.NET Web Application in Visual Studio .NET, and use the Add Existing Item feature to add `SimpleReport1.rpt` to the project. Make sure that the report is looking to the Customers table for its data.

Next, rename `WebForm.aspx` to `CustomersByCountry.aspx`, and add a Web Forms `CrystalReportViewer` control to it. Unlike the Windows Forms `CrystalReportViewer` control, the Web Forms variant doesn't have a `ReportSource` property that's exposed at design time. You can only set it in code, usually in the `Page_Load` event:

```
CrystalReportViewer.ReportSource = Server.MapPath("SimpleReport1.rpt")
```

Run the application and you'll see that it works as before. The output sent to the browser is, of course HTML; but search, navigation, zoom—all of the features except printing—are supported through the use of trips back to the server.

Exporting to a PDF

If you want users to be able to print a copy of the report, browser output is usually not a very good option. A better one is to export your report to Adobe Acrobat (PDF) format. You simply export the report to a PDF file and redirect the browser to that same file. Listing 10.13 shows the code to do this.

LISTING 10.13   Exporting a Report to a PDF

```
Private Sub Page_Load(ByVal sender As System.Object, ByVal e As _
  System.EventArgs) Handles MyBase.Load
    Dim destopts As New _
      CrystalDecisions.Shared.DiskFileDestinationOptions()
    Dim FName As String = GUID.NewGUID().ToString
    destopts.DiskFileName = FName
    With cbsMain  ' Name of the CrystalReport object
        .ExportOptions.ExportDestinationType = _
          CrystalDecisions.Shared.ExportDestinationType.DiskFile
        .ExportOptions.ExportFormatType = _
```

LISTING 10.13 Continued

```
            CrystalDecisions.Shared.ExportFormatType.PortableDocFormat
        .ExportOptions.DestinationOptions = destopts
        .Export()
    End With
    Response.Redirect(FName)
End Sub
```

Because several users may request the report at the same time, you need to provide unique names for PDF files. I used the NewGUID() method of the GUID class that comes with .NET. (I had to use the ToString cast because technically, a GUID is a type and a string is a different type.)

Other Report Experts

So far, we only looked at the Standard Report Expert. Crystal Reports comes with seven experts:

Standard

Form Letter

Form

Cross-Tab

Subreport

Mail label

Drill Down

Each of these walks you through the process of building a slightly different kind of report. The wizards permit you to build a variety of display output from your data with little or no coding. We've already looked at the standard wizard, so we'll now look at samples of some of the other types of report output produced by the wizards.

Create a Windows Form project called OtherReports. Change Form1.vb to MainForm.vb, size 790 × 510, no MinButton or MaxButton, autocentered on the screen, and with a fixed 3D border. Add a MainMenu control with a File, Exit option, and then add a Reports pad with three menu bars: Form Letter, Cross-Tab, and Drill Down. (These three are pretty interesting and will illustrate how the Report Experts work.) To make the code easier to read, you might want to select Show Names from the menu's context menu and assign meaningful names. Now you're ready to build some new types of reports.

The Form Letter Wizard

Form letters (called mail-merges in the FoxPro world) are a useful addition to many database applications. They're easy to do in FoxPro, and they're easy to do in .NET.

Add a new Windows Form called frmFormLetter. Make it 780×500 and sizeable, no `MinButton` or `MaxButton`, autocentered. Add a `CrystalReportViewer` control and dock it to all sides. Next, right-click on the project and select Add New Item, Crystal Report. Select Form Letter from the Experts dialog, as shown in Figure 10.31. Enter the data connection information for the Northwind database, and then select the Customers table.

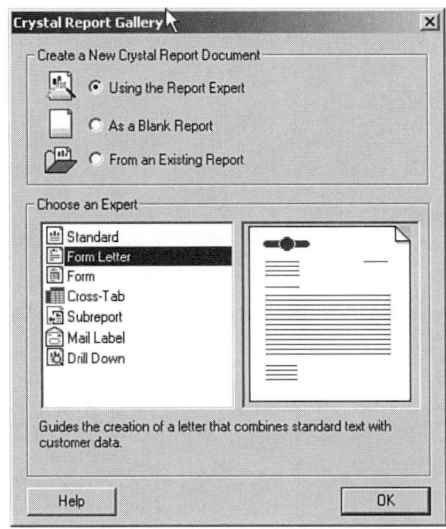

FIGURE 10.31   Running the Form Letter Expert.

We're going to do a form letter to all customers, so all we really need are the fields that are going to be printed on each page. So include the fields shown in Figure 10.32.

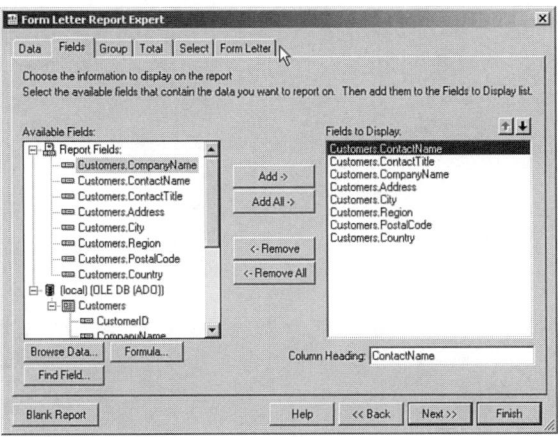

FIGURE 10.32   Selecting the fields to be printed in the form letter.

10

The rightmost tab of the Expert page is specific to the Form Letter expert. On it, you select the band in which to put the content (select Detail), and then type text and insert field placeholders to be filled in with data from each selected record when the report is run. Figure 10.33 shows the detail band I built for the form letter; save the report.

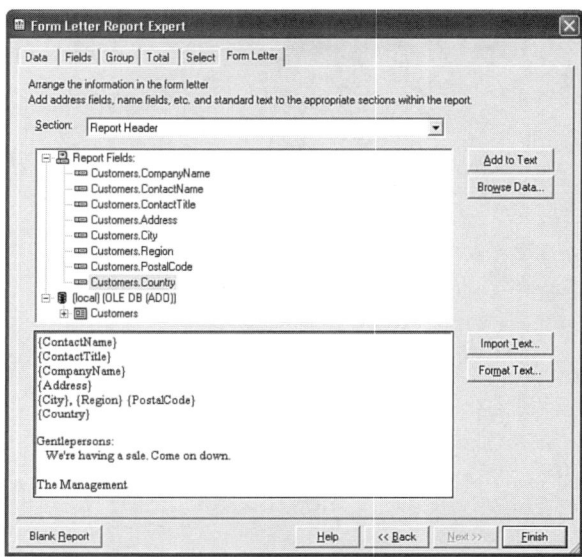

FIGURE 10.33 The finished form letter in the Form Letter Expert dialog.

When you close the expert, you'll be looking at the report. The text and placeholders that you created are by default inserted into the report's Detail band (Section 3).

We have one more thing to do. If you consider that the form letter will try to fit multiple objects on a single page if they're small enough to fit, you'll understand why you need to either expand the detail band to 9 inches in height or do something else. Something else is preferable in this case; right-click on the Detail Band and you'll see the Properties sheet shown in Figure 10.34. Check the New Page After option, and you'll get exactly one letter per page.

Finally, go to MainForm and add the following two lines of code for the `mnuFormLetter` menu code:

```
Dim frm As New frmFormLetter
frm.Show()
```

> **CAUTION**
>
> There's a gotcha here that got me, so I'll try to save you the pain: Don't name your form and your report both FormLetter, even though they have different file extensions. The reason for

those endless object prefixes in the Visual Studio .NET world (besides the fact that because a form in Visual Studio .NET just has an extension of .vb or .cs, you can't tell if a file is a form or not without the prefix) is that the filename is usually used as the default class name. Because both the report and the form will be converted to classes, you'll end up with two FormLetter classes.

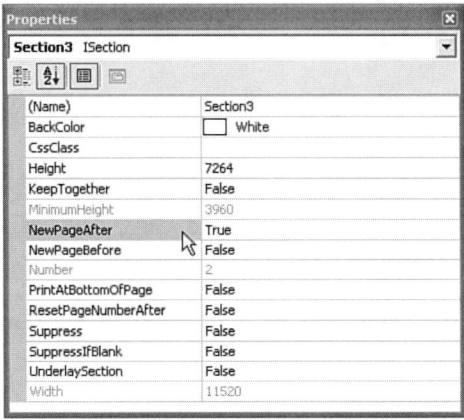

FIGURE 10.34   Forcing a new page after the detail band for a record prints.

Figure 10.35 shows a sample page produced by a form to which I've added a CrystalReportViewer component with the ReportSource set to the form letter report created previously. When you run a form letter, the entire batch is printed in a preview format; you can then send it to the printer.

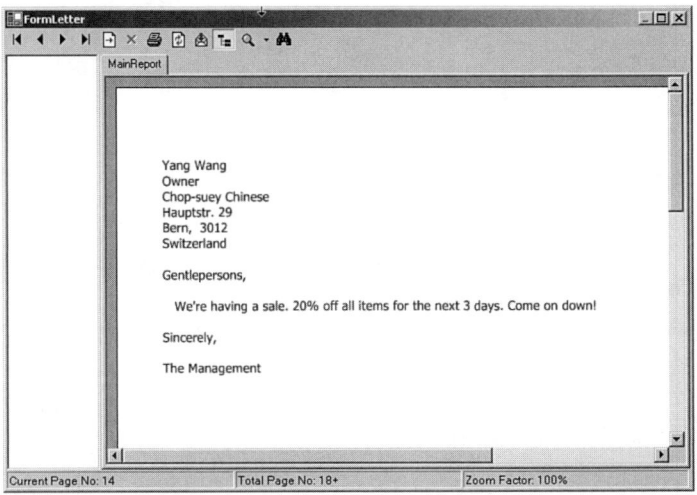

FIGURE 10.35   The finished form letter in the Form Letter Expert dialog.

Mail merges are a part of many database applications. FoxPro has a pretty good mail-merge feature, but .NET's implementation is at least as easy to use, and maybe even a little easier.

The Cross-Tab Expert

Add a new Windows form called frmCrosstab to the project. Drag a `CrystalReportViewer` object onto it and dock it to all sides. Next, right-click on the project in the Solution Explorer and select Add, Add New Item, Crystal Report. Select Cross-Tab from the Expert dialog.

The report then asks you to select a table. The Products table has some useful fields to tabulate, so I'll use it. Pick the Supplier ID and Category ID as the row and column tabs. But there's no meaningful value to add; adding quantities of different items is literally adding apples and oranges.

However, if we multiply on-hand quantity times unit price, we have an extended value that can be totaled. You can open the Formula editor, create a "formula" called Extended, select UnitPrice from the list of table fields, type in an asterisk, and then select UnitsInStock from the list of table fields (Figure 10.36). You can then save the formula and use it in the cross-tab.

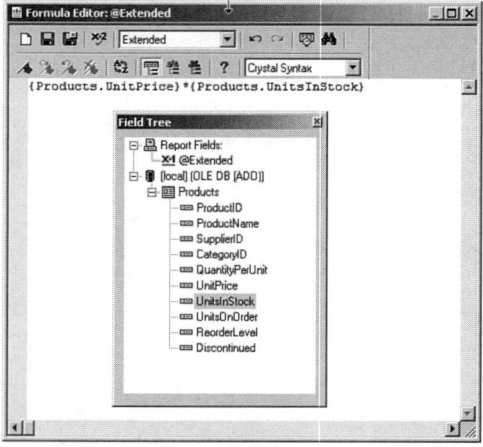

FIGURE 10.36   Defining a "formula" (a calculated variable) for use in the report.

In Figure 10.37, I've entered the two control fields at the top and left, and the value to be totaled in the Summarized Fields box.

The finished product appears in Figure 10.38. For good measure, I included a graph that the expert offered me at no extra charge.

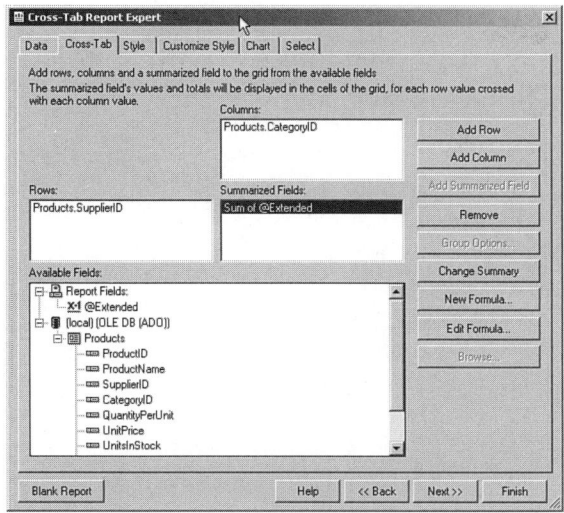

FIGURE 10.37   The finished cross-tab in the designer.

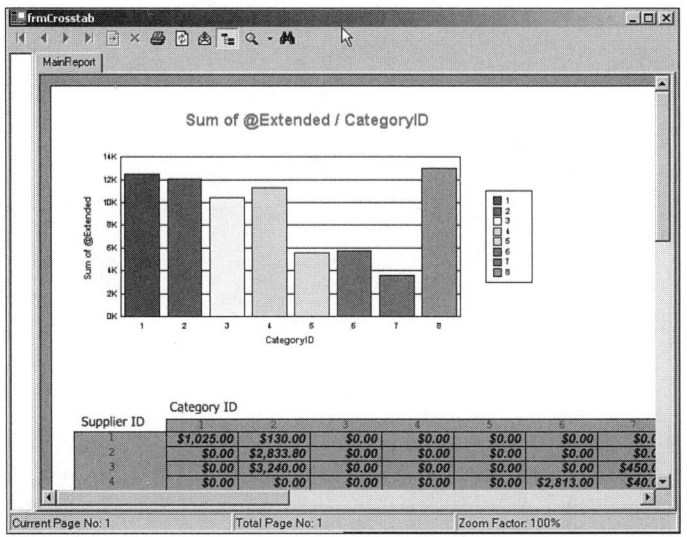

FIGURE 10.38   The cross-tab report.

The difficulty of building cross-tabs has long been a frustration for database developers. If the Cross-Tab Expert were the only feature in Crystal Reports, it would be an important tool. The fact that it's just one of many types of reports that Crystal can build is a tribute to how far this product has come.

The Drill Down Expert

It's easy to create links in Web pages that pass parameters to other pages in such a way as to give the illusion of "drilling down" into the data. This feature is one that users are accustomed to, and ask for in our applications. Unfortunately, it's not as easy to do in Windows Forms applications as it is in a Web page. But Crystal Reports' Drill Down Expert builds reports that do just that. I've added a new form called frmDrilldown with a CrystalReportViewer control on it, docked to all sides as usual. In Figure 10.39, I've added a Crystal Report to the project, and selected the Drill Down expert.

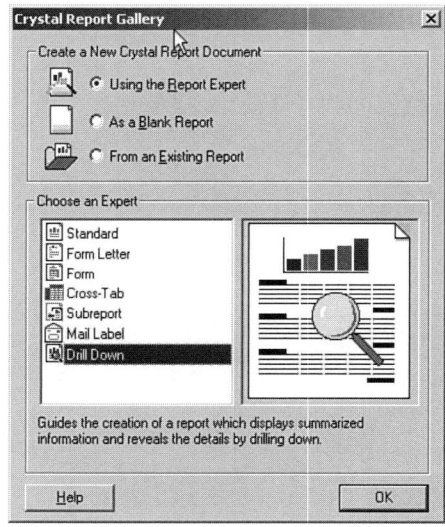

FIGURE 10.39   The Drill Down Expert.

I added the usual database connection, then selected the Customers and Orders tables. The expert correctly linked the two tables on CustomerID. I added the Customers table and the Orders table, and the expert correctly linked the two using their CustomerID fields (see Figure 10.40).

The report's data selector is going to do a JOIN on the two tables. As you know, a JOIN puts all of the selected fields in both records into a result cursor. The report will group on the fields in the Customers table and present those fields at the first level; when you double-click on any row, all of the records for the group will be shown, but only the columns from the detail record. It's a simple concept, elegantly executed. In Figure 10.41 you see the field selection.

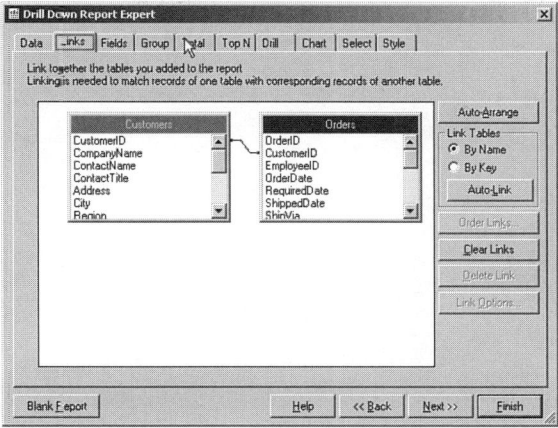

FIGURE 10.40   Joining the two tables on `CustomerID`.

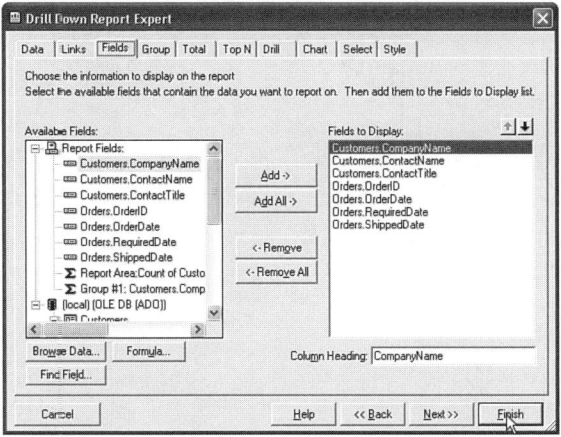

FIGURE 10.41   Selecting fields for the Drill Down report.

The Drill tab shown in Figure 10.42 is where you specify which records to show and which to hide.

Finally, set the `ReportSource` property of the form to `Drilldown.rpt` and add the following code to the MainForm menu:

```
Dim frm as New frmDrilldown
Frm.Show()
```

In Figure 10.43, I picked one of the 10 custom formatting options, which gave me drop shadows on some of the text displays.

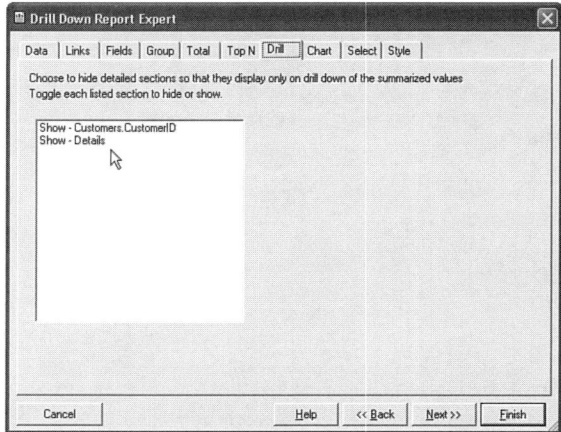

FIGURE 10.42   The Drill tab: Show the Customer fields, hide the Orders fields.

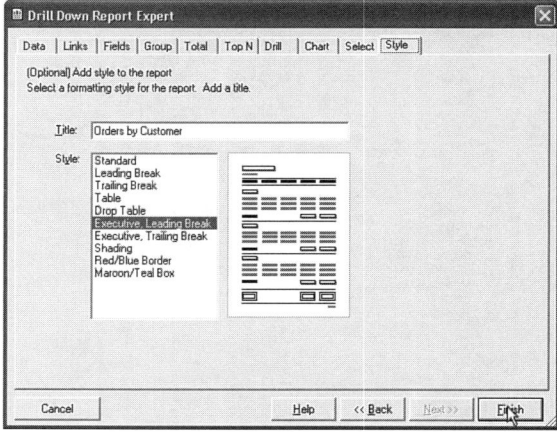

FIGURE 10.43   Selecting a report style.

The resulting report layout is shown in Figure 10.44. Group and detail records share the same column headings. It looks strange when you first run the report because the column headings for the detail records show even though the detail records don't.

Press F5 to bring up MainForm and select Reports, Drill Down from the menu, and you'll see the high-level customer summary data, as shown in Figure 10.45.

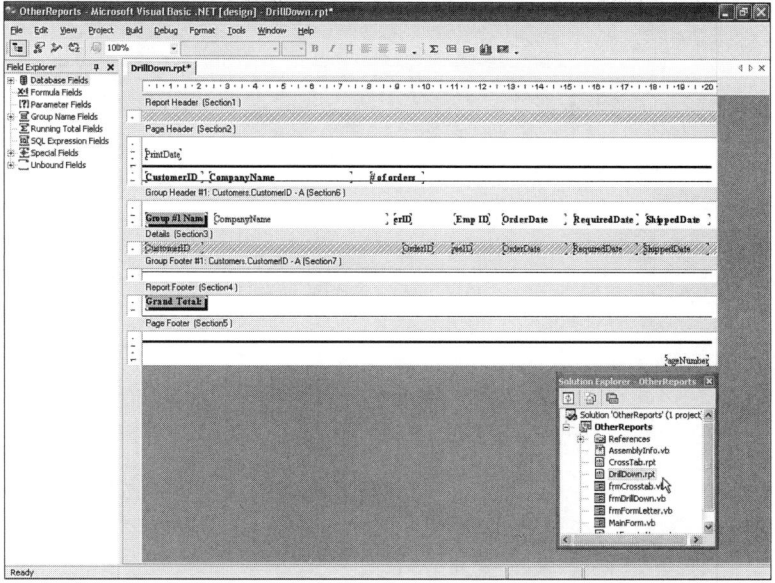

FIGURE 10.44   The final report layout.

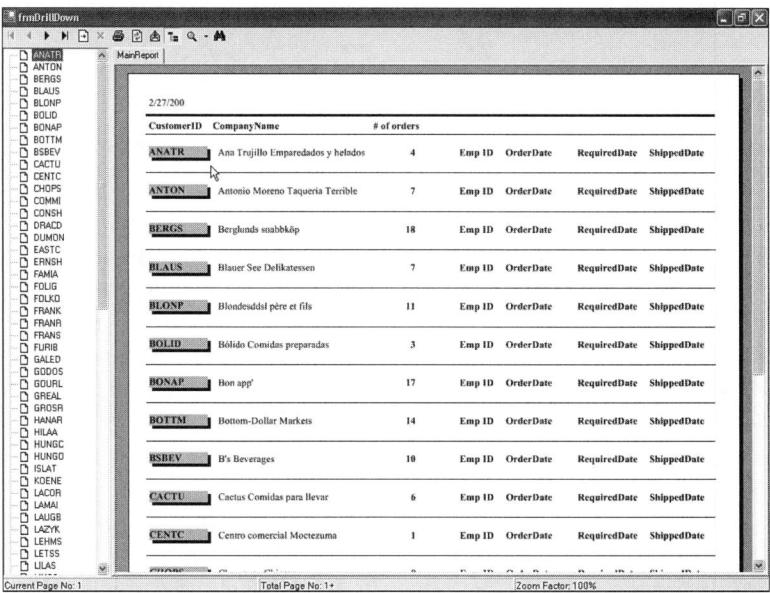

FIGURE 10.45   The top-level customer data.

Double-click on the heading row, and the detail rows appear, as shown in Figure 10.46.

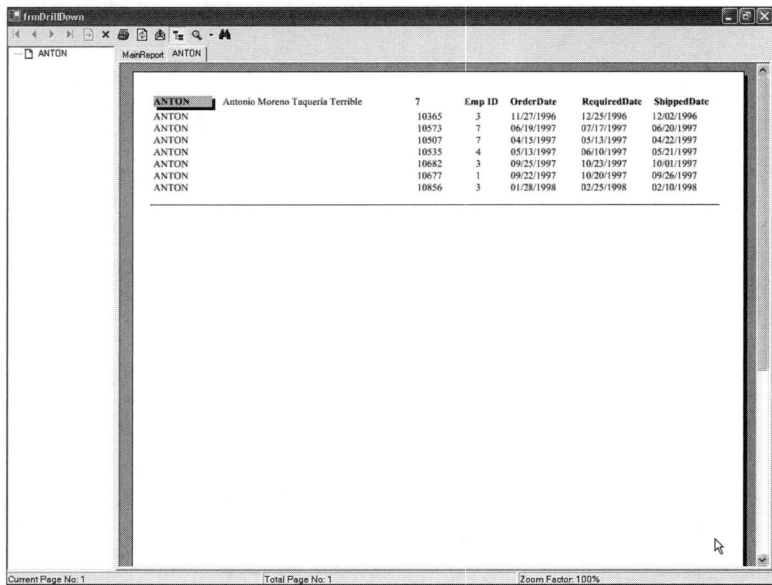

FIGURE 10.46   The drill-down detail report.

This is an amazing result for no programming.

Summary

In this chapter, we've learned that building reports with Visual Basic .NET using Crystal Reports is no more difficult than it is in Visual FoxPro. In fact, for my money, Crystal Reports is a little better.

In the next chapter, we'll look at the competition: thin client. It's important to know what it is and how it works because many of your competitors will try to sell thin client applications as the solution in cases where a smart client (the same kind of applications we've been developing for years, but using an Internet-based data server) would better serve their needs. You need to understand how they work in order to understand their considerable shortcomings.

Index

A

How can we make this index more useful? Email us at indexes@samspublishing.com

How can we make this index more useful? Email us at indexes@samspublishing.com

How can we make this index more useful? Email us at indexes@sampublishing.com

Q - R

How can we make this index more useful? Email us at indexes@samspublishing.com

How can we make this index more useful? Email us at indexes@samspublishing.com